From Norman Conquest to Magna Carta

From Norman Conquest to Magna Carta is a wide-ranging history of England from 1066 to 1215. Starting with the build-up to the Battle of Hastings and ending with the Magna Carta, Christopher Daniell traces the profound changes that England underwent over the period, from religion and the life of the court through to arts and architecture.

This survey uses a combination of original sources and sharp analysis to trace England's transformation after 1066. The papacy became powerful enough to proclaim crusades and to challenge kings. New monastic orders revitalised Christianity in England and spread European learning throughout the country. The Norman conquerors built cathedrals, monasteries and castles, which changed the English landscape for ever. By 1215 the king's administration had become more sophisticated and centralised. Between 1066 and 1215 Normandy was a major concern of the English kings, who either had to defend or conquer the Duchy. The acceptance of the Magna Carta by King John in 1215 would revolutionise the world in centuries to come.

This volume will make essential reading for all students of medieval history, casting new light on a crucial period in England's development.

Christopher Daniell is Research Associate with the Centre for Medieval Studies, University of York and a Researcher for the Continuum Group. He specialises in the study of medieval cemeteries and twelfth-century York. His last book was *Death and Burial in Medieval England, 1066–1550* (1998).

From Norman Conquest
to Magna Carta
England 1066–1215

Christopher Daniell

Routledge
Taylor & Francis Group

LONDON AND NEW YORK

First published 2003 by Routledge
11 New Fetter Lane, London EC4P 4EE

Simultaneously published in the USA and Canada
by Routledge
29 West 35th Street, New York, NY 10001

Routledge is an imprint of the Taylor & Francis Group

Typeset in Garamond by Exe Valley Dataset Ltd, Exeter
Printed and bound in Great Britain by MPG Books Ltd, Bodmin

British Library Cataloguing in Publication Data
A catalogue record for this book is available from the British Library

Library of Congress Cataloging in Publication Data
Daniell, Christopher
    From Norman Conquest to Magna Carta: England 1066–1215/
        Christopher Daniell.
            p. cm.
    Includes bibliographical references and index.
    1. Great Britain–History–Norman period, 1066–1154. 2. Great Britain–History
    –Angevin period, 1154–1216. 3. England–Civilization–1066–1485. I. Title

    DA195.D36 2003
    9342.02–dc21   200215539

ISBN 0–415–22215–X (hbk)
ISBN 0–415–22216–8 (pbk)

For Alison

Contents

Illustrations

Plates

Figure

Maps

Table

Introduction

This book explores England between 1066 and 1215 and the changes that took place across the political, religious and cultural landscape of England. It provides a lively and engaging account of a fascinating and dynamic period of English history.

In both 1066 and 1215, dates which form the time limits of this book, there were seismic shifts in perspective. The Norman Conquest of 1066 is remembered not only because it was the last time an uninvited foreign power seized control of England by force, but also for the far-reaching changes that the new conquerors brought with them. At the other end of the time period King John bowed to pressure from the rebellious barons and assented to the demands of the barons at Runnymede. For the first time in English history a king had agreed to limit his own power. As importantly, his assent was agreed in writing in the Magna Carta (which means 'Great Charter'). The physical document meant that the details could be widely distributed and remembered. The importance of the event was apparent immediately, but the long-term consequences across the centuries were unforeseen. Four hundred years later the Magna Carta was used as a crucial political weapon in the fight between Parliament and Charles I during the English Civil War.

The changes that occurred in England between 1066 and 1215 were remarkable. The Norman conquerors imposed their will, sweeping away the old Anglo-Saxon culture and language. The period was also a time of evolving customs and culture. By the end of the twelfth century heraldry and the glamorous world of the Arthurian legends had become popular with the nobility. They were the start of a long tradition which still powerfully captures the imagination.

Other institutions were also evolving. Government changed from the Anglo-Saxon method in which all the offices of state travelled with the king, increasingly to being based in one place and independent of the king's control. The church too saw huge changes. Internationally the Pope's power increased across Europe and in England the authority of the bishops over their own dioceses made them influential regional figures. The court and justice systems became more ordered following the changes made by Henry II, who increased the power of the courts. It was during his reign that the codification of the law began. During the twelfth century there was a subtle but profound shift in the Anglo-Saxon language which evolved and re-emerged in the later twelfth and early thirteenth centuries as Middle English. This is the foundation of the English language we have today.

Following the Norman Conquest England was also tied into a much larger European network. The connections with the Continental lands became stronger through trade, links between churches, marriage alliances and learning. Knowledge spread throughout England as part of the European-wide Renaissance. Some Englishmen, such as Adelard of Bath, sought Arabic knowledge in the Mediterranean lands. The Crusades further widened people's horizons and the willingness to embark on military adventures was a feature of the period, whether in the Holy Lands or Europe. One military disaster occurred in 1204 when King John was defeated by the French king, Philip Augustus, and lost Normandy. England still had a few coastal possessions on the Continent, but the heartlands of the dukes of Normandy and counts of Anjou were no longer owned by the English kings. For centuries afterwards English kings tried to reclaim their ancestral lands.

Despite England's size and wealth, the importance of the Norman and Angevin possessions to the English kings between 1066 and 1204 has resulted in England being described as a 'colony' (Holt 1997). The impression is made stronger by the amount of time and resources the English kings spent in protecting their Continental lands. However, England was larger, wealthier and more powerful than either Normandy or Anjou and pioneered methods of government and laws which were unknown in other lands.

Fundamental changes were also taking place within people's attitudes. People began to form specialised groups in ways not seen in the Anglo-Saxon period. Individual craft guilds were started, clergy increasingly saw themselves as a defined group separate from the laity and ranks of noblemen became more defined through heraldry. Different positions in society began to be regulated, whether it was how many horses a bishop could have, or how much a nobleman should pay to take part in a tournament.

At the same time there was a movement towards centralisation. The power of the monarchy spread throughout England through military action, political actions of the sheriffs and the legal system. The papacy too became a focal point for all ecclesiastical decisions with the help of the bishops to implement policy.

The combination of specialised groups and centralisation were part of the desire to create hierarchical structures. The creation of hierarchies is one of the most characteristic and powerful forces at large in the changes brought about in twelfth-century England. The ultimate change came in 1215 when King John assented to Magna Carta. The centuries-old power of kingship as the final arbiter in the law had been replaced in the hierarchy by a concept of the law. This change has been a determining factor in the history of England ever since.

Map I.1 Map of Normandy.

1 Hastings and after, 1066–1100

The Battle of Hastings was one of the great turning points in English history, which still generates analysis and debate. It was also a unique event, for it was the only time that a crowned sovereign king (Harold) was defeated on his own soil by a foreign duke (William) (Loyn 1992: 17). Most of the speculation concerns Harold. What if he had died fighting King Harald Hardrada of Norway three week's earlier at Stamford Bridge? What if he had waited for the rest of his forces from London before fighting William? What if he had retreated into the Midlands, drawing William after him? What if Harold had not died? These can only be answered by 'counter-factual history' which looks at other possibilities, rather than what actually happened. What can be said is that the best outcome of 1066 was that there was only one king ruling at the end of the year with the authority to reign effectively across the whole of England – an outcome which was achieved. The worst scenario would have been the three protagonists to have all survived, or for them all to have died. Either way the country would have been left in chaos.

Background and battle

Although England was ruled by an Anglo-Saxon elite before the Conquest, Norman influence had been present in England ever since the arrival of Edward the Confessor's mother, Emma, with her entourage in 1002. Furthermore, Edward himself had been brought up in the Norman court as a child. As a consequence there was often a tension before 1066 between the Anglo-Saxon nobles and the Norman courtiers. The 1051 rebellion by the Anglo-Saxon Earl Godwine was in part a reaction to the power of Norman courtiers (Maund 1988: 181), one of whom was Robert of Jumièges, Archbishop of Canterbury. The movement of people between the English and Norman courts resulted in a 'conspicuous cultural overlap' between England and Normandy (Lewis 1990: 212; Lewis 1994: 123). However, towards the end of Edward the Confessor's reign the Anglo-Saxon nobility were in the ascendant. Harold, the son of Earl Godwine, had obtained almost regal status in court and following Edward's death in 1066 Harold took over and proclaimed himself king. This did not go unchallenged and two leaders in particular prepared to seize the throne for themselves: Harald Hardrada, King of Norway, and William, Duke of Normandy.

Harald Hardrada had forged a formidable reputation by fighting for the Byzantine emperors. The emperors paid him well for his services and he returned to Norway with so much gold that twelve young men could scarcely lift it (Shepard 1992: 281). Hardrada was certainly serious about his invasion of England even though the tradition that he claimed the throne was first recorded in the thirteenth century. The catalyst for Hardrada's invasion may well have been Tostig, Godwine's son and Harold's brother. Tostig was made Earl of Northumbria in 1055, but following a rising of Northumbrians in the autumn of 1065 he was expelled from England and fled to Baldwin V, Count of Flanders. From there he launched unsuccessful attacks on the Isle of Wight and Sandwich, before joining forces with Hardarda and launching a joint large-scale attack on York (Higham 1997: 162–7, 184–95). The relationship between Tostig and Hardrada is disputed. *The Anglo-Saxon Chronicle* mentions that Tostig submitted to Hardrada as his vassal (i.e. Hardrada was Tostig's lord), but modern commentators have seen the York attack as more of a pact (Williams 1978: 164).

There were other claimants for the English crown, though without the force or political power to pose a serious threat. Swein Estrithson of Denmark, nephew to Cnut and one of the last survivors of the royal house of Denmark, claimed that Edward the Confessor had promised him the kingship of England in 1042. An Anglo-Saxon claimant was Edgar the Ætheling, the grandson of King Edmund 'Ironside' who ruled in 1016 before being defeated by Cnut. As a 12-year-old Edgar's claim was never a strong one, but he did have royal blood (Williams 1978: 164–5). On the sidelines was Baldwin V of Flanders, who was related to Harold and Tostig (Tostig had married Baldwin's half-sister), and to Duke William of Normandy (William had married Matilda, Baldwin's daughter). Baldwin allowed Flemish mercenaries and ships to fight for both William and Tostig, but Baldwin remained neutral and neither actively supported nor hindered either party (van Houts 1995: 843; Nip 1998: 151). The two strongest contenders for the throne were the de-facto king, Harold Godwineson, and Duke William of Normandy. Both believed that Edward the Confessor had promised them the throne, and therefore they were the rightful heirs.

At the centre of the dispute was the relevance of the dying King Edward the Confessor's wishes. At this point the Anglo-Saxon and Norman traditions clashed. Duke William had been promised the crown by Edward the Confessor in 1051 and Edward's magnates – including Stigand, Archbishop of Canterbury and the powerful earls, Godwine of Wessex, Leofric of Mercia, Siward of Northumbria all swore to accept him on Edward's death. William's position was made stronger by the fact that he had rescued Harold after he had fallen into the hands of Guy, Count of Ponthieu. Whilst in William's court he swore an oath that he would be William's deputy in Edward's court and would ensure William received the throne (Davis and Chibnall 1998:

67–77). In Norman tradition once a bequest or oath had been made it could never be revoked, even by deathbed testament. The combination of Edward's promise and Harold's oath took precedence over all other forms of bequest (Williams 1978: 165). This version of events has been disputed as Norman propaganda in order for William to claim the throne, but the facts leave the issue open to doubt (Golding 1994: 15–26).

In Anglo-Saxon England an oral deathbed bequest (*verba novissima*) by the testator to the priest who administered last rites took precedence over all over bequests, so long as it was executed in the correct legal form. Harold therefore claimed his nomination took precedence over all previous promises. Harold, using Anglo-Saxon tradition, and William, using Norman tradition, each believed they had been legally promised the crown (Williams 1978: 166–9).

Whatever the truth of the matter, Harold succeeded to the crown when Edward granted it to him on his deathbed. The E version of *The Anglo-Saxon Chronicle* states that 'Earl Harold succeeded to the kingdom of England, just as the king had granted it to him – and also men chose him for it' (Swanton 2000: 196).

William and Harold prepared for the forthcoming fight. Harold readied the fleet and called out the fyrd, the trained militia, along the south coast. During the summer there was a phoney war, with both sides preparing for action but nothing of consequence happened in military terms.

Duke William had by far the greatest challenge in front of him. Although he could raise an effective army, the ships needed to carry that army and their provisions had to be constructed or acquired. One document, known as the Ship List, is reputedly a list of William's barons with the number of ships they should supply. The list has often been seen as a later invention, although van Houts has argued that it is a contemporary text written in Normandy, after 13 December 1067 or c.1072 (van Houts 1987: 174). The list shows that three barons along the Seine were expected to supply a total of 160 ships between them, a feat which would have required half the forest reserves of the Seine basin. The likelihood is they might have purchased or hired ships from Flanders (Gillmor 1984: 116, 119–21). If the ships were indeed built from new (as shown in the Bayeux Tapestry) then the speed of working was incredible. In early February 1066 Roger II of Montgomery promised sixty newly constructed ships in less than six months, on average one being built every two working days (Bachrach 1985: 17).

The campaign logistics

The logistical problems facing William in gathering ships, men and horses were enormous. Modern estimates of the numbers of men needed for the invasion put the total at about 14,000 with 3,000 horses. A camp was set up at Dives sur Mer. A reference by the contemporary writer, William of Poitiers, indicates an organised supply of provisions at the camp, for he states that 'an abundant provision was made for the soldiers and their hosts and no one was permitted to seize anything' (Davis and Chibnall 1998: 103). In other words, the soldiers did not have to scavenge or plunder the neighbourhood. It has been suggested by Bachrach that the internal organisation of the camp was masterminded by Roger II of Montgomery and that it was likely that every person was assigned to a tent and unit within the camp. To make 1,000 ten-man tents, 36,000 hides were needed (Bachrach 1985). For a month's stay, the material requirements for the camp have been calculated as: 420 tons of firewood; 210 carts of wine; and a daily minimum (assuming routine and very boring diet) of 28 tons of unmilled wheat grain and 14,000 gallons of fresh water. The horses in turn produced 5,000,000 pounds of faeces and 700,000 gallons of urine and required 8,000–12,000 horseshoes, which in turn required 75,000 nails and 8 tons of iron (Bachrach 1985: 11–14).

The order and scale of the camp have led historians to query what template William was using, for it is unlikely that such a successful camp was created without any model to follow. There are two basic theories: William was using either Byzantine/Roman or Viking systems. William's Roman template may have come from the military writings of Caesar and Vegetius, which were known in Normandy (Bachrach 1985: 5). However, the alternative is that William was following the logistics of large Viking 'round forts', which could house hundreds of men. A round fort has been discovered on one of the Dutch islands, relatively near to Normandy (Roesdahl 1986). There have been similar discussions as to whether the design of the ships to transport the horses came from Byzantine and Sicilian practices (Waley 1954; Bachrach 1985) or previous Viking practice (Gillmor 1984; Grainge and Grainge 1999: 120) and whether the Norman vessels used rowers or only sail (Gillmor 1984: 110; Grainge and Grainge 1999: 120).

The size of William's fleet is also unknown. The late twelfth-century poet, Wace, was told by his father that the Conqueror's fleet had 696 ships, which sounds more accurate than the undoubtedly over-inflated report of 3,000 by William of Jumièges and the extravagant 11,000 claim by Gaimar (Gillmor 1984: 105). However, how realistic is the figure of 696 ships? In an analysis of Wace's work, Bennett suggests that Wace 'does little better than most medieval authors when dealing with numbers. . . . It was simply not fashionable to count. Even his figures of seeming exactitude, like the like the 696 of Duke William's invasion fleet . . . are dubious' (Bennett 1988: 44). Even though the number might not be exact, most commentators take the figure as a good starting point.

With the fleet built, the waiting game started because the winds were constantly in the wrong direction for sailing. As well as military preparations, William also commenced a diplomatic offensive, winning the support of the papacy for the venture and converting most of public opinion in Latin Christendom to his cause (Allen Brown 1980: 6; van Houts 1995: 832). Potential enemies were also neutralised through marriage, wars or alliances (Douglas 1964; Beech 1986: 14). Spiritual concerns were also important and the dedication of La Trinité in Caen on 17 June 1066 in front of the Norman assembly has been seen as a key element in William's spiritual preparation for invasion (Danbabin 1993: 111). Pope Alexander II sent William a banner to ensure God's protection for the army and thus an overlay of Holy War to William's plans of conquest (Maccarini 1983: 173). To increase further his chances of winning, William of Poitiers reported that William wore round his neck 'the relics whose protection Harold had forfeited from by breaking the oath that he had sworn on them' (Davis and Chibnall 1998: 125).

Voyage and arrival

Meanwhile in the north of England another threat had suddenly emerged for Harold, for Harald Hardrada and Tostig had joined forces and landed in Yorkshire. The puzzling element about Hardrada's invasion, and then Harold's attack at Stamford Bridge, is the element of surprise in both cases (Allen Brown 1980: 6). Harold was informed of the invasion as he disembarked in London, but there had been no early warning system, no moves to mobilise the forces in the north and nothing comparable to the calling out of the fyrd on the south coast. Even the northern earls – Edwin and Morcar – did not put a system of defence into operation. Moreover a fleet of more than 300 ships collecting in Norway and meeting in Scotland with Tostig's forces would have been hard to conceal. That Harold should have no intelligence of such a dangerous opponent as Tostig, his own brother, is perplexing. Whatever the reasons, a surprise it was and Harold marched north to meet the threat. Hardrada marched on York, defeating a local force in a bloody skirmish led by the northern earls Edwin and Morcar on 20 September at Fulford Gate. Some of the victims were probably buried in the local cemetery of St Andrew's Fishergate, just outside York (Daniell 2001).

Victorious, Hardrada claimed York and then retreated to Stamford Bridge, presumably to await hostages. The reason why Stamford Bridge was chosen is problematic. Apart from a bridge crossing the Derwent there is no obvious tactical advantage in retreating from York with its superb fortifications. Perhaps there was the fear of an uprising by the local inhabitants who had previously ousted Tostig from his position as Earl of Northumbria. Another possibility was that Stamford Bridge was a deliberately provocative choice as it was probably part of Harold's estate of Catton. The Vikings had therefore moved onto Harold's own land to show they were in control (Williams 1980: 184–5).

Harold marched north and surprised Hardrada at Stamford Bridge. The battle, fought on 25 September, was long and vicious. Initially a single Viking warrior held the bridge until an English soldier climbed into a barrel, floated under the bridge and 'stabbed him through under the mail-coat', as *The Anglo-Saxon Chronicle* records (Swanton 2000: 198). The English stormed across and in the ensuing battle Harald Hardrada, Tostig and large numbers of Vikings were killed. The Battle of Stamford Bridge marked the end of the era of large-scale Viking invasions (Allen Brown 1980: 7). In the meantime William was preparing to sail from his base camp at Dives sur Mer.

But before the crossing the fleet collected at St Valéry. Some scholars have suggested that St Valéry was deliberately chosen to improve the chance of a south wind and to avoid Harold's ships at the Isle of Wight (Gillmor 1984). However, a counter argument has been made which states that after William brought the fleet out of harbour at Dives he was forced northwards by the winds. This was far from ideal, for the shoreline of St Valéry was notoriously treacherous and some men may have been drowned (Grainge and Grainge 1999: 136–7).

As a straight line St Valéry to Pevensey is 97 km, but an additional 30–40 kms should be allowed for tidal currents (Neumann 1988: 127). Some incidental details of this momentous crossing have survived: the ships were fitted with lanterns on their masts for the night sailing and when the ship carrying Duke William lost contact with the others – a potentially disastrous occurrence – a sailor climbed up the mast to see the other ships. Taking into account all the calculations about tides and winds, there is general agreement that the crossing was straightforward, though the actual date of arrival at Pevensey is unclear, being either 28 September 1066 (Neumann 1988: 221) or the morning of the 29 September (Grainge and Grainge 1999: 139).

The shape of the Sussex coastline today is very different to that of 1066 and little is known about the coastal ports of the south coast in the eleventh century (Neumann 1988: 227; Gardiner 1999: 88–93). On his arrival at Pevensey, William quickly set up a secure base, built a wooden castle, organised patrols and added to the fortifications of the captured Roman fort (Bachrach 1985: 21). William's choice of Pevensey to base his fleet was probably governed by the fact that it was a good harbour away from strong Anglo-Saxon settlements. Of equal importance may have been that Pevensey was in easy striking distance of Harold's lands. The following day William's forces marched to Hastings, built a castle and began to ravage the countryside as an act of provocation. Like Hardrada at Stamford Bridge, William was dishonouring Harold by attacking his homelands, which in turn would demand retaliation and a rapid response (Allen Brown 1980: 10)

Meanwhile the Anglo-Saxons under Harold were in disarray. There are many unanswered questions about the Anglo-Saxon preparations and their response to the invasion. Harold had called out the Anglo-Saxon militia (the fyrd) along the south coast as he had expected an invasion from Normandy during the summer. Both William and Harold were probably fretting about the lack of wind. Harold's fleet was based at the Isle of Wight, but *The Anglo-Saxon Chronicle* recorded that 'in the end it was to no avail. Then when it was the Nativity of St Mary (8 September), the men's provisions were gone, and no one could hold them there any longer. Then the men were allowed to go home, and the king rode inland, and the ships were sent to London'

(Swanton 2000: 196). The 'all or nothing' nature of the fyrd was a serious drawback to Anglo-Saxon defences, for there seems to have been no element of rotation of the troops, or any ability to mobilise extra troops in rapid response to any threat. The Anglo-Saxon troops went home, having used their provisions. It seems that whereas William had ease of acquiring men and horses, but difficulty in finding enough ships, Harold had the ships, but the fyrd was more of a problem. With the fyrd back home the south coast was left without adequate defences.

The Battle of Hastings

After a forced march from the north, Harold arrived to confront William's army at Senlac Hill – or Battle as it was called soon after. The numbers facing each other are broadly agreed by historians. Each side had roughly 7,000–8,000 soldiers. Calculations suggest that William had brought 14,000 men over with him, with 1,000 men manning the garrisons at Pevensey and Hastings, 3,500 sailors (five for each of the 700 ships), and then a contingent of non-combatants, including cooks, servants, carpenters, smiths, clerks and monks (Gillmor 1984: 106; Bachrach 1985: 2). A contemporary account by the Poitevin chronicler of St Maixent also records 14,000 men, but how he came to know this figure is a mystery (Beech 1986: 16).

Although the core of the invasion force was Norman, as many as one-fifth of the army may have been non-Norman. The Flemish connection was a strong one as William's Queen, Matilda, was the daughter of the Count of Flanders (Rowlands 1980: 146). There were probably three main contingents of nationalities, Franco-Flemings, Normans and Bretons, each deployed with archers and crossbowmen in front, heavy infantry behind, knights/cavalry in the rear (Cook 1978: 100). Other nationalities included a Poitevin contingent led by the Count of Poitou, Aimeri.

On the English side the professional core of the army consisted of Harold's own housecarls and those of his brothers, Gyrth and Leofwine, as well as of the other great lords. There would also have been troops from the provinces. The traditional view of the status of the housecarls was that they formed a distinctive element in the Anglo-Saxon military organisation, though this has been challenged and they have been described as 'indistinguishable from their neighbours, and together with their tenants the thegns the housecarls formed the shire hosts' (Hooper 1984: 175).

At the time of the battle the two sides had roughly equal numbers. However, if Harold had waited he might have greatly increased his army's strength. The E version of *The Anglo-Saxon Chronicle* states that Harold fought 'before all the army had come', and Florence of Worcester reported that Harold 'gave them battle, before a third of his army was drawn up' (Allen Brown 1980: 8). A case has even been made for a potential Anglo-Saxon manpower pool of 375,000 (25 per cent of a population of 1.5 million in

Saxon England) with a select fyrd ranging from 14,000 to 20,000 (Bachrach 1985: 25). The Norman explanation for Harold's speed of action was that Harold intended to take William by surprise, a view suggested by the Norman chroniclers William of Jumièges, William of Poitiers and Orderic Vitalis, the last two adding that Harold even considered a night attack (Allen Brown 1980: 8).

At sunrise on 14 October 1066 the two armies met with Harold gaining the higher ground and forming his army upon the crest of a ridge, with the Normans some 600–800 yards away. The battle itself has provoked many debates about the strength, effectiveness and tactics of the opposing sides. Some historians have viewed the Normans as more technologically advanced (especially in terms of cavalry warfare), William as the more able general, and the Normans as the superior army (Round, Fuller, Allen Brown) whilst others have argued that the sides were much more evenly matched (Glover, Morillo). (For the discussions see Morillo 1999.)

Pitched battles between opposing leaders were a rare event in the Middle Ages. The potential decisiveness of the result and the possibility of death often caused hesitation on the part of the participants. Death of a leader was a vital consideration. Even the rumour of death could be serious. During the battle William only refuted the rumour that he had died by taking off his helmet so that all could see him. Whilst both leaders had fought in war, only Harold had led an army into battle previously – a few weeks before at Stamford Bridge (Gillingham 1999: 96–101).

As the armies stood before each other, their composition and chosen tactics were radically different. Harold's Anglo-Saxon army had marched and ridden from the north, but all stood on foot forming a shield wall through which axes could be wielded. A shield wall presented a continuous front to the enemy but allowed the use of weapons and movement of men behind it. Even groups of inexperienced troops could offer strong resistance using this tactic (Hooper 1978: 92). A few archers were also part of the force. In essence Harold was following traditional Anglo-Saxon tactics of using foot troops, though Graham Campbell has argued that the Anglo-Saxons may have used cavalry if their horses had not been exhausted after the ride south from Stamford Bridge (Cook 1978: 97; Graham Campbell 1991: 89).

William's army was made up of three main components: archers and crossbowmen, heavy infantry, and heavy cavalry. Old Anglo-Saxon tactics met new Continental tactics. The archers not only aimed directly at the enemy, they also shot their arrows on a high trajectory forcing those in the shield wall to cover their heads and thus were exposed to a cavalry charge. The cavalry's weapons included a straight slashing sword – most frequently mentioned in accounts – and an ash lance about 8–9 feet in length, which was thrown as a javelin at the opposing lines (Cook 1978: 97–100). However, despite William's innovative use of cavalry at Hastings, late eleventh- and twelfth-century military tactics did not permanently change and in the twelfth century battles were normally fought on foot. In the Battle of the

Standard of 1138 the Anglo-Norman knights all dismounted and fought behind a shield wall, in the same way as the Anglo-Saxon army at Hastings (Graham Campbell 1991: 89). The Battle of Hastings did, however, highlight the effectiveness of the cavalry as a fighting force.

William's tactics involved the skilful coordination of infantry and cavalry, shown through the disciplined attacks and retreats by cavalry units (called 'conroi'). The most likely groups were the households of individual lords who could train together. Other battles where feigned retreat or concerted action was used by the Normans included St Aubin-le-Cauf near Arques in 1052–3, near Messina in 1060 and by Robert le Frison of Flanders at Cassel in 1071 (Allen Brown 1980: 16). William of Malmesbury also mentions Baldwin – whom William described as 'not far short of the best soldier who ever lived' – making feigned retreats on crusade (Mynors *et al.* 1998: 669).

The Norman horses were considered to be of amazing quality. That there was differentiation amongst Norman horses is shown by the different monetary values for different types of horse, whilst the Anglo-Saxon references treated all horses equally (Davis 1987: 81). Modern historians estimate that the horses were no more than 14 hands high (Davis 1987: 69). (A hand is four inches and 14 hands high is about the size of a large modern pony.) Archaeological evidence confirms this (Graham Campbell 1991: 78). Sometimes horses could be smaller. Richard son of Ascletin, the Norman Count of Aversa, preferred to ride horses so small that his feet almost touched the ground (Davis 1987: 69). The indigenous species in Europe was about the size of the present Shetland pony and so for the Normans to achieve horses of 14 hands high there must have been selective breeding on stud farms. Further height was gained by the Normans using metal stirrups so that they could stand up in their saddles, which also increased the leverage for a sword slash or lance thrust (Cook 1978: 98). (Stirrups were not a Norman innovation as they were also known to the Anglo-Saxons (Graham Campbell 1991: 79).) Although soldiers were heavily armoured, horses were not and the death and injury of the horses during the Battle of Hastings is graphically depicted on the Bayeux Tapestry.

The different tactics made it a peculiar battle. The Bayeux Tapestry shows how the Normans were in constant motion with cavalry charges and troop movements, whilst the Anglo-Saxons were rooted to the spot (Bernstein 1982: 41). It could be said that the shield wall acted as an immovable object against the unstoppable force of the Norman cavalry assault. During the battle the Normans made little headway until a feigned retreat tempted the Anglo-Saxons in the shield wall to pursue the fleeing cavalry. With the shield wall broken, the cavalry turned and attacked.

It was an unknown archer, however, who dealt perhaps the greatest blow by hitting King Harold in the eye. The depiction of Harold's death on the Bayeux Tapestry shows two figures, one has an arrow in his eye and the other is being hacked down by a knight. Careful study of the Tapestry has shown that they are the same man, for the warrior being hacked down did at one time have an arrow in his eye before the stitching was removed (Bernstein 1982). The Anglo-Saxons, realising they were beaten, turned and fled. Duke William had won the crown of England.

It is likely that for most Normans the Battle of Hastings was the largest and bloodiest engagement they would ever experience (Strickland 1992: 59). Later the poet Baudri wrote:

> Victory without injury is granted to neither side,
> and the dry earth runs with the blood of the slain
> (Brown and Herren 1993: 66)

Even so, the casualties on the Norman side were remarkably light; their only significant casualty was Engenulf of Laigle (Thompson 1995: 180).

For the Anglo-Saxons the battle was a disaster. King Harold was dead. His brothers, earls Leofwine and Gyrth, also lay dead. Their combined earldoms covered the greater part of southern and eastern England (Lewis 1990: 216). With Harold, Leofwine and Gyrth dead at Hastings, and their brother Tostig dead at Stamford Bridge, the House of Godwine had been smashed.

Despite the historic consequences of the battle and that it is the best known event in English history, little is known about the people who fought. Douglas identified only twenty-seven people whose presence is established by specific evidence, and five other people who probably fought (Douglas 1943; Cook 1978: 95). Ten of the twenty-seven men are given in a famous catalogue of warriors, listed by William of Poitiers, for their bravery and prowess (Martindale 1984: 224).

Aftermath

The two months between the Battle of Hastings (14 October) and William's coronation (25 December) in 1066 were a period of turmoil. Gradually, important Anglo-Saxons submitted to William – Stigand, the Archbishop of Canterbury, submitted to William at Wallingford, and then oaths of allegiance were given by the chief men of London, Archbishop Ealdred of York, Edgar the Ætheling and the Anglo-Saxon earls Edwin and Morcar. Neither side could have misunderstood the importance of the oaths as William began to secure his power (Nelson 1981: 117; Davis and Chibnall 1998: 147–9).

William faced a fundamental decision: should he crown himself king? Despite his overwhelming victory his followers were wary of him elevating his title from Duke of Normandy to King of England, for with kingship came greater powers. Alternatively, the Anglo-Saxons expected William to become king, for them kingship was the traditional, authoritative centre of power (Nelson 1981: 118). In some accounts the deciding moment came in a speech by Aimeri, Count of Poitou, who urged William to have himself crowned without delay (Beech 1986: 9). William was crowned in Westminster Abbey on Christmas Day 1066. On his being crowned, the Anglo-Saxons in

the Abbey let out a tremendous shout which nearly had disastrous consequences, as William of Poitiers described: 'But the men, who, armed and
mounted, had been placed as a guard round the minster, on hearing the loud
clamour in an unknown tongue, thought that some treachery was afoot and
rashly set fire to houses near the city' (Davis and Chibnall 1998: 151). As the
fire blazed outside, William may have feared that God had turned against
him. The moment passed, William was alive and still king. His king-
making was not only to demonstrate his power, but also an act of reconciliation in an (initially unsuccessful) attempt to mark the end of harrying
and war, inaugurating peace between conquerors and conquered (Nelson
1981: 122–3, 128).

For the rest of his reign William used the title King of the English (not
England) whilst in England and could issue writs as King of the English
whilst in Normandy, but there was always a careful distinction – he was
never titled King of the Normans. Very occasionally the titles of King and
Duke were used jointly on documents (Garnett 1985: 112).

Even though the papacy had supported William, its attitude to the
shedding of blood between Christian enemies was very ambiguous. The
church insisted upon a penance for those who fought and killed at Hastings
and in the subsequent campaigns. Bishop Eremfield of Sion drew up the
'Penitential Ordinance' (normally dated to 1067, and possibly issued at
the Fecamp Easter assembly) (Nelson 1981: 129; Chibnall 1984: 127). The
ordinance was aimed at those men who owed military service to William as
Duke (van Houts 1987: 160). This accords with the concept of a 'public
war', which could only be fought on the orders of a legitimate ruler against
those who were subverting Christian peace (Garnett 1985: 115). That such
an ordinance was drawn up at all suggests that in ecclesiastical and church
minds the carnage of Hastings was greater than most battles. The last such
ordinance was for a bloody battle in 924 (Strickland 1992a: 55–6). Penances
included founding monasteries, convents or endowing churches, both for the
actions of battle and for gaining lands which were not inherited. The
chronicler Orderic Vitalis considered that the foundation of Shrewsbury
Abbey by Roger of Montgomery was partial reparation for acquiring the
earldom from the Conqueror, rather than through inheritance (Chibnall
1984: 127; Thompson 1993: 226). William the Conqueror's foundation of
Battle Abbey on the spot where Harold fell may be part of his penance,
though the legend of its foundation was first recorded over a hundred years
after the event, casting doubt upon its authenticity (Searle 1979: 155; Allen
Brown 1980: 3; Nelson 1981: 129).

William's policy in the first few years of his reign suggests that he
attempted to integrate the Anglo-Saxon and Norman nobles in the government of England. Providing subjects gave him allegiance, they were allowed
to retain their positions. Edwin and Morcar remained earls of Mercia and
Northumbria and, in total, five of William's earls were English (Lewis 1990:
216). The archbishops of Canterbury and York also continued in office, despite

grave misgivings about the state of the Anglo-Saxon church. Whereas, sixty years earlier, King Cnut had immediately executed potential enemies after his conquest, William was lenient with Anglo-Saxon nobles until the revolts of 1068–71. Furthermore, as William depicted himself as the true heir to Edward the Confessor, he respected the pronouncements of the previous Anglo-Saxon kings, with the exception of Harold (Hayward 1998: 90).

Bayeux Tapestry

One result of the Conquest which can still be seen is the magnificent Bayeux Tapestry. The Bayeux Tapestry is technically an embroidery on a linen cloth, over 70 m long and 50 cm high. The detail and intricacy is superb, incorporating 626 people, 202 horses, 555 other animals, 37 buildings and 41 ships. Despite its fame and uniqueness today, it 'would have been considered quite ordinary by the Anglo-Saxons, for it lacks the preciousness of gold thread which was one of their hallmarks of excellence' (Dodwell 1982: 139). The consensus amongst art historians is that it was made in Canterbury under the auspices of William the Conqueror's half-brother, Odo, Bishop of Bayeux. The Tapestry shows the political and military events leading up to the invasion, the detailed preparations, the sailing to Hastings, followed by the battle. The last scene shows the Anglo-Saxon army fleeing. Opinion is more or less equally divided as to whether it is Norman or Anglo-Saxon propaganda, but, as has been recently pointed out, perhaps its most important theme concerns the role and status of kingship and associated perjury. Indeed, the first image on the Tapestry is that of Edward the Confessor enthroned as king. The end is missing, but might have had William enthroned (Thompson 1999). The imagery has been used by many to show actual events and details from the Conquest, even down to William the Conqueror's figurehead on the prow of his ship (van Houts 1987: 166). However, a note of caution has been sounded by Hart (1999) who has pointed out the many similarities in detail between the Bayeux Tapestry and the illustrated manuscripts known to have been at Canterbury, notably the Utrecht and Harley Psalters and the Old English Hexateuch. Hart has also cast doubt on how contemporary the details and practices depicted on the Tapestry were. This caution applies to many famous scenes, including the carpenters building the ships.

The first known documentary reference to the Tapestry occurs as Item 262 in the 1476 Inventory of the Treasure of Bayeux Cathedral, but there is a strong possibility of a prior reference to it in the poem 'Adelae Comitissae'. The poem was written by the late eleventh-century poet Baudri of Bourgeuil (d. 1130) for Adela, William the Conqueror's daughter and Countess of Blois. Baudri says he is describing a pictorial wall hanging (Brown and Herren 1993: 55–7) and adds details, such as in a passage about the construction of the ships he describes how:

the ash, the oak and the ilex fall,
the pine is uprooted by the trunk.
The aged fir is hauled down from the steep mountains;
labour gives value to all trees.

(Brown and Herren 1993: 62)

Anglo-Saxon options

With William crowned King there were four possible options for the noble
Anglo-Saxons still in England: be captured, flee, fight or join the ranks of
the Normans. It was not an easy decision. The Normans themselves have
been described as 'cruel, greedy, proud, domineering, oppressive, class-
conscious, usually race-conscious, extraordinarily self-confident – except on
their death beds' (J.F.A. Mason 1990: 261), and against this background
individual Anglo-Saxons had to judge which possibility would lead to the
best outcome for themselves.

As captives, important Anglo-Saxon nobles were a rich political prize.
William of Poitiers describes how William paraded his captives and the
spoils of his victory in Normandy, much in the style of a Roman general
parading his captives in Rome (Dumville 1993: 85). William also took two
Anglo-Saxon earls, Edwin and Morcar, to Normandy in 1067 to ensure good
behaviour of their respective earldoms, Mercia and Northumbria, though
they returned to England in 1068 (Lewis 1990: 216). After the show came
the practicalities of what to do with the captives. For many the answer was a
'genteel captivity' in Normandy (Dumville 1993: 97). In a foreign land,
with foreign customs and a different language the political power of the
Anglo-Saxon captives was neutralised. An alternative was to be imprisoned
in a monastic community: Æthelric, Bishop of Durham, was imprisoned in
Westminster Abbey, his brother Æthelwine in Abingdon Abbey (Mason 1998:
115) and Godric, Abbot of Winchcombe, was deposed in 1068 and imprisoned
at Gloucester and then Evesham (Hayward 1998: 92). Secular enemies could
also be confined in a monastery and circumstantial evidence points to
Wulfnoth, Harold's remaining brother, being imprisoned in Winchester
Cathedral Priory.

Another possibility was to flee the country. The nearest safe haven was
Scotland and William of Malmesbury described how King Malcolm 'had a
warm welcome for all the runaways on the English side . . .' including the
last of the Anglo-Saxon royal line, Edgar the Ætheling and his sisters
Margaret and Christina. King Malcolm married Margaret about 1069
(Mynors *et al.* 1998: 463). Some Anglo-Saxons fled further afield. Harold's
mother, Gytha, fled to Flanders in 1068 and Robert the Frisian welcomed
political exiles such as Gospatrick of Northumbria (Nip 1998: 153). Other
Anglo-Saxons with Viking or Anglo-Saxon sympathies migrated to Denmark
and Norway, one of whom was Abbot Alsin of St Augustine's Canterbury

who left in 1071 (Godfrey 1978: 68). Another was Abbot Ælfwold of St Benet, who had been entrusted by Harold with a naval command, who fled to Denmark before returning and resuming office (Williams 1980: 179).

The largest exodus was a group of Anglo-Saxons who left the country in the 1070s in a fleet said to number 235 ships. Such a fleet would have been impossible to conceal from William and if the figure, given in the Byzantine *Latin Chronicle*, is correct they must have been given permission to leave. The chronicle describes their journey to Byzantium where they remained (Godfrey 1978: 69).

Lower down the social scale the villeins, small tenant farmers, and medium landowners had no choice but to cooperate with their new Norman masters and it is quite possible that they viewed their Norman lords as a not unwelcome replacement for their Anglo-Saxon masters. On the estates of Norman nobles Anglo-Saxons were probably important and two reeves, 'both clearly Englishmen, and somewhat acquisitive', have been identified as working for Richard de Clare in 1086 (Mortimer 1980: 133). Anglo-Saxon expertise was also used by royal administrators or Norman sheriffs to inform them of local duties and service (Green 1982: 132).

Some middling Anglo-Saxon landowners accepted the Normans and prospered. The two best known are Thorkill of Arden (Williams 1988) and Colswein of Lincoln, both of whom held some political influence. At a slightly lower level of importance there were many others, such as Alfred of Marlborough, Osbern fitz Richard and Swein of Essex, Azor and Oswald, who are often described as Norman by historians but could equally be of Anglo-Saxon lineage (Mortimer 1980: 124; Lewis 1994: 138). At a lower level there were many Anglo-Saxon landowners who survived on their estates, albeit in more straitened circumstances, and evidence from Wiltshire in particular shows this (Loyn 1987: 231).

The final option, favoured by many Anglo-Saxon nobles, was to fight the Normans, either internally or through raids from overseas. The remaining sons of Harold launched a raid on Devon in 1069. Exeter was attacked by the men of Devon and Cornwall; Shrewsbury was attacked by the men of Chester and Eadric the Wild. William quelled these attacks by sheer force, though their complete lack of coordination allowed him to pick them off one by one (Williams 1997: 24–44).

However, it was the revolt of the Northumbrians which was the most serious. In 1068 and 1069 the rebels ransacked Durham and at York the Norman castle garrison was killed. William's response has become known as the Harrying of the North. The extent, impact and lasting consequences have been disputed. It was certainly considered by near contemporaries as a devastating campaign. The chronicler Orderic Vitalis, citing William the Conqueror's supposed deathbed speech, wrote:

> I [William] treated the native inhabitants of the kingdom with unreason-
> able severity, cruelly oppressed high and low, unjustly disinherited

many, and caused the death of thousands by starvation and war, especially in Yorkshire . . . I descended on the English of the north like a raging lion, and ordered that their homes and crops and furnishings should be burnt at once and their great flocks and herds of cattle and sheep slaughtered everywhere . . . alas! was the cruel murderer of many thousands, both young and old of this fair people.

(Chibnall 1973: 95)

There may well be a substantial element of exaggeration in this account. However, Symeon of Durham recorded that the countryside remained empty and uncultivated for nine years. The Harrying has been used to describe many features of northern life, for example it is given as a reason why there are no slaves recorded in the Yorkshire sections of Domesday Book (Moore 1988:200). Such an explanation is probably too easy however, for true slavery was declining fast throughout England, and it may never have been a feature of Yorkshire society, or it may simply not have been recorded. One indicator that has been used to determine the extent of the Harrying is the large number of villages in Yorkshire described as 'waste' written in Domesday Book of 1086. Unfortunately there are a large number of reasons why the term 'waste' could be applied to a village, for example it may not have rendered tax.

The one remaining outpost of revolt was in the fenlands of East Anglia. The Anglo-Saxon forces were led by Hereward the Wake. Hereward himself and some of his followers, such as Thorkell of Harringworth, were substantial land holders who had been dispossessed by the Normans of their lands, or feared dispossession. The revolt of 1070–1 was strengthened by Earl Morcar of Northumbria and his brother, Earl Edwin of Mercia, who was disappointed not to have been given William's daughter in marriage (Searle 1980:163). Edwin died before the last battle, but Hereward and Morcar's forces were defeated by a combined land and water attack led by William himself. One of the results of the defeat was that the earldoms of Mercia and Northumbria began to be dismantled (Head 1997; Williams 1997:45–57).

As well as Anglo-Saxon revolts, William the Conqueror had to deal with uprisings amongst his former friends. In the autumn of 1067 Eustace of Boulogne, who was reputed to have killed Harold at Hastings, launched an attack on Dover. The attack failed and cost him the territories granted to him by William, though they were later reconciled. In 1086 Eustace was one of the ten wealthiest magnates in England (Tanner 1991:272–4). In 1075 three earls rebelled against William; Waltheof, Earl of Northumbria, Roger, Earl of Hereford, a Norman and eldest son of William's most trusted friend William FitzOsbern, and Ralph Guader, a Breton who benefited by the Conquest and was Earl of East Anglia. Each of them had individual grievances, though the common grievance was that they received less land than they thought they deserved. The revolt was quickly crushed, and

Waltheof was executed, a cult developing around his shrine at Crowland (Chibnall 1984: 108; Williams 1997: 55–67; Hayward 1998: 92). He was the last of his line to rule in Northumbria.

The impact of the Conquest

The Conquest had a dramatic effect over the next twenty years upon the make-up of society. The introduction of castles, the building of churches and the plundering of England were more obvious signs of the Norman presence. Contemporaries were well aware of the changes and Hermann, the chronicler at Bury St Edmunds, wrote: '[King William] implanted the customs of the French throughout England, and began to change those of the English' (Gransden 1981: 68). However, within the day-to-day lives of the resident population the change produced by Conquest is very hard to see. Pottery is often the best indicator of innovation or new contacts, but in the case of the Norman Conquest there is no evidence of the Conquest in the pottery record at all (Mahany and Roffe 1982: 216).

One immediate result of Conquest was that the Normans seized what they could, especially from the richer churches of the kingdom. Harold's foundation of Waltham Abbey was ransacked, the Normans taking three gold shrines and four silver gilt shrines, relics, precious jewels, four books covered with gold, silver and jewels and four large gold and silver censers (Rogers 1992: 163). The quality of the looted treasure was considered remarkable by the Normans (Dodwell 1982: 217–34). William of Poitiers stated that 'Treasures remarkable for their number and kind and workmanship had been amassed' in England and that after the Conquest gold crosses, jewels and vessels were given to churches on the continent (Davis and Chibnall 1998: 153–5). Though the spoliation of the great churches was usually commented upon, it is likely that many chapels, churches on estates and smaller monasteries were also looted.

A study of Anglo-Saxon books has shown that plundering of books following the Conquest is one of the reasons that Anglo-Saxon books can often be found abroad. Over forty high-class, late Anglo-Saxon manuscripts travelled to the Continent in the late eleventh and early twelfth centuries, though by the middle of the century this had ceased. Not all were looted and some could have been sent to be copied. Interestingly, one category of Anglo-Saxon book does not seem to have been exported – the vernacular illustrated book, possibly showing that content and intelligibility of the manuscript was an important factor in determining what was taken to Normandy. Moreover, the pattern of exported books is uneven, with none from Durham or Exeter, but some from Canterbury and Winchester. This may be because a powerful bishop was able to defend church possessions and lands, whereas the absence of a strong bishop resulted in looting (Dumville 1993: 88–93).

Tenurial revolution and land disputes

The Norman Conquest resulted in a large number of Anglo-Saxon landholders of the upper and middling ranks being dispossessed, with their lands
and wealth being given to comparatively few nobles. By the time of
Domesday Book in 1086 the dispossession of the Anglo-Saxon nobles was
practically complete (Holt 1997). The scale of the change can be expressed
in numbers. Around 5,000 pre-Conquest estates were concentrated into the
hands of less than 200 major lay tenants-in-chief, who between them
controlled 54 per cent of England in 1086. The twenty richest lords and
twelve richest prelates held some 40 per cent of land as expressed in value.

Some Norman barons did spectacularly well. William the Conqueror's
half-brother, Odo of Bayeux, was pre-eminent amongst the nobility and his
English lands far exceeded those of any other Norman noble. Domesday
Book lists his estates in twenty-two counties, mainly south-east of a line
from the Humber to the Severn, which was worth about £3,050 in 1086
(Bates 1975). The geographical scattering of Odo's estates was exceptional,
but many of the great lords had estates across several counties. The spread of
estates across counties can be seen as an attempt by William to weaken the
nobility by dispersing any potential power base, but it is noticeable that the
King and his closest nobles all had scattered estates – the wide dispersal of
estates meant that all areas of the kingdom had a royal or noble presence.
This was not new and the Anglo-Saxon kings had followed similar policies,
though mostly in the south. William expanded his sphere of influence
throughout the kingdom. A consequence of the scattering of estates meant
that nobles could not govern them all personally, so many less wealthy
estates were let out at extortionate rents, whilst the more profitable estates
were controlled directly by the nobleman (Lennard 1959: 51; Mortimer
1980: 132; Mason 1990: 259). The relative scarcity of compact estates across
the country also led to a growth of local tenants governing their own affairs.
Whilst still bound to the lord, tenants had more independence than if the
lord was standing over them.

As part of the process of distributing lands, important consolidated lordships were created in key military locations around the borders of the
kingdom, such as Kent and Cornwall, East Anglia and Northumbria. The
threat from the Welsh border led the Conqueror immediately after the
Conquest to devise a system whereby counties were given to individuals to
administer and control. Within four years, William the Conqueror had established Roger Montgomery at Shrewsbury and Hugh, Vicomte of Avranches,
at Chester. However, the compactness of Norman lordships in the West
Midlands was considerably broken up by the holdings of the church. As
William portrayed himself as the legitimate successor to Edward the
Confessor church lands were not officially seized, though individual lords
could illegally seize lands, resulting in long-running disputes, or negotiate
with the church (Wightman 1966: 127). The earls of Cheshire and

Shropshire were all-powerful within their shires with little or no external interference and as the king held no land in the shires, there was no sheriff either, for there was no royal land to administer (Lewis 1984: 196). Herefordshire has been described as a compact single entity similar to Cheshire and Shropshire, but Lewis (1984: 195–7) has argued that it should be seen as William the Conqueror's way of trying to place William FitzOsbern into Harold's position in Herefordshire: 'FitzOsbern was therefore given Harold's rank, Harold's lands and Harold's responsibilities. He stood nearly as high in the first year of Norman England as Harold had done in the King Edward's last days' (Lewis 1984: 197).

Under-tenants also had an important role. One such tenant was the Lacy family whose estates lay in a triangle from north Shropshire, to the Severn estuary, to south-east Oxfordshire in compact enclaves of land. It has been suggested that in the case of the Lacy family, their lord, William FitzOsbern, was creating smaller fees within his earldom so that he had a strong force to call upon when needed (Wightman 1966: 145). Following FitzOsbern's fall from grace after the rebellion of 1075 no new earl was appointed, but rather the under-tenants were promoted to become tenants-in-chief. They could further extend their power by advancing into Wales. The Lacy family advanced and named the settlement Ewyas Lacy after themselves and built a castle there. In Domesday Book of 1086 Roger de Lacy had pleas over his own men, showing his comprehensive jurisdiction in the area. Apart from the king, often hundreds of miles away, there was no higher authority in Ewyas Lacy than Roger de Lacy himself (Wightman 1966: 139–40).

Sometimes the landholdings of former Anglo-Saxon nobles were radically changed. In Sussex Anglo-Saxon nobles held lands straddling the administrative units called 'rapes'. The Normans reorganised the system into power blocks where one rape was controlled by a single lord (Searle 1979: 157). When the Honour of Clare was formed Richard fitz Gilbert amassed many estates of his predecessors and rearranged his lands and redistributed lands to his supporters to create a new lordship in Kent and new land blocks in East Anglia. It was not a particularly quick process – taking over twenty years to accomplish fully – but the changes were obvious to those on the ground (Mortimer 1980: 141). Some lords also parcelled out lands to their own supporters from the Continent. This not only brought in new landowners but also increased local loyalty to the lord. The tenants in England of Robert, Count of Eu, were men whose names reveal the origin of their families in Creil-sur-Mar, Floques, Normanville, Ricarville, Sept-Meules and Mesnires, which lie in a circle round Eu itself (Douglas 1977: 270). The same pattern can be seen in East Anglia, with the tenants of the Breton Earl Ralph the Staller, and in Herefordshire (Williams 1997: 63).

There has been considerable analysis of how the lands were redistributed and how much continuity there was between the previous Anglo-Saxon estates and the post-Conquest estates of the new Norman lords. A Norman lord might acquire his estate in a number of ways: by writ or charter directly from the king, marriage to an Anglo-Saxon heiress, or simply by force or guile (Holt 1997:5). The question can be summed up as: was there a tenurial revolution following the Norman Conquest? Peter Sawyer advocated that there was substantial continuity although he recognised that many estates were broken up, but his view was challenged by Robin Fleming who saw Sawyer's evidence as exceptional, with less of a continuity than Sawyer suggested (Sawyer 1985; Fleming 1986).

An alternative way to view the land holdings is to look at the tenurial and legal rights of the new landowners. Roffe (1990) argued that, despite the overriding power of the king's writ, the vast majority of grants of manors were passed with their rights to the new Norman lord. As the manors and their rights were passed, they included many pre-Conquest characteristics, renders (i.e. payments in kind) and legal rights. Roffe argued that 'the greatest indication of continuity lay in the renders of the estates', analysis of which leads to the conclusion that there was no radical change in land tenure and 'probably [in] most instances there was direct continuity of tenure and service' (Roffe 1990: 174).

One of the key areas studied in the continuity of land holding is the lands of Worcester Cathedral, under the control of Bishop Wulfstan. New Norman landowners simply assumed responsibility for the traditional obligations of fyrd and ship-service. The obligations remained until at least 1086 when they are mentioned in Domesday Book despite attempts by the tenants to convert their leases into hereditary fees (Mason 1985: 163–4).

At the lower level of land holding the bulk of Anglo-Saxons kept their lands under much the same conditions as previously, and it is likely that the newcomers and new subtenants held their estates following Anglo-Saxon custom (Roffe 1990: 171). A similar point has also been made by Holt, who emphasised that 'English institutions might survive where there were Englishmen to preserve them' (Holt 1997: 103–11). This is an important point for it puts the debate back to the people on the ground and the influence they had, but also shows how an Englishman might adapt to the systems of the new·Norman rulers.

In the granting of land, money was always a powerful incentive. In Anglo-Saxon times there had been a strong link between the security of tenure and the payment of geld – a payment ostensibly to secure peace from the Vikings and the Danes. Lawson has pointed out a passage in Hemming's cartulary whereby people with desires upon church property simply paid the geld on it and secured the title, regardless of the church's wishes (Wormald 1992: 75–6). The process of selling land to the highest bidder was described in *The Anglo-Saxon Chronicle*:

> [William] granted his land on such hard terms, the hardest he could. Then a second came and offered more than the other earlier gave, and the king let it go to the man who offered him more. Then a third came and offered yet more, and the king let it go into the hands of the man

who offered most of all, and did not care how very sinfully the reeves got it from the wretched men.

(Swanton 2000: 218)

It is not surprising therefore that there was considerable cause for future disputes as to who owned the land. One such dispute lasted a century, as in 1163 Thomas Becket laid claim to Rochester and Saltwood Castles, which had been taken from the estates of the archbishop and Christchurch, Canterbury during the Conqueror's formation of consolidated military lordships around Saltwood, Tonbridge and perhaps Folkestone (Eales 1985: 96). The monastic chronicles are full of the crimes of the Normans, either in imposing their will upon the population or seizing lands – especially church lands. However, even though land was redistributed, it did not need to be permanently alienated and in at least one case it reverted back to its original owner. In 1086 the Abbey of Shaftesbury's manor at Beechingstoke in Wiltshire was held by Turstin and Harding was cited as the former owner. However, in the reign of Henry I it had reverted to Harding (how is unclear) who originally held it on a 'life-lease' (Williams 1985: 227).

The seizure of land was a common complaint following the Conquest. At Bury St Edmunds a Norman baron called Rannulf indulged in indiscriminate marauding and another Norman courtier 'moved by greed, as was typical of his race' invaded one of St Edmund's manors. In this case the abbot, a Norman appointed by Edward the Confessor, was strong enough to recover some land and gain confirmation of the Abbey's privileges. The Abbey's saint, St Edmund, was also a powerful force and he appeared in visions warning of the dire consequences of invading the Abbey's lands (Gransden 1981: 67–8). The Abbey also received the patronage of William the Conqueror who granted the land of an Anglo-Saxon landowner on his death to the monastery of Bury St Edmunds 'so that the abbot might give it to his Frenchmen to go in service of the saint where and when necessary' (Mortimer 1980: 140).

The perception of Norman land seizure is often more complex than first appears, because Anglo-Saxon nobles had sometimes seized the land before the Conquest. When the Norman nobles were granted the lands of Anglo-Saxon nobles, they also received the disputed lands. The encroachment upon the lands of Worcester Cathedral by Urse d'Abetot, the Norman Sheriff of Worcestershire, has sometimes been portrayed as a Norman invasion of the Cathedral's property. However, whilst he was responsible for taking some land, in many cases he was continuing Anglo-Saxon practice of holding long leases from the Cathedral or taking over lands formerly encroached upon by Anglo-Saxon landholders (Mason 1985: 161).

It is exactly this scenario of seizure of land during Edward the Confessor's reign, which was then complained loudly about following the Conquest, that seems to be behind the famous trial on Pinnenden (or Penenden) Heath in 1072 (Douglas and Greenaway 1981: 481–3). The trial was ostensibly to recover lands and rights seized by Odo, Earl of Kent and Bishop of Bayeux, from the churches of Kent. The memory ran deep for over a century later in about 1200 an Evesham writer described Odo as a 'ravaging wolf' against the Church of Canterbury. However, modern research has shown that Odo had merely taken over encroachments of land undertaken by Earl Godwine and his sons during the period of the sickly Eadsige's rule (1038–50) and then Stigand's rule (Bates 1975: 9; Eales 1985: 94). The willingness of three of the most important people in the country – King William, Lanfranc, Archbishop of Canterbury and Odo, Bishop of Bayeux, Earl of Kent and William's half-brother – to negotiate for three days about the lands has been seen as an example of the care and attention to detail that often took place in order to resolve long-standing differences and create an orderly transfer of lands (Bates 1978).

Change and continuity

The Norman Conquest marked a dramatic change in the leadership of England, but thereafter there is considerable debate about how much change there really was. It is likely that the Anglo-Saxons themselves did not foresee sweeping changes: to them the Conqueror was just the head of another dynasty (Holt 1997: 3). Culturally there was also little to concern the Anglo-Saxons for both Anglo-Saxons and Normans were at the court of Edward the Confessor. The lack of concern on the part of the Anglo-Saxons has been seen as a major reason for the lack of a coordinated Anglo-Saxon response on a national scale to the Norman invasion and why a national leader never emerged to challenge William (Williams 1997). Indeed, the belief that Harold had escaped from Hastings and become a hermit in Chester and then a missionary was 'the quietest literature of a defeated nation' (Holt 1997: 3–4).

The Conqueror did bring some innovations to England, noticeably castles, the attitude to the forests (see Chapter 7) and new methods of legal punishments, in particular trial by battle (Bartlett 1986: 104). However, William encouraged Anglo-Saxons to join his cause and began a deliberate policy of continuity, for he promoted himself as the rightful heir of Edward the Confessor. Continuity of laws was therefore an important element in the stability of rule. Continuity was emphasised in a number of ways. William continued the crown wearing ceremonies at the seasonal festivals, predominantly at Westminster, Winchester and Gloucester, a custom started by the Anglo-Saxon kings (Cownie 1994: 146). Even one of the classic supposedly Norman innovations (Garnett 1985), the murdrum fine, which was a fine on a village or region if a Frenchman was murdered, has been seen as a continuation of a policy started by Cnut. By its continuation William showed that he was not a foreign tyrant but a good and traditional lord of the English (O'Brien 1996: 354). Personnel from Edward's reign also continued to serve the new king. In the Confessor's reign, Regenbald (whose name is either French or German in origin) was a royal priest of importance and may have been the Conqueror's first chancellor until December 1067 (Keynes 1987: 196, 211). The other priests of Edward's chancery also remained in office and were producing documents written in Anglo-Saxon beyond the Conqueror's reign. Along with the staff, Anglo-Saxon diplomatic practices continued and between 1066 and *c.*1070 writs were not only drawn up in Anglo-Saxon, but under the same principles as those issued by Edward the Confessor. The appointment of Lanfranc as Archbishop of Canterbury was the probable reason for the abrupt ending of large-scale production of writs written in Anglo-Saxon (Keynes 1987: 220; Bates 1998: 50). There were other changes to the documents, such as witnesses and the place of issue being more frequently mentioned, but even so 'there was no documentary revolution in William's reign' (Keynes 1987: 217; Bates 1998: 109).

The Norman Conquest and the church

The Conquest marked a turning point for the English church. The Archbishop of Canterbury, Stigand, was deposed in April 1070, along with his brother Æthelmær, Bishop of East Anglia and several abbots. Stigand was pilloried by Norman writers for his wealth and unecclesiastical behaviour and was replaced as archbishop by Lanfranc, a passionate reformer from Normandy (Gibson 1978; Smith 1993: 199). Other bishops and abbots either fled, were deposed or died. The Archbishop of York, Ealdred, who had crowned William, was confirmed in all his rights by the Conqueror (O'Brien 1996: 355). Following Ealdred's death in September 1069, Thomas of Bayeux became archbishop. The two most important posts in the English church had been quickly filled by Normans. Thereafter the attitude and ability of Anglo-Saxon churchmen to reform was important in determining how long they would keep their positions: Wulfketel, the Abbot of Crowland appointed by Edward the Confessor was 'English and vile to the Normans' causing his deposition at a council at Gloucester in *c.*1085 (Hayward 1998: 92).

The scale of the change is shown by the origins of the abbots and priors of important religious houses: in October 1066 only one abbot (Baldwin of Bury St Edmunds) had come from abroad, whereas by 1087 all the heads of the thirty most important religious houses were either trained or born abroad. Moreover, all had been chosen by the king and his ecclesiastical advisers (Loyn 1994: 96).

Like virtually all the Norman bishops and abbots, Lanfranc, on his accession, faced three problems in his own church, which were echoed in England as a whole: discipline, rivalry and property (Ridyard 1986: 202). In response to these problems Lanfranc replaced the standard Anglo-Saxon monastic rule, the *Regularis Concordia* (Symons 1953) with his own rule, the *Decreta Lanfranci* (Knowles 1951). This brought his church up to date with the reformed Continental church, and Lanfanc tried to disseminate the *Decreta* throughout England, with some success. Many Norman abbots had problems with their Anglo-Saxon monks. At Glastonbury the new Norman

Abbot Thurstin tried to impose Norman chants, whereas previously the monks had sung the more familiar Anglo-Saxon chants which had been hallowed by tradition (Hiley 1993: 137, 154). He met with great hostility and sent in archers to bring the monks to order. Whilst this was a dramatic event, the dispute was about Thurstin attempting to impose Norman customs. Thurstin was forced from office, but returned a few years later and William of Malmesbury puts Thurstin's account into perspective: 'The rest of Thurstin's acts we are inclined rather to admire, and we must not dwell on this one only in which he sinned rather by accident than by design' (Lomax 1992: 123–7).

Other Norman abbots had a greater contempt for their Anglo-Saxon monks and some Norman abbots were more like warrior lords than church-men. In 1070 William the Conqueror had sent Turold to be abbot of Peterborough Abbey. The region was rebellious and Turold not only brought with him 160 knights, but then proceeded to build a castle near the abbey and also parcel out nearly half the abbey's lands to his kinsmen. Not surprisingly, after his death in 1098 the monks paid 300 marks to the king so that they could choose their own abbot (Hollister 1987: 150–1). At St Albans the Norman Abbot Paul was described as being 'lord over barbarians whom you cannot instruct in words because of the diversity of language' by Archbishop Anselm (Loyn 1994: 95). Anselm also thought that if Bishop Maurice died in England he would be buried amongst 'barbarians' (Luscombe 1995: 9) and in 1089 the abbot expelled the monks from St Augustine's Canterbury and replaced them with a new community (Cownie 1996: 55). Previous Anglo-Saxon abbots were also looked upon with suspicion. At St Albans the new Norman Abbot Paul, 'destroyed the tombs' of his pre-decessors, at Malmesbury Abbot Warin 'belittled' the deeds of his predeces-sors and moved them from their burial place on either side of the high altar to an obscure corner of the church (Ridyard 1986: 189, 193).

As well as predecessors, the new Norman abbots also had suspicions about many Anglo-Saxon saints. Some Anglo-Saxon saints – such as St Cuthbert of Durham – were honoured, and Bishop Maurice (the first Norman Bishop of London) actively supported the Anglo-Saxon cult of St Osyth and enriched her shrine (Hayward 1998: 83). However, Archbishop Lanfranc expressed hesitancy about some English saints as accounts of them did not constitute grounds for veneration (Ridyard 1986: 200) and he intentionally removed Anglo-Saxon saints from the calendar of Christchurch, Canterbury (Bishop 1918: 227; Klukas 1983: 139). Abbot Warin of Malmesbury was initially doubtful about Saint Aldhelm, but was then 'converted' after hearing about the saint's miracles. Thereafter he actively promoted Aldhelm's cult. One of the most extreme reactions was by the new Norman Abbot, Walter of Evesham (1077–1104). He subjected relics 'about which there was doubt' to ordeal by fire (Ridyard 1986: 204). However, his actions seem to have been caused by puzzlement, for he began to wonder how 'a people sprung from the blood of so many holy men had been defeated by the Franks and subjugated by them'. If England had really been so full of saints, their divine help would have meant defeat for the Normans at Hastings. As the Normans had won, some of the Anglo-Saxon saints must be false. The procedure of testing relics by ordeal by fire was known to Walter from being a monk at Cerisy where in 1048 the relic of St Vigor had been tested (Hayward 1998: 91). The ordeal at Evesham was carried out and those which passed the test were treated with honour, those which failed, were not.

Generally the Normans respected the Anglo-Saxon cults (Crook 2000: 176–8). A study of the feast of saints from five churches before and after the Conquest has shown that there was no suppression by the Normans of any established Anglo-Saxon saints' cults in the long term and there was no attempt to replace Anglo-Saxon saints with Norman saints (Hayward 1998: 90). Even in the dedications of churches there were no new fashions for Norman saints, though some cults, such as the Holy Trinity, did become more popular (Hayward 1998: 90).

Local rivalry between churches could be intense, and the status of the relics of a church was often of crucial importance. A popular and powerful saint encouraged pilgrims who by their gifts increased the wealth of the church. Lanfranc became a major promoter of the cult of St Dunstan, the tenth-century Anglo-Saxon Archbishop of Canterbury. The cult became a vehicle for Lanfranc's aims of raising the status of the Cathedral above that of the rival monastery in Canterbury, St Augustine's (Ridyard 1986: 203).

The status of patrons was an important consideration for the well-being of Anglo-Saxon churches. Patronage was never uniform and some churches – such as Gloucester and Abingdon – gained the patronage of William the Conqueror and important Normans. Other churches, especially those patronised by dispossessed Anglo-Saxon nobles, were not so fortunate and many had their possessions and lands taken from them, such as Ely or Glastonbury (Cownie 1994: 157; Cownie 1995: 50).

Even though some Anglo-Saxon churches were looted by the Normans there were also some tremendous success stories of English monasteries surviving the Conquest, such as St Albans, Abingdon and Gloucester, which all gained the widespread backing of small and medium-sized land holders in the vicinity. Bury St Edmunds did especially well with Abbot Baldwin's close connections with Archbishop Lanfranc and William the Conqueror, and Baldwin largely rebuilt the town. Domesday Book of 1086 demonstrates some measure of the wealth of monasteries after the Conquest. Seven were wealthy, with £500 plus a year income, seven between £200–£500, seven between £100–£200, seventeen between £50–£100 and eight below £50 per year (Knowles 1966; Loyn 1994: 98, appendices).

The Conquest also opened the way for a wave of new monasteries in the north. Before the Conquest there was no regular Benedictine house north of a line from Worcester, Burton on Trent and the Wash (Burton 1997: 6; Cownie 1996: 49), although there were communities of secular canons as in York, and Beverley and Durham. As one of the furthest north Benedictine monasteries in Anglo-Saxon times, Peterborough held a great importance and was visited by many of the Anglo-Saxon archbishops of York. After the Conquest the north gained an increasing number of monasteries, for example St Mary's, York, and Selby, though monastic growth on a large scale was a twelfth-century phenomenon (see Chapter 6). The monasteries could also have a calming effect in trouble spots, which is implied by the founding of St Mary's in York, the city having been in a state of revolution. In other areas the abbot or bishop played a vital role in securing Norman power and keeping, or attempting to keep, the peace (see Chapter 6).

The fate of the bishops also varied. The longest surviving Anglo-Saxon bishop, Bishop Wulfstan of Worcester, complained bitterly about the invasion of Normans upon the Cathedral's lands. If Anglo-Saxon bishops were supportive of the new regime, keeping them in place had its advantages and Wulfstan's knowledge of the diocese and the language has been suggested as the reason for the request by Thomas, Archbishop of York, for Wulfstan to make a visitation through the remoter parts of the diocese (Mason 1985: 172). However, Wulfstan was the exception and from William, the Bishop of London (1051–75) being the only Norman bishop at the time of the Conquest, within twenty years all the bishoprics except Worcester had bishops of Continental origin in post. The bishops were given the backing of William the Conqueror, Bishop William gained a castle (Bishop's Stortford), had seized lands and was allowed to buy lands which made up the Bishop of London's estates (Taylor 1991: 303).

The change in the backgrounds of the bishops before and after the Conquest is representative of the changes in the country. The bulk of the clergy, and population, remained Anglo-Saxon, but following the Conquest at the highest levels of power there was an almost total change in personnel. The newcomers saw their role as holding onto power, creating change where necessary, but also legitimising their power by continuing Anglo-Saxon methods of government. William the Conqueror was aided by the strong bishops and sheriffs throughout the country, but also because there was no strong unifying leader to carry forward the Anglo-Saxon opposition. By the end of William's reign any Anglo-Saxon opposition had been crushed.

2   Peoples and families, 1066–1215

Normans and Anglo-Saxons

The Norman Conquest of 1066 was only one of a long line of assaults and invasions throughout the eleventh, twelfth and thirteenth centuries. A man of sixty standing on the south coast watching William the Conqueror's fleet land would have heard of the Danish Thorkill the Tall's raids in 1009–11, the return of the Danish King Swein and his army in 1013, Swein's son Cnut attack on Wessex in 1015, Godwine's invasion of 1052 and Harald Hardrada's invasion in the north in 1066. The man's son would have heard about Robert Curthose's successful landing in 1101 with an invasion fleet against Henry I. The man's grandson would have heard about the invasions and campaigns of the Empress Matilda, and then of her son the future Henry II in the 1140s and 1150s. The largest and most dangerous invasion to take place since 1066 occurred in 1216 when the French Dauphin Louis invaded and almost succeeded in defeating the forces loyal to the young boy king, Henry III.

The Conquest was, however, the most devastating of the invasions because it pitted one nation against another – the previous and later invasions tended to be part of an already existing civil war. Speed, surprise and decisiveness mark the Norman Conquest as an extraordinary invasion. However, before and after the invasion the English chroniclers barely mentioned Normandy, with the more generic term of 'France' being used more frequently. After the Conquest two terms – 'the French' or 'the English' – distinguished the different peoples. This terminology occurred widely, for example in Domesday Book of 1086 or in the chancery records; and *The Anglo-Saxon Chronicle* never uses the term 'Norman' before or after the Conquest, but does occasionally mention 'Normandy' (Garnett 1985: 114; Matthew 1994: 2). Occasionally other groups are mentioned, for example Flemings or Bretons. The fluidity of terms and confusion of meaning is well shown by the twelfth-century chronicler, Florence of Worcester. who consistently translated the term 'Frenchman' into 'Norman' whether they were Norman or not (Lewis 1994: 129–32).

For Anglo-Saxon nobles the Conquest was a disaster. The Normans succeeded in creating an immediately widespread and simultaneous conquest across England in the midst of great hostility (J.F.A. Mason 1990: 259). Contemporary views about the Conquest in the twelfth century can be broadly divided into favourable and hostile. The background of the chroniclers and their patrons inevitably influenced their views. One of the most favourable opinions of William the Conqueror in England came from the *Chronicle of Battle Abbey*, the abbey that the Conqueror had personally founded on the spot where Harold fell.

> At the command of the authority that governs the secular world, there arose, like the morning star, the most pious Duke William out of the glorious lineage of the Normans, scion of their mighty prince Rollo. William well deserved to be called father of his country, bulwark of his duchy and kingdom.
>
> (Searle 1980: 33)

One theme pursued by Continental churchmen was that the Norman church had, in the words of the twelfth-century Bishop Ivo of Chartres, brought the 'light of upright conduct [to a] barbarous nation' (Barker 1990: 33). Religious reasons were an important part of the explanations for the success of the Conquest. Harold had given William the Conqueror an oath, made over precious relics, which he had then broken. William had been careful to gain papal support for his expedition and had carried the papal banner into battle. Later in the twelfth century the chronicler Henry of Huntingdon saw the Norman invasion as a divine punishment against the sinful Anglo-Saxons – the five plagues of God's punishments were the successive invasions of Romans, Picts and Scots, English, Danes and Normans (Greenway 1995: 110). Anglo-Norman writers also rewrote the history of the Anglo-Saxon church by emphasising its great achievements, such as the seventh-century saints so vividly portrayed by Bede, but also highlighted the decadence into which they saw the church had fallen in the decades before the Conquest: Orderic Vitalis, who came from Shrewsbury but was a monk in the Norman monastery of St Evroul, wrote that Stigand, the last Anglo-Saxon Archbishop of Canterbury, was accused of murder (Gransden 1989). The similarities between the Anglo-Saxon and Norman churches were rarely mentioned, such as giving churches to loyal favourites, a disregard for canon law and fostering powerful and wealthy bishops (Smith 1993: 215). Even though there were failings in the Anglo-Saxon church, Orderic Vitalis was critical of the looting of Anglo-Saxon possessions. Whilst the victory at Hastings could be seen as God's will, Orderic believed the defeated should be treated justly, along with Norman penance and reparation (Chibnall 1984: 126, 183).

Following the Conquest there were anti-Anglo-Saxon jokes based on drunkenness, cowardice, treachery, lechery, irreligion and dog-like barking which passed for speech. The Anglo-Saxons were depicted as abstracted and dreamy because of the damp and foggy land they lived in and the lack of military skill was a common Norman insult (Crouch 1994: 64). They were also taunted as having tails as a punishment for mocking the first missionary to England, St Augustine, as in Wace's, *Roman de Brut* (Short 1995: 153). The stereotypes survived. In Jordan Fantosme's poem, written in the 1170s, the Norman wife of Robert Earl of Leicester described the English as better boasters and guzzlers than fighters (Johnston 1981: 73). The Normans too had certain attributes – they were clean-shaven in contrast to the mustachioed Anglo-Saxons – and William of Malmesbury said that they were 'well-dressed to a fault, and particular about their food . . . [and the] whole nation hardly knows how to live without fighting' (Mynors *et al.* 1998: 461).

Throughout the twelfth century the Conquest was an event that was not forgotten and it was still politically important in the later twelfth century. The poet Wace wrote a long poem called the *Roman de Rou* (1160–70) about the Conquest, but the purpose of the poem seems to have been to attribute special prestige to the noble families of the twelfth century whose ancestors took part in the Conquest. Furthermore the poem seems to have been written for Henry II, who wanted to align himself with the great Norman historical tradition (Holt 1997: 172).

Following the Conquest Anglo-Saxon nobles, language, architecture and culture were all crushed, but different elements were targeted at different times. There was no universal or instant destruction of the Anglo-Saxon past. The different timings can be seen by the examples of architecture, politics and literature. In the twenty or so years after the Conquest Anglo-Saxon cathedrals were physically destroyed to such an extent that virtually nothing remains (see Chapter 8). The fate of the local parish churches was less severe as some still remain (Taylor and Taylor 1965) but there is no way of knowing how many Anglo-Saxon churches were deliberately pulled down by the new Norman lords. From 1090 onwards Anglo-Saxon styles begin to reappear in greater numbers within the architectural repertoire of large buildings so that it has been said that 'post 1090 building in England . . . had a great deal in common with pre-Conquest architecture' on large building projects such as Ely Cathedral (Fernie 1986: 73).

Whilst Anglo-Saxon architecture was barely considered between 1066 and *c.*1090, some of the Anglo-Saxon nobility lasted until the late 1070s. The period between 1080 and 1120 was 'the lowest point' of the fortunes of the Anglo-Saxon aristocracy (Stenton 1944). By the reign of Henry I the fortunes of the nobility began to recover, especially when the Norman king, Henry I, married the Anglo-Saxon heiress Matilda, who was also known as Edith or Maud (Tsurushima 1991: 313). Matilda had a clear interest in her ancestry and most chroniclers described her lineage and relationship to Edward the Confessor. Moreover she displayed an interest in her West Saxon roots, received a genealogical table from the monks of Malmesbury and was eventually buried at Westminster Abbey near Edward the Confessor (Huneycutt 1990: 93). The marriage seems to have been a deliberate attempt by Henry I at reconciliation between the peoples, and William of Malmesbury's history made the Norman kings direct descendants of the

Anglo-Saxon kings (Matthew 1994: 3). That there was a contemporary political dimension to the match can be gauged by the fact that nobles taunted Henry and his new wife by calling them Godric and Godgiva – distinctly English names (Clark 1978: 232; Thomas 1998: 231). The birth of their son William the Ætheling was seen as a joining together of the two blood lines of the Normans and the Anglo-Saxons. Furthermore, from the early twelfth century onwards men with Anglo-Saxon backgrounds began to serve in local government (Stenton 1944).

The survival of Anglo-Saxon culture and power continued during the twelfth century, though it is only sometimes seen by reaction against it. Eadmer of Canterbury wrote of the prejudice against English churchmen in Henry I's reign, Osbert of Clare stated that the English were still experiencing the effects of the Norman Conquest, William of Malmesbury reported heated debates between the English and Normans over the actions of individuals during the Conquest and Richard de Lucy appealed to Norman solidarity and warned against the English in an account of his 1157 speech written in the 1180s (Thomas 1998: 213). Literary works supporting the Anglo-Saxons in the twelfth century were few, though one was the 'Gesta Herewardi', which gave a clear message that the English 'are . . . a worthy, civilised and noble people . . . and deserve to be treated honourably in their own country by the descendants of those who conquered them' (Thomas 1998: 232). Unfortunately this was an unlikely dream.

Following the Conquest Anglo-Saxon cultural tradition was kept alive by the monasteries, which preserved the traditions of their own communities against the changing religious and political world (Chibnall 1984: 109). It has also been suggested that the sense of loss of lands and rituals 'drew English monks together in defence of their past' (Southern 1973: 247). Some cases seem relatively clear, such as Abingdon Abbey which became a focus for disaffected English men and the abbot, Ealdred, was arrested for treason. Later traditions about Ely suggested there was a close association between the monks and rebels who supported Hereward the Wake. Another indication of anti-Norman feeling occurred when Abbot Thorkell entertained the invading King Swein of Denmark in 1069. Ely continued to be a monastery whose lands were often attacked by local Norman landowners, but after the appointment of a new Norman abbot in 1069 the issue of different nationalities became irrelevant as the Norman abbot tried to protect the Abbey's lands from Norman lords (Ridyard 1986:184). Many disputes within monasteries – often between a Norman abbot and Anglo-Saxon monks – were more about the introduction of new liturgical practices, or simple character clashes (Rubenstein 1995: 40) than a strong sense of national consciousness on either side (see Chapter 1). More often the Norman abbot and Anglo-Saxon monks worked together to defend the rights of the religious house.

However, it was in the monasteries that the Anglo-Saxon traditions and language were preserved for longer than elsewhere in England, and the last substantial piece of literature in Anglo-Saxon was written at Peterborough Abbey in 1155, finished eighty-nine years after the Conquest (see Chapter 8). Thereafter there is silence in the Anglo-Saxon language with only the occasional Anglo-Saxon words, phrases or letter forms punctuating documents. From 1200s onwards a new literature developed: Middle English.

One of the defining works of the twelfth century was Geoffrey of Monmouth's *History of the Kings of Britain* (*Historia Regum Britanniae*), which built on the increasingly popular myths about King Arthur and other ancient kings. The Arthurian romances were a web of intrigue, romance and chivalry and became very popular at court and amongst the nobility (see Chapter 8). An important element of the political power of the stories was that Arthur had not died but waited to return to overthrow the oppressors. Arthur therefore could be used by rebels trying to replace the king. The name of Arthur was a powerful symbol in its own right. Richard I's nephew and Henry II's grandson was called Arthur of Brittany, a powerful piece of propaganda, and his cause proved to be a thorn in King John's side. However, the myth of Arthur's ability to return was shattered by excavations at Glastonbury which discovered Arthur's tomb and body. It was known to be Arthur by the inscription found upon his coffin, and the body showed signs of terrible wounds. Not surprisingly, these have since been proved to be a twelfth-century forgery, but at the time contemporary opinion was that Arthur was not only found, he was provably dead and buried (Gillingham 1990: 103). Henry II was reputedly one of those interested in the excavation, for the myth was very much alive. In his propaganda Henry used Arthur's reputed conquest of Ireland to match his conquest. Richard the Lionheart also used Arthur as propaganda and associated himself with the mythological Arthur by giving Arthur's sword Caliburn (Excalibur) to Tancred, King of Sicily. In his description of the event Roger of Howden identified Richard with Arthur, aligning the Angevin king with the great British king of the past (Warren 1998: 268).

The Conquest of England was but one incident in the Norman expansion across Europe. As well as England, the other great Norman military success was the conquest of Sicily (see Chapter 3). Therefore, by the first half of the twelfth-century there existed a Norman world with influence from northern England to the Mediterranean. The Normans were one of a large number of peoples in the geographical region which is now France. Others included the Angevins and the Poitevins, but it was the Normans who amongst all others in the eleventh century defined themselves as a separate people, by the mythology of their origins and social codes of the elite (Lewis 1994: 130). However, by the mid-twelfth century the dynamism amongst the Normans diminished. The writing of the chronicles and original accounts of the history of the Norman people, such as the *Deeds of the Norman Dukes* (*Gesta Normannorum ducum*), ceased by the 1140s, although the *Deeds* were frequently copied later and were known at both Durham and Reading (van Houts 1980: 106). The loss of Norman momentum was symbolised by the new French Gothic architecture in the Île-de-France which superseded the Romanesque Norman styles (Bates 1994: 30) and the provincial councils of the Norman church at Rouen – frequent until 1118 – ceased after that date (Foreville 1996).

In the late twelfth century an affection for the Normandy homeland remained in Henry II's court (Bates 1994: 31). Copies were circulating of the Norman histories of Dudo of St Quentin (*Gesta Normannorum*) and William of Jumièges, which emphasised Norman history and the conquest of England (Huisman 1983: 122). Wace's poem the *Roman de Rou*, written for Henry II and his court, concerned the Norman Conquest (Bennett 1982), though reference to historic Normandy may equally have been because Henry's father had conquered Normandy and Henry himself was Duke of Normandy.

By the end of the twelfth century Anglo-Saxon and Norman history had begun to be combined. The poet Gaimar had written *L'Estoire des Engleis*, thereby annexing the Anglo-Saxon past whilst still cherishing Norman traditions (Chibnall 1984: 214). Even though some individuals might emphasise a difference in language or place of birth, as peoples the Normans and Anglo-Saxons in England had lost their sharp cultural differences.

With any group invading a native population there is always the possibility of intermarriage and cultural assimilation. The chronicler William of Malmesbury had parents of mixed nationality and tried to be impartial because of this fact:

> The Normans and the English, spurred on by different motives, have both written of King William. The former have praised him excessively, extolling to high heaven his good and bad actions; the latter, out of enmity between peoples, have heaped undeserved reproach on their lord and master. I, on the other hand, since the blood of both peoples flows in my veins, shall steer a middle path in my writing about him.
>
> (Short 1996: 162)

However, even with mixed parentage, William thought of himself as English (Matthew 1994: 3). Other chroniclers too had mixed parentage, such as Orderic Vitalis and Henry of Huntingdon, but whilst mixed marriages are known about amongst the aristocracy both William of Malmesbury and Orderic describe mixed marriages as common. By the 1170s the accounting treatise *Dialogus de Scarrario* claimed that the two peoples were indistinguishable, though unfortunately this was probably referring to specific rules about a fine relating to murder, known as murdrum (Johnson 1950: 52–3; Clark 1978: 224–5).

There was little to hinder intermarriage or cultural assimilation, except perhaps social stigmatism. In 1086 Domesday Book records that at Bury St Edmunds there were thirty-four knights amongst the 'French' (i.e. Norman) and English, showing at least a degree of co-operation (Clark 1978: 240).

There was also some cultural demarcation. In Southampton a 'French Street' runs in parallel with 'English Street'. In Shrewsbury Englishmen objected to the tax exemptions given to foreigners. Throughout England Normans settled in the major towns. This was possibly for security as many towns had castles. In 1086 Domesday Book lists some of the Continental communities – 145 Frenchmen were in York, 65 at Southampton, 41 in the 'new town' at Norwich and 86 elsewhere in the city, as well as communities in Shrewsbury, Hereford, Dunwich and Wallingford (Clark 1978: 241).

Whilst the Anglo-Saxons and Normans lived side by side, with some intermarriage, the notion of 'Englishness' as a concept is difficult to assess. As seen above, William of Malmesbury thought of himself as English, even though he was of mixed parentage. For those arriving in the country 'Englishness' might just have meant being in England. Archbishop Lanfranc, Italian by birth and resident for many years in Normandy, described himself as a 'new Englishman' within a few years of living in England (Lewis 1994: 139). With kingship being so itinerant it is difficult to know what the kings themselves thought, though William the Conqueror was careful not to use his royal designation of 'King of the English' when in Normandy. Normally the chroniclers do not indicate what nationality they thought the king to be, though in the entries of the *Peterborough Chronicle*, the chronicler has described William Rufus as 'our king' (*uran cynge*) (Clark 1979; Short 1995: 162–3; Swanton 2000: 228).

One measure of cultural assimilation is the choice of names, as on a broad scale names can mirror patterns of cultural allegiance and demographic movements (Clark 1979: 22). When Edith (Matilda) married Henry I her four elder brothers all had names from the last century of Anglo-Saxon kingship (Baker 1978: 124). There are various difficulties, however, in assigning a name to a particular group. One is that names can be changed during a person's life (for example the chronicler Orderic became Orderic Vitalis when he went to Normandy and Christina of Markyate's original name was Theodora) (Short 1995: 161). A further problem is that some Normans had similar names to the Anglo-Saxons, such as Azor or Osmund, because both peoples had Viking ancestry (Lewis 1994: 132). Writing a different language could also cause problems. A case in point is the Anglo-Saxon name Æelfwine or Æethelwine, the first element of which the scribes of the Domesdsay Book wrote as 'Al' and the second element as either 'win' or wig'. Therefore the pre-Conquest Sheriff of Gloucester appears both as Alwin and Alwig (Williams 1988: 282).

The Anglo-Saxons had four sorts of name: Christian name, a name associated with their office or occupation, a name associated with a certain location and nicknames (Williams 1992: 237). The Normans had the same range of names but importantly the concept of the toponymic name (which named the individual after the place of their most important lands) became much more common amongst the conquerors. It was an important cultural shift as it conveyed a sense of Norman ownership of land. The 'toponymic served home sickness, family tradition, political domination and social snobbery at one and the same time' with the change becoming pervasive in noble society (Holt 1997: 185). The second change to names brought about by the Normans was that names were passed on from father to son in a way rarely seen in Anglo-Saxon times. A further development took place in the 1140s when the four sons of Robert chose to take as their surname after 'Gerald' an ancestor, rather than using their father's name. The FitzGerald family's name is one of the earliest examples of an ancestral Christian name being used as a proper surname (Vincent 1998: 251).

During the twelfth century another trend became commonplace across the Continent, that of using Christian, and more specifically Biblical, names such as John, Stephen and Thomas (Clark 1978: 235). The rise in the use of Christian names has been shown by the low number in the early twelfth century (6–7 per cent in surveys of Winchester and Battle) rising to 16 per cent at Winchester in 1148 (Clark 1979: 28). For the first generation after the Conquest names can give a reasonable picture of a person's nationality but by the twelfth century Anglo-Saxon names had been discarded across the social spectrum (Clark 1978: 234). The change seems to have been most dramatic in the mid-twelfth century with Norman or Continental names becoming much more common, for example amongst key families in York (Daniell 1995), though generally the names of women were slower to change than names of men (Clark 1978: 235).

Family politics

Between 1066 and 1215 the majority of the politics of the time can be seen as a continuing inter-familial strife between the noble families, and especially between kings, queens and their children. One of the themes of late eleventh- and twelfth-century English royal history is that of sons rebelling against fathers, or brothers rebelling between themselves. Royal sons were notoriously hungry for more power than their fathers gave them, and their actions led to a continuing tradition of rebellion (see Chapter 4). Sons were not the only source of family problems, and William's half-brother, Odo of Bayeux, frequently rebelled and was imprisoned by William the Conqueror.

On William the Conqueror's death, the titles of the Duke of Normandy and the King of the English were divided between his two eldest sons: Robert Curthose received Normandy whilst the Conqueror's second son, William Rufus, was given the larger but less prestigious England. The Conqueror's third son, Henry, received no lands but was provided with a monetary settlement. The chronicler Orderic Vitalis described the reaction of the Norman nobles as one of panic on Curthose's accession, and there was some looting, though his account was probably exaggerated with hindsight (Thompson 1990: 269). Even so, accounts reveal a real unease amongst the nobles, many of whom had lands either side of the Channel, now under the control of two separate rulers. William Rufus's accession took place peacefully on 26 September 1087 at Westminster Abbey, seventeen days after his father's death.

As part of an amnesty, Odo of Bayeux was released from prison following William the Conqueror's death and on regaining the earldom of Kent, he started fermenting trouble. Odo and Robert of Mortain (both Rufus's uncles) rebelled in 1088. Their reasons, as given by William of Malmesbury, were that they feared losing their lands in Normandy (Wareham 1994: 225). There were outbreaks of revolt across the country, but the most serious were in Odo's earldom of Kent and Robert of Mortain's lands in Sussex. The rebellion was ostensibly in support of their nephew, Robert Curthose, but Curthose failed to provide military backing for their venture. The rebels gathered at Rochester to attack London, but Rufus reacted quickly and the rebels surrendered (Mason 1998: 122). They were treated leniently and only Odo was banished from the kingdom.

With England secure, Rufus now turned his attention to attacking his brother in Normandy. He effectively bought his way in by buying and bribing various of the nobility to hand over their strongholds, such as St Valéry at the mouth of the Somme. Even in the powerful city of Rouen there was a rising in favour of Rufus, which, although crushed, turned out to be an indication of things to come. When Rufus crossed to Normandy in 1091 the barons flocked to him in large numbers and Curthose was forced to come to terms. The brothers then turned on their younger brother Henry (who had bought lands from Curthose) forcing him to become landless again. Then, amazingly, all three temporarily united and crossed the Channel together in 1091 to fight the Scots.

The situation changed dramatically in 1096 when Curthose decided to go on the First Crusade (see Chapter 3) and mortgaged Normandy to Rufus for 10,000 marks of silver. Rufus now set about expanding his territory at the expense of the French king. He may also have had serious plans for building his own extensive empire in the late 1090s (Vaughn 1993). However, on 2 August 1100, whilst Rufus was out hunting, Walter Tirel, Lord of Poix, shot an arrow which killed Rufus. Whether it was an accident or part of a conspiracy has not been determined, but hunting accidents were not uncommon.

Rufus's brother, Henry, seized the opportunity and rode to Winchester and gained the royal treasury. This gave him the means, if necessary, to buy support and troops, but in the event he was peacefully crowned as king at Westminster Abbey three days after Rufus's death. Henry still had to contend with his brother, Robert Curthose, Duke of Normandy who had returned full of glory from Crusade and had reclaimed Normandy as his own. Curthose even tried to go one step further and invaded England in 1101 (see Chapter 4). On landing at Portsmouth with a considerable army Curthose marched towards London, but Henry was waiting for him. No fighting took place and a negotiated peace was achieved by the Treaty of Alton (Newman 1988: 14). A second Battle of Hastings had been averted, which in turn allowed Henry I to strengthen his position by ridding himself of rebellious nobles.

In 1104 the position was reversed and Henry launched his own invasion of Normandy against his brother. The decisive battle for both Henry and Robert Curthose occurred in 1106 at Tinchebrae where Henry captured Robert (Newman 1988: 14). Robert was effectively neutralised as a political figure and remained in captivity until his death in 1134.

At this point Henry thought he should become the undisputed King of England and Duke of Normandy. However, family politics once again emerged: Henry's title in Normandy was challenged by William Clito who arguably had a better claim to the title than Henry as Curthose's eldest son. Clito gathered around him discontented nobles and gained the help of Louis VI, King of France. Fulk, Count of Anjou, also married his daughter Sybil to Clito and endowed him with the county of Maine, until Clito recovered his lawful inheritance. Clito led two very serious risings against Henry in Normandy in 1117–19 and 1123–4. Clito's cause, however, swung like a pendulum between power during the rebellions to poverty and helplessness when he was defeated (Leyser 1990: 226). Clito took refuge with the Count of Flanders, but the attitudes of the three successive counts (Robert, who died in 1111, Baldwin VII, who died in 1119, and Charles the Good, who was murdered in 1127) to Clito's cause varied greatly. Even so, Clito was a constant source of irritation to Henry.

On 15 November 1120 the sinking of the *White Ship*, and the drowning of Henry's only legitimate son, William, was to have an effect upon politics for the next thirty years. The sinking occurred because of a drunken prank when the crew of the *White Ship* attempted to overtake the king's ship and then foundered (Leyser 1990: 225). The death of William, Henry's heir, had two results. The first was that William Clito's claim not only to Normandy but also to the English throne suddenly became much stronger. By 1127 Clito had become more powerful still as he married the sister of the wife of the French king and as part of the deal had been given the Vexin, a borderland area of Normandy. However, in 1128 Clito died and Henry was now undisputed King of England and Duke of Normandy. Normandy remained at peace for the rest of his reign (Hollister 1983: 78; Nip 1998: 162).

The second consequence had more serious and long-lasting consequences, for Henry's heir was now his daughter Matilda. There were several possible courses of action open to Henry. The first was to remarry after the death of his first queen, Matilda, in the expectation of a son. He married Adeliza of Louvain, daughter of Duke Godfrey of Lower Lotharin, but the marriage remained childless. Therefore, towards the end of his reign Henry realised that his daughter Matilda was the natural choice to succeed him. She had strong credentials as a ruler of England. In 1110 she had been sent to Germany as an 8-year-old girl and four years later (when she was 11, before the official canonical age of marriage of 12) she was married to Henry V, the

Holy Roman Emperor, thirty years her senior. She therefore took the title of Empress, a title she used for the rest of her life. It was a highly prestigious match and Henry V loved and trusted wife to the extent that when she was 16 years old he left her in charge of his possessions in Italy (Leyser 1990: 226–8). In 1125 Henry V died. Matilda returned to England where her father, Henry I, sought out other marriages for her. Geoffrey, the son of Fulk, Count of Anjou, was Henry's first choice. The union of the English and Angevin lands had been attempted previously by Henry as before William the Ætheling's death he had been betrothed to Matilda, the Count of Anjou's daughter. (After William's death she had stayed some years at Henry's court before returning to Anjou (Leyser 1990: 227).) A political alliance with Anjou had many benefits. First Anjou bordered southern Normandy, and so a marriage would reduce the threat of attack. The marriage would also break a feared coalition between William Clito, the King of France and the Count of Anjou. On 10 June 1128 Matilda was duly married to Geoffrey. After her illustrious marriage to the Holy Roman Emperor she may have thought that she was marrying someone of lower social standing, though Geoffrey used her title of Empress to his political advantage.

Gradually it became apparent that in order to secure the succession Henry would have to have to ensure the nobles supported Matilda by an oath of allegiance, which was recorded in 1127, 1128 and 1131. With the oath given, the succession was as secure as it could be. However, despite the oaths there were major problems, one of the most intractable being that no woman had ever held England or Normandy in her own right. The tradition was that it should pass to the nearest male heir. There was much unease amongst the nobility about the issue, as it was entirely possible that through her remarriage her husband would become King of England. Moreover, Geoffrey of Anjou seems to have become distanced quickly from his new wife (though they were later reconciled) and was distrusted by the nobility in England because in the past the Counts of Anjou had sided with the French king. Matilda's first marriage to the Emperor Henry V had remained barren, but following her marriage to Geoffrey they had two children: Henry (the future Henry II of England) was born in 1133; and Geoffrey who was born in 1134.

If Henry I had lived another ten to fifteen years he could have passed the succession on peacefully to his grandson Henry, but on 1 December 1135 he died after surfeiting on lampreys (eels). His death was sudden and unexpected, the succession unclear. The political situation was thrown into greater confusion by Henry I himself, for two chroniclers, Ralph Diceto and Henry of Huntingdon, record that the powerful nobleman Hugh Bigod swore that on his deathbed Henry had disinherited Matilda in favour of Stephen of Blois (Wareham 1994: 233). The disinheritance may have occurred because of a dispute between Henry and Matilda concerning some castles on the Norman border, which led to a minor war. This in turn caused a diplomatic break in the mid-1130s between Henry and Matilda, and also made the Norman nobles fearful of Angevin aggression. The combination of the border dispute, Matilda's impetuousness and the rumour of Henry's change of mind on his deathbed made Stephen's path to the crown of England easier (Hollister 1979: 106). Whatever the truth of the matter about Henry's deathbed decision, there are strong echoes of the situation in 1066 when Edward had promised England to William in his lifetime, but then gave the kingdom to Harold on his deathbed (see Chapter 1).

Following Henry's death, Matilda took no action at all and remained in Anjou. The reasons for this have never been fully explained, but she may have been ill, or had the perception that she was the mother of the future king, rather than ruler in her own right. Her inaction caused political confusion and several chroniclers wrote of anarchy. In Normandy her claims to the Duchy were ignored and the nobles approached Theobald, Count of Blois, Henry I's nephew. However, it was Theobald's younger brother Stephen who took the initiative and sailed for England to claim the crown. Stephen was Count of Mortain and had married Matilda, the Boulogne heiress, in 1125, and soon after he became Count of Boulogne (Leyser 1990: 226). In England Henry I's illegitimate son Robert, Earl of Gloucester, attempted to stop Stephen by refusing him entry into Dover and Canterbury, but Stephen entered London in triumph. The support of the Londoners throughout Stephen's reign proved crucial, and Stephen in return allowed the Londoners to form a commune which allowed them greater freedom to control their own affairs. The Londoners called an assembly and elected Stephen as king. Stephen then journeyed to Winchester where the royal treasury was kept in the castle and his brother – Henry of Blois – was bishop. Stephen successfully entered the city, took control of the treasury, and was more formally proclaimed king.

The final step was to be consecrated king by the Archbishop of Canterbury, William of Corbeil. At this critical juncture the archbishop hesitated and was only persuaded on hearing that many nobles felt they were not compelled to honour their oaths to Matilda, not only because they had sworn unwillingly, but also because Henry had nominated Stephen over Matilda on his deathbed. Twenty-two days after Henry's death, Stephen was crowned King of England. The nobles of England now had to decide as to which oath was the greater: those they made to Matilda during Henry's lifetime, or the coronation oath of an anointed king (Chibnall 1997: 36). The coronation oath was a powerful reason for nobles to join Stephen's cause because now Stephen was the Lord's anointed representative on earth. Even one of Stephen's bitterest future opponents, Robert of Gloucester, only defied Stephen after a period of soul-searching, and he only excused himself because he stated that his homage had been conditional (Dalton 1991: 49). With Matilda not pressing her claim and Stephen the anointed king, the nobles of England supported his coronation. The nobles of Normandy switched their allegiance from Theobald to Stephen, fearing divided loyalties between a separate King of England and Duke of Normandy.

The Anarchy

The first two years of Stephen's reign were successful in England. Law and order were maintained, Stephen received the support of the majority of nobles and a Scottish invasion was beaten by the forces led by the Archbishop of York at the Battle of the Standard on 22 August 1138 near Northallerton in Yorkshire. However, Stephen's rule in Normandy was immediately challenged by Geoffrey of Anjou, who attacked in 1136 and 1137. Stephen managed to maintain power in Normandy and his presence enabled him to mend relations with his brother Theobald. Furthermore, Stephen's son, Eustace, did homage to Louis the King of France, thereby securing the family's hereditary claim to Normandy over Geoffrey and Matilda. Stephen left Normandy in 1137. He never returned and within seven years Normandy had fallen to Geoffrey of Anjou.

In England, the political situation deteriorated. William of Malmesbury wrote that Stephen attempted to ambush Robert of Gloucester, possibly because Stephen feared a treacherous plot. The ambush failed and Robert formally renounced his loyalty to Stephen and joined with his half-sister Matilda. Others began to join Matilda's forces, including the powerful nobles Miles of Gloucester and Brian fitz Count. Although open war had not yet broken out, loyalties were becoming divided.

Up until this point the church had not become involved, but in 1139 Stephen suspected treason and arrested three bishops, Bishop Roger of Salisbury and his nephews Nigel, Bishop of Ely, and Alexander, Bishop of Lincoln. Between them they had effectively run Henry I's administration, but they also held many well-fortified castles across the country, such as Sherbourne, Devizes, Malmesbury, Salisbury, Ely and Newark. Stephen seized their castles, which were eventually legally handed over to him following the Archbishop of Rouen's argument that there was no provision in canon law for bishops to hold castles, and that even if they did, the king should hold them as it was his duty to fight for the rights of all.

During the years 1138 and 1139 a series of rebellions broke out, most of which had strong connections with Robert of Gloucester, who was testing Stephen's resolve and ability. Stephen systematically defeated the rebellions, but when Matilda herself landed at Arundel in 1139, in company with her half-brother Robert of Gloucester, the conflict worsened. The three key protagonists were all now on English soil. Stephen laid siege to Arundel but Robert escaped to Bristol. The war had effectively begun. The war ebbed back and forth with most of the fighting in the West Country and the Midlands, with towns and castles being captured and re-captured. The only major battle of the war occurred at Lincoln on 2 February 1141 when Robert of Gloucester led a relief force to break Stephen's siege of the Angevin garrison at Lincoln. Rather than retreating to gather reinforcements, Stephen chose to fight, even though outnumbered. The battle was a disaster for Stephen, who was captured and held prisoner (Bradbury 1996: 90–8). The

Angevin cause was triumphant, both in England, where Matilda processed through southern England, and in Normandy where her husband Geoffrey marched in to Normandy. However, although Stephen and his supporters had been defeated, they fought on and Empress Matilda herself inadvertently aided Stephen's cause by her 'insufferable pride'; her arrogant treatment of the Londoners hardened their determination to continue to support Stephen's cause. Stephen's Queen, also called Matilda, and his commander, William of Ypres, gathered a force in Kent and marched to London. The Londoners themselves rebelled against the Empress who was forced to flee, as did Stephen's brother Henry, Bishop of Winchester. Henry had initially supported Stephen; he had then nominally supported the Angevin cause by being with them in London. However, when Matilda fled, he also fled and now allied himself with Stephen's queen. The royalist force now besieged the Angevins in Winchester. During August 1141 and the early part of September the siege continued. Then on 14 September Matilda managed to escape, but Robert of Gloucester was captured as he fought a rearguard action.

The results of the fighting at Winchester were as devastating to the Angevin cause as the capture of Stephen had been to the royalists. With both Stephen and Robert captured the two sides were at a stalemate and it underlined the fact that the sides were evenly balanced, with neither being able to deliver the decisive blow. The two sides were almost back to their original positions, although the Angevin cause had established a firm hold in England. Following negotiations a mutual exchange was arranged of Stephen for Robert in November 1141. The church viewed the period of Stephen's capture as irrelevant and that the magnates were still bound to Stephen, despite the homages that nobles may have given to Matilda (Dalton 1991: 51). Matilda now set up her base at Oxford. Stephen besieged the town, but just before Christmas 1142 Matilda made a daring escape. With only four knights she left the castle (possibly by scaling the walls by a rope) and dressed in a white cloak as camouflage against the snowy landscape she crossed the frozen Thames. They walked to Abingdon through the harsh winter night, and then rode to safety.

The war descended into skirmishes and sieges, with Stephen nearly being captured again at Wilton, but escaping just in time. Both sides had gains and losses; gradually Stephen gained the upper hand. London, which funded Stephen's campaigns, and Kent remained loyal to Stephen and served as a valuable power base for his operations (Eales 1985: 92). Gradually the tide turned in England against Matilda and the Angevin cause. An important supporter, Geoffrey of Mandeville, Earl of Essex, who had caused Stephen considerable trouble in the Fenlands, died from a crossbow wound to the head. Robert of Gloucester's castle of Faringdon was captured in 1145 and Robert's son, Philip, joined Stephen's cause. In the following two years the Angevin cause crumbled as magnates joined the king, castles surrendered and, worst of all, Robert of Gloucester died on 31 October 1147 at Bristol. In 1148 Matilda retired to Normandy, having failed to entice her husband,

Geoffrey, from his conquests in Normandy to join her in England and fight for the crown.

However, Stephen too suffered setbacks, notably in Normandy where Geoffrey of Anjou finally conquered the Duchy in 1144. The loss of Normandy was probably an important reason for the withdrawal of support by the nobility from Stephen's cause, especially those nobles who held lands either side of the Channel, for now they held lands ruled by enemies.

Henry of Anjou, Geoffrey and Matilda's son, from 1142 had frequently been in England. In 1142 he had visited Robert of Gloucester for several years. His first military expedition in 1147 had ended in humiliation when neither Matilda nor Robert would financially support Henry; he appealed to his enemy, King Stephen, who paid Henry's troops for him. Henry returned to England in 1149 and made his way to Carlisle to be knighted by David, King of the Scots, on 22 May (Dalton 1991: 53). Afterwards he stayed in England, attempting military action for the Angevin cause. His power and status increased in 1151 when he was formally recognised by the French king as Duke of Normandy, and in the same year he became Count of Anjou after the death of his father in 1150. In 1152 Henry married Eleanor of Aquitaine, who was the heiress to the great duchy in southern France. When Henry sailed for England on 6 January 1153 with his moderate force of thirty-six ships he already ruled an area from the English Channel to the Pyrenees.

Despite attempts by Stephen and Henry to have a decisive battle the two armies never fully engaged. The closest they came was at the last major encounter of the war at Wallingford. The nobles on both sides refused to fight and both Henry and Stephen complained about the disloyalty of their respective nobles. The nobles themselves had probably adopted a policy of neutrality. The *Gesta Stephani* describes how Stephen's nobles were 'slack and very casual in their service and had already sent envoys by stealth and made a compact with the duke' and how at Wallingford 'the king and duke . . . being sensible of the treachery of their adherents, were reluctantly compelled to make a peace between themselves' (Potter 1955: 234–8). The nobles seem to have followed the suggestion of the church, whereupon they remained loyal to Stephen in that they obeyed his summons to the army, but they refused to fight against Duke Henry because he was the lawful heir to the kingdom. The refusal of the magnates to fight has been described as 'the magnates peace' (Davis 1980: 118–20; King 1991: 119; Dalton 1991: 56).

Both Stephen and Henry were reluctantly forced to make a truce. The documents surrounding the truce have caused confusion. The two most important are the Treaty of Winchester, which Holt argues came first, followed by the charter issued at Westminster which was the 'administrative consequence' of the Winchester treaty and as such the charter gives what has been agreed (Holt 1994: 295). In the charter Stephen recognised Henry as his successor, a move made easier, if sadder, by the death of Stephen's own son, Eustace, on 17 August 1153. (Stephen's queen, Matilda, had died the year before on 3 May 1152.) Stephen's second son, William, did homage to

Henry, but in return William kept the family's hereditary lands and those from his marriage to Isabel de Warenne. In return, Henry of Anjou did homage to Stephen and agreed to abide by the conventions of the treaty and charter, a successful compromise which lasted until Stephen's death in 1154.

The period of the civil wars between Stephen and his Angevin opponents is known as the Anarchy. During and after the period there was a strong sense that it was a period of war and different to anything since the Norman Conquest. The legal cases of the thirteenth century which refer back to the Anarchy suggest that it was an event of major importance during the twelfth century (Brand 1993: 52). Despite the violence, it has been suggested that the term the Anarchy can only really be used when local tensions rose so high through political unrest or military operations that figures like Robert fitz Hildebrand could cause local chaos (Earles 1985: 90). Whilst brigandage did exist it was in no one's interest (except the brigand's) for such a situation to continue. The most powerful nobles attempted to maintain law and order in their own territories but to ferment lawlessness in their opponents.

Family politics dominated the political and military fighting of the period. Matilda and Robert of Gloucester, sister and half-brother, fought against the brothers Stephen and Henry of Blois. Later two of the key players were Eustace, son of Stephen, and Henry of Anjou, the son of Geoffrey and Matilda. One of the greatest crises of Stephen's reign came when he arrested three bishops who were all part of the same family: Roger of Salisbury and his nephews Nigel, Bishop of Ely, and Alexander, Bishop of Lincoln.

The greatest nobles could usually count on their tenants and members of their families for support. The family connections probably played a much bigger role than the texts reveal and at times neighbouring families deliberately took opposing sides. Two such families were the Bigods and the Warennes who fought on opposing sides, as much for their own interests as those of Stephen or Matilda (Wareham 1994: 235–6). This is well illustrated by the actions of Hugh Bigod: in 1141 he rebelled against King Stephen, but rather than the reason being support for the Angevin cause, it is most likely that he was pursuing his own agenda (Warren 1983: 66). Another important participant was Ranulf, Earl of Chester, who frequently changed sides because he was fighting primarily for his own self-interests rather than any particular cause. It has been suggested that allegiances he gave to either side were limited and he may have given his allegiance to both sides simultaneously. 'The primary objective of Earl of Chester and his half-brother and ally, William of Roumare, in Stephen's reign was the preservation and expansion of their power in the localities, rather than resolution of the succession dispute' (Dalton 1991: 41). It was an important point that when private interests were at stake, it was possible to fight against their lords without necessarily rejecting the lord, and without considering themselves traitors (Dalton 1991: 48–9). Family rivalries could also exist within the same 'side'. Richer of Laigle was imprisoned by the Earl of Leicester because of a previous rivalry, even though both supported King

Stephen (Thompson 1996: 188–9). The attempts by families to seize power in the regions through military action have been seen as revealing the politics of the twelfth century in greater detail than at other times, but it was only the methods that had changed – before and after nobles achieved their ends through less obvious means (Holt 1974).

One of the features of the period of the Anarchy was the private agreements that nobles made between themselves to try and lessen the impact of the wars. One of the most remarkable was the 'Conventio', or pact, of 1149 between the earls of Chester and Leicester, both of whom had substantial power bases in the Midlands. The basic problem that many nobles faced during the Anarchy was who to support during the succession. Whilst not ignoring their duties, many only gave the minimum amount of support required in order to be seen to behave honourably (Dalton 1991: 54). The agreements were worked out by the officials of the nobles and probably communicated by the clergy who journeyed frequently between enemies (King 1991: 124). Whilst not common, such pacts were a legitimate way of defining loyalties and expectations between opposing lords. There seems to have been a rash of such private treaties after the Empress landed when loyalties between powerful neighbours were about to be tested. One such pact was made between the earls of Gloucester and Hereford. Both earls looked to the end of the war, to the time when both of them 'would have their lands and their rights again'. Other instances of such conditional pacts include Stephen's peace treaty with David, King of the Scots, and that between Henry of Anjou and the Earl of Chester (King 1991: 119–21; Dalton 1991: 56). Such agreements were not unknown in Normandy and one existed between the counts of Eu and Poitiers, without any reference to the Duke of Normandy (Power 1994: 190).

However, even though the earls seem to have been dividing up the territory and securing their boundaries into consolidated blocks of power, in reality the shallowness of the power blocs is shown by the ease with which Henry II re-imposed royal authority (Eales 1985: 89). After the accession of Henry II changes in common law resulted in the royal courts simply refusing to recognise the private treaties between nobles, a change which happened quite suddenly and abolished a previously legal practice (King 1991: 128).

The role of the church during the Anarchy can be broken down into two separate arenas: the papacy and Continental influence, and the churchmen in England. At the beginning of Stephen's reign Pope Innocent II gave approval to Stephen, especially as Stephen was officially crowned by the time of the Angevin party's objections. It was always one of Stephen's greatest strengths that he had been crowned by the Archbishop of Canterbury, for an anointed king was very difficult to depose in the eyes of the church. As was stated in a papal hearing 'What had been done with such ceremony could not . . . be undone' (Chibnall 1956: 84). However, the Angevin party was able to block papal approval for Stephen's son, Eustace, to be crowned. In England the church's position was complicated, for although Stephen had been consecrated by the archbishop, his treatment of individual churchmen was much more ambiguous. The arrest of Bishop Roger of Salisbury and his nephews caused serious concern. Even King Stephen's own brother, Bishop Henry of Winchester, was incredibly ambivalent, in turn supporting the royal and then the Angevin causes.

The political and religious spheres merged during Stephen's reign in a way rarely seen before. The number of monastic foundations increased with nobles on both sides eager to secure their territories by founding local monasteries, often on disputed areas of land which had in certain cases been taken during the wars (Vincent 1998: 247) (see Chapter 6). Sometimes the foundations were surprising. William of Ypres, one of King Stephen's most trusted allies, founded a Cistercian monastery at a time when relations were worsening between Stephen and the Continental Cistercian leaders Bernard of Clairvaux and the newly elected Cistercian Pope Eugenius III (Eales 1985: 100). Matilda was a patron to several churches on the Continent, notably the monastery at Bec, and she was known for her desire for church reform and religious renewal (Leyser 1990: 236; Chibnall 1987: 43; Chibnall 1988). In return the monks at Bec were steadfast supporters of both Matilda's and Henry's causes.

Theobald, Archbishop of Canterbury, managed to remain on good terms with both sides, and although formally an abbot of Bec, a monastery which supported the Angevin cause, Theobald acted in the way he thought best. He even successfully argued with the Pope not to excommunicate King Stephen. The election of the Archbishopric of York turned into a cause célèbre as it polarised support between the supporters of Stephen and the Cistercian order. The initial election was won by William FitzHerbert who duly became Archbishop of York. William was the son of Herbert, chamberlain to Henry I, and his mother was half-sister to King Stephen. William also had impeccable York connections: he had been treasurer at the Minster since before 1114 and his family had large estates in Yorkshire. Even though William was successfully elected to the position of archbishop by the canons of the Minster, his election was disputed, mainly by the supporters of the new Cistercian order. The ripples of claim and counter-claim spread to the papacy in Rome and to Bernard at Clairvaux. On the one side was royal favour and his uncle, Henry of Blois, Bishop of Winchester, and on the other side the massed ranks of the Cistercians including Bernard, Pope Eugenius III (a disciple of Bernard) and the Yorkshire Cistercian abbots, Richard of Fountains, William of Rievaulx, Ailred, later Abbot of Rievaulx, and Henry Murdac. Eventually the competition proved too strong for William FitzHerbert and Henry Murdac replaced him as archbishop. In 1153 the situation dramatically reversed when Murdac, Bernard and Pope Eugenius III all died. With the major obstacles gone to his election William made a triumphal return into the city. William's rapid and suspicious death on the 8 June 1154 led to the rumour that he had been poisoned.

The clergy of London were also courted by both sides. Stephen's illegitimate son, Gervase, was appointed Abbot of Westminster in 1138, and Stephen's brother, Henry of Blois, became dean of the collegiate church of St Martin Le Grand. Two of Stephen's children who died young were buried in Holy Trinity Church, Aldgate. Despite Stephen's hold on London, in 1141 Matilda managed to secure the see of London for her supporter Robert de Sigillo (Green 1991: 107).

The Plantagenets

Stephen died on 25 October 1154. Henry was then effectively king, although he did not immediately cross from Normandy. He first set the dukedom's affairs in order and only then, six weeks later, sailed for England. On 19 December 1154, Henry and his wife Eleanor of Aquitaine were crowned together in Westminster Abbey. King Henry II was undisputed King of England and Duke of Normandy. Henry immediately began appointing people to major governmental posts, some of whom had been administrators for his grandfather Henry I. Nigel, Bishop of Ely, was recalled to restart the workings of the treasury and exchequer. Some nobles had been in government for both Henry I and Stephen, and now joined Henry II. One such was Eustace Fitz John, who had witnessed at least one of Stephen's charters, and in Henry II's reign gained a series of judicial and governmental posts, and finally died campaigning for Henry in Wales (Dalton 1996: 379–80).

The war had caused confusion and instability. Lords had fought to gain the upper hand in their localities, and they had determined policy rather than the crown, a situation which Henry II set about changing by reinforcing the power of the crown. He ordered: that strongholds should be demolished; the departure from England of the hated Flemish mercenaries (including William of Ypres, one of Stephen's commanders); and that the barons should hand back castles which belonged to the crown. One baron, William Aumale, attempted to stand against Henry, but as Henry led his troops north he submitted and William's Scarborough stronghold was given to Henry. Even Henry's supporters were not immune, and nobles from all sides submitted to his will. By such swift and prompt action the peace of the country gradually became secured.

As well as the military response Henry implemented the resurrection of administrative power, both for law and order, but also to boost the finances of the treasury. During the Anarchy land had been seized by nobles, both between themselves and from the crown and Henry set about recovering and restoring lands to their rightful owners, not least the crown. The principle behind the land restoration was that lands which had been seized should be restored to those who possessed them at the end of Henry I's reign (Warren 1983: 62). The reference to his grandfather, Henry I, linked Henry II to a powerful king, but to restore the lands to the status quo of decades ago was impractical: rather Henry II's policy was more a presumption of right which could then be modified to suit the current situation.

The country was brought back under royal control and the horrors of civil war passed, but over the following decade the crown came into increasing conflict with the church to an unprecedented degree. The affairs of church and state had been one of a roller-coaster ride since the close co-operation and friendship between William the Conqueror and Archbishop Lanfranc. However, it was during William's reign that the desire was expressed that church matters should be judged in church courts, rather than the secular courts:

> no bishop or archdeacon shall henceforth hold pleas relating to the episcopal laws in the hundred court; nor shall they bring to the judgement of secular men any matter which pertains to the government of souls, but anyone cited according to the episcopal laws, for whatever cause or fault, shall answer at that place which the bishop shall appoint or name.
>
> (Douglas and Greenaway 1981: 604–5)

The division of power between church and state became an increasingly acrimonious issue and during the late eleventh and twelfth centuries there were frequent occasions when archbishops or bishops had fled the country out of fear of the king. Anselm, whilst Archbishop of Canterbury, both fled from William Rufus and Henry I. In the twelfth century the church took an increasingly firm stance in resisting the king's wishes, though royal pressure was brought to bear in certain cases. Archbishop Theodore wrote to the Pope that 'we just and only succeeded in recalling the case to the judgement of the Church' in the case of Osbert who supposedly poisoned Archbishop William of York (Warren 1983: 461). During Henry II's reign, however, the king became involved in the dispute, not only because individual cases came to his attention, but also because of rising crime throughout the country.

By the 1160s the underlying tensions between church and crown were brought to the fore by the issue of whether the church or state should punish churchmen who had committed a crime. Henry II proposed that the church should disown those clerks who were found guilty and let the state punish them. This brought the king into conflict with the Archbishop of Canterbury, Thomas Becket. Becket had previously been Henry II's chancellor and Henry had proposed Becket as Archbishop of Canterbury in the full expectation that Becket would continue to support the king and royal policy. However, in what has been seen as one of the most remarkable changes in character in history, Becket changed from a loyal royal supporter into a determined and relentless advocate of the rights of the church. Becket argued for the church's immunity from all secular jurisdiction, for the clergy were 'set apart from the nations of men' (Warren 1983: 469). The arguments steadily built with a potential compromise being reached that the bishops would observe previous customs but with the key phrase added 'saving their order' – i.e. excepting the church's customs and laws, which in effect negated the king's power. Henry's response was to produce a written document, the Constitutions of Clarendon, which set out the customs and privileges of the realm. Within the Constitutions there are three main groups of clauses: machinery of royal control over ecclesiastical communication with Rome (for example the king's permission had to be sought before a churchman could leave the country), the defining of limitations regarding ecclesiastical censure (for example application had to be made to the king before excommunication of a subject was carried out), and defining the ecclesiastical jurisdiction between lay and secular courts.

The novelty of the Constitutions was that they were written. Whilst verbally and through memory there is a chance of compromise and flexibility, with a written document there is one text to refer to with little possibility of compromise. The king was attempting to fix the position once and for all, but it also hardened the battle lines and made a solution much more difficult. The bishops refused to accept the Constitutions. It was at this point Becket changed his mind in dramatic fashion, for after arguing fiercely against the Constitutions for three days, he suddenly and without consulting the other bishops accepted them. A few days later he changed his mind again, and once more argued against the Constitutions. He then fled the country and during his six-year absence both sides attempted to win the backing of the Pope and gain adherents in England and Europe.

A defining moment came with the coronation of Henry II's son, also called Henry, a privilege usually performed by the Archbishop of Canterbury but in Becket's absence performed by the Archbishop of York. By allowing the coronation of the Young King Henry, Pope Alexander III had hoped to gain concessions from Henry which did not materialise. The Pope therefore planned to excommunicate those who had taken part in the coronation and lay an interdict upon England. However, Henry quickly sent word after the coronation that he was ready to make peace with Becket. After seven months of negotiations Becket returned to England, and on his way back he excommunicated the Archbishop of York and the bishops of London and Salisbury for their part in the Young King Henry's coronation. Becket was now in England, but Henry was abroad and the excommunicated bishops travelled to him to complain of their treatment at the hands of Becket. It was at this meeting that Henry was supposed to have said 'Who will rid me of this turbulent priest?', though the accounts of the conversations differ. Such outbursts had happened before with no ill consequences but this time four knights took it literally. They sailed for England by different routes and arrived in Canterbury. Their plan is unclear, but a strong possibility is that they simply meant to capture Becket or send him back into exile. They journeyed to Canterbury Cathedral and pursued Becket through the church in the gathering evening gloom. Becket stopped to pray at an altar and the knights found him there. The result of the ensuing struggle was the death of

Becket, his brains lying over the pavement. The date was 29 December 1170.

Becket immediately achieved Europe-wide fame for his stand against Henry II. Becket was canonised in 1173 and on 12 July 1174, in a carefully stage-managed affair, Henry II did penance for the murder by praying, weeping and being beaten at Becket's tomb. The next day, 13 July 1174, the Scottish king, William the Lion, was captured by English forces at Alnwick and was sent south as a captive. It seemed that Becket had forgiven the king and produced this miracle.

In 1173, the year of Becket's canonisation, England was once again rocked by a royal family rebellion. Henry II's son, Young King Henry, was impatient to acquire lands to rule and in exasperation of not being given Anjou to rule (his younger brother John was promised it instead), he rebelled. Others joined him, including his two brothers, Richard and Geoffrey, and his father in law, King Louis of France. Even his mother, Henry II's queen, Eleanor of Aquitaine, attempted to join them but was captured on the way. The campaign was short but bloody with armies and mercenaries marching back and forth across England. In the north the Scottish King William invaded the border areas down to Carlisle and Alnwick, until his capture on the 13 July 1174. Thereafter the rebellion quickly faded with terms being agreed in September.

At the end of Henry's life, family politics once again involved rebellion and warfare. Henry's queen, Eleanor, and sons Richard and John, allied themselves with the French King Philip Augustus in 1189 in an effort to wrest Normandy and Anjou from Henry for themselves. They had considerable success, but Henry's death in the same year meant that Richard was now King of England and Duke of Normandy. The collaboration with the French king broke. Richard was crowned in 1189 at Westminster Abbey and thereafter went on the Third Crusade (1189–92), also with Philip Augustus. On the return journey Richard was captured by the Holy Roman Emperor, Henry VI. Richard was imprisoned for over a year until the 150,000 mark ransom was paid. During his absence the international situation had changed as dissatisfied nobles in England, including Richard's brother John, were waiting to seize power. In true Angevin fashion the family was once again set against itself. John managed to capture Windsor Castle, but his mother Eleanor of Aquitaine, although over seventy years old, mobilised the defence and besieged John. In Normandy the French king, Philip Augustus, had managed to capture a large slice of the Duchy. A ransom of 150,000 marks was asked for the restoration of the land and the majority of it paid. Following Richard's release by the Holy Roman Emperor, he quickly regained control of the kingdom, forcing Philip back to the borders of Normandy. Thereafter Richard was constantly in Normandy and the Angevin Empire securing its borders. It was as part of these campaigns that Richard was struck in the shoulder by an arrow from which he died on 6 April 1199.

Richard's younger brother John made his way to a peaceful England and on the 27 May 1199, Ascension Day, he was crowned as King of England in Westminster Abbey. Whilst the situation in England remained peaceful almost immediately the French King Philip Augustus began to attack and probe the borders of Normandy. The ensuing treaty of Le Goulet in 1200 resulted in John paying Philip 20,000 marks for securing John's succession to Normandy, and recognising that Philip was John's overlord for his Norman possessions. The marriage also was arranged between Philip's son Louis and John's niece Blanche (and thereby Philip received her dowry lands in Normandy).

During the relative peace John then made a disastrous mistake. His childless marriage with his Queen, Isabella of Gloucester, was annulled, on the basis that she was his second cousin, and on 24 August 1200 John married Isabella of Angoulême. This was potentially a wise tactical move, for Angoulême and the surrounding counties of Lusignan, La Marche and Limoges were all sensitive areas and a marriage would secure their support. Unfortunately, the marriage did exactly the opposite for it enraged Hugh IX, Lord of Lusignan (reputedly because he and Isabella had been betrothed) and when he complained, John not only failed to compensate Hugh and his family, but declared them traitors. The family then looked to Philip Augustus, as John's overlord, for support. Philip had gained valuable allies.

Family issues also weakened John's position with the death of Constance of Brittany in 1201. Constance was the widow of John's elder brother, Geoffrey of Brittany, who had died in 1186, and with Constance's death their son, Arthur, came of age. Arthur was a potential heir to all the Angevin empire and as such posed a threat to John, especially as in 1202 King Philip received Arthur's homage for Brittany, Anjou, Maine and Tourraine.

Further pressure was applied when Philip demanded John's presence at court following a formal appeal to the French king by the Lusignans. John refused to attend the court of his overlord. Philip therefore had the option to punish his over-mighty subject and attempt to force him to attend. The resultant campaigns between 1202 and 1204 saw Philip systematically drive John out of not only Normandy but all his Angevin possessions. There were two key events which took place during the campaigns. The first was John's great success of his forced march (eighty miles in forty-eight hours) to capture the castle of Mirabeau, which held Arthur of Brittany. This was a stunning victory, but John's vicious treatment of prisoners and Arthur's mysterious death (which rumour turned into the fact that John had murdered Arthur) caused severe disaffection amongst the nobles and support continued to drift away. A second decisive event was Philip's capture of the magnificent castle of Chateau-Gaillard, which guarded the river Seine and the heartlands of Normandy. The castle had been built by Richard I but was captured by Philip through a combination of military ingenuity and heroism, which included a knight called Peter Bogis climbing through the chute of a toilet into the castle. He let down a rope for his companions and they in turn let down a drawbridge for the main force to enter. The fall of the castle on 6 March 1204 was a major blow to King John and thereafter the towns and castles of Normandy rapidly fell to Philip. John himself had left Normandy in December 1203. He was never to return. In 1206 John raided Gascony, Poitou and Anjou, and gained control of Gascony and parts of Poitou. After the loss of Normandy it was a small success, but did give the English king a toehold from which to launch other campaigns.

Meanwhile, a crisis had erupted in the English church in 1205 with the death of Hubert Walter, Archbishop of Canterbury and a long-time chancellor of both Richard I and John. John favoured the Bishop of Norwich, John de Gray to be the new archbishop. The monks of Canterbury, who resented royal intervention, elected their prior, Reginald. Appeals went back and forth to Rome with the Pope choosing his own candidate, Stephen Langton, who was consecrated by the Pope as Archbishop of Canterbury on 17 July 1207. The king refused to confirm his appointment, forced the monks to abandon Canterbury and seized the Cathedral's revenues. John's half-brother – Geoffrey, Archbishop of York – also fled to the Continent after complaining about taxes. The Pope had given power to the bishops of London, Ely and Worcester to impose an interdict, but they withheld the threat for seven months before declaring it on Sunday 23 March 1208. All ecclesiastical rites – baptisms, marriages, burial and the Mass – were suspended. For the first time in England the papacy had used the interdict as a political weapon though it had been threatened before, and the Pope had issued an interdict against France in 1200). Negotiations between the sides faltered and the Pope issued a formal excommunication upon King John in November 1209. Despite continuing negotiations in 1213 the Pope threatened to depose John if his terms were not accepted. The threat was made real by Philip Augustus who was planning to invade England as well. Caught between religious and secular power, John sided with the Pope. However, John went further than merely agreeing to the return of Stephen Langton, he resigned the kingdoms of England and Ireland to Pope Innocent III, and received them back under the bond of homage and a large annual payment. John was now under the protection of the papacy, having been shortly before under excommunication. It was a remarkable change in fortune. From then on the Pope would support John unswervingly.

During the dispute with the papacy John had continued his military activities, securing his power in the British Isles by operations in Ireland (1210), Wales (1208 and 1211) and along the Scottish border in 1209. With the borders secure and considerable influence in Ireland and Wales from 1212 onwards John turned his attention to his Continental lands, at the same time as Philip Augustus was preparing for the invasion of England. Philip had collected an impressive fleet of some 1,700 vessels stocked with arms and provisions for the English campaign. A lightning raid by an English fleet disabled a large number of the ships, postponing the invasion attempt. Instead John gathered his forces for an invasion of France, which would attack Philip as part of a coalition which included the Holy Roman Emperor, Otto IV, whose agents were constantly at court.

However, King John's preparations were hindered by English barons who were unwilling to serve an excommunicated king. Even after John's excommunication was lifted a group of northern barons ('The Northerners') rebelled against a cross-Channel campaign, with a key point in their argument being that they were only liable for campaigns in England, not overseas (Holt 1961). The eventual overseas campaign proved a disastrous failure. The strategy was sound enough, with a main attack in the north-east of Normandy and a diversionary attack in the west. The Battle of Bouvines (27 July 1214) proved the decisive moment for all parties (Duby 1990). Otto IV was completely defeated by King Philip. The battle had major implications for the three main protagonists – it secured the French monarchy and dominions, Otto's rule as emperor ended and King John, who remained near La Rochelle, had lost the chance of recovering Normandy.

In England the barons were increasing their campaign against John, and their position was much stronger by their discovery of Henry I's coronation charter, supposedly revealed to them by Archbishop Langton. The charter, in reality a statement of promises by Henry following the lawlessness of William Rufus's court and rule, seemed to the barons to be a self-imposed limit by Henry I on his own power. The barons seized it as the basis for their demands. Not surprisingly John rejected their demands, and in return required a renewal of the oath of fealty to ensure their obedience. The barons refused and the two sides gathered their forces, with the rebels gathering at Stamford and seizing London.

Magna Carta

The baronial opposition was too strong either to ignore or defeat and on 15 June 1215 the royal and baronial parties met at a meadow beside the Thames called Runnymede, chosen because it was between the royal castle at Windsor and London, which the barons held. Previous discussions between the two sides, in which Stephen Langton, Archbishop of Canterbury, had been involved, had led to the king conceding on 10 July a series of points which were written down in a document now known as the Articles of the Barons. This document carried no legal force, but it was a breakthrough and formed the basis for Magna Carta which King John agreed to five days later on 15 July 1215. Copies were rapidly made and sent out into the provinces, four of which still survive (two are at the British Library, one at Salisbury Cathedral and the other at Lincoln). The importance of the document was enormous: for the first time a king had agreed to abide by limitations on his power which had been set down in writing. However, Magna Carta's contents are hardly inspiring. There is a large range of subjects in its sixty-one clauses, ranging from the king's council, taxation, abuses of power, administration and relations with the church at the generalised level of government and at the other end specific details about fish weirs.

It is worth pausing in the hectic pace of events to consider the huge implications of what had happened. Before Magna Carta the only person able to modify the amount of power a king had was the king himself. Of course in some ways this was a pretence, for a king needed to consult and gain acceptance from powerful nobles. But in assenting to Magna Carta John acknowledged that the king was not above the law and that in certain cases subjects were given a legal right to resistance. Magna Carta thereby limited the king's power through the rule of law.

Following his assent to Magna Carta the barons gave homage to King John, which in turn should have meant the end of the war. However, neither side trusted the other. Both sides stayed armed and the barons organised a tournament at Stamford as an excuse to keep their weapons. The papacy considered that the charter was illegal because it had been assented to under duress illegal, and by the end of 1215 the papacy had excommunicated thirty of the rebellious barons. The barons in turn rebelled and the war once again flared up, but this time the barons were determined to rid the country of King John and replace him with the French Dauphin Louis (who later became King Louis VIII of France). The barons' campaign began disastrously with Rochester Castle falling to the king after a seven-week siege and thereafter none seriously resisted the king as he subdued the north and the east. King John was in the ascendant and he prepared to atack the barons' power base of London.

However, Louis of France landed at Thanet (21 May 1216) and joined the barons in London. The pendulum swung again, with castles and barons surrendering to Louis. One of John's staunchest allies was Pope Innocent III who excommunicated Louis and released John from his oath of Magna Carta in September 1216. Even so, John was forced onto the defensive with a succession of bad news about the campaigns, not least having his baggage train, which included his treasure and wardrobe, his chapel and relics, being overtaken by the tide as it crossed the Wash. Following a long campaign, King John fell ill and died on 18 October 1216.

King John's death was arguably what saved England from being captured by Louis. With King John's death the main reason for fighting had gone and the crown was now in the hands of John's 9-year-old son Henry. The situation for the royalist cause was, however, still dire, though the young king's advisers, led by William Marshall, were still strong in the north and west. The coronation of the boy king took place on 28 October in Gloucester, with its long royal associations with the crown wearings of Anglo-Saxon kings. Counsellors, bishops and magnates all gave formal oaths of allegiance to the boy king and on the 12 November 1216, Magna Carta was reissued in the king's name. What had begun as a statement of rebel objectives had been changed into a royal policy document. It was a clever move, for Louis could not now claim to reissue it, and the French prince was increasingly seen as a royal pretender. Papal support was also firmly behind the royalist cause and gradually the royalists, led by William Marshall, gained the upper hand, relieving a siege of Lincoln and defeating an expeditionary naval force at Sandwich. In the Treaty of Kingston, King Philip Augustus made peace and Louis returned to France. He was never to return.

After the wars Magna Carta was not forgotten, indeed it was reissued with variations in 1217 and in 1225 – it was the 1225 version which was lodged in the statutes of England in *The Confirmation of Charters* in 1297 by Edward I. The first use of the name 'Magna Carta' (i.e. Great Charter) was recorded soon after in 1218, when the name 'Great Charter' was used to differentiate it from the physically smaller 'Forest Charter' which was issued on 6 November 1217 (Hindley 1990: 176). The 1225 edition was issued according to the king's 'own spontaneous goodwill'. Magna Carta's importance continued throughout the thirteenth century, but its significance began to wane. By the end of the sixteenth century the Magna Carta was no longer associated with King John, so much so that in Shakespeare's play, *King John*, the Magna Carta does not figure at all. Rather, legal textbooks cited Henry III's reissue of 1225. It came back to prominence in a way that would have been completely unexpected to the medieval barons when Coke and others in the Parliaments of James I and Charles I seized on it in an attempt to limit and define the king's powers – a battle which eventually led to another conflict, the Civil Wars of the 1640s.

3   Boundaries and networks

The Norman Conquest forged the link between England and Normandy which would remain in the English political psyche for centuries. Long past the loss of Normandy in 1204, kings of England – notably Edward III and Henry V – attempted to regain their Norman inheritance by invasion and conquest. Even when the kings of England held Normandy, such was their concern for the duchy that one historian has described England between 1066 and 1204 as 'Colonial England' (Holt 1997). However, the colony itself grew. The kings of England may have concentrated the majority of their efforts in securing their dukedom of Normandy, but through campaigns in the north and towards Wales, as well as the conquest of Ireland, the territory within the British Isles under the control of the King of England markedly increased. By 1215 the boundaries of kingdoms, especially in the north between Scotland and England, had become firmly defined. In England as a whole in 1215 there was also a much greater consciousness of lands beyond the English Channel and Normandy than there had been in 1066. The Crusades opened up the Holy Lands, pilgrimages were becoming popular, and the families of Norman nobles had influence across Europe. The new monastic orders – all Continental in origin except the Gilbertines – further tied the localities of England into a European framework. Whilst the importance of the Viking lands of Scandinavia rapidly diminished after the Conquest, new cultures and lands opened up in Europe and the Holy Lands.

Anglo-Norman aristocracy

One of the consequences of the Conquest was that the incoming Normans and their allies replaced the Anglo-Saxon elite. Many of the Normans held lands in both England and Normandy which has led historians to ask the question: was there a cross-Channel 'Anglo-Norman culture'? Le Patourel (1976: 195) believed there was and that the cross-Channel aristocracy was 'one homogeneous, aristocratic community'. The two realms were certainly seen as a single unity by the Pope in Rome 'since they were subject to a ruler who personally had kingly rank' (Cowdrey 1998: 459). As an idea it has the attraction of simplicity. The theory stresses that the constant flow of people and ideas across the English Channel between Normandy and England allowed the aristocratic community to develop. Channels of communication existed within the royal and political spheres, in religious contacts and through trade. The court journeyed back and forth between Normandy and England and was composed of nobles with lands in both countries, for example Hugh Bigod, an important East Anglian nobleman, witnessed forty-five charters between 1120 and 1135, one-third of which were issued in Normandy (Wareham 1994: 232). The scale of some landholdings can be seen by the example of the Earls of Chester were also the 'vicomtes' of Avranches and so powerful in both England and Normandy. Furthermore, French was the language of nobles either side of the channel and there were strong cultural influences unifying Normandy and England, such as in art (see Chapter 8) and the adoption of heraldry. Heraldry arose in north-west France in the late eleventh century and spread to England and northern France in the early twelfth century as a means of identifying nobles. Heraldry was confined to the greatest nobles of the realm until the 1160s, and as such it was a commonly understood means of symbolic communication between nobles on both sides of the Channel, which supports Le Patourel's view of a single aristocracy bound together by a sense of their own culture. However, the late twelfth century, the families at county level also began to take devices – often from their lords – to show allegiance. Any thought of a cross-Channel heraldic community disintegrated as the heraldry became more localised (Crouch 1994: 66–7).

Le Patourel also proposed that the cross-Channel nobility wanted political stability and so worked together to unite Normandy and England, especially when they were under different rulers in the years 1087–96, 1100–6 and 1144–54. The first two periods occurred when Normandy and England were inherited by different members of the same family (Robert Curthose was Duke of Normandy and his brother William Rufus was King of England; from 1100 Robert Curthose was again Duke of Normandy whilst his brother Henry I was King of England.) The third period was the result of military conquest when Geoffrey the Count of Anjou captured Normandy from King Stephen of England in 1144. The lands were united when Geoffrey's son, Henry, Duke of Anjou and Normandy, became King Henry II of England.

This fundamental idea of a cross-Channel aristocracy working in unison has come under attack from many different directions. Rather than acting as a unified group recent research has shown that most noble families acted in what they saw as their own best interests. The pattern of burial location amongst noble families in England has established how quickly English interests gained prominence in families with English lands after 1066 (Golding 1986: 40–8), which also ties in with new patterns of patronage to English religious houses. Furthermore the newcomers married English women and it is 'probable that an aristocracy with predominantly British interests emerged relatively quickly after 1066' and became firmly entrenched in local society, and, by extension, their lands overseas rarely dominated their policies (Bates 1989: 860; Bates 1994: 30). The formation of dynasties over generations also meant that families naturally focussed on their key lands, devoting more time and energy to specific landholdings either in England or Normandy. Whilst undoubtedly some nobles held large amounts of lands either side of the Channel, many others did not. Even in the period immediately after the Conquest, some of the most important Norman nobles held no lands in England at all by 1086, such as Roger of Beaumont, and these families would have concentrated solely on their position in Normandy rather than on English politics (Bates 1994: 854–5).

Nobles also had international links beyond the borders of Normandy and England, as the Laigle family demonstrates (Thompson 1995). Gilbert of Laigle married Juliana, daughter of the Count of Montagne and their daughter Margaret married Garcia Ramirez, who inherited the kingdom of Navarre. In England another of Gilbert's sisters married Robert Mowbray, Earl of Northumbria, shortly before his rebellion and downfall. For a short time Laigle power stretched over thousands of miles. However, keeping power meant supporting the winning side and Gilbert switched service from Robert Curthose to William Rufus and then to Henry I. Unfortunately, following generations kept supporting the wrong sides, with subsequent reprisals by the victors leading to loss of Laigle power and status. The penalties for supporting the wrong side could be severe. Robert of Bellême supported Robert Curthose throughout Curthose's rule of Normandy even when defeat was imminent, and then again when Curthose invaded England in 1101. Rather than losing everything Robert then supported Henry I. However, Henry was suspicious of him and imprisoned Robert who died in prison in 1112 (Thompson 1990: 266).

The political affiliations of neighbours also complicated local and regional politics. The enmity between the Montgomery family and their neighbours the Grandmesnil and Courcy families resulted in the Montgomery family siding with William Rufus and the Grandmesnil and Courcy families siding with Robert Curthose (Thompson 1990: 271).

Over time some families naturally drifted apart, with different branches holding lands in England and Normandy and suffering differing fortunes. The Paynell family was one such noble family. The original member who arrived with the Conqueror held lands in Normandy and England. By 1204 the Paynell family lands were split between two cousins. Both had lands in England and Normandy – one, Hugh, supported King John and so lost his Norman lands, the other, Fulk, supported the French king and so lost his English lands (Chibnall 1994: 46–7).

In a few exceptional cases a lord might be powerful enough to dictate terms. The Count of Meulan was able to pay homage to the French king and to the Duke of Normandy, thereby ensuring possession of his lands in both areas. The power of the count allowed him to achieve this, though few others had the power to achieve this satisfactory solution (Crouch 1990: 86–7).

Boundaries

At the boundaries of the kingdom the situation becomes more confused, for the nobles were pulled in many different directions in deciding how to protect and promote their best interests. Viewed from the centre the situation at the boundaries can often be seen as stable and definable. When Powicke wrote *The Loss of Normandy* the records he used were those of central government at Rouen and Caen, which showed an organised and defined state owing allegiance to the Duke (Powicke 1913). However, the boundaries of countries and regions were rarely firm in this era and it has been said in relation to Wales 'Countries and boundaries are not laid up in heaven. They are shaped by men: and what men shape they may also choose to reshape' (Davis 1991: 4). One of the effects of studying border regions is to emphasise the regional aspect of culture. It is often possible to pinpoint a particular place as following one influence or other, but taken as a whole the map is blurred and unclear as individual details alter (Power 1994: 183–4).

The Norman conquerors of England had a large number of borders to contend with. Bordering England were Scotland, Wales and Cornwall. Normandy, too, had many volatile borders: the Île-de-France controlled by the French king; Brittany, Maine, Blois and, to the north, Flanders and the increasingly independent cities. Arguably the most important borders for the English rulers between 1066 and 1215 were those of Normandy, for the Norman homelands had much greater political and cultural influence upon the English kings than their actual size suggests. When the Norman homelands were attacked, money and troops would frequently be sent across the Channel from England.

The defining of a boundary is not always easy, for religious, political and cultural areas of influence may all be different. In the case of Normandy, the border can be defined either as the area of ducal administration, as shown by the areas covered by the exchequer rolls, or as the diocesan boundaries of the archdiocese of Rouen, or third as the areas that followed the Custom of Normandy (*Coutume de Normandie*). By the late twelfth century the Custom had become divorced from political power so that areas outside Norman control continued to follow it (Power 1994: 185, 191–3).

Around Normandy was a patchwork of warring states and the borders between them were rarely static for any length of time. Whilst the core heartlands of Normandy were well defined, the edges were blurred. During the twelfth century the struggles between the Duke of Normandy and the Lord of Mayenne created a boundary which was constantly altered by oaths, bargaining, truces, hostage-taking – any of which could alter family allegiance and the regional balance of power (Power 1994: 188–90). During the late twelfth and early thirteenth centuries the border of Normandy became more threatened as the French king, Philip Augustus, built ever more intrusive castles to mark the extent of his own territory along the eastern border of Normandy (Power 1994: 190). A monarch's own presence in a region could have a decisive influence in changing the allegiances of nobles in a border region and during 1200 and 1201 Philip Augustus journeyed from Senlis, to Vernon, Gisors, Mantes and Pontoise putting pressure on the noble families who spanned the border to join his cause (Bradbury 1998: 137–9; Bradbury 1999: 356). This careful preparation meant that he could, and did, strike into Normandy when he was ready.

Along the borders the noble families were extremely powerful in their own right, as their allegiance was often essential to competing powers, but they were also to some extent pawns in the battle for the control of the border. Many noble families had an indifference to the political frontier, being mainly interested in their own security and power. They could there-fore be bought or compromised. Power (1994: 197–8) has shown how between 1168 and 1181 the counts of Évreux were changed from Franco-Norman magnates with no English lands into Anglo-Norman lords with no French lands by Henry II's policy of marriage alliances and giving lands. However, the situation was reversed when Count Robert of Alençon, who held extensive lands along the French/Norman border, changed his allegiance from King John to the French King Philip in 1203, which signalled, in the words of Powicke, 'the beginning of the end for John' in Normandy (Powicke 1913: 233–4).

Scotland and the northern border

The situation concerning the northern border of England changed over time. Following the Norman Conquest the kings of England constantly attempted to push the limits of their control northwards. Immediately following the Conquest the northern boundaries were ill-defined and a case can be made that York was initially outside William's control, for the burning of the two castles in the city and the slaughter of the garrison was the only time that two of William's castles were destroyed. William quickly gained the initiative, but even by 1086 Domesday Book shows that the Norman influence to the north of York fades away.

Over the following decades the border between England and Scotland was generally considered to be the river Tweed on the eastern side. On the western side the ancient kingdom of Cumbria was disputed territory, although historically the Scottish had had more influence over it than the English kings. There was a fluidity across the border, determined by the political or military power of kings, for culturally the lowlands of Scotland were similar to those of northern England, all having once been part of the Anglo-Saxon kingdom of Northumbria. *The Anglo-Saxon Chronicle* described the Lothian region as 'Lothian in England' and Cumbria was disputed, sometimes being called 'between England and Scotland'.

The Scottish king had the title of King of Scots and during the twelfth and thirteenth centuries he consolidated his power in the lowlands of

Scotland. In the twelfth century the places from which royal acts of the Scottish king were delivered rarely strayed outside the zone bounded by the rivers Tay, Clyde and Tweed, i.e. the lowland fertile zone (Barrow 1991: 28). Some charters do mention revenues from Moray, Argyll and Kintyre, and judicial sessions were held at Banff and Aberdeen, but these are fragmentary references in the whole set of evidence. Outside his jurisdiction were the Western Isles from the Isle of Man to the Isle of Lewis, which were controlled by the kings of Norway. By the late twelfth century there was a strong cultural divide between the Scottish king in his court in the lowlands and the peoples of the Gaelic-speaking upland areas and Western Isles. Similarly, the kings had little influence where strong lordships existed, such as those of Galloway and Nithsdale, and the various earldoms such as Lennox, Menteith, Strathearn, Atholl, Mar and Buchan.

As the Normans controlled territories further and further north, areas of their control were marked by new fortresses. A castle at Newcastle was built in 1080 and further north still the castles at Norham and Wark marked the Tweed as the boundary between Scotland and England (Strickland 1989: 189). In 1092 William Rufus captured the north-western town of Carlisle and proceeded to build a castle there. This act was to prove decisive for determining the western border. The river Solway became the boundary between Scotland and England. The building of castles can therefore be seen as an offensive move to push forward the boundary and mark it by a fortification at the limits of Norman rule. However, although the fortifications might be points on a map acting as local bases, the control of the border region was by 1100 still very limited. To control the border more effectively great baronies were created, for example that for Alnwick, which was given by Henry I to Eustace Fitz John in order to defend the borderlands. Eustace was also given castles across the north-east and Yorkshire, which included Malton, and the custodianship of Bamburgh, Knaresborough and Tickhill (Dalton 1996: 365).

In order to extend their influence various tactics were used by the English and Scottish kings. David, King of Scots, was a patron to religious houses in Cumberland and Westmorland, for example those of Wetheral, Holt Cultram and St Bees, perhaps in an attempt to extend his influence further south (Barrow 1991: 26). The Scottish kings also launched military campaigns against the English in the years 1070–93, 1136–9, 1153, 1173–4 and 1215–17, the latter three periods all at a time when there was civil war in England and Scotland was aiding the king's enemies. However, compared to the violent and frequent military campaigns across the borders of Normandy, the Scottish border was remarkably free of major warfare.

There were two recurring issues of dispute: the status of Northumbria (claimed by both English and Scottish kings) and the relative authority of the kings. The earls of Northumbria, who acted as a buffer between England and Scotland, were nominally English in their allegiance, but centuries of independence had produced an independent spirit. The intrusion of the

Vikings into Yorkshire in the ninth and tenth centuries had further isolated the region. Following the Conquest, Waltheof, Earl of Northumbria, initially supported William but then rebelled and was eventually beheaded for treason. Scottish claims to the earldom derived from Matilda, daughter of Waltheof, who held Northumberland and the earldom of Huntingdon. Matilda's second husband was King David of Scotland who successfully pursued his claim to Northumbria when in 1136 King Stephen granted King David's son, Henry, the earldom of Northumbria. Stephen also granted him part of Cumbria, which King David had seized from Stephen and made one of his most important seats of power, minting coins and dying even there in 1153. Stephen's decisions regarding the Scottish border were swiftly reversed when Henry II came to the throne. Henry re-established the border at the Tweed and Solway, as it had been between 1092 and 1136. However, the issue of Northumbria was a potential thorn in the king of England's side. One explanation of the Scottish invasion in 1173–4 was that the Scots wanted to seize back Northumberland (Duncan 1999: 249).

The second dispute was that of the homage and status between the kings. At times the Scottish kings paid homage to the English kings – for example the Scottish King Malcolm Canmore declared homage to William the Conqueror – thereby declaring that the English king was their overlord. However, as the concepts and ideas connected with homage became more concrete during the twelfth century the Scottish kings were very reluctant to pay homage for Scotland. Occasionally it was forced upon them, for example when King William the Lion of Scotland was captured at Alnwick in 1174. Henry II imposed stringent terms upon William for his release, requiring homage from him and the nobles of Scotland, along with handing over five key Scottish castles. When Richard I came to the English throne his desire for crusading money meant that William was successfully able to buy his way out of the agreement and retrieve his castles.

When King John came to the English throne King William of Scotland threatened to seize the earldom of Northumbria. During the civil war of John's reign, the new king of Scotland, Alexander II, sought the earldom from Louis of France who was fighting John. In 1216 Alexander crossed the Pennines and moved south, passing through London (the only conceivable explanation is that there was a treaty between himself, the barons and the City of London). At Canterbury there was the extraordinary meeting of Alexander, the King of Scots, with Prince Louis, son of Philip Augustus King of France, on English soil whilst fighting the King of England. At Dover Alexander did homage to Louis (Duncan 1999: 267). Such a meeting in such circumstances was unique in English history, and showed the terrible weakness of King John's position. Louis's attempts failed to gain the crown of England and with the failure went Alexander's possibility of the earldom. There was little long-term advantage following the Scottish campaign and the issue of the earldom and the location of the border was finally resolved in the Treaty of York in 1237 (Duncan 1999: 251, 268).

The nobles living near the English–Scottish border had to decide which king to support. As in Normandy, cross-border links were common with both marriage and hostage-taking being important. On a regional scale, Eustace Fitz John was close to Henry I and owned considerable lands in the north of England, but fought for the Scots at the Battle of the Standard in 1138. He effectively maintained his power in Northumberland through allegiances with the Scottish crown. Eustace's son, William de Vescy, maintained strong links with Scotland and his cousins Philip and Roger de Valoignes gained lands there (Dalton 1996: 370–81).

Noblemen joining the Scottish king could be a serious threat. Some saw the Scottish court as a refuge, as had happened after the Norman Conquest and thereafter throughout the twelfth century. During Stephen's reign Robert, Lord of Bampton in Devon, took refuge from Stephen at the court of the Scottish king, and incited him to invade. There is also evidence that the Empress Matilda communicated with the Scottish court in her attempt to overthrow Stephen (Barrow 1991: 30, 32). The subject of the shifting power bases and political alliances of the Scottish border area is one which needs further exploration because allegiances could be divided, limited and con-ditional, as well as dependent on time and circumstance (Dalton 1996: 370).

The intermingling of nobles along borders, alliances and refugees also resulted in changes at the Scottish court itself. The migration brought with it Norman and French culture and views, and their power was such that Barnwell Chronicler wrote that: 'more recent kings of Scots profess them-selves to be rather Frenchmen both in race and manners, language and culture; and after reducing the Scots to utter servitude, they admit only Frenchmen to their friendship and service' (Duncan 1999: 247).

The migration of Anglo-Normans to the Scottish court had largely petered out by the late twelfth century, especially as new lands in Ireland became available for the English nobles to explore and conquer, though there were still opportunities in the Scottish church. Roger, the son of the Earl of Leicester, served King William of Scotland and was promoted to Bishop of St Andrews. A probable relative of Roger's, John of Leicester, became Bishop of Dunkeld in 1212, and William Malveisin – also associated with Roger – was appointed Bishop of Glasgow, and then Bishop of St Andrews. There are indications of the closeness of administrative procedures between the English and Scottish, for example the Scottish chancery in 1195 adopted a recent English royal practice of giving the month date in royal charters and when Hubert Walter introduced the oath for keeping the peace in England in 1195, the oath was adapted and extended for Scotland in 1197. These administrative changes most likely came from the clerics who had joined the Scottish King William's service from the English court. William favoured them, partly because they acted as a buffer against the power of the clerics of the Scottish church (Duncan 1999: 248).

However, English chroniclers may have overemphasised the impact of the incomers into Scottish society. Even though Barrow (1980) has traced the migration of Anglo-Norman families to Scotland from about 1120 (who replaced all but the very highest levels of native Scottish nobles) there was no dramatic cultural shift. Duncan (1999: 248) has pointed out that there is little evidence for the reception of French culture into Scotland. There is only one Scottish romance, 'The Roman de Fergus', but it is written in Picard French and both manuscripts are of French provenance.

The Scottish kings, following the Norman and Angevin example, increasingly adopted the social, political and military institutions of the Normans in England (Strickland 1989: 177). One consequence of copying the English systems was that with increased wealth and administrative abilities the Scots could gather large armies, which in turn meant that they could carry invasion and war into England. The border was crossed several times by major military campaigns, usually launched by the Scottish kings into England. King Malcolm III of Scotland attacked Cumbria and plundered Teesdale, Cleveland and Hartness in both 1070 and 1071. The Scots attacked again in 1079 and 1091. In 1091 the Scots reached Durham before being repulsed by William Rufus, after which Rufus annexed southern Cumbria and Carlisle in 1092 (Aird 1993: 14, 18). Further periods of Scottish invasion occurred between 1136 and 1153. The chroniclers reported an especially vicious campaign in 1138 which resulted in Archbishop Thurstan of York organising the defence of the north. The resulting battle near Northallerton (North Yorkshire) was known as the Battle of the Standard because the Standard of St Cuthbert was taken into battle. The use of religious standards in battle was relatively common on the Continent, but rare on English soil and the reason for its use in this case is unknown. During the battle a disastrous and uncoordinated attack by the Galwegian contingent of the Scottish army resulted in a rout of the Scots (Strickland 1989: 192). Another serious Scottish incursion into England occurred in 1173–4 during the civil war in England known as the Young King's Revolt. The campaigns were vividly described by a contemporary poet Jordan Fantosme (Johnston 1981).

The portrayal of the Scots altered over time. John Gillingham (1997) has traced the start of English xenophobia of the Scots to 1138 and their invasion. Following this attack the attitude of English writers changed and became more hostile in general to the Scots, though the Scottish king was seen as master of his own house and on the whole less troublesome that the French king (Strickland 1989: 192). The hostile attitude was sometimes altered by chroniclers who became familiar with the Scots. Gillingham has traced the attitude of the chronicler Roger of Howden, who probably entered Henry II's service during the 1170s and was sent on several diplomatic missions to the Scottish court. Initially he was hostile to the Scots and in his early writings he mentions the atrocities during the 1174 campaign and in particular the massacre at Warkworth. Over time and acquaintance with the Scots his views were modified and in his writings of the 1190s he is generally more positive and omits the Warkworth massacre entirely (Gillingham 1997: 161; Gillingham 1999b).

Wales

The Welsh were a very different proposition to the Scots for they could offer a serious challenge only if a powerful ruler united the people, but more often the Welsh fought amongst themselves. Just before the Norman Conquest the Welsh border had been a source of considerable weakness for Edward the Confessor as Gruffydd ap Llewelyn of Gwynedd took control of all of Wales in 1055 and attacked the border. The danger was only averted when Harold and his brother Tostig combined to destroy Gruffydd's power and Gruffydd died (Walker 1978: 132–3; Lewis 1984: 213). Thereafter Wales reverted to its normal infighting, which included sporadically attacking the English across the border. The memory of Welsh power and the potential of Welsh attack were such that the Normans saw the border as a weakness. Edward the Confessor had attempted to strengthen the border by giving the Norman Ralf de Mantes lands to settle and Ralph introduced the innovation of ditch and pallisade castles in Herefordshire. A further innovation was that Earl Ralf trained his English soldiers in cavalry warfare in the French fashion, something which was deplored by the chroniclers of the day. Even though Ralf was bringing French warfare to English soil, Edward still thought of him in terms of the usual fighting force, for example in a writ of 1062 Edward referred to him as 'my housecarl', which put him in the same category as other English warriors. What Ralf thought to this description is unknown (Mason 1985: 155–6).

Unlike the Anglo-Saxons, the Welsh suffered no single calamitous defeat and although the frontier could be pushed into Wales or political alliances changed, there was always the possibility that the Welsh would regroup (Rowlands 1980: 144). The border area was known as the Welsh March. The lands were dominated by Norman, and then later English, lords but there were still extensive Welsh communities either side of the border and the border was perhaps more fluid than a static line on a map suggests (Rowlands 1999: 274).

The first Norman involvement in Wales occurred in 1072, when assistance was provided to Caradog ap Gruffudd of Gwent against Maredudd ab Owain ab Edwin, followed soon after by Norman attacks on Deheubarth, Ceredigion and Dyfed (Babcock 1993: 24). Thereafter the Normans pressed ever forward. In 1081 William the Conqueror travelled to St David's to offer prayers. There is no indication that the journey was a problem and that an English king could penetrate so far into Wales shows either overwhelming force or a defeated south Wales. South Wales was also vulnerable to Norman incursion from the south-west of England and a number of families held lands either side of the Bristol Channel (Walker 1978: 134).

As the Normans advanced, the previous Welsh areas were changed into Norman marcher lordships, so Brycheiniog became the lordship of Brecknock; Morgannwg became the lordship of Glamorgan (Walker 1978: 134). The advance into Wales can be seen by the status of Hereford. In the eleventh century Hereford was an outpost, and it was named after the ford that the army used ('here' means 'army' in Anglo-Saxon). By the mid to end of the twelfth century Hereford had lost its frontier character and become fully integrated into England. The only remnant of its former frontier status was that it was still sometimes called 'Hereford in Wales' and Welsh was a part of the oral culture (Walker 1978: 143).

The movement of the Normans westward continued after William the Conqueror's death as William Rufus did nothing to restrain the Norman advance of lords eager for land (Babcock 1993: 27). In 1093 Roger of Montgomery, Earl of Shrewsbury, and William fitz Baldwin, Sheriff of Devon, invaded and quickly overran Dyfed and Ceredigion, building castles and fortifying them. The Welsh response to their new lords was not enthusiastic:

> The people and the priest are despised by the word, heart and work of the Normans. For they increase our taxes and burn our properties. One vile Norman intimidates a hundred natives with his command, and terrifies (them) with his look . . . Families do not now delight in offspring; the heir does not hope for paternal estates; the rich man does not aspire to accumulate flocks.
>
> (Rowlands 1980: 142)

There were frequent incursions into England and Wales by both sides and the fortunes of war on the Welsh border ebbed and flowed. The first invading forces were Normans, followed by Bretons and Flemings in the twelfth century (Walker 1978: 131). At first the marcher lords drove the expansion into Wales. This was particularly true of the southern and eastern seaboards which were seized by the earls of Shrewsbury, and the northern coastal plains being taken by the earls of Chester.

The profits from the marcher lordships could be high. An analysis of the holdings of the Clare family, who were earls of Hereford and Gloucester in the late twelfth century, showed that their Welsh or border estates produced £825: about half the total income of the family. The income from the lordship of Glamorgan rose steadily and in 1317 it alone was producing 40 per cent of the Clare's income. The marcher lordships were valuable commodities (Altschul 1965: 202–5; Walker 1978: 141).

In the early twelfth century Henry I pursued an active policy of controlling Wales. This he did by a combination of giving lands to nobles – such as the family of Clare in Ceredigion – or groups, such as Flemings in Pembrokeshire. Henry also tamed the Welsh princes by force or gifts. However, the civil war between Stephen and Matilda was accompanied by a renewal of Welsh native power, and even with Henry II's rule and military expeditions in 1157, 1163 and 1165, the Welsh princes managed to retain more independence than under Henry I. Occasionally a strong Welsh leader would emerge to unify the Welsh, such as Lord Rhys, whom Henry II granted the title of 'justiciar of all Deheubarth', but on his death the Welsh chiefdoms once again fought amongst themselves. During King John's reign a new Welsh leader, Llywelyn ap Iorwerth, appeared. During the civil wars of 1215–17 Llywelyn expanded his power and captured several important castles. After the civil war Llywelyn retained his power by performing homage to King Henry III.

Ireland

Politically, Ireland was not important to the English kings until the 1160s, but in ecclesiastical politics Lanfranc, the Archbishop of Canterbury, attempted to establish Canterbury's primacy over the Irish church in the decades after the Norman Conquest. Lanfranc wrote to Gofraid, King of Dublin, that he had consecrated Patricius (Gilla Pátraic) as Bishop of Dublin – the date of which is pre-1074. Lanfranc tried to justify his actions by stating that the consecration was in 'the custom of our predecessors' (*more antecessorum nostrorum*). The lack of evidence about the custom suggests otherwise (Philpott 1997: 190), though the sources are difficult to interpret and there may have been earlier involvement during Cnut's reign (Abrams 1997: 27–8). Thereafter correspondence between archbishops of Canterbury and the Irish church was intermittent and there were obvious differences in practice. In a letter to the Bishop of Munster, Lanfranc was forthright in his condemnation of the Irish belief that babies were not baptised until they had had the consecrated bread and wine (Clover and Gibson 1979: 157).

Worcester Cathedral had a greater claim of earlier involvement with Ireland. The port of Bristol lay at the southern end of Worcester's diocese and it is likely that contacts with religious foundations would have existed over the centuries. The Bishop of Dublin had been a monk at Worcester and his writings speak of Bishop Wulfstan and Worcester (Philpott 1997: 200). Wulfstan took an active interest in Ireland and the Irish, stopping slave sales to Ireland, having contacts with Irish kings and keeping contact with Gilla Pátraic. Material evidence of this link has been found in archaeological excavations in Dublin where a pilgrim flask from Wulfstan's shrine has been unearthed (Emma Mason 1990: 250–1).

Even though there were personal links with Ireland, the country was largely ignored by English rulers and nobles until 1166. In that year the defeated King of Leinster, Dermot MacMurrough, travelled to the court of Henry II to ask for assistance and to recruit Henry's nobles to his cause. Henry agreed and Dermot began a series of successful campaigns using Anglo-Norman troops in 1169 (Duffy 1997).

The year 1169 was a turning point for Irish history. The subsequent events in Ireland have been termed an invasion. In reality it was a steady process of settlement. There was not one decisive battle as at Hastings, nor were areas conquered by a long drawn-out piecemeal entrenchment as in Wales, but in Ireland large compact lordships were rapidly formed (McNeill 1990: 99). The Norman nobles of Pembroke formed the most important group. The most prominent was the dispossessed Earl of Pembroke, Richard of Clare (nicknamed 'Strongbow') who had remained Lord of Chepstow. Other Pembroke nobles included the fitz Gerald family, Robert fitz Stephen and Meiler fitz Henry. A series of successful attacks led to Dermot and his allies capturing land and the important cities of Waterford and Dublin, and Dermot's realm rapidly increased until his death in 1171. The Anglo-Norman nobles thus spanned the Irish sea in territory and rather than return, Strongbow and the other Anglo-Norman leaders decided to set up their own, practically independent, lordships in Ireland.

Henry II reacted strongly against his nobles creating power bases in Ireland and led his own expedition in 1171–2. Strongbow was forced to submit to Henry's authority, but his submission allowed him to keep his lands. Henry set about parcelling out lands to other nobles: Hugh de Lacy was given Meath whilst Strongbow remained in control of Leinster where he parcelled out land to his followers based on native Irish units of land (Flanagan 1997: 122). Most of the Irish kings made formal submission to Henry at Christmas 1171.

The church too was exploited as a vehicle of conquest and Henry II instigated a national synod at Cashel at which Irish practices were brought into line with English liturgical practices and new communities of monks (nine Cistercian, nine Benedictine), canons (twenty Augustinian houses) and military orders such as the Templars were introduced into Ireland, often by expansionist and aggressive Anglo-Norman lords (Ó Néill 1997:179). John de Courcy, Earl of Ulster, rebuilt Inch Abbey in 1180 (after destroying it by fire in 1177), and Grey Abbey was founded by de Courcy's wife. Both were linked to Cistercian houses in the north of England, rejecting Irish links (Mallory and McNeill 1995: 277–8). Saints too were used as political symbols and in 1185 the bodies of Ireland's three most prestigious saints – Patrick, Colum Cille and Brigit – were supposedly discovered in a cave, at which point John de Courcy obtained them for his own churches (Ó Néill 1997: 183).

Ireland became an attractive proposition for other nobles who set out on their own acquisitions, either with royal approval or from their own sense of adventure. John de Courcy had been part of the Dublin garrison, until he decided to head north following an invitation of the King of Ulaid. De Courcy seized the kingdom and turned it into his own earldom of Ulster. At its height in the thirteenth century the earldom covered the north-eastern seaboard (Mallory and McNeill 1995: 249–59). South of Ulster Hugh de Lacy controlled Meath in central Ireland and was Constable of Dublin, from where he fuelled further colonist expansion (Duffy 1999: 233).

The English perception of the Irish or Ireland was not a favourable one. Irish marriages were depicted as polygamous or incestuous (possibly because of inter-marriage between Irish nobility). Irish politics were depicted as kin-slaying and Ireland itself was a land of mountains, bogs and rain which the English could control if the will existed (Gillingham 1997: 164).

Henry II tried various tactics concerning Ireland. The High King of Ireland, Rory O'Connor, was forced to submit to Henry at the Treaty of Windsor in 1175. The treaty recognised O'Connor as the king of the unconquered parts of Ireland, in return for a payment of one hide in ten; the treaty in effect defined the extent of Irish and English rule. The situation changed in 1177 when Henry's 9-year-old son, John, was to be made King of Ireland. This title never materialised and instead his formal title became Lord of Ireland.

When John was seventeen, in 1185, he led an expedition to Ireland to impose his will – an expedition which turned into a disaster. Politically the Irish kings were humiliated by the English who pulled their long beards in jest, but the military campaign collapsed because it had no clear plan and the soldiers were left unpaid. The campaign did, however, clearly show that John considered the English to be masters over the Irish – the prospect of English and Irish being equal partners was crushed (Duffy 1999: 232). When John became King of England in 1199 his titles were merged – he was now King of England and Lord of Ireland, a joint title which continued until the sixteenth century when Henry VIII declared himself King of Ireland. John supported an expansion of English settlement and influence, which in turn set up serious tensions within Ireland, both between English and Irish, and the Irish themselves, which flared into civil war during the first decade of the thirteenth century (Duffy 1999: 238).

In response to the unrest, King John made a second expedition to Ireland which was more concerned with controlling the Anglo-Norman baronage. With more limited objectives and better planning the expedition was more successful, capturing or expelling key Anglo-Norman nobles (such as William de Broase and Hugh de Lacy, Earl of Ulster) as well as receiving the submission of many Irish kings. Some of the details of the organisation of the campaign have survived in an account roll, known as the prestita roll (from the money or 'prests' which the king gave to men to carry out his business). The assumption has been that these were loans, to be repaid at a future date, though Church has argued that these were wages, disguised as loans. If correct, this is the first evidence of wages and costs of campaigning being paid by the king to nobles (rather than lowly mercenaries), thereby initiating the beginnings of an army separate from the feudal levy (Church 1998).

Empire building

As well as Ireland and Wales, kings and nobles looked to the Continent for alliances and conquests. A powerful case has been made that until his death in 1100 William Rufus was actively creating a European empire in the 1090s (Vaughn 1993).

The greatest empire of the English kings in the twelfth century was the Angevin Empire, but it was an empire which expanded and collapsed within sixty years. However, whilst the term 'empire' implies common characteristics between lands and the imposition of a culture, in practice the huge variations in records make comparisons between areas impossible. The survival of large numbers of financial and governmental records in England and Normandy is in contrast to an almost total lack of financial and governmental records from Anjou and Aquitaine.

The origin of the empire was the marriage of the Empress Matilda – the daughter of Henry I – to Geoffrey, Count of Anjou. (This was her second marriage: she retained her title from her first marriage to the Holy Roman Emperor.) Geoffrey was determined to conquer the neighbouring lands of Normandy and succeeded after a series of successful campaigns between 1141 and 1144 during the civil wars in England. Geoffrey and Matilda's eldest son Henry inherited Normandy from his father in 1150. Henry was not content with Normandy and Anjou and invaded England (see Chapter 2) and was eventually crowned King of England on 19 December 1154. For a second time in a hundred years the Duke of Normandy had become the King of England, though the contrast between William the Conqueror and Henry's accession to power could not have been greater. William arrived, conquered and crushed a culture and people. Henry took over from where Stephen had left off, harking back to his grandfather's day in terms of laws and landed possessions.

Henry now had Anjou, Normandy and England under his command, and his marriage to Eleanor of Aquitaine – previously separated from King Louis of France – meant the inclusion of Aquitaine into Henry's empire. In theory Henry's realm stretched from the Scottish border to the Pyrenees. However, whilst the theory of Henry's command is viable for England, Normandy and Anjou, the lands further south were a complex patchwork of lordships, many of which might give lip-service to Henry but in practice he probably had little power unless he was personally present. The geographic spread and diversity of lands meant that to govern them Henry was constantly on the move. Detailed itineraries are not possible for Henry, but the itineraries for Henry's son John are known and probably reflect the same pattern of movement as Henry. Between April 1199 to the end of 1202 King John spent approximately 45 per cent of his time in Normandy, 25 per cent in England, 22 per cent in greater Anjou and 8 per cent in Aquitaine. Although it is dangerous to project data backwards, the surviving evidence suggests a similar programme for Henry II, whilst Richard I spent three years in Normandy, one in Anjou, eight months in Aquitaine and just two months in England (Gillingham 1994b: 54).

In all calculations, it is Normandy which was the focus of the king's attention between Henry II's accession to its loss in 1204. Normandy was the key to the Angevin empire because from the Duchy the kings could have rapid access to all parts of the Empire. However the heart of the empire can be narrowed down further to a twenty-mile stretch between Rouen and Andeli (Gillingham 1994b: 56). Less developed, but rising in importance, was a stretch of the Seine Valley with the great castle of Chinon, where John spent more time than at any other single place, but also the Abbey of Fontevrauct which became in practice a family mausoleum for the Angevin dynasty (see Chapter 4).

The French kings did not idly stand by and watch the Angevin Empire increase in size, but continually probed and attempted to disrupt the Angevin kings. Warfare between Henry II and the French king was one of continual border incursions. The French kings, Louis VII, and then Philip Augustus, were most successful when allied to Henry II's sons, whether the Young King Henry in 1173–4 during the Young King's Revolt or Richard in 1189. The death of Henry II dissolved the alliance between Richard I and Philip Augustus, though they both went on the Third Crusade together (where they quarrelled incessantly). Normandy became a prime target for the French king, not only for itself, but also because it was the hinge between England and the other sections of the empire. After serious incursions throughout the latter half of the twelfth century the French kings managed to capture Normandy in 1204. Despite King John's attempts to recapture the Duchy, his defeat at the Battle of Bouvines in 1215 made the loss of Normandy by the English kings permanent (see Chapter 2).

Networks: dynasties and church

The details of many international networks in the twelfth century remain hidden from view, for example those connected with trade (see Chapter 7). Two, however, give an indication of the scale of the networks across Europe. The first is the dynastic networks formed by marriage between members of different royal and noble families. The second is that of the new monastic orders.

A feature of power politics of the Middle Ages was the theoretical power of marriage to unite families against a common enemy and families were linked in extensive networks across Europe. Often the spouses only knew of each other beforehand by reputation before they travelled to their new homes. Map 3.1 and Table 3.1 show the areas from which marriage partners were sought for English monarchs and they show the range of influence that the English kings sought to exert across Europe between 1066 and 1215. The concentration of marriages is noticeable in the northern part of the map, showing the importance of the region until the middle of the twelfth century. This map is a minimum, for betrothals and intentions occasionally did not succeed (for example Richard I stopped his betrothal to the King of France's sister) as the power politics shifted and changed. The map in effect shows the areas that mattered to the kings – there were few marriages to Scandinavian royalty for there was no advantage at all politically.

The practice of marrying children to political allies often had unseen political consequences. When William the Conqueror married his daughter Adela into the family of the Count of Blois, the families united. In the future the counts supported Henry I in his battles, but the dynastic link also led to

Map 3.1 Origins of spouses for the English rulers (for key, see Table 3.1).

Stephen claiming his inheritance to rule England, thereby resulting in the wars against Henry's daughter Matilda, which in turn led to the Angevin conquest of Normandy and England. Another marriage, that of Geoffrey, Henry II's third son, to Constance of Brittany meant that their son, Arthur, had a claim to Brittany and he was a regular thorn in King John's side. His 'disappearance' proved devastating for King John (see Chapter 2). Loyal

Table 3.1 Marriages of the rulers of England, 1066–1216

Number on Map 3.1	Ruler of England	Married
1	William I the Conqueror	Matilda, d. of Baldwin V, Count of Flanders
	William II Rufus	Not married
2	Henry I	(1) Edith/Matilda (English)
3		(2) Adeliza of Louvain
4	Stephen	Matilda of Boulogne
5	Matilda	(1) Henry V, Holy Roman Emperor
6		(2) Geoffrey, Count of Anjou
7	Henry II	Eleanor of Aquitaine
8	Richard	Berengaria of Navarre
9	John	(1) Isabella of Gloucester (English)
10		(2) Isabella of Angoulème

subjects turned against him and a Breton force joined the French King Philip Augustus to conquer Normandy in 1203–4 (Bates 1994: 28).

The greatest permanent pan-European network was that of the church. There had been some Anglo-Saxon links with Continental churches but following the Conquest the links greatly intensified and diversified (Dumville 1993: 97). Occasionally one place had a particularly profound effect, such as the monastery at Bec which produced many educated and resourceful men who helped to transform the church in England. The Bec community included many men who went on to become bishops in England and elsewhere: Lanfranc, previously the prior of Bec, became Archbishop of Canterbury; Thomas, a pupil of Lanfranc's at Bec, became Archbishop of York; William Bona Anima became Archbishop of Rouen; both Gundulf and Ernulf became successive bishops of Rochester; and Fulk became Bishop of Beauvais (Barker 1990: 19). In the century following the Conquest Bec supplied three of the five archbishops of Canterbury (Chibnall 1987: 37).

Whilst there were no formal ties between Bec and other associated religious houses there was a constant movement of people between them – some monks from Bec transferred to Canterbury and vice versa – producing a community of ideas across Europe (Hollister 1987: 152). The movement of monks and other religious men and women was a common feature of twelfth-century monastic life for, with the abbot or prior's permission, a monk could travel widely to visit other monasteries. The letters of Lanfranc (Clover and Gibson 1979) frequently mention how monks travelled to deliver messages, seek his permission or ask advice. The geographic range of Lanfranc's network of contacts can be mapped from letters received and written. Even though many letters are probably missing and in some the place cannot be determined, Lanfranc's network of contacts with bishops and abbots was wide: Thetford (4 letters), York (3), Durham (2), Lincoln (2), Abingdon (1), Bury St Edmunds (1), Chertsey (1), Chester (1), Chichester (1), London (1), Rochester (1), Winchester (1) and Worcester (1). Lanfranc's network also spread abroad and there are letters to and from Rouen (5), Bec (2), Bayeux (1), Caen (1) and Poitiers (1). Lanfranc's letter collection also contains correspondence with the Pope (5), the King of Dublin (1), the King of Munster (2), Queen Margaret of Scotland (1) and Roger, Earl of Hereford (3). The range of people and places indicates Lanfranc's, and Canterbury's, assumed sphere of influence throughout England. The letters also indicate how Lanfranc's advice was sought from abroad, showing how the English church came into close contact with churches on the Continent.

Lanfranc's network was an informal one, being based on contacts created whilst at Bec and because he was Archbishop of Canterbury. During the twelfth century monastic orders, such as the Cistercians and Cluniacs, also began to develop formal networks. These new monastic networks were of a different magnitude in influence across Europe compared to the informal Benedictine contacts. The key change was that the Cluniac and Cistercian monasteries all looked to their mother house for guidance and inspiration. A mother house could send out monks to found monasteries elsewhere, and with the repetition of this process great family trees of monastic houses were formed (Burton and Stalley 1986: 394–401). One of the largest families of monastic houses in Britain was that of Rievaulx, which was itself founded in 1132 from Clairvaux. Rievaulx had four daughter houses, monks from which founded ten grand-daughter houses and two great-granddaughter houses. The family of the mother house of the monastery at Mellifont in Ireland contained twenty-three monastic foundations.

At the centre of the Cistercian order was Citeaux, but the single greatest and most powerful Cistercian was Bernard of Clairvaux. Bernard's influence was felt across Europe as an overall analysis of his letters reveals. Archbishops, bishops, abbots, priors, kings and queens all felt the power of his pen. Many of his letters concerned various situations in England and for a while Bernard was particularly concerned about the situation regarding the election of the Archbishop of York (James 1998).

As well as the formal networks, there were other ways that churches could join together or communicate. A popular, and flexible way, was by the formation of prayer unions. After the death of a monk, a member of the monastery would take a roll of parchment to other members of the group, not only to announce the death of particular individuals but also to obtain prayers from each house. One such roll was circulated through England and northern France to announce the death of Matilda, daughter of William the Conqueror, in 1113 (Southern 1953: 24). Religious houses also had a duty to give hospitality to travellers. Pilgrims were becoming an increasingly common sight on European roads journeying to the great shrines, such as St James at Compestella or St Thomas at Canterbury. Other religious institutions had their own networks as well, notably the military orders of the Knights Templar and the Knights of St John, both of which initially formed in the Holy Land to protect and comfort pilgrims (see below). Their influence spread and by the end of the twelfth century they had gained a significant presence in England. In the twelfth century there were also frequent visits to Rome by clergy and Rome therefore became a natural location for the exchange of ideas and objects. One small group of twelfth-century door-knockers shows this. At All Saints Pavement, York (Plate 3.1) and Adel in West Yorkshire there are two very similar doorknockers and it is thought that they were made in York *c*.1200. The third one of the group, also made in York, occurs at Luborzyca in Poland. It has been suggested that the Polish one was given by the Archbishop of York to the Bishop of Cracow when both attended Rome for the Fourth Lateran Council in 1215 (Zarnecki 1984: 256).

The importance of these networks was that they allowed information and learning to reach across Europe. There are many examples of this. Travellers might be monks or clergy, or important visitors bringing news. William of Newburgh wrote at the end of the twelfth century 'I well remember . . . in my youth, a venerable monk returning from the East full of information' (Stevenson 1996: 428). Similarly, the monks or clergy might have been connected with the courts of kings, giving an insight into the politics of the day.

The Mediterranean and the Crusades

The Mediterranean lands increasingly came into the consciousness of the people of northern Europe from the middle of the eleventh century onwards. Mercenaries and warriors sought employment in Constantinople, a journey which took on average forty days from northern Europe (Ciggaar 1986: 58). Harald Hardrada, the future King of Norway and who died in 1066 at the Battle of Stamford Bridge, was reputedly in the Varangian Guard of the Greek General George Maniaces in 1043. There was also a tradition amongst some Norman families of serving as mercenaries in the Byzantine Empire (Ciggaar 1982: 83). After the Norman Conquest some Anglo-Saxons set sail for Byzantium (a Byzantine source, *The Latin Chronicle*, said it was a 'large force') and the Byzantine Emperor gave them lands six days' sailing away, probably in the Crimea. The group founded 'Nova Anglia' ('New England') and gravestones existed until the nineteenth century, but were destroyed during the Crimean War (Godfrey 1978: 70).

The first Norman to acquire a permanent title in southern Italy was William de Hauteville ('Iron Arm') who became Lord of Apulia in 1043 after a military conquest. His brothers (Drogo, Humphrey and Robert Guiscard) all increased Norman possessions in the area, and Pope Nicholas II gave Robert the duchies of Apulia and Calabria. He was also given the island of Sicily which was yet to be conquered. In the following campaigns the Arabs were displaced from Sicily by the Norman invaders between 1060 and

Plate 3.1 Doorknocker from All Saints Pavement, York.

1091. In 1130 Roger II was proclaimed the first King of the Kingdom of Sicily, which covered the island and southern Italy. There was contact between Sicily and England and Normandy, for example the English administrators Robert of Selby and Thomas Brown were employed by Roger II of Sicily (Bates 1994: 30). William FitzHerbert, the prospective Archbishop of York who had been ousted from his post, travelled to Rome to state his case to the Pope. William then visited his kinsman Roger, King of Sicily. It was from this contact that the York Minster sculpture of the Virgin and Child might have been influenced, for although 'the work is Romanesque in every detail, [it] is nevertheless strongly Byzantine in character' (Zarnecki 1984: 188). However, the new rulers of Sicily were much more interested in forging links with Byzantium and conquering north Africa than with political or trade connections with northern Europe (Abulafia 1984: 35; Loud 1992: 177). The kings of Sicily showed an almost total lack of interest in their Norman past and had not the slightest desire to appear Norman (Hermans 1979: 80).

The eastern Mediterranean world was known to a few northerners in the eleventh century, as there had been a history of pilgrimage, but contact increased dramatically through the Crusades. The Crusades were a series of military campaigns by Christians to capture lands and free them from non-Christian influences. The First Crusade resulted from a sermon by Pope

Urban II who, in 1095 at the Council of Clermont, called on Frankish knights to liberate Christians from Islamic rule and to free the tomb of Christ from Muslim control. An army was gathered and in six years Christian forces had captured Jerusalem. It was a successful military campaign against all the odds. Thereafter there were a whole series of military campaigns to capture lands in the East: the Second Crusade (1147–9); the Third Crusade (1189–92); the Fourth Crusade (1202–04); and the Fifth Crusade (1217–29). As well as these, there were a wide range of other military actions against other religions or heretics: in the East (1107–8, 1120–5, 1128–9, 1139–40); in the Spanish peninsula against the Muslims (in 1114, 1118, 1122 and until 1187); against the Wends in northern Germany (in 1147); in the Baltic region (at various times between 1193 and 1230); and in southern France against the Albigensian heresy (between 1209 and 1229).

Pope Urban's sermon was revolutionary and sent a shockwave throughout Christian Europe because for the first time a Pope associated warfare with pilgrimage to Jerusalem. Furthermore the soul of a knight who died would gain salvation in Heaven. Guibert of Nogent summed up the attitude

> In our time God has instituted holy warfare so that the knightly order and the unsettled populace . . . should find a new way of deserving salvation. No longer are they obliged to leave the world and choose a monastic way of life, as used to be the case, or some religious profession, but in their accustomed liberty and habit, by performing their own office, they may in some measure achieve the grace of God.
>
> (Morris 1989: 337)

All those who went on crusade would be given remission for their sins, and as a sign of their inward faith and intentions they would wear a cross on their garments.

The sermon set Europe aflame with religious excitement. The linking of military action with salvation combined warfare and religion, two of the most potent concepts of the age. The sermon and resultant military pilgrimage were to cause centuries of warfare as Christians fought Muslims for the control of the Holy Land. William of Malmesbury described the impact of the sermon as the fields became deserted and the cities emptied as people flocked to join the First Crusade (Mynors *et al.* 1998: 607–9). Whilst William of Malmesbury's estimate of 6 million people is of course a wild exaggeration, the figure does give a feel for the impact that later commentators thought the sermon had.

In England there was little organised royal support for the Crusades until the late twelfth century. Crusaders did leave from England and Normandy, but it is noticeable that the First Crusade was led by important dukes and nobles, such as Robert Curthose, Duke of Normandy, rather than by kings. In the Second Crusade of 1147 the French and German kings took part (though for an argument that there was not a defined Second Crusade but rather a series of individual initiatives see Tyerman 1995). Although there were many family ties between English royalty and the kings of Jerusalem – for example King Stephen's wife Matilda was the niece of the first two rulers of Jerusalem – English royalty did not actively become involved until the Third Crusade (Bartlett 2000: 112). The spur to the involvement by King Richard of England came in 1187 when Saladin conquered key cities and destroyed the crusader army at the disastrous Battle of Hattin.

The details of the battles and campaigns of the crusaders in the East, and elsewhere, lies outside the scope of this book, but the Crusades involved more than just fighting overseas, for there was a huge network of support in England and the other European crusading nations. Initially this support was fragmentary and unorganised. In the early twelfth century, pilgrim knights began to band together to help other pilgrims and crusaders. These bands of men, living under a monastic rule, created a series of knightly monastic orders. The two best known in England were the Knights Templar (founded *c.*1120) and the Knights of St John. The Knights of St John, or Hospitallers, were founded during the First Crusade to care for pilgrims, but they assumed military responsibilities from the 1130s. Each order maintained its own fighting force and 230 Templars were killed at the Battle of Hattin in 1187. Each order equipped its own knights and built impressive castles across the Holy Land, the funds for which came from a European network of farms and estates as well as patronage. Nobles and laity across Europe were anxious to help and fund the military orders in the East (Walker 1998). One of the greatest noblemen of the twelfth and early thirteenth centuries, William Marshall, was buried in the Temple Church in London after a lifetime of his interest and support of the order (Crouch 1990). Gifts could be of money or items such as horses or armour. The influence of the orders throughout England can be seen in the nobles who gave gifts. Even small gifts, such as that made by the Yorkshire nobleman Henry de Lacy to the small order of the leper hospital of St Lazarus, shows how the Holy Lands had gained a real presence in the mentality of the times (Wightman 1966: 112). From these gifts, land was purchased and Templar houses (called preceptories) were set up to manage the estates. By 1150 seven preceptories had been established in England (Barber 1998: 22).

To go on crusade was not only dangerous, it was also very expensive. Money was needed for travel, provisions, armour and horses. This need could change the fortunes of royalty and nobility overnight. When Robert Curthose, Duke of Normandy, decided to go on the First Crusade he allowed his brother, William Rufus, to buy Normandy from him for three years for 10,000 marks of silver. Rufus raised this sum, partially by raiding gold and silver from various monasteries, much to the consternation of the chroniclers of the day. The nobility too needed money and mortgaged or leased out estates, or borrowed money from the Jewish moneylenders. Taxes too were raised and in England and France in 1188 a compulsory tax, known as the

Saladin Tithe, was levied on income and movable possessions in order to fund the Third Crusade.

The later crusading taxes, such as in 1199 when Pope Innocent III required the clergy to pay a fortieth of their revenues for one year, showed an organisation which was lacking for the earlier Crusades. Following the disasters of the Third Crusade the papacy took the initiative in advance planning for the Fourth Crusade. One aspect of this was the care and attention given to preaching in order to gain money and recruits (for thirteenth- and fourteenth-century sermons see Maier 2000). In order to gain maximum coverage planned itineraries were worked out and the first detailed description of a preaching tour was recorded by Gerald of Wales as he toured Wales with Baldwin, the Archbishop of Canterbury, in 1188. The mission was considered successful for not only were 3,000 men signed up to the Crusade, but those who could not go through age or infirmity often gave money to the cause. The crusaders themselves were described by Gerald as 'highly skilled in the use of spear and arrow, most experienced in military affairs and only too keen to attack the enemies of our faith' (Thorpe 1978: 205). Whilst the quality of the fighting men was to be applauded, the fact that 'the most notorious criminals of those parts [around Usk Castle] were amongst those converted, robbers, highwaymen and murderers' must have stored up problems in the future (Thorpe 1978: 114).

Analysis of recruits going on crusades has revealed distinct patterns. Until the Fifth Crusade (1217–29) it was common for large numbers of non-combatants to accompany the knights, such as their wives and members of their household, because it was wise for followers to go to in order to preserve their status and win the lord's favour. These people too could claim to have been on crusade and yet took no part in fighting. The church had attempted to limit the numbers of non-combatants going on crusade during the twelfth century, but with little success. In 1213 Innocent III ruled that anyone could take the cross, but that their vows could be redeemed, deferred or commuted into a monetary payment. Crusaders now did not have to go on crusade (Lloyd 1995: 49–50).

Another identifiable pattern was the involvement of families in deciding who should go on crusade (Lloyd 1995: 52). Sometimes one son might stay at home to look after the estates whilst the other was away. Without firm family loyalty this could be dangerous and Richard I attempted to give his brother John enough power to keep him satisfied, but to limit his actions. Richard therefore gave him lands and revenues in England and Ireland and made him Count of Mortain but ordered him to stay out of England for three years. Crusading could also be a family tradition. Sons could accompany fathers, or went on crusade later, thereby continuing the family tradition. Roger de Mowbray journeyed to the Holy Land on crusade several times, first during the Second Crusade, then after the failed Young King's rebellion in 1173–4 and finally in 1186. His son, Nigel, also went on crusade and died during the siege of Acre in 1186.

Whereas the passion of the preaching of the cause had resulted in recruits eager to fight, the circumstances of the Crusades were often terrible. After the long description of his preaching tour and the successful recruitment campaign, in his last chapter Gerald describes how Archbishop Baldwin made his way to Acre, only to find the soldiers 'in a state of desolation and despair, for they had been deserted by their leaders. They were worn out with waiting so long for supplies, sadly afflicted by hunger and want, and made ill by the inclement climate' (Thorpe 1978: 208). Leaders such as Richard I would soon be with them, but the want of supplies, food and water in an unbearable heat was constant.

The desire for information about the events in the Holy Land was relentless and the chroniclers wrote about the miracles, successes and failures in great detail. Even though there was so much written, sometimes chroniclers felt ignorant about what was really happening: 'for in our distant lair beyond the British Ocean, scarcely a rumour comes to enlighten our ignorance of events in Asia' (Mynors *et al.* 1998: 655). The chroniclers were also aware of the danger of 'traveller's tales' which would 'trade upon the credulity of the hearer', and William of Malmesbury was so conscious of the need for 'accurate knowledge of the facts' that he would only repeat what he had seen 'written down' (Mynors *et al.* 1991: 681).

There was one other type of crusade, which was to have a profound influence in England following the death of King John. This was political crusade, instigated by the Pope against his political enemies to remove them from power or hinder their cause. The first occurrence may have been when Innocent II proclaimed a crusade against Roger II, the Norman King of Sicily, in 1135. Pope Innocent III also proclaimed a crusade in 1199 against Markward of Anweiler and his supporters in Sicily (Lloyd 1995: 41). In England in 1213 King John became the Pope's vassal, so any attack on John was also seen as an attack on the Pope. The baronial revolt therefore became an attack on the crown and the papacy. After King John died in 1215, his 9-year-old son was proclaimed King Henry III. The war between the barons, supported by Prince Louis of France, and the Henricians continued, with Pope Honorius actively supporting Henry. In 1217, Pope Honorious granted Guala, the Papal Legate in England, the power to remit the sins of those fighting for Henry. Guala also signed them with the cross 'as if they were fighting against pagans'. The fact that the Henrician side were crusaders stimulated their morale. They were also visually different to their opponents, wearing crosses on their clothes (Carpenter 1990: 28). It was an important factor in re-establishing royal control over England.

4   Court life and power

Kingship

Kingship consisted of two powers: secular and religious. On a secular level, the English king was simply the greatest lord in England, and as such the king could extract the same revenues for special purposes (such as marriage or ransom) as other lords could. However, the king was distinguished from other lords in two important ways. The first was that whilst the king was owed homage by other lords, he owed homage to nobody for his English possessions. A complexity arose, however, with the Duchy of Normandy as the Duke of Normandy (whether he was also the King of England or not) owed homage to the French king.

The second way in which the king differed from other lords was in the sacral nature of kingship, conferred on the king during his coronation. During the ceremony he was anointed with holy oil and the chrism (sacred oil consecrated by a bishop and used for baptism, confirmation or ordination). The coronation ceremony gave the king a divine power denied to all other lords and nobles. The Bible made it plain that the king ruled by the power of God (Romans 13: 1) and the sign of that power was the anointing of the king with holy oil. From the moment of coronation the king's reign began. The link between the divine and royalty also became evident in monarchies across Europe allying themselves to a particular saint. The French monarchy in the mid-twelfth century had vigorously promoted St Denis. The English monarchy had many potential saints to choose from: St Edmund, who was killed by Vikings, Edward the Confessor and St Cuthbert to name but three. Henry I and his family had established a familial interest in the rapidly growing cult of the Virgin Mary. One indication of this is that the first known representation of the Coronation of the Virgin comes from Henry's royal foundation of Reading Abbey (Zarnecki 1984: 159; Chibnall 1987: 45). St George did not become the patron saint of England until the mid-fourteenth century, when Edward III associated St George with the Order of the Garter. However, he was known in England in the eleventh century and as early as 1000 Aelfric wrote the legends of St George. However, the saint first came to national prominence in England after the First Crusade and it is at this time that there are representations of the saint fighting the dragon, an early representation of which is given over the doorway of the church at Fordington in Dorset.

If the king was a combination of the greatest lord and God's representative on earth, the death of a king was a potentially traumatic time. Nature itself was seen to warn of such a calamitous event, and *The Anglo-Saxon Chronicle* records how 'the day darkened over all the lands and the sun became as if it were a three-night-old moon' a year before Henry I died (Swanton 2000: 262–3). The lack of a king could also result in lawlessness because the ultimate power in the land had gone. After Henry I's death the land 'grew dark, because every man who could immediately robbed another' (Swanton 2000: 263). In order to ease the succession the French kings crowned their heirs before their own death. The only occasion when an English king attempted to follow this tradition of crowning his son was when Henry II crowned his eldest son, also called Henry (although King Stephen had attempted to crown his son Eustace). Henry's experiment was not a success as the Young King Henry attempted to seize power in a series of revolts in 1173–4. Whilst revolts by younger sons against their fathers were not uncommon, that the young king had been crowned made the threat to Henry II all the greater. The crowning of a young prince whilst the king was still alive was not tried again in England.

Until the thirteenth century there was no firm tradition that the eldest son should automatically rule the kingdom, though it was generally understood that only members of the royal family could be kings. This manifested itself in several ways. During the early years of the minority of Henry III the most powerful man in England was William Marshall who saw his own role as protecting the infant Henry III rather than seeking the crown himself (Carpenter 1990: 14–15). In the case of William the Conqueror, he divided up his kingdom so that his eldest son, Robert Curthose, received the Dukedom of Normandy (which as the homeland was the most prestigious) and gave England to his second son William Rufus.

There were two further problems connected with the succession. The first was that a king might designate his heir, but then change his mind or events might overtake him. Edward the Confessor reputedly chose Duke William, but then changed his mind in favour of Harold on his deathbed (see Chapter 1). Richard I initially chose Arthur of Brittany as the next King of England, partly through a determination to keep his younger brother John from the throne, but recanted and by the time he died had cited John as the next king (Warren 1998: 266–71). Henry I's eldest son William was the natural heir to his father, but he died in the tragic *White Ship* disaster. Henry I therefore designated his eldest daughter, Matilda, who was Empress as she was married to the Holy Roman Emperor. However, even though an heir might be chosen the speed of events might alter the situation. Following Henry I's death Stephen of Blois seized the initiative by sailing for England and was crowned. Stephen's speed of action had caught Matilda completely off guard and she was never crowned queen. Henry I himself had reacted extra-ordinarily quickly following his brother's death during a hunting trip in the New Forest. Upon hearing of William Rufus's accidental death (he was shot by Walter Tirel), Henry instantly rode to Winchester to seize the treasury and was crowned in three days.

The second problem was that of the uncle–nephew relationship (Holt 1997). This problem occurred during the reigns of both Henry I and John. Although Henry and John had seized the throne, their nephews William Clito and Arthur of Brittany were a constant source of political trouble because they too had a strong claim to the throne and were a cause around which enemies of the kings could gather (see Chapter 2). Both nephews died in suspicious circumstances, but whilst Henry was strong enough to remain almost untainted, John's supposed murder of his nephew provoked a strong reaction amongst many nobles (Bradbury 1999: 353).

Once chosen the king was crowned in the coronation ceremony which took place in Westminster Abbey, usually on a Sunday, except for William the Conqueror and King John. William the Conqueror followed a Continental tradition of being crowned on Christmas Day, a date also chosen by Charlemagne in 800, Otto II (967), Otto III (983) and Henry III (1046), as well as by some Byzantine emperors (Ciggaar 1986: 57). Whether the choice of date by William the Conqueror was part of the tradition or because Christmas Day was the both a major religious festival and the start of the New Year is unclear.

Despite considerable debate, it is generally accepted that the coronation service from Harold onwards followed the liturgy of the 'Third English Ordo' which stressed both the religious and secular aspects of kingship (Nelson 1981: 128; Garnett 1985: 109). The king swore a threefold coronation oath to protect the peace, prohibit crime and maintain justice, thereafter he was anointed with holy oil (see above), followed by being crowned, girded with a sword and being invested with ring, sceptre and rod. The chronicler Roger of Howden described the coronation of Richard I in considerable detail and it survives as the longest account of a twelfth-century English coronation. A king could be only be anointed with holy oil once, but he could have many coronations without holy oil. After release from capture both King Stephen and King Richard held second coronations to reassert their positions and King John held three coronations in all.

Thereafter the king would wear his crown at formal 'crown wearings' which in the late eleventh and early twelfth centuries took place three times a year (Biddle 1985). The normal tradition was for the crown wearing ceremonies – a huge and impressive gathering of the important churchmen and nobles of the kingdom – to be held at Winchester, Westminster and Gloucester. This pattern could be varied as the need arose and at Christmas 1069 William the Conqueror wore his crown in York to symbolise his victory over the north. The assemblies were a combination of decision making, pronouncements and royal image making. One decision is still in evidence, for at the Christmas gathering in Gloucester in 1085 the order was given to compile Domesday Book. The image of the king wearing his crown was intended to convey Christ in majesty seated as judge, though the court jester who called out in adulation 'Behold I see God! Behold I see God' when he saw the king in robes went too far. Lanfranc, the Archbishop of Canterbury, was less than amused (presumably because he saw it as insulting to God) and asked that the jester be flogged (Nelson 1981: 131). The crown wearings were great ceremonial occasions. When the crown wearings occurred in Winchester the kings probably stood on the cathedral's high stone balcony which was visible from both the square outside and the nave inside. As well as being seen by the greatest number of people, the balcony may have been symbolic because the king was near heaven, and because the balcony was both part of the holy cathedral and outside it in the secular world (Klukas 1983: 152; Biddle 1985). Whilst these formal crown wearing ceremonies were part of the royal year in England, William the Conqueror was careful to distinguish his ducal status in Normandy from his status as king in England. He did not wear his crown in Normandy as there he was Duke and his overlord was the King of France (Nelson 1981: 131).

Itineration

The king and the household were constantly on the move. The movement of the royal household in England was a centuries' old part of royal life and it had some important benefits, for example the king was a visible presence across his territories. There were other practical reasons, such as the necessity of moving to new hunting grounds and to new food sources, though the traditional payments of food were increasingly commuted to cash during the twelfth century and items bought separately.

There were many people travelling with the king and his household. The queen, when with him, also had her household. Towards the end of the century, Eleanor of Aquitaine's household contained a steward, constable, butler, knights and serjeants, almoners, chaplains, clerks, damsels, nurse and cooks (Richardson 1959: 208). There would also be royal family members, the princes and princesses and their entourage, and then possibly the wives and families of the permanently resident members of the royal household. Apart from royalty there were the officials visiting the king: judges, sheriffs, barons of the exchequer and vicomtes (Le Patourel 1976: 133–8). In addition there were ecclesiastics and noblemen with their entourages, men looking for preferment or honours, and the hangers-on such as traders and peddlers. The prostitutes of the household were mentioned as people who knew the secrets of the palace. Traders and merchants also flocked to the court and Walter Map described how merchants sailed from beyond the sea to court with wares and luxuries for sale, as well as drawing in merchants from across England (James *et al.* 1983: 473). The role of king as the final arbiter in decision making resulted in a constant flow of petitioners seeking his favour or judgement, and it was not uncommon for them to follow him abroad. The monastery at Durham received a writ from the king in their favour written at Salisbury and another from across the Channel at Pont l'Arche (Mason 1998: 139).

The size of a king's or nobleman's household was also a measure of power. When Henry I was expelled from western Normandy in 1091, his poverty and vulnerability were described by Orderic Vitalis in terms of his household: he was accompanied by only one knight, one clerk and three squires. For the wealthy during times of war the household was an indication of military might for it included soldiers and commanders who could give tactical advice or fight. One particular group which has been identified is the younger landless sons of the nobility who sought military fame and glory in the service of a wealthy and powerful king. However, the household was unlikely to be large enough to fight large independent actions (Prestwich 1963: 50–1; Prestwich 1981: 6). After Henry had become King of England and Duke of Normandy his large military household played a central role in his military campaigns. The same themes are reflected in literature. In Geoffrey of Monmouth's *History of the Kings of Britain* both Constans and Arthur prepared for defence and attack by enlarging their military households (Prestwich 1981: 32).

Royal itineration in England mainly concentrated upon southern England and London, with Gloucester being an outpost for the regular crown wearings. The knowledge of the itineraries of kings becomes more and more detailed as the twelfth century progresses. The itinerary of King John is known in greatest detail, both during his travels in the Angevin Empire and in England. Whilst Normandy was still in English royal hands, the Duchy was the focus of the king's attention (see Chapter 3). However, even though King John travelled extensively around England he still conformed to the general tradition of concentrating his movement in the south of the kingdom.

One of the most detailed descriptions of an entourage on the move is that of William FitzStephen's account of Thomas Becket's wagon train. Whilst Becket was Henry II's chancellor he journeyed through France and had with him eight wagons each pulled by five horses. Two wagons were for ale (a drink which the French admired), one wagon each was for the chapel, chamber, bursary and kitchen. The others carried food and drink, cushions, sacks with nightgowns, bags and baggage. There were also twelve carthorses to carry the treasure, gold and silver tableware and sacred vessels of the chapel. As well as goods there were numerous grooms, youths and 250 foot servants. Animals were an integral part of the train, whether horses, dogs, birds or monkeys. There was a defined order to the wagon train as it approached a town or village. The foot servants went first, followed by the huntsmen and dogs, then the wagons, which were covered by great hides of animals sewn together, and last of all the carthorses (Staunton 2001: 56). Such a wagon train passing through a small town or village was an impressive spectacle.

Detailed records of the frequency and routes of ecclesiastics and nobles are rare and only one survives from the late twelfth century from an unknown household. The first to survive in detail concerns the household of Hugh de Neville of Essex, the master of the royal hounds and the chief justice of the forests. The journey closely follows the movements of King John. The itinerary starts at the hunting lodge at Geddington in Northamptonshire on 1 March 1207 and by its end, on 27 April, the household had travelled through Cambridgeshire, Hampshire, Wiltshire and Buckinghamshire (Woolgar 1992: 110–16).

At each stopping point for the royal household there was the disruption of finding somewhere to sleep. Accommodation occasionally caused arguments between the different households: when the men of Bishop Roger and Alan of Pentievre both claimed a particular lodging, a fight broke out between them (Bradbury 1996: 53). An alternative was to set up tents or temporary accommodation – in Ireland there is a reference to the men of Henry II building a structure for him from branches and twigs (Duffy 1997: 82). In Henry II's case, everything was dependent upon his decision. This often led to exasperation on the part of his courtiers, as graphically portrayed by Peter de Blois. Peter wrote that if Henry II had decided not to travel the previous night, he would suddenly change his mind and decide to move on, thereby causing panic. However, if he had decided to move on the following morning everything would be packed up, only for him to sleep on, causing the courtiers, packhorses and carts to idly wait.

The beginning of the end of the process of itineration came in the early years of the twelfth century when the innovation appeared that a group of administrators dealing with the exchequer accounts remained static whilst the king was still journeying around the country. Furthermore, meetings could be held without the king's presence. At first the administrators met twice yearly at Winchester to take the accounts of the sheriffs but by the reign of Henry II the exchequer was permanently based at Westminster in London. The static nature of the department was a significant change, for kingship and the associated offices had been itinerant until the early twelfth century. Gradually, other departments also went 'out of court' and remained in one place rather than following the king, for example the chancery remained static at Westminster in the thirteenth century.

Court life

Members of the itinerant court could, if not restrained, inflict terrible abuses upon townspeople and villagers. The household of William Rufus is said to have plundered the land and villages as if in enemy territory. Under Henry I reforms took place and looking backwards from the end of the twelfth century Walter Map wrote a nostalgic, but probably reasonably accurate, account of the court of Henry I. Map described how in the 'forenoon [the court was] a school of virtues and of wisdom, and in the after noon one of hilarity and decent mirth' (James *et al.* 1983: 439), showing that the court was organised so that business was conducted in the morning with leisure in the afternoons. Furthermore a schedule was devised for Henry I's court a month in advance giving dates and stopping places – an admirable system though not one followed by his grandson Henry II. Henry I also set prices of goods that the retinue could buy (Prestwich 1981: 30).

Fashions at court changed through the period. The Anglo-Saxon fashion for moustaches was not taken up by the Normans but instead during William the Conqueror's and William Rufus's time long hair and pointed shoes were fashionable. When Henry I came to the throne Bishop Serlo denounced the court fashions as indications of moral depravity, which led to Henry I's court becoming more sombre in its fashion. Another person to bring an austere standard of food and dress to Henry I's court was the powerful Lord Robert of Beaumont. William of Malmesbury, who wrote of Robert's changes, considered the new ideas to have come from Byzantine emissaries to Robert, though modern commentators have thought Robert was more concerned with financial and political considerations (Prestwich 1981: 29).

One feature of the household was the richness and sumptuousness of the clothing and items. There are only hints given at what was a magnificent sight. Accounts for the king's wardrobe late in the twelfth and early thirteenth centuries describe the buying of furs, cloths and items from goldsmiths. At Henry II's coronation he wore cloth of green and scarlet, Spanish cloth and sable. King John adorned himself further, sleeping in silk and wearing rare furs. He even dressed his horses in silk with the lions of England in gold on them. His food would be presented on golden plates. In 1205 the Christmas feast cost over £700 – more than the clothing Henry II paid for his son's coronation (Jolliffe 1963: 261–4). Whilst John's tastes and expenditure were exceptional, the king had always risen above his subjects in extravagance, indeed not to have done so would have diminished the status of the king.

The royal or noble household was also one of entertainment, including feasts, hunting expeditions and amusement. Hunting was one of the greatest of royal and noble pastimes. At the end of the 'Establishment of the King's Household' (see Chapter 5) of Henry I is the section on huntsmen, which included the horn blowers, keeper of the kennels, the huntsmen of the stag hunt and the wolf hunt, and 'the bowman who carries the king's bow'. The hunt was a serious business and the creatures (from the huntsmen's horses, to the dogs, birds of prey and hunted animals) were all carefully defined by social status. The deer and the boar were considered as the king's personal animals whom none could touch without special permission, whilst the king more often granted (for a price) the right to hunt foxes, hares and wildcat. During the twelfth century the first books survive detailing aspects of the hunt and Adelard of Bath wrote 'On the Care of Falcons' which gave detailed instructions on their training and care (Cochrane 1994: 52–61).

Tournaments also grew in importance both as entertainment and as a training ground for the younger knights. As early as the 1130s English knights were journeying to Normandy for tournaments and the first recorded tournament in England occurs during Stephen's reign. From the 1170s the first detailed descriptions emerge and tournaments were fought in national teams (Crouch 1994: 66). Fame and fortune could be won or lost: William Marshall, the colossus of the late twelfth century, rose to fame through tournaments. However, tournaments could also be threatening to the crown if not controlled and in the 1190s Roger of Howden described how Richard I's government attempted to impose restrictions upon tournaments in England, specifying five sites where they could be held (Bartlett 2000: 243).

Jesters were an important part of the amusement of noble households and two feature in Domesday Book as being given land by their patrons: Berdic the King's jester and Adelina, a female jester who had been given land by the Earl of Hereford. Other entertainers were the *jongleurs*, who recited or sang epic poems of romance or adventure and were part of every royal or noble's retinue which aspired to culture. It was a *jongleur*, Taillefer, who was reputedly the first person to ride into battle at the Battle of Hastings and fought in single combat with an Anglo-Saxon warrior (Chibnall 1984: 204; Damian-Grint 1998: 23). An alternative was for a noble, such as William, Duke of Aquitaine, to compose his own poems. This was not confined to men and Marie de France was a noble poetess of distinction. From the middle of the twelfth century historical verse histories were also becoming popular with poets such as Gaimar writing his *Estoire des Engleis* for his patron, Ralph fitzGilbert, before 1140. Wace wrote his epic poem *Roman de la Rou* for the court of Henry II (Chibnall 1984: 204).

Storytelling was popular, with the wild and fabulous mixing easily alongside the political. Even the most detailed chronicler of political life, such as William of Newbrugh (who ridiculed the Arthurian legends of Geoffrey of Monmouth), could include accounts of devils and the fabulous. One such story was the descent into the underworld by a villager who brought back a valuable cup, a common literary theme (Otter 1996: 93–128).

Music played an important role in court. The employment of minstrels was not solely to entertain, but also to glorify magnates or lend prestige to an occasion. William of Malmesbury complained that Henry I's queen, Matilda, paid money to foreigners (probably Frenchmen) so that they might 'sing her praises in all lands'. This idea of prestige and announcing your presence may be behind a puzzling account given by Gerald of Wales. On arriving at a potentially dangerous wood, Richard de Clare thought the trackway was safe: 'Ahead of him went a singer to announce his coming and a fiddler who accompanied the singer' (Thorpe 1978: 108). Richard was wrong. He was ambushed and killed.

There was also a symbolic function to music. Music during large-scale feasts symbolised joy, which in turn symbolised honour. A court without music was sad or dishonoured. Musicians were a crucial part of maintaining the honour of the household and they have been described as 'one of the pillars of the court and courtly life' (Wright 1986: 105). A particular musical piece, sung at coronations and on great public occasions, was that of the 'Laudes regiae', which was probably first performed at the coronation of Matilda, William the Conqueror's queen, on 11 May (Pentecost) 1068 (Nelson 1981: 129).

Board games, such as chess and backgammon, were common amongst the elite of society. A superb backgammon set has been discovered at Gloucester Castle which probably dates to before 1120 (Stewart and Watkins 1984). There are many references to the playing of chess (Eales 1986). Chess came into Europe in the tenth century and by the eleventh and twelfth centuries it was played predominantly by the military elite, yet there is manuscript evidence that it was known and played in monasteries. Chess also seems to have influenced accounting procedures in England for the exchequer (*scaccarium*) took its name from the Latin name for the chessboard. In the *Dialogue of the Exchequer* Richard of Ely ties chess and the exchequer process together: 'Just as on a chess-board battle is joined between the kings, here too the struggle is mostly between two men, namely the treasurer and the sheriff' (Eales 1986: 27). In 1831 the remains of four sets of chess pieces were found in a sand dune on the Isle of Lewis. They probably date to between 1150 and 1200 and were made in Scandinavia but were brought to Scotland to be sold. The chess sets are unusual because of their life-like design, as pieces were normally abstract in design or shape before this date, such as the late eleventh-century whalebone set from Witchampton in Dorset.

At the opposite end of the spectrum was that of the zoo with its exotic animals. It is possible – from bones found by archaeologists – that the first zoo in Western Europe was at Winchester and there was a zoo at Woodstock in the early twelfth century. Yet like so much in the Middle Ages a zoo probably was also symbolic: it represented a miniature paradise with creatures from the regions of paradise – in essence a miniature world. Furthermore, the importance is heightened by the zoo being the king's – in essence it is symbolising a miniature world over which the sovereign ruled (Ciggaar 1986: 53).

Rebellion

There was a considerable danger to the king from his sons and rebellious nobles. With the exception of William Ætheling, son of Henry I, who died in the *White Ship* disaster, every royal male heir to reach puberty between 1066 and 1215 made trouble for his royal father (Holt 1997: 237). Even William, however, had gathered round him eldest sons of noblemen who had been deprived of their inheritances, such as William Bigod (Wareham 1994: 232). As soon as heirs came of age they rebelled against their fathers to gain more power. One of the greatest threats during Henry II's reign came when his eldest son, Young King Henry, rebelled and sided with the French king.

After the Young King's death, Henry's sons Richard and John joined forces with their mother Eleanor of Aquitaine to fight against Henry II. Nobles joining such revolts often had a sense of grievance against the king, feeling that they had been overlooked or snubbed.

Hollister analysed the groups of nobles who supported the Duke of Normandy, Robert Curthose, against his brothers William Rufus in 1088 and 1095, and Henry I in 1101. Hollister discovered that nobles conspicuously absent from Rufus's or Henry's entourages were more likely to rebel as they were excluded from the court circle. Another finding was that there was a continuation of personnel between Rufus and Henry I, and in 1101 Henry had surrounded himself with more less prestigious middle men of the court (the 'curiales') – stewards and sheriffs who had witnessed Rufus's charters 140 times. There was therefore a split between the magnates and the curiales. Following the rebellion of 1101 Henry I sought to remedy this and thereafter Henry's eleven most powerful magnates were among the most frequent witnesses (Hollister 1979: 96, 99). Henry had managed to bind the magnates and their loyalty into the court structure.

The king did have a powerful weapon in his armoury to keep nobles loyal, and that was the power of patronage. The rewards for loyalty, especially when others had deserted the cause, could be great. In the Anglo-Norman civil war of 1101 Henry I was supported by Hugh d'Avranches and Richard de Redvers. Hugh was rewarded with the earldom of Chester and Richard was given the lordship of the Isle of Wight (Hockey 1982: 146–7). Patronage could also be extended to trustworthy courtiers.

Sometimes similar tactics secured the support of enemies. When Curthose attempted to conquer England in 1101 William of Warenne supported him against Henry I. Henry seized Warenne's lands and held his younger brother. These tactics changed William's allegiance and William fought for Henry at the Battle of Tinchbrai in 1106. Henry rewarded William with the castle and lordship of Saint-Saens in upper Normandy. The success of Henry's policy can be seen by the number of times William witnessed charters. He witnessed only a very few for Rufus, but frequently attested charters for Henry I and in 1111 William sat as a judge in Henry's court in Normandy (Hollister 1979: 101–2). Henry I employed similar tactics against the Clare family, who had supported Robert Curthose against William Rufus and Henry I, but after they were given lands and power by Henry changed their allegiance to him (Hollister 1979: 101).

There was also one other type of rebellion, described as 'ritual rebellion' (Wareham 1994: 233). This occurred when a nobleman had a grievance, but his rebellion or actions were in a framework which recognised royal authority. An example of this is Hugh Bigod during the early years of the reign of King Stephen. Bigod seized Norwich Castle in 1136, which has been interpreted as Bigod becoming Stephen's first rebel, but before and after seizing the castle Bigod attended court and witnessed nine charters. He also stated that he would hand back the castle, but only if the king arrived in person. Even though he was rebelling because of a grievance, he was portraying himself as a loyal subject of the king. The concept of ritual rebellion also explains the curious phenomenon of nobles rebelling and then receiving greater amounts of land or status.

Feudalism

Feudalism is a fundamental theme in England from the late eleventh century onwards through the twelfth and thirteenth centuries. There is, however, a long and continuing debate about what it means, what it meant to people of the twelfth century, and how and when it changed. The word 'feudalism' was coined in the nineteenth century in an attempt to give an abstract term to the system of relationship between lord and tenant following the Conquest. (The word derives from the Latin *feudum* or fief, meaning a group of lands or estates owned by a lord and his tenants.) Academic debate about feudalism occurs about almost every point, and even the usefulness of the word feudalism has been challenged (Reynolds 1994; Flanagan 1997: 110).

The relationship between lord and tenant was the foundation of twelfth-century politics. The relationship was formalised by the act of homage, when a tenant gave an oath of fealty to the lord by kneeling, placing his hands between his lord's and giving the oath. The system had evolved on the Continent following the collapse of the Carolingian Empire in the ninth century when the lack of a strong central authority had resulted in a system of protection between a lord and his vassal. In Anglo-Saxon England there was a looser, less formal, bond between lord and tenant. Following the Conquest, the Normans imposed their own feudal practices: all land was in lordship; there was no tenure without service; and the Anglo-Saxon way of distributing lands amongst the family was replaced by the lands passing to the eldest male heir (Holt 1997: 4). However, the new Norman feudal systems did not cause comment amongst chroniclers such as William of Poitiers, Orderic Vitalis and William of Malmesbury, a fact which is puzzling given the enormity of the changes historians have since observed (Prestwich 1981: 31).

The act of homage was a formal procedure, but the feudal relationship between lord and tenant could be negotiated. The late twelfth-century poet Wace in his poem *Roman de Rou* has William the Conqueror interviewing his most powerful nobles individually before the Conquest. This description of personal discussion has been seen as epitomising the feudal arrangement of a series of personal and individual agreements between lord and vassal (Bennett 1982: 34). In theory the personal link was only for the lifetime of the tenant (and in extreme cases could be broken) and after the tenant's death the lord could redistribute the land. In practice the lands became hereditary and it is the hereditary nature of the lands being passed through generations of the same family which has been seen as a key feature of the feudal system in England. Holt wrote that 'The very language of feudalism, from its inception in Norman England, implied inheritance. A non-hereditary fief was a contradiction in terms; it might occur in practice, but it was not what men normally intended when they gave or accepted fiefs' (Holt 1997: 116). The legal formulae only gradually emerged (the initial land-owners with the Conqueror had gained their lands by Conquest, not inheritance) and was becoming more common in the mid-twelfth century, and was standard and necessary by the late twelfth century.

The services that a tenant rendered in return for land could vary and in some cases land could be given piecemeal to tenants without a precise definition of the service due (Chibnall 1999: 81). A common service was for a tenant to work on the lord's land, but it is the tenant's military obligations that have been the subject of most debate. The most important is that of 'knight service' – how many knights would be supplied by a tenant for how long. The term 'knight' (in Latin *miles*, plural *milites*, in French *chevalier*) is, however, confused by the various meanings of the word knight. On a military level the knight owned a horse and armour and formed part of the cavalry but on an economic level a knight was somewhere below a baron but above a rich freeman. The distinguishing factor was that a man was made a knight at a formal knighting ceremony during which the man was girded with a sword and belt. In the entry for 1147 the *Gesta Stephani* recorded that King Stephen, 'in the presence of the magnates, ceremonially girded with the belt of knighthood his son Eustace . . . endowing him with lands and possessions, and giving him the special distinction of a most splendid retinue of knights, advanced him rank to the dignity of an earl' (Potter 1955: 137–8). The sequence of events recorded in the *Gesta Stephani* indicates that becoming a knight was the first stage of acquiring even higher office, but also the fact that as a knight Eustace had knights under him shows that within the term 'knight' there were men of different wealth and standing. Knighting could take place at any time in a man's life, and was not unusual before or after a battle, but sons of royalty were often knighted in their late teens. The act of being knighted also marked a coming of age and Glanvill wrote that a knight came of age at 21 (Hall 1965: 82). Towards the end of the twelfth century knights were also expected to play a prominent part in the system of justice, being called upon by the sheriffs to discover facts or being members of juries. In King John's reign (1199–1216) there were approximately 4,500–5,000 knights, but there was a sharp decline in numbers between 1215 and 1230 as the military and judicial requirements became more expensive and onerous. By 1230 knighthood had become an expensive rank (Faulkner 1996).

In England the total number of knights available from knight service in the decades after the Conquest was approximately 5,000. However, despite the potential 5,000 knights available, it is difficult to find examples of the call out of the full feudal levy, although a famous example is that of William the Conqueror's command in 1072 to the Abbot of Evesham. The abbot was to bring before William at Clarendon 'all those subject to your administration and jurisdiction . . . all the knights they owe me duly equipped' (Douglas and Greenaway 1981: 960).

In practice there were many obstacles to gathering the full feudal host, such as sickness or old age. In 1100 the first known evidence occurs of the commutation of knight service into payment known as scutage (Stenton 1961: 179). As there is so little evidence for knights actually being called out and serving, the importance of knight service may always have been a financial one (Reynolds 1994: 362), for with money knights could be replaced with battle-hardened mercenaries.

The number of knights a lord had to send is sometimes straightforward (five or ten, or multiples) whilst others were expected to send or pay for fractions of knights, as if lands had been split between members of a family. The initial imposition of knight service probably occurred *c.*1072 (Loyn 1994: 99) and the imposition was not only upon lay landlords, but also on Anglo-Saxon monasteries. The service does not seem to have been levied in ratio to wealth and the allocation seems irrational and confusing, for example Peterborough was charged with sixty knights, Ramsey, which was more prosperous, with four, St Albans six, Coventry, which had less than half St Alban's income, with ten. There may have been other consider-ations apart from wealth in the equation, for example Peterborough may have needed a high number as it was in the fens, a hot spot of Anglo-Saxon resistance; but against this explanation Ramsey too was in the fens. The imposition of the initial knight service seems to have been completed by the time of Domesday in 1086, but there was always movement in the allocation of knight service as estates were amalgamated or split (Loyn 1994: 99). Following a detailed analysis, Holt came to the conclusion that 'quotas were mostly known and fixed by the end of the eleventh century at the latest'. He also concluded that the decimal quotas (for example five or ten) were the most ancient in origin, with non-decimal quotas being later, either through accretion of lands and associated knight service, or through the division of lands (Holt 1983: 99).

Ideally the feudal chain of command was straightforward – for example a tenant held of a lord, who held from the king – but it was rarely so straightforward for one tenant could have many different lords if his lands were scattered. There was therefore a real possibility that in the event of conflict a tenant's loyalty could be divided. This scenario occurred during Stephen's reign when nobles found themselves caught between the opposing claims of Stephen and Matilda. To make matters more complicated, their lands in Normandy were seized by Geoffrey of Anjou. By the end of the twelfth century the situation had been rationalised and the legal author known as 'Glanvill' described the situation: 'A man may do several homages to different lords for the different fees held of these lords; but there must be a chief homage, accompanied by an oath of allegiance, and this homage is to be done to that lord of whom he holds his chief tenement' (i.e. his liege lord) (Hall 1965: 104).

Homage included the tenant's promise not to attack his lord except in self-defence, or by royal command if the king's army marched against his lord. If two lords were in conflict and a tenant had performed homage to both, then his duty is to his liege lord, saving to his other lord the service that is due to him (King 1991: 124). Glanvill states that 'women may not by law do homage . . . though they generally swear fealty to their lords' (Hall 1965: 103). The difference between fealty and homage has been explained by Bloch:

> Unlike homage, which bound the whole man at a single stroke and was generally held to be incapable of renewal, this promise [fealty] – almost a commonplace affair – could be repeated several times to the same person. There were therefore many acts of fealty without homage: we do not know of any acts of homage without fealty.
>
> (Bloch 1965: 146)

The feudal idea of homage and loyalty to one's lord remained a powerful force throughout the Middle Ages, but the personal service of tenants began to be anachronistic by the late twelfth century. The situation regarding knight service had become so confusing that Henry II ordered an inquiry into the amount of knight service he could expect, which resulted in the lists of 1166 known as the 'Cartae Baronum'. The demands for information were sent to the sheriffs who then inquired of the local landowners, some of whom were very wealthy with great estates, others very poor. The survey went to the grass roots of English knighthood and some replies give a vivid impression of impoverished knights: 'To his dearest lord Henry, king of the English, William son of Robert sends greeting. You should know that I hold of you the fief of one poor knight; and I have not enfeoffed anyone on it since it is barely enough for me, and thus my father held it. Farewell' (Warren 1983: 277).

Much like Domesday Book eighty years before, the Cartae Baronum shows an instant in an ever-changing pattern. In in analysis of the Honour of Clare, knight service owed ranged from fourteen knights by one tenant to one-thirtieth of a knight by another. Yet even though knight service could be small, it was a powerful symbol of the feudal hierarchy in which a knight, however poor, had a different status to others. A pattern emerged that the nobles with the most knight service remained relatively stable, whilst those with small amounts of knight service show chaotic change. However, it is entirely feasible that a lord could give a large amount of land to a tenant with a very little knight service as a reward or bribe. The direct link between knight service and the amount of land held could therefore easily be broken (Mortimer 1985: 188–94).

By the end of the twelfth century the concept of personal military service for knights was breaking down. In 1181 Henry II issued the Assize of Arms which specified the weapons each soldier was supposed to bring to battle: a holder of a knight's fee was to have a hauberk, a helmet, a shield and lance, and all burgesses and freemen were to have a quilted doublet, a headpiece of iron and a lance (Douglas and Greenaway 1981: 449–51). Both Henry II and Richard I had difficulty in persuading English men to fight in Normandy and overseas and both Richard I and John demanded only one knight in ten for their Normandy campaigns, who were supposed to fight for at least forty days. In practice fewer knights than could have been raised went for a longer period. By John's reign the traditional system of service being required from the knights fee had broken down and in 1205 John issued a writ that ten knights were to equip and maintain one of their number at 2s a day for defence of the realm so long as was necessary. Moreover, scutage – the payment by knights so they did not have to serve – became a separate tax, divorced from the obligations of the knight service (Church 1998: 52, 55).

The feudal relationship was, however, wider than purely land or service, for a landlord could ask for money for certain agreed events. These 'feudal incidents' or monetary gifts could be demanded for various aspects of family life: the knighting of an eldest son, marriage of an eldest daughter or as a ransom payment. As well as being able to demand payment, the lord had rights over his tenants. As technically a tenant only held his land and property for the duration of his own life, if he died the lord could look after the estate until the heirs came of age (known as wardship). If a tenant's child got married, the tenant also had to seek the permission of the lord, and permission was usually granted after a payment. With large estates wardship could be very profitable and combined with the power of marriage the lord had a way of keeping a firm political grip upon the estate. Marriage of widows was also a potentially lucrative business, for rich suitors would pay handsomely for a wealthy widow, or the king could offer a widow as a reward for a particular service. Occasionally a rich widow might buy the right not to marry again whilst also keeping control of her lands.

Women, marriage and family

The higher the social level of a woman, the more likely she was to leave some trace in the historical record, though the majority of women remain hidden from view. Status and wealth, however, gave freedom from social constraints. Noble women could go on crusade and there are references to Eleanor of Aquitaine leading 300 of her women dressed as Amazons during the Second Crusade. She also took part in strategy sessions, siding with her uncle Raymond of Antioch instead of her husband Louis on the question of whether to attack Jerusalem. At the highest social levels women were expected to fulfil certain duties. One of these was to be a peacemaker between their husbands and enemies, thereby allowing, without loss of face, a legitimate reason for the male enemies not to seek revenge (Leyser 1990: 230). Matilda, queen of Henry I, fulfilled this role and was praised on her ability to keep the peace (Huneycutt 1990: 90). Through Eleanor's intervention as his mother and former queen, Richard I magnanimously pardoned his brother John for rebellion (Martindale 1999: 146).

Abstractions of women also began to form during the twelfth century. The queen began to be seen as the mother figure for the nation. Archbishop Anselm suggested a queen ought to be seen as a mother, nurse, kind mistress and a queen to the churches placed under her care (Huneycutt 1990: 91). In theological terms by the end of the twelfth century the iconography of women had become polarised, between Eve, the sinful temptress, and the Virgin Mary, the most holy mother of God. The Virgin Mary rose steadily in prominence during the twelfth century, partly because of secular veneration (Henry I and his family especially seem to have promoted her cult), but also in religious terms as the Queen of Heaven, a recurrent theme in the powerful visions of Christina of Markyate (Talbot 1959).

Nor surprisingly, however, few women conformed to the religious stereotypes and some determinedly led their own lives. One of the most famous English countesses of the twelfth century was the formidable Hawisa, daughter and heir of William le Gros, Count of Aumale, whose lands were based in Holderness, East Yorkshire. Her character was described as 'a woman, who was almost a man' and it is suggested that she is unique, for not only did she issue charters in her own name (sometimes in parallel with one of her three husbands), but her ladies in waiting, who were the wives or daughters of important tenants, also witnessed charters (English 1991: 37). Normally, however, when women are included in the texts of the charters they are a man's nameless wife or widow.

Women in the lowest levels of society receive only the briefest of comment from contemporary writers: the prostitutes who were part of the king's travelling court, and the washerwomen who were allowed by the Second Lateran Council to go on the Second Crusade. In the increasing records of government, however, women are mentioned. In the Pipe Rolls for Yorkshire for 1184–85, Albreda, along with Benedict and his wife, and Hugh son of Lewin and his wife, took over her husbands estates for £12 14s 1d and in the Yorkshire Pipe Roll of 1191–92 (3 Richard I), Agnes, the ale wife (*braciatrix*) of Ovingham was fined 3s 8d for taking wood from the forest. The role of women in the rural economy also comes to light in the thirteenth-century estate book, the *Seneschancy*. The most significant role of women is that of dairymaid. The dairymaid was in charge of the under-dairymaids, and was expected to make and salt cheese, look after the vessels of the dairy, know on which day to make cheese and be ready to answer questions from the bailiff and reeve when they inspected the dairy. Other duties of the dairymaid were to winnow the corn, keep the geese and hens, and to keep and screen the fire (Oschinsky 1971: 287–9).

Higher up the social scale women still remain shadowy, but odd references show they could command real power, often looking after estates and households whilst their husbands were away on business. Mabel of Bellême, who married Roger II of Montgomery, Earl of Shrewsbury, brought to the marriage lands in France, Normandy and Maine, and may well have been in control of her property before 1077 as Roger concentrated upon his English lands (Thompson 1990: 268). Wives being apart from their husbands may have been an expedient way of a couple controlling their far-flung lands, and this is a possible reason for Agnes, wife of Robert of Bellême, taking their newly born son back to her father's house (Thompson 1990: 282). Long separations during noble marriages were not uncommon, though Agnes may just have wanted to escape from Robert.

Wives were also responsible for the homes and estates whilst their husbands were away. In a story in the *Life of St Wulfstan*, Wulfstan sent his servants ahead to find accommodation, but the 'Sheriff as it chanced, was from home, but his good wife honourably received the messengers' (Piele 1934: 65). In the foundation story of Selby Abbey some nobles 'instructed their wives to assign carpenters to Benedict for the purpose of building a chapel . . . Their wives soon acted upon this and, after sending carpenters, saw to the construction of the little oratory' (Neale 1984: 21). Wives of nobles could also be in control of castles, though not always in their husbands' best interests; Roger of Beaumont collapsed and died at the court of King Stephen when he heard that his wife had handed over Warwick Castle to Henry of Anjou (Mason 1979: 128).

Women's lives become visible in detail when they are nobility or royalty. A study of dowager countesses between 1069 and 1230 revealed that over half (34 of 59) married twice or more, with seven marrying three times and one marrying four. Remarriage was usually following the death of the husband, often in battle, on crusade or, in the case of Geoffrey, fifth Earl of Essex, jousting. Of the sample, one of the longest marriages (and one would hope happiest), was that of William Marshall and Countess Isobel of Pembroke who produced ten children (five boys and five girls). The total of children known for the dowager countesses was 182, giving an average of just over three per dowager countess, of which 111 were male and 72 female. The male/female imbalance of numbers is probably a reflection on the under-reporting of female children (DeAragon 1994).

However, whilst it is possible to analyse the families of royalty or the nobility (though even here there are many uncertainties), to generalise about families in the twelfth century is particularly difficult. Although increasing numbers of records survive, such as charters or the Pipe Rolls, they usually only list males who have reached maturity. The situation before 1200 is unknowable in any sort of detail because records have not survived, but there are four main classes of records that can be used to cast some light on family size and structure: the 'libri vitae' ('Books of Life') and records of religious confraternity; cartularies and original deeds; the unique *Rotuli de Dominabus* of 1185 (which was an inquiry into the lands held by widows, minors and heiresses, which unusually gives ages); and finally the royal judicial records at both national and county level. The largest households were those of the king and the richest nobles. Not only would they have their own family –

often a large one as the relatively better diet and living conditions gave them a better chance of survival – but they would also have a potentially large contingent of servants and visitors or guests. The nuclear family was likely to be surrounded by domestic servants, chaplains, estate officials, scribes, men-at-arms, squires undergoing military training and knights not yet given land. The normal household size for a middling knight was probably ten to twenty people, whilst baronial households probably ranged from fifty to several hundred (Moore 1991).

Down the social scale household size reduced. A rich trader may have had a servant or two but at the bottom of the scale it was most likely to be just parents and children. However, at all social levels the norm in the later twelfth century was the nuclear family of husband, wife and unmarried children. Social differences were reflected in different family sizes, with smaller families at the bottom of the social scale, possibly because of poor living conditions and diet (Moore 1991).

The birth of children, and especially sons and heirs, was crucial for the continuance of the family name and honour. The study of the families of dowager countesses revealed that of fifty couples, fourteen were childless and ten earls faced a potential succession crisis, with the king often being able to decide between various claimants (DeAragon 1994: 92). Such a situation was potentially disastrous, leading to the power and wealth of a family built up over the generations, passing out of the family altogether.

Illegitimacy, whilst not endorsed by the church, was accepted. Kings (whose children are known in the greatest detail) often had many illegitimate children and some reached high office: Robert, the illegitimate son of Henry I, achieved great wealth and power. He was a key player in the civil wars between Stephen and Matilda and was Matilda's most important supporter. Nobles also had illegitimate offspring, though details are harder to discover. The actual birth was a potential source of great propaganda, especially if a son and heir was born. There was always the danger that enemies would declare that a baby had been smuggled in and the real baby had not survived, though few would go as far as Constance, the Empress of the Holy Roman Emperor. She set up a birthing tent in the market square of Jesi and welcomed any lady of the town who wished to be present at the birth. Her son was born in 1194 in public view and a day or two later she publicly breast fed her son (Fröhlich 1992: 113).

Following birth, families sought baptism (at this period also known as confirmation) as soon as possible, because it was thought that an unbaptised baby could not go to heaven. Hugh, Bishop of Lincoln, was also particularly conscious of the importance of confirmation and his biographer, Adam of Eynesham, described people flocking to him, bringing their babies for confirmation (Douie and Farmer 1961: 127). Hugh would dismount (a sign of humility) and then summon the children and their godparents to him, one after another. In contrast, the actions of other bishops could be much more haphazard:

I (Adam) saw a certain young bishop . . . when the spot and the weather were both admirable and he had no reason to be in a hurry, sprinkle children with the sacred chrism whilst on horseback. The children howled and were terror-stricken, and in actual danger amongst the fiery and kicking horses. The ruffianly retainers cuffed and struck these innocents, but the bishop took no notice of their danger and panic.

(Douie and Farmer 1961: 127)

Records or accounts of childhood tend to be fragmentary and incidental. Children's games and other antics are occasionally recorded. The chronicler William of Newburgh described how the boys of York stoned Archbishop Gerard's hearse because he was accused of witchcraft and later William wrote that young boys were appointed into clerical positions, but they were better suited 'to build childish houses, to yoke mice in little wagons, to play together indiscriminately' (Stevenson 1996: 517). The image of boys catching mice and harnessing them to small wagons is an amusing one. Children's imagination can also be seen in a description by Gerald of Wales of his brothers who were tracing or building, in sand or dust, now towns, now palaces, whereas the holy Gerald designed churches or built monasteries instead (Wada 1997: 223). Other glimpses are afforded through anecdotes, for example Matilda, queen of Henry I, visited the building site of Merton Priory and often brought along her young son so that he might be inspired by happy childhood memories and remain a lifelong patron of the foundation (Huneycutt 1990: 91).

The coming of age of children differed according to status. In the law book attributed to Glanvill, he gives the coming of age of a range of individuals. In the case of a son or heir of a lordship or military fee the coming of age occurred at 21. The significance of this is that the estates may have been in wardship and by having so late a coming of age the person with the wardship would gain maximum profit from it. There were, however, one or two benefits to being under age, notably that if a minor was accused of a felony, he could not answer for it until he came of age – potentially giving time for passions to subside or the crime to be forgotten or amended.

Glanvill concentrates on the coming of age of nobility, but also mentions that the 'son and heir of a sokeman is deemed of full age at fifteen, the son of a burgage tenant when he can count money carefully, measure cloth and generally do his father's business', presumably in their middle or upper teens. The specific link between being a burgage tenant and a merchant/businessman and the cloth trade is an interesting one, though generally burgesses were not confined to the cloth trade (Hall 1965: 82).

Whilst birthdays were not usually celebrated, a child's age became crucial in cases of wardship following the death of the child's parents. A study of noble marriages showed that although it varied – from a few weeks to forty-seven years – the average length of a marriage was seventeen years – long enough to raise children but not long enough for a child automatically to inherit the estate (DeAragon 1994: 91). This was a potentially serious situation where the lands were held and exploited by the guardians without necessarily any regard for the ward. As the wardships could be very expensive – for the right to hold the guardianship was to be paid to the king – the guardians often exploited their opportunities to the full. For this reason it was essential to know how old a child was, for to under age a child was to leave the lands in another's hands until the child came of age.

If a growing child was parentless then he or she had little authority over their own lands, and equally they might have little choice as to whom they married, their lord or guardian determining their choice. The control of marriages was a powerful weapon as the giving of a wealthy bride could be a rich reward for service or loyalty (Searle 1980: 170).

It was accepted that families and lords had the right to arrange marriages for their daughters and womenfolk, so long as the marriage did not conflict with canon law. For important lords the king had to give his assent (Holt 1997: 249–50, 262). Of course arranged marriages often did not please everyone. Robert Curthose, Duke of Normandy, had arranged the marriage of Bertrade de Montfort, niece of William, Count of Evreux, to Fulk of Anjou, much against the Count of Évreux's wishes. Orderic Vitalis reported William as saying:

> My lord duke, you ask something which is repugnant to me, for you wish me to give my niece, who is entrusted to my guardianship by my brother-in-law and is a young virgin, in marriage to a man who has already twice been married. The truth is you are solely concerned with your own interests, and think nothing of mine. You wish to use my niece as a pawn to take away my inheritance from me. Is this a just proposal? I will not grant your request unless you restore me Bavent and Noyon-sur-Andelle, Gace and Gravencon, Ecouche and other estates of my uncle . . . and restore my nephew . . . properties which we can reasonably and lawfully prove to be ours by hereditary right.
>
> (Chibnall 1973: 185)

This passage highlights many of the issues surrounding arranged marriages – the lack of control over the marriage partner, the political manoeuvring, but most important of all for the family the dispersal and loss of estates, potentially to one's enemy.

Theoretically the key age after which a child could be married was 12. It was not uncommon for royal or noble children to be married or betrothed at a very young age as a political measure by their parents. In 1175 the Synod of Westminster specifically banned the marriage of female children in the cradle to male infants as neither child was at an age of discretion. Even following a legitimate marriage some chroniclers were deeply suspicious. The comments of the chroniclers about the age of Isabella of Angoulême, whom King John married in 1200, suggest that she may have been as young as 8 or 9 (Vincent 1999: 166). Another young royal bride was Henry II's 11-year-old daughter Joan who was betrothed to William II of Sicily (Warren 1998: 265).

Even at the time such marriages were exceptional and caused comment. Usually marriage would have occurred from the couple's late teens onwards. The marriage itself was a secular vow between two people and so it could take place in secret without any witnesses. However, the church was concerned that a vow could be rescinded and without witnesses it was one person's word against another, and so it sought to make marriages public (for example at the Council of Rouen), by the priest openly performing the marriage with witnesses present. The witnesses were a vital component, for there was no formal written documentation and later disputes could turn on their memory. Normally the marriage took place at the door of the church with an exchange of rings. A symbol of the women's dowry could also be given. The dowry was usually land or money from her father or relative, which on marriage was joined to the husband's possessions. In 1088 Ramsey Abbey gave to William Pecche and his wife Alfwen the land of Over in Cambridgeshire, and the wording of the grant suggests that they were given the land on their wedding day (Hudson 1990: 68).

In England certain estates, for example round Exeter, were traditionally given to the queen, a custom which stretched back into the Anglo-Saxon past (Vincent 1999: 185). In 1200, however, there was a particular problem for there were three queens of England – John's new queen, Isabella of Angoulême; Richard I's Queen Berengaria of Navarre; and Henry II's Queen Eleanor of Aquitaine – a situation which proved to be complicated for John, especially as Eleanor of Aquitaine had been granted these estates. Following Eleanor's death in 1204 Berengaria and Isabella fought for control of her estates (Vincent 1999: 185).

The final part of a legal marriage was the consummation. Christina of Markyate's parents attempted to get her so drunk that she would agree to the consummation of the marriage with her husband later that night. On her arrival in the bedroom, Christina became cold sober and she suggested they live chastely for several years. The marriage remained unconsummated and fell apart (Talbot 1959; Holdsworth 1978: 187).

During the twelfth century the theories ebbed and flowed as to the form of a legal marriage and the grounds of annulment. One of the most powerful prohibitions to marriage was the canon law that people could not get married within the seven degrees of consanguinity. This was announced in 1072 at the Council of Rouen and then more widely in 1095 at the Council of Clermont (Chibnall 1984: 130). However, the laws on marriage were at a formative stage and the intermarriage of the nobility of Europe over the centuries meant that within the seven degrees was the norm. In effect there was little to stop marriage amongst the nobility, though the seven degrees could be a useful barrier if anyone really objected. Henry I of England prevented the politically disastrous marriage between his nephew William Clito and Sibyl of Anjou by alleging that the degrees of consanguinity forbade the union. Henry's threats, pleas and 'an enormous quantity of gold and silver and other valuables' also helped his cause and it was 'ruled that they could not to be married by Christian law'. However the same objection could have been raised against the marriage of Henry I's son William to Fulk's daughter, and Henry I's daughter Matilda to Fulk's son Geoffrey. Fortunately neither was challenged in the courts as the succession of the English crown depended upon the marriages. In 1199 King John also used the degrees of kinship to annul his ten-year marriage to Isabella of Gloucester (Vincent 1999:166). A further way to stop a marriage was by giving money to the father – Richard I paid King Philip of France 10,000 marks to buy his way out of a twenty-year betrothal to his sister (Warren 1998:269).

If the passion was strong enough, marriage could withstand social disapproval: Bavent, who was married to Fulk of Anjou, eloped with the King of France and, in defiance of papal prohibitions and excommunication, was married to him (Chibnall 1984:129). Equally couples could part. When Eleanor of Aquitaine left King Louis of France and married Henry (later the II of England) it caused ripples of condemnation across Europe.

The death of a husband could lead to the king or lord forcing a widow to remarry. The forced marriage of widows by the king was one of the grievances of the rebels against King John and articles seven and eight of Magna Carta specify that the widow was to receive her dower, marriage portion and inherited property quickly after the death of her husband, without payment and that she should not be compelled to marry again. Thereafter the abuses of the system were greatly reduced (DeAragon 1994: 98).

The death and burial of a lord was a traumatic one, not only for his immediate family, but also for his tenants: the death of a king had the potential to throw the kingdom into anarchy if there was no obvious successor. The burial of a king was normally treated with great solemnity but the burial of William the Conqueror had been something of a travesty. A fire had disrupted his funeral procession, a local man claimed the plot where William was to be buried had been stolen from him, and William's corpse had to be stuffed into a coffin, causing such a stench that the service was brought to a hurried end (Hallam 1982: 359). This was, however, an exceptional case and previously the deaths of Anglo-Saxon kings such as Edward the Confessor had been treated with considerable respect and care, both over his body and the funeral arrangements as depicted in the Bayeux Tapestry. By the mid-twelfth century kings were taking care over the locations for their burials. Both Henry I and King Stephen built churches for their interment (Reading Abbey and Faversham Abbey respectively). The idea of a royal family mausoleum became increasingly powerful and by the end of the century the English kings had chosen the Abbey of Fontevrault in Normandy. At the abbey were buried Henry II, his queen, Eleanor of Aquitaine, and children, Richard I and Joan, as well as Isabella of Angoulême, the widow of his son John, and his grand nephew (Raymond VII of Toulouse) (Gillingham 1994b:

56; Church 1998: 50–1). When John lost control of Normandy in 1204, the loss included the heart of the Angevin Empire and the family mausoleum. King John was the first king since 1066 to be buried in England whereas his choice would probably have been at Fontevrault.

The nobility also chose their burial places with care. With lands split between Normandy and England, and the many religious foundations which families created, it was not always a straightforward choice. An analysis of the burial locations of 104 people (Golding 1986) has revealed that the choice was often a political one. A key factor in the decision was the link between a person, or family, and a particular church. The founder of a church usually wanted to be buried there, so for example the family of Warenne were buried at their Cluniac foundation of Lewes. Powerful families might found or be patron to more than one religious house, and there was a trend for nobles to favour the newer orders, such as the Cistercians or Augustinians, over the older Benedictine monasteries. In the case of the Cistercians, the burial of a layman in their church was forbidden in their early statutes, though this rule increasingly was broken. This shift can be seen in the burial places of the de Ferrers family. Robert's predecessors were buried in the Benedictine house of Tutbury (Warwickshire) outside their castle, whereas Robert chose to be buried wrapped in an ox hide in the Cistercian foundation of Merevale. (Burial of the nobility in an ox hide was not uncommon in the twelfth century.)

Warfare

England during the late eleventh and twelfth centuries was a largely peaceful country, though at times the peace was punctuated by noble rebellion or outright civil war. Border incursions by the Welsh and Scots, with attempted invasion from Normandy, or the invasion of Ireland can give an impression of a society permanently at war. Yet compared to Normandy, which was a constant theatre of war, England was remarkably peaceful.

When warfare did break out the normal mode of attack was to waste the opponent's possessions. This had several advantages for the attacker. The first was that it reduced the economic prosperity of the defender, whilst the attacker could live off the land or plunder the possessions. Wasting and plundering could also foreshadow a siege of a castle and in his description of the Young King's Revolt, Jordan Fantosme has Philip of Flanders saying 'Let him not leave them, outside their castles, in wood or meadow, as much as will furnish them a meal on the morrow. Then let him assemble his men and lay siege to their castles. They will not get help or succour within 13 leagues around them' (Strickland 1989: 186).

The plundering of churches in the ownership of an opposing lord might also reward the attacker with items of gold and silver, though the ecclesiastical censure might be great. The second advantage was that it revealed the weakness of the defender. A lord was supposed to protect his tenants and their possessions – a policy of wasting showed that the lord was incapable of preserving his lands and tenants. These two factors combined may have been the reason why William the Conqueror wasted lands around the Pevensey countryside, in the heart of King Harold's lands, a deliberately provocative act which brought Harold quickly to battle.

The core unit of military strength and expertise lay in the household of a king or noble, a unit which could grow or diminish as the need arose (see above). The feudal host was also a potential source of military strength, though as has been seen, knight service was probably more important as a source of money than as a fighting force in itself. Mercenaries, often from overseas, were usually the bulk of the army, though they were seen as the lowest of the low by knights and nobles, for they received payment for their services, rather than fighting as a duty to the king. Orderic Vitalis described Henry I's forces as '*pagenses et gregarii*' (rustics and commoners) because they received payment, in comparison with the French army which contained the 'flower of all France and Normandy' in 1124 (Church 1998: 56). Flemish mercenaries had a particularly fearsome reputation and were used extensively during the Young King's Revolt of 1173–4.

Castles

Wasting was a rapid and easy policy, but if the lands were to be held then castles had to be besieged and captured. Except for a few castles on the Welsh borders (Hereford, Ewyas Harold, Richard's Castle, Clavering) built by Norman favourites of Edward the Confessor, the Normans introduced castles into England. (Castles had long been known in Normandy, with the oldest known castle at le Mans constructed before 1015 (Barton 1994: 46) and the donjon at Loches has been redated by dendrochronology from early twelfth to the early eleventh centuries (Fernie 1998: 7).) However, Norman and Continental castles cannot have been unknown to Anglo-Saxon nobles or ecclesiastics as they travelled through Europe. The reason why castles were not imported into England by the Anglo-Saxons was that Anglo-Saxon defence was based on a communal system (Williams 1992: 239). In contrast, a castle was an individual's fortress, a psychologically imposing statement of an individual's will towering over a conquered community (Beresford 1981: 33; Coulson 1983: 30). Therefore castles also symbolised a more dramatic shift in power, because the Anglo-Saxon administrative system had been based on areas: shire, hundred and vill. However great an Anglo-Saxon lord, he did not have administrative centres in his private manors. Part of the outrage against castles was directed against the imposition of new power structures which cut across the jurisdiction of the old areas and included administrative centres within a single lord's castle (Williams 1992: 239–40).

The standard type of castle was the motte and bailey castle which consisted of a high mound (the motte) with a fortified building on top, access to which was by a large defended enclosure (the bailey). An example of a small reconstructed motte and bailey castle can be seen at the Ulster History Park in Omagh, Northern Ireland. This gives a vivid impression of the buildings and fortifications of a motte and bailey castle. Looking down from the motte – the highest point of the castle – the bailey could be seen with its buildings for accomodation and horses (Plate 4.1a). Entry to the bailey was by a stoutly defended gateway. Looking up from the bailey to the motte the attackers had to cross a narrow bridge which spanned the moat. On top of the motte was a building which was the administrative and defensive heart of the castle (Plate 4.1b). Around both the motte and the bailey were water-filled moats. The manpower needed to construct a motte has been calculated: fifty men working a ten-hour day for forty-two days could build a small motte 5.6 metres high and 39.5 metres at the base (English 1998: 52). An alternative to the motte was the ring-work, where ditches and banks created a defended enclosure – a bailey writ large without the motte. However, the notion that Saxons did not have castles has been challenged. Whilst it is true they did not have motte and bailey castles, the description of a thegn's seat as a 'chapel, kitchen, bell-house and burhgeat' (i.e. defended gateway) can be seen as a design similar to Norman castles without mottes, such as Richmond, Chepstow and Ludlow (Fernie 1998: 7). However, the key differences between large Anglo-Saxon defensive works and Norman castles were that the new Norman motte and bailey castles were small, high and personal.

New motte and bailey castles were built right across England, often within Anglo-Saxon defences (Renn 1973). An excellent example occurred at Goltho, a manor house in Lincolnshire which has been extensively archaeologically excavated. Pre-Conquest there was a strong Saxon defended enclosure which had ramparts 25 feet thick and an 18-foot wide and 6-foot deep ditch. With a new Norman owner the defence was changed to a timber and earth castle, with a moat 40 feet wide and 12 feet deep. The new castle had a bailey (60 feet long and 50 feet wide) which had in it two aisled halls, probably providing accommodation and the manor court. The size of the castle was very small and rather than the lord's residence it was probably the residence of his steward who looked after the estates in the region. The severe burning on the hearths showed that it was in permanent use (Beresford 1981: 27, 30). In the mid-twelfth century the status of the site was upgraded to the 'caput' (i.e. chief residence) of Simon fitz William. The defensive capabilities of the castle were reduced by lowering the motte, but the building of a large aisled hall showed its upgraded status. Despite the changes it was only occupied for short periods before the site was abandoned in favour of one three-quarters of a mile away (Beresford 1981: 35).

The four earliest castles following William's landing were built as part of his progression to London – Pevensey, Hastings, Dover and London. A strong case has been made that the initial castles built by William were all of the ring-work type, only later being changed to the motte and bailey design

Plate 4.1(a) and *4.1(b)* below. Reconstruction of a motte and bailey castle, Ulster History Park, Omagh, Northern Ireland.

(English 1998). Thereafter there was a proliferation of early castles to protect the lords and their garrisons. By 1086 there were over seventy castles in England, fifty of which were recorded in Domesday Book (Harfield 1991). The castles were probably built by forced Anglo-Saxon labour or by changing the Anglo-Saxon duty of 'burh bot' into castle building, a burden which fell upon the shire (Colvin 1963: 24–5). Both York and London had two castles, and as well as the White Tower and Baynard's Castle London may have had a third castle at Montfichet (Taylor 1991: 304). The vast majority of late eleventh- and twelfth-century castles were made of wood, though there were occasional exceptions of castles built in stone, such as the White Tower, the great donjon at Colchester and Richmond in Yorkshire (Cook 1978: 96).

The castles were incredibly effective, and in the years following the Conquest only the castles at York were overcome by invading forces. The castles themselves were usually independent self-contained units during times of war rather than being organised as a planned network as a strategic masterplan (Beeler 1956; Hollister 1965; Strickland 1989: 179). Castles were, of course, mainly for defence – castles were the immoveable objects against the unstoppable force of a cavalry charge (Cook 1978: 97). But they were also an excellent base for active operations, which was why it was dangerous for an attacker to leave an uncaptured castle in conquered lands. However, sometimes commanders did pass castles without capturing them. When King David of Scotland failed to take Wark Castle he marched further south and devastated the land without opposition (Strickland 1989: 183).

Castles could also be used as bases for attacks into new areas. William FitzOsbern's castles on the Welsh border where primarily for defence, but they also served as bases for the earliest advances into Wales. Thereafter they were used as centres of administration and organisation for territory beyond the frontier (Walker 1978: 135). The building of a castle on disputed land could also turn a tentative claim to land into a reality of possession, which in turn could lead to settled dominance of an area (Coulson 1994: 68). Furthermore they could act as supply bases, a tangential indication of this occurred in 1074 when Edgar the Ætheling and his household journeyed from Scotland to William in Normandy, as *The Anglo-Saxon Chronicle* records: 'And the sheriff of York came to meet them at Durham, and travelled all the way with them, and had them found food and fodder at each castle they came to, until they came across the sea to the king' (Swanton 2000: 210).

The scale of castles varied tremendously, from the small castle built to give defence from a small raiding party to the great castles, such as the White Tower in London, which was built to withstand prolonged siege. In the northern border areas were Newcastle, Wark and Norham, all of which had considerable amounts of money spent on them to make them as impregnable as possible. In times of need and panic earthworks with timber superstructures could be thrown up. If an invasion was being planned castles could even be made before the expedition and carried overseas. In the Pipe

Rolls of 1170–1 there is a reference to two wooden castles being ferried overseas during the expedition to Ireland, and although there is no contemporary evidence the poet Wace, writing for the court of Henry II, describes the Normans disembarking and constructing a wooden castle at Hastings from pieces ready cut and transported in barrels (Bennett 1982: 37).

There was a general principle that a royal licence was needed for a castle to be built and the Laws of Henry I describe how building a castle without licence put the offender at the king's mercy (Downer 1996). When kings were strong enough, this law could be enforced, but in times of civil war nobles either built castles without licence or could easily sway a weak monarch to allow them to build. When William Rufus acquired Normandy from Robert Curthose, he banned fortifications in Normandy and England as part of the attempt to reassert the rule of law. During the Anarchy between Stephen and Matilda the rule of law had been weakened and there had been a major surge in castle building by nobles across England. Exact figures are not possible because the dating evidence for the majority has not been discovered, and moreover many were so small that they would have been practically useless against anything other than a small local attacking force. However, even a small castle could cause great local disruption. A major complaint of the citizens of York during the wars of Stephen's reign was that a new castle had been built downstream at Wheldrake, which seriously impeded traffic along the River Ouse into the city. Along with the castle came the castle garrison – often little more than thugs with a lord's protection, who could wreak havoc with a local area. At Selby the garrison 'applied themselves to robbery, spending their time plundering the area, oppressing everyone weaker than they' (Bartlett 2000: 284). The scale of castle building and oppression was nationwide and *The Anglo-Saxon Chronicle* recorded that in Stephen's reign 'every powerful lord made his castles . . . and filled the land full of castles . . . then when the castles were made, they filled them with devils and evil men' (Swanton 2000: 264).

Following Henry II's accession to the throne, both he and his sons Richard and John had a systematic policy of seizure, confiscation and demolition of noble castles. The scale of this policy has been described as a deliberate 'castle-policy' which resulted in a dramatic reversal of the balance of power in favour of royalty. In 1154, when Henry II came to the throne, the crown possessed forty-nine castles, but by 1214 the crown possessed ninety-three castles, as well as having destroyed a large number of non-royal castles (Coulson 1983: 12).

The military capability of a castle depended upon its construction as well as the size and determination of the defending garrison. A surprisingly small number of men were needed to defend a castle. In 1174 ten knights and forty sergeants held Wark against a sustained assault by William the Lion. The chronicler Richard of Hexham records that although a castle was held by only nine knights, they were disgraced by surrendering too easily since they had plenty of provisions, and ditches and keep were very strong

(Strickland 1989: 185), a testimony to the art of castle building for defence. No castle, whatever its size or garrison, could withstand an indefinite siege and so it was important to mobilise military support to relieve the castle (Strickland 1989: 178). In some instances the attacking force was sandwiched between the castle and the relieving force, as at the Battle of Lincoln in 1141.

Within castle studies there is a continuing debate about the balance between the military aspects of a castle and its other functions, whether administrative, residential, political or symbolic. Coulson has emphasised that a castle maintained the honour and status of a lord, thereby becoming a powerful political symbol (Coulson 1994: 65–6). The sheer massiveness of the defensive structures have also been seen as much for show as their military practicality and that all castles can be viewed as primarily grand residences of the powerful (Fernie 1998: 7). Part of a castle's power and prestige was due to the associated rights that came with possession, including judicial and feudal rights which changed the make-up of power in the locality (Coulson 1983; Power 1994: 189).

One recent trend is to view the castle not only as a building, but also as a building in a designed landscape. This approach was first highlighted in the report about the later medieval Bodiam Castle, but increasingly other castles have been placed into their landscapes. Whereas the trend is normally portrayed as occurring between 1300 and 1550, a ground-breaking article has shown that the castle at Castle Rising in Norfolk, built *c.*1140, was set amidst a designed landscape with its own park and settlement. Other early castles too portray similar arrangements, such as Castle Acre (*c.*1070), Mileham (*c.*1110) and New Buckenham (*c.*1146) where the design of the landscape seems to have mattered more than the military considerations (Liddiard 1999: 167, 186).

The pride felt about an individual's castle and the life within can be seen from a letter written by Adam of Balsham. Outside the castle, in the fields and pastures, were horses of different breeds. The castle itself had a rampart and ditch, and on entry he was greeted by a multitude of relatives, with others in the great hall. He listed the food eaten, and whilst eating there were musicians. He then describes visiting the tower where the armoury was, followed by the library, chapel, storehouse, granary, yard, stables, wine cellar and kitchen. Back in the hall he describes the weaving implements, clothes and ornaments, then finally he went to the chamber to sleep (Lendinara 1992: 165).

The design of castles did not stand still and over the following decades and centuries continually evolved. One example is that of Prudhoe Castle. In the mid-eleventh century the site was cleared and timber buildings were protected by a substantial timber palisade, which following the Conquest was changed into a ring-work with a large entrance tower, probably when it came into the ownership of the Umfraville family. In the second quarter of the twelfth century the defences were strengthened by a stone curtain wall and a stone gatehouse, but the entrance tower was kept. Further changes were made in the last quarter of the twelfth century (after the Young King's Revolt in 1173–4) when a keep was constructed and the entrance tower was demolished (Keen 1982: 183).

By the end of the twelfth and into the thirteenth centuries occasionally features such as the keep on top of the motte were retained, but increasingly the great central tower was giving way to a stronger curtain wall and strong gatehouses. The curtain wall also had closely spaced rectangular towers, all with excellent communication. Since the introduction of castles by the Normans the design had evolved into a powerful system of defence. Castles remained for centuries a vital part of a lord's status and an effective form of defence until the introduction of gunpowder in the fifteenth century.

5   Government and justice

Between 1066 and 1215 there were fundamental changes to the systems of government and justice in England. Their development was not always smooth and certain periods of time have been seen as more important than others. The first was in the twenty years or so after the Conquest when William the Conqueror extended the power of the English crown throughout England. This was achieved by a combination of county sheriffs (who replaced the regional Anglo-Saxon earls) and bishops. The court itself grew in power and personnel. The norm during the Anglo-Saxon period was for the king and all associated offices to travel round the country but in the early twelfth century a change took place which altered the concept of government: the exchequer became permanently located at Westminster in London. Although the king and court still itinerated through the country the mould had been broken and gradually other large offices of state became fixed in one place.

The court system too became more structured, though the courts of the magnates estates (either the larger honourial courts or smaller manorial courts) could cut across the ancient Anglo-Saxon court system. A major leap forward in the processes of the law occurred during the 1160s to 1180s with the reforms of Henry II. Trial by jury became a regular feature of legal life, thereby forming the basis of the English legal system. Until 1215, when King John assented to abide by Magna Carta (see Chapter 2), the king remained the most important secular judge, though the church – especially Thomas Becket – had secured the right to try people in its own courts without royal interference. The law itself evolved. The first attempts to codify the law, such as the *Laws of Henry I*, were largely chaotic, but by 1215 the law had assumed a much more defined and codified structure.

The king and the curia regis

The king in the king's court – the curia regis – was the centre of government and justice for the Norman kings. The court could vary in size, from the normal household of a king to great set piece occasions when William I, William II and Henry I wore their crowns in crown wearings three times a year (Biddle 1985). It was at such an occasion in Christmas 1085 at

Gloucester that the orders for Domesday Book to be made were given (see Chapter 7). However, in the day-to-day business of the king's court, William the Conqueror had with him a small group of powerful magnates who travelled with him, forming an inner circle of advisers. The duty of the advisers was just that – to advise, and there was no compulsion on the king to take their advice, although it was important not to alienate powerful nobles unduly. For Henry I at least, formal consultation was an important part of his rule, though the assemblies of nobles 'were more concerned with ratification and publicity than with debate' and it is rare to find instances of the king changing his mind (Green 1989a: 23–4).

The workings of the courts, including the king's court, in the early twelfth century are not known in detail, though some general themes do emerge. Whereas the Anglo-Saxon kings had divided the country into areas almost solely governed by earls, for example Wessex, Mercia and Northumbria, the Norman kings were more active in governing the whole of the country. The Norman kings were determined to control from the centre, and if a region or person transgressed, the response was normally vigorous. Part of this process was to monitor the localities closely by having centralised systems in place. The most formidable of these was the exchequer, which controlled the annual audits of the county sheriffs, the records of which were written on sewn rolls of parchment and were known as the Pipe Rolls. The earliest surviving Pipe Roll dates from 1129–30, though its form indicates it was not the first. Such controls were important for there was a real danger that, away from the court, powerful local men could rule effectively untrammelled.

Following Henry I's death and Stephen's accession, Stephen's policy shifted to one where central authority was weakened in favour of creating large territorial earldoms across England, with the individual earls having great power in the regions under their control. This was a retreat from the previous policies of the Norman kings. William the Conqueror had dismantled the powerful earldoms of Wessex, Mercia and Northumbria and instead had implemented a system of sheriffs governing individual counties. Whilst Stephen did not initiate the creation of new earldoms (Henry I had created eight), he rapidly increased the numbers between 1136 and 1140 by adding fourteen more. His opponent, the Empress Matilda, also added some in territories under her control. By the end of Stephen's reign only five counties did not have an earl (Kent, Hampshire, Berkshire, Middlesex and Shropshire). The motive behind the creation of so many new titles is not clear, though it is possible that Stephen was seriously worried by the local loyalties of the sheriffs in the kingdom. There is no indication of Stephen's original intentions concerning the powers of the earls but they became the most important people in the counties. In 1154 the sheriffs in half the counties were under the authority of the earls, in effect acting as their agents (Davis 1980: 129–44; Green 1991: 92). The actions of many earls are open to question. One such is Earl Reginald of Cornwall who submitted no revenues to the king during his time as earl. There is therefore the suspicion that he pocketed all the royal income, but it may be that this was a legitimate way of recouping money spent on his successful defence of the county (Green 1991: 102).

In the north King Stephen created the position and title of Earl of York for William of Aumale after William's part in the Battle of the Standard. William was a useful ally to have, having great power in the region. He was even able to bar Murdac, the Archbishop of York, from entering York following Murdac's successful election against King Stephen's choice of archbishop, William FitzHerbert. The comparative standing of sheriff and earl can be seen by the chronicler William of Newbrugh's description of William Aumale as 'more truly the king beyond the Humber' and that the only sheriff positively identified during the earl's 'reign' was Robert of Octon, a tenant of the earl (Green 1991: 94–5).

When Henry II acceded to the throne he made it clear that he would rule as his grandfather, Henry I, had done by following his grandfather's policies. Henry II quickly restored the power of the exchequer, and the Pipe Rolls, which had been discontinued during Stephen's reign (unless none has survived), were restarted under Henry II. Furthermore the earldoms created during Stephen's reign were dismantled, either by Henry reasserting his power or by being allowed to lapse when the holder died. Henry II was determined to make the court and its administrative offices the centre of power, thereby restoring royal authority over the whole country.

Henry II steadily recovered royal power, but the interval between 1166 and 1180 have been seen as the key years in which the system of government was transformed rapidly. Before these years the king and his administration had only occasionally intervened in the judicial systems within the shires. After 1180 the king and his justices took over direct management of justice, both criminal and civil, as well as much of the work of government in the localities (Warren 1987: 106) (for the legal reforms, see below).

The king's household

The nucleus of government until the late twelfth century travelled with the king as part of his household. The king's entourage was broadly divided into two: the 'familia' of the king and the 'domus'. The 'familia regis' is the most difficult to define. A 'familiaris' was an intimate or close associate, but one who did not necessarily have any direct feudal obligation to the king. The familiaris could either give advice, be part of the council or carry out important tasks such as members of the king's court or itinerant justices who went out into the provinces. The men who made up the familia regis were a fluid group with the result that they are often hard to identify. But the fluidity also meant that there was no contention about the definition as to who a 'familiaris' was, whether they should take an oath or how such men would relate to the other nobles, all issues which would become important in Henry III's reign in the mid-thirteenth century. A familiaris had the trust of the king and might hear his thoughts or be asked his opinion when others would not (Jolliffe 1963: 166, 188; Warren 1983: 305). Another important aspect of the familia regis was that it could also incorporate a fighting force of knights, some of whom were paid for their services; such knights have been seen as of central importance during the reign of Henry I (Chibnall 1977; Prestwich 1981; Green 1989a: 26–9).

At the end of Henry I's reign two descriptions were written detailing the familia regis and the king's domus or household. Only the description of the household of the king has survived for the reign of Henry I (though it was probably written just before Stephen's coronation). Walter Map, writing towards the end of the twelfth century, wrote that Henry I 'had the customs of his house and household, as ordained by himself, kept in writing' (James *et al.* 1983: 439). 'The Establishment of the King's Household' (*Constitutio Domus Regis*) (White 1948; Douglas and Greenaway 1981: 454) is a remarkable document which lists in detail the payments for over a hundred individuals within the king's household. The list can be divided into groups which can be graded in significance by their pay and allowances, which is invaluable in assessing the relative importance of the offices (Newman 1988: 7). The most important group included the chancellor – who received 5 shillings a day with loaves, wine and 40 pieces of candles – and then the steward, master-butler, master-chamberlain, constables, master-marshal and treasurer who all received 3 shillings and six pence, a loaf, wine and 24 pieces of candle. Below these headings were members of the various branches of the household, such as the bakers, the waferer and the cooks. An alternative way of analysing the list is by the five main offices: the chapel, the chamber, the hall, the buttery and the constabulary-marshalsea. The detail in the list is remarkable, for example, the description of duties and allowance of the chaplain reads:

> The chaplain in charge of the chapel and of the relics shall have the provision of two men; and the four servants of the chapel shall receive double food, and for each of the two packhorses assigned to the chapel they shall have an allowance of a penny a day, and also a penny a month for shoeing. For their service of the chapel they shall have 2 wax candles on Wednesday, and two on Saturday; and 30 pieces of candle; and a gallon of clear wine for mass; and a sextary [four gallons] of ordinary wine on Maundy Thursday for the washing of the altar; and on Easter day 1 sextary of clear wine for Communion, and 1 of ordinary wine.
>
> (Douglas and Greenaway 1981: 454)

Part of the fascination of the list is that it includes rarely mentioned occupations such as the usher of the turnspit, the turnspit, the servant who takes in beasts killed in the chase, the slaughtermen and the cellarmen. In King John's reign an alternative comparative measure of the importance of the household offices is given by the composition of his wagon train. The

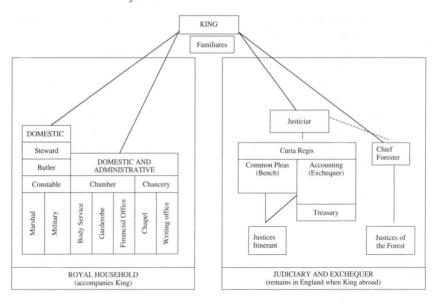

Figure 5.1 Diagram of governmental structure under Henry II.

largest of the wagons was the 'long-cart' which carried the king's personal goods and valuables which formed the core of the chamber and the wardrobe. When the long-cart was not used, three smaller carts ('carette') pulled by one horse each were used. The kitchen needed one or two carettes whilst the other branches of the household of butlery, 'dispence' and 'dinerium' only used one. The chapel and the forge went on packhorses. On average the wagon train travelled twenty miles a day (Jolliffe 1963: 141). Noblemen and important churchmen such as archbishops or bishops also had their own households and attempted to emulate the structure of the royal household, though their success depended on their wealth and status.

During the course of the twelfth century the household offices became more defined and by the end of Henry II's reign the association between departments can be described using a diagram (see Figure 5.1, adapted from Warren 1983: 307) which, although simplified, is helpful in understanding the system.

Whilst the diagram of the structure of government is logical, it masks the personal nature of the court and government, which saw the government more as a network of men than as a structure of different departments. Even though each was semi-independent there was mobility of staff between them (Warren 1987: 127; Mortimer 1990: 133). Moreover, if the king wanted someone to do something, he could command whom he wanted, independent of the structure. There may also be several men in the same post (especially in the lower echelons, such as constable), or none at all, for after Becket's dismissal no chancellor replaced him for many years. As well as the expertise within the country, in the twelfth century there was also the possibility of administrators rotating between different Norman areas of influence, such as between England, Normandy and Sicily (Haskins 1916: 122; Gillmor 1984: 111).

Even though the structure was potentially chaotic, by the end of the twelfth century there was enough of an independent machinery to continue in the king's absence. Whereas Henry II was seen to have played a great part in the legal and governmental reforms, Richard I's long-term absence from England meant that any administrative changes were made in his absence. When King John came to the throne, the chronicler Roger of Howden wrote that John's accession made little difference to the routine conduct of government (Gillingham 1999a: 12), which had grown too large for the king to control or watch every aspect of its workings. Even so, the notion remained that all the workings of government were directed by the king, so even the exchequer was not seen as a separate office, but rather as a special session of the king's court convened twice a year. When justices journeyed into the shires to judge cases in Henry II's reign and later, they did not hold independent sessions of court, rather they brought the king's writ out into the provinces (Warren 1987: 128).

The justices who were sent out into the provinces on defined circuits (the circuits were called 'eyres') were just one way in which the king could make his authority felt. The most direct way was for the king to command that an individual or group follow an action by issuing a writ. As well as a direct order, the king could issue a writ to find out the truth of a case. If a lord failed to act, the sheriff might be directed to enforce the king's writ, and if that failed the king's own advisers might be called upon as the most powerful nobles in the land (Chibnall 1986: 176). Charters were a way for the king to grant or confirm landholding. However, until King John's reign there was no attempt by royal government to keep copies of writs or charters and therefore collections have to be pieced together from the remaining copies in private hands, a long and laborious process. A remarkable recent achievement is the edited collection of 'acta' issued by William the Conqueror (Bates 1998).

The growth of the administrative records was part of a longer-term trend in the twelfth century of the written word becoming important as proof of transactions. Society increasingly moved away from an oral, memory-based culture to one where there was more emphasis upon the written word as proof. This process is well shown by the attempts of monks and churchmen to write down what they thought, or remembered, to be true, which often resulted in blatant forgeries (Clanchy 1993). Earlier in the twelfth century the beginnings of the trend can be seen by the increase in written charters produced by the chancery. Between the thirty-four years from 1066 to 1100 there were only approximately 490 charters (Newman 1988: 19), though of course there was the magnificent Domesday Book. In comparison, in the following thirty-five years of Henry I's reign, Newman identified three categories of documents: surveys, exchequer records and chancery documents – the chancery alone produced over 1,520 charters.

The scale of government documentary activity rose continually through the twelfth century and beyond, except during the disruption of war. Two particularly sharp rises in government record-keeping came in the later years of the twelfth century. The first major leap forward came in the 1170s when duplicate records of 'fines' (i.e. promises to pay the king in return for his granting of land or other favours) were kept. The second advance occurred in 1195 when the justiciar, Hubert Walter, ordered that a third copy of a fine be made for the treasury, the first of which was written on 15 July 1195. Extracts were then sent to the exchequer to be copied and 'enrolled' (i.e. sewn together end to end on sheets of parchment and rolled up and stored). When Hubert Walter became chancellor (1199–1205) the keeping of almost all administrative documents became commonplace. For the first time historians can begin to see the intricate workings of government. Documents kept included charters (transcriptions of which were sewn together into rolls – hence the name Charter Rolls – from the first year of John's reign), Patent Rolls (from the third year of John's reign), grants and authorisations by the king ('letters patent') and instructions to officials ('letters close'). By the end of the twelfth and early thirteenth centuries the English administrative system was the most impressive in Europe (Warren 1987: 126).

In conjunction with the rapid escalation of records, the complexity of government increased. By 1200 the business of the exchequer had grown so much that the officers in the king's household had to have permanent deputies at Westminster and communication was by written instruction and memoranda. The amount of business also increased the length of time of business, so that an Easter session of the exchequer could continue until August and the Michaelmas session continued from September to March. The formal business of government departments was becoming a year-round routine.

The two main household offices were the chancery and the chamber, which were overseen by the chancellor and the chamberlain respectively. In the list of 'The Establishment of the King's Household' the chancellor is the most senior official and as such he received the greatest daily allowance. The chancellor – in theory at least – kept the Great and Exchequer seals and copies of the records sealed with them. However, by the end of the twelfth century the sealing of documents was usually delegated to subordinates (Vincent 1993: 105). The importance of the function of sealing documents can be seen by the reference in the 'The Establishment of the King's Household' to Robert 'of the Seal' who was the keeper of the seal in the chancery throughout Henry's reign. The expansion of the office meant that by King John's reign the king needed a personal seal and so he had his own private – or 'privy' – seal, with which to authenticate documents. By the use of this seal the king was able to bypass the chancery completely if the need arose.

The best known chancellor of the twelfth century was Thomas Becket before his appointment as Archbishop of Canterbury. Following Becket's martyrdom many accounts of his life and death were written which included details of his role as chancellor. William FitzStephen described in some detail Becket's duties: he had custody of the seal, which in turn meant that he signed and sealed documents, he was in charge of the arrangements and order of the royal chapel, and he kept charge of all the vacant archbishoprics, bishoprics, abbeys and baronies which fell into the king's hands (Staunton 2001: 48–53). The chancellor was also critical within the exchequer, being 'next in importance' to the treasurer in all exchequer business (Johnson 1950: 34). The chancellor was a key man in the king's court whom the king could trust. Henry II sent Becket to Paris to negotiate and Becket was also a leader on the military campaign to Toulouse. Yet despite the importance of Becket, once he had left the post there was no position of chancellor for ten years, which shows how a man could rise through the ranks carving out his own position, when in effect there was no permanent role there, especially as document production and administration were continued by more junior royal clerks. Whilst Becket's biographers indicate that the position was one of great importance, two other chancellors, Ralph de Warneville and Henry II's son Geoffrey, made very little impact on the administration on the kingdom. It is likely that Ralph and Geoffrey viewed the post as one in which to make a profit, rather than the great administrative role that Becket considered it (Mortimer 1990: 131).

Chancery was for the writing of records, but at a cost. The king expected a payment if he granted a charter, and a further payment was expected if a document was written out confirming the grant. It is possible that a reduction was allowed for those people who provided their own parchment and scribe to write out the charter (Mason 1998: 138). A scale of charges during John's reign has survived because the chancellor, Hubert Walter, lessened the charges to those of Henry II's reign. A simple confirmation (i.e. copying an existing charter) with nothing added resulted in a payment to the chancellor of a mark (two-thirds of a pound), a 'bisancius' each for the vice-chancellor and the protonotary, and one shilling for the wax used. For a new charter the costs soared. The chancellor received a mark of gold or 10 marks, and to the vice-chancellor and 'protonotharius' a silver mark each, with a charge of 5 shillings for wax. There was therefore a degree of categorisation of document writing to reflect the work involved, and also to produce a profit for the chancellor (Mortimer 1990: 131).

Even though potentially expensive, the chancery was open to anyone who could afford it and even soon after the Conquest it was not unusual for small landowners to obtain a royal writ. One such was Modbert who, shortly before 1120, produced a royal writ to support his case against the Cathedral Priory of Bath (Hudson 1990: 77). Even though he produced a royal writ judgement went against him, which probably shows that he had just paid for, and received, a writ, without the details of the case being investigated at the time. The writing of documents was a function of the chancery, but the alternative was for the beneficiary to write their own after royal assent to an action had been given. This option was frequently carried out, especially after the Norman Conquest, by monasteries who had their own scribes (Bates 1998: 97).

The scribes working for the king were based in the scriptorium (writing chamber), at first overseen by the chancellor but by the end of Henry I's reign there was a master of the writing chamber. He was in charge of a number of chaplains or clerks who worked either in the scriptorium or the chapel. However, the king did not have a monopoly of scribes and they could move around, both within government and beyond. As well as by the chancery, scribes were used by the treasury to keep financial records, by the justices in eyre and sheriffs who required records to be kept, and, outside government, by nobles and the church (Mortimer 1990: 133). T. A. M. Bishop was a pioneer in the field of tracing scribes by identifying traits within their handwriting. He identified the hand writing of a large number of scribes and so could piece together their careers (Bishop 1961; Mortimer 1990: 120). One scribe (CIV) shows the range of employment he undertook. He began his work in the chancery during the reign of Henry I, then during the Anarchy became a scribe for Matilda, before later joining the service of Archbishop Theodore (Mortimer 1990: 128). However, the chancery and its scribes dominated the output of royal writings, and increasingly through Henry II's reign came to dominate the writing in all walks of life, especially of writs. The only real alternative was the ecclesiastical scriptoria of cathedrals or monasteries which mainly produced their own documents, but for the layman the chancery was more popular (Mortimer 1990: 124).

The chamber was the heart of the king's finances and was responsible for the payments connected with the king's household, whether the day-to-day or for exceptional expenditure as in warfare. As the king moved through his domains the chamber drew upon treasure stored in treasuries scattered at strategic locations across the kingdom. Throughout the twelfth century the most important treasury was at Winchester, and in Henry II's reign there were also castle treasuries in Gloucester, Colchester, Salisbury, Oxford and Guildford, as well as scattered through his Continental lands. The chamber records survive from King John's reign, but are known to have been compiled from the eleventh century. The lack of twelfth-century records means that the true role and scale of the chamber then cannot be assessed. During times of war the chamber would have handled very large sums of money but the lack of records means that the chamber has been forced into the background behind the abundance of records connected with the English, and then later Norman, exchequers.

Associated with the chancery were the exchequers, one based in England and the other in Normandy. From these two exchequers large quantities of material have survived, from 1154 in the case the English Pipe Rolls (with one in 1129–30). In Normandy the first surviving exchequer rolls date from

1180, though the system was instigated earlier, possibly in 1176 or the 1160s (Green 1989a; Moss 1994: 186–8). These records dominate analysis, and simply by their preservation can falsely given the impression of greater importance. As Gillingham stated 'compared with the chamber, the exchequers of England and Normandy were merely useful auxiliaries' (Gillingham 1994b: 51–2).

Some details of the treasuries have survived. The physical keeping of the treasure was the responsibility of the chamberlains or the treasurer, both of whom were household officers. The treasure could be moved around between England and Normandy and often followed the army (later King John moved the treasure around the country with disastrous effect as it sank in the Wash). In the early twelfth century Robert Mauduit was the chamberlain to the exchequer and owned Porchester, a necessary staging point on the way to Southampton from where treasure was to be carried across the Channel (Mason 1976). During the early thirteenth century, however, the chamber gradually lost its role of transporting and keeping the treasure which accompanied the king and a new department formed called the wardrobe. The personal nature of the treasury is shown by an account from the Scottish court: Queen Margaret pilfered coins from the treasury for charitable causes, whereupon the king, who greatly loved this type of trick, would lead her to mock justice (Huneycutt 1990: 85). The treasury also meant power. William Rufus personally viewed his treasury at Winchester, which not only contained gold and silver, but also purple cloths and gems (Swanton 2000: 222) and after Rufus's death, Henry immediately seized the treasury at Winchester before claiming the crown.

The physical location of the king's treasure did not equate with the king's exchequer however, and early in the twelfth century there is the first evidence that annual accounts were being calculated from Winchester. This grouping of administrators was known as the exchequer from the chequered tablecloth upon which were columns for pounds, shillings and pence. There was also a 'zero' column, which got round the problems faced when using the Roman system of counting, which does not have a symbol for zero. The system rapidly developed into a sophisticated system which effectively kept track of the finances from across the country (Chibnall 1986: 125–7).

By the mid-1120s the title of treasurer was beginning to be applied, and like other offices the position was practically hereditary – Roger of Salisbury, then his nephew Nigel, and then his son Richard fitz Nigel were all in effect court treasurers. Richard fitz Nigel wrote the famous treatise the 'Dialogue of the Exchequer' which was the first book describing administration in Europe (Johnson 1950).

The office of chamberlain was created to keep the treasury but by the middle of the twelfth century the office had diverse financial powers and responsibilities. Details of the FitzGerald family, who were for a while hereditary chamberlains, have been unearthed (Vincent 1998: 233). When Henry II came to the throne he officially made Warin FitzGerald his chamberlain. Interestingly, Warin had been with Henry previously, but then joined King Stephen before returning to Henry when Henry became king. The fact that Henry lavished lands upon Warin has given rise to the suggestion that Warin was a 'plant' within King Stephen's camp (Vincent 1998: 233), but equally it may be that both Stephen and Henry valued his knowledge. Whatever Warin's motives, his cross-over between the kings meant that there was a continuation within at least a part of the administration. Under Henry II, Warin's duties as chamberlain included being part of the hearings about the liberties of Battle Abbey, receiving money from the City of London, paying the king's knights and huntsmen and overseeing the expenses of the queen in Hampshire. After Warin's death *c.*1158–9 he was succeeded by his brother Henry. Henry witnessed charters, accounted for the finances of a royal manor, went to the Pope as part of the king's envoy in 1164, paid the king's knights in Kent and levied fines and amercements in Kent along with royal justices (Vincent 1998: 238).

As well as the officers responsible for the chancery and the chamber, there were other important servants to the king. The steward (dapifer) was the principal officer of the hall. He looked after the king's needs and so tended to be well rewarded by the king. Eudo fitz Hubert was, in turn, steward for William the Conqueror, William Rufus and Henry I, and acquired lands in over ten counties (Vincent 1998: 243). During Henry I's reign there were probably four stewards who served in rotation (Green 1989a: 35). The butler was responsible for the butlery or wine stores (the name is a corruption of the French for bottle *bouteille*). Within the list of 'The Establishment of the Household' the keepers of the wine barrels and the keeper of the wine butt come under the general heading of the butlery. It was the marshal's job to organise the king's horses and stables, a vital job for a king always on the move.

The role of the individual and family in government

Yet, for all the offices of state, in the last resort responsibility fell to those whom the king could trust. The personal element of patronage cannot be overstated. The king's patronage could rise a man of humble beginnings to the very highest position of power, but equally the lack of patronage could mean the loss of power and influence. Men in all ranks of society could rise or fall on a whim of the king or powerful noble. Roger of Salisbury, one of the most powerful bishops and courtiers in Henry I's court, was elevated by the king, who favoured him initially because of the speed with which he said the Mass as a parish priest. Gilbert Strongbow was also given rapid advancement by King Stephen, so much so that between 1135 and 1138 he rose from a poor knight to earl (Ward 1988: 274). When Henry I died the royal treasure was personally supervised by Robert of Gloucester, his favourite royal bastard, rather than being housed in the royal treasuries of Winchester or Rouen. The reverse of this was that individuals could fall rapidly out of royal favour, in which case social isolation and financial poverty could be the result.

The role of individual families was an important one, for many families held the same position through different generations. The power of Roger of Salisbury's family through the generations has already been seen in the exchequer. A second example is where three brothers, Payn, Eustace and William Fitz John all held posts in Henry I's government. Payn Fitz John's duty was to serve Henry I with wine every night, should the king so wish (James *et al.* 1983: 440). Payn became an itinerant judge, may have been a sheriff of Shropshire and Herefordshire, and was a frequent attendee at Henry I's court. William was an itinerant judge in the west for Henry I and probably in Normandy for Henry II. The third son Eustace worked with Walter Espec in Yorkshire, Northumberland, Carlisle and Westmorland, and heard pleas in Durham. Their work took them the length and breadth of England and between them they could give information about all areas except the south-east and East Anglia. Moreover, it is likely that each helped the other to progress as there are several charters were they all witnessed together (Dalton 1996). A final example is that of the FitzGerald family, based in Windsor, who focused on stewardship. Positions held by the family included steward to: Queen Adeliza, widow of Henry I; Queen Eleanor of Aquitaine, queen of Henry II; the monks of Bury St Edmunds; and the bishopric of St David's in Wales (Vincent 1998: 248). These three examples could be replicated many times between different families, and the role would have been made easier for subsequent members to follow as there would be guidance and help within the family to further the career of siblings or future generations.

Absence of the king, family members and the justiciar

The Norman Conquest meant that the ruler of England also had lands across the Channel and several kings, notably William the Conqueror, Henry I, Henry II and Richard spent large amounts of time away from England. For the country to continue to be administered, individuals were given powers to complement the king's own. Family members played an important part in running the country during the king's absence. During William the Conqueror's reign there were well-organised methods for the delegation of authority, usually to other family members such as William's half-brother Odo of Bayeux, or nobles such as William FitzOsbern (Green 1982: 138). The opposite could also occur when the king was in England and in the case of William the Conqueror the vacuum in Normandy was filled by William's queen, Matilda, with the help of other family members, such as her son Robert Curthose, or powerful nobles such as Roger of Montgomery. How much separate power the regents had is debatable, as they may simply have put into effect orders from William (Bates 1981: 6, 8). Other powerful queens could also wield regency powers. There is evidence that Henry I's

Queen Matilda and Henry II's Queen Eleanor also held regency powers whilst their husbands were away – a large number of writs issued in the name of Eleanor shows her importance in the rule of the country (Bates 1981: 11).

The second group who were given powers in the king's absence were important nobles, but it seems likely that rather than having regency powers, they were given heightened powers of government, which in turn led to the evolution of the governmental administration. An example of such a noble is Roger of Salisbury who was in charge of a group of administrators based on the exchequer, but although he had great power, it was less than the regency powers of a family member (Bates 1981: 12).

Following Henry II's accession to the English throne there was a change in attitude towards appointing family members as regents. Increasingly, Henry looked to people within the administration to appoint both as a royal deputy who was not a member of the royal family and as a permanent head of the exchequer when he was not in the country. As Henry II's reign progressed, the power of regent became regularly devolved to a justiciar who was not part of the royal family (West 1966). Why this occurred is debatable. It is possible that Henry did not trust members of his own family, a not unnatural emotion given their rebellious nature, or it may have been implemented as an Angevin reform. However, it came to be such a prominent position, it was a solution to the delegation of authority by the king (Bates 1981: 12). The office, however, had a disjointed history, for after the loss of Normandy in 1204, King John rarely travelled outside England so the need for a justiciar holding regency powers was lessened. Henry III thought the post redundant and abolished it in 1234, but it was remembered as an effective post and its re-establishment was one of the demands of Simon de Montfort during his rebellion of the 1260s. The power of the justiciar in England at the end of the twelfth century was probably unique in Europe, for although the term 'justiciar' was used elsewhere, for example in Ireland and Brittany, a careful analysis of the usage of the word indicates that the position in other areas was one of 'principal royal agents' rather than holding the powers of regent (Everard 1997: 87).

The church and administration

The king was the fount of all law, security and military action, but in England through the twelfth century there was often a vigorous debate about the role of the church in governing England. A particularly fierce exponent that the king and archbishop ruled side by side was Anselm, Archbishop of Canterbury. Anselm used the analogy of a plough drawn by both men, the king who ruled by secular justice and the archbishop who ruled by divine doctrine and teaching. Unsurprisingly, this approach was anathema to William Rufus and he accused Anselm repeatedly of 'robbing the king of the jewel of his sovereignty', an accusation Rufus and his barons made at the Council of Rockingham (25–8 February 1095) (Vaughn 1993: 249). The argument reached a climax with the struggle between Thomas Becket, Archbishop of Canterbury, and Henry II. In the Constitutions of Clarendon in 1164 Henry declared that the crown and the secular courts were the overriding legal system in the kingdom, a declaration passionately disputed by Becket.

Even though there was often serious dispute between the church and crown the clergy were an important group at court. During the reign of William Rufus, the abbots from the major Benedictine monasteries regularly attended the court (Mason 1998: 139). It was also the clergy from the court that produced the majority of bishops between 1066 and 1216. It has been calculated that of the 136 bishops consecrated between 1066 and 1216 seventy-four came from court circles and many of the remaining number became part of the king's circle after they were elected. A figure of 60 per cent has been calculated of bishops who were committed royalists, more often than not taking the king's side in disputes (Walker 1982: 220).

However, the pattern of appointment was not a uniform one: William the Conqueror, William Rufus and Henry I made a large number of episcopal appointments from court circles, whereas Stephen made few and Henry II tended to favour drawing the bishops into the court after they had been appointed (Walker 1982: 221). Sometimes the links between the crown and a bishop were personal: King Stephen's brother was Henry of Blois, the powerful and influential Bishop of Winchester, and Henry II's illegitimate son, Geoffrey, was made Archbishop of York.

The ecclesiastical link with the court was important for the government and control of the country. William the Conqueror, Rufus and Henry I all had need of able men who could effectively rule their territories in the provinces. Furthermore, the bishops were a powerful, usually unified, group within their own right who could command respect. Coming from court they could also usually be trusted to side with the king, though in the case of Thomas Becket, who was Henry II's chancellor, this spectacularly backfired.

Along with the ecclesiastics were the laymen of the court who were called 'curiales'. The term covers a huge range of status, from great barons to minor administrators. Many of the curiales were given appointments across the country, whether as sheriffs or castellans, which gave them tremendous power within a local radius and a power base on which to build. By the end of the twelfth century many former curiales had reached baronial status and their local or regional wealth and prestige meant that they could further their prospects by marrying into the families with older titles and wealth (Mason 1979: 118).

Rule of the provinces: sheriffs

Arguably it was the Norman kings who permanently extended the rule of the king throughout England. The Anglo-Saxon system of powerful regional earls resulted in the Anglo-Saxon kings often having limited power if they were not strong enough to impose their will. Sheriffs were used in Anglo-Saxon administration (the term sheriff derives from the Anglo-Saxon *scir gerefa* or 'shire reeve') but they were held in check by the greater authority of the Anglo-Saxon earls. The earls were powerful enough to subordinate even the bishops in the various courts. Following the Norman Conquest William took up and extended the system of Anglo-Saxon sheriffs across England. But the Conquest also changed the nature of the sheriffs from a meagre landholder with moderate power into one of the most powerful secular positions in the shires. By the end of the Conqueror's reign it was the sheriffs who were powerful, and the Anglo-Saxon earls were becoming a distant memory.

The backgrounds of the new sheriffs varied. Initially some were from the Anglo-Saxon regime such as Edric of Wiltshire, Tofi of Somerset, Swawold in Oxfordshire and Edmund in Hertfordshire. In some cases it is, at present, impossible to know whether sheriffs such as Gamel, son of Osbern, the first Sheriff of Yorkshire (1066–8), were a new creation or a continuation of Anglo-Saxon tradition. After the great rebellions of 1069–71 the pendulum swung towards favouring men from across the channel, though some Englishmen (to judge by their names) did continue, such as Alwine or Agelwine the Sheriff of Warwickshire witnessed a charter purportedly dated to 1072, and other sheriffs may have married Englishwomen, such as Ivo Taillebois, Sheriff of Lincoln. Alternatively, some sheriffs may have had mixed-race parents, such as William Malet, the first Norman Sheriff of Yorkshire, who may have had an English mother (Green 1982: 131–2).

However, it was sheriffs from across the Channel who dominated the local power in the shires. After the Conquest, William the Conqueror only chose sheriffs who were Norman, with the exception of the Sheriff of Surrey, Ansculf of Picquigny, which shows that William was obviously cautious of putting Bretons, Frenchmen or Flemings into such key posts (Green 1982: 138). Some sheriffs such as Urse d'Abetot and Robert d'Oilly seem to have been connected with the households of William the Conqueror and William Rufus. However, in most cases no information is known about the background of the sheriffs during William Rufus's and Henry I's reigns, indicating that the sheriffs rapidly rose in status by royal patronage from humble origins. This had the advantage that a sheriff's power was not combined with the great wealth of a magnate, which would have made a sheriff virtually unassailable in a county – a few joining together would have been a dangerous threat (Green 1982: 138–40).

Some sheriffs had terrible reputations in their localities. Two in particular were mentioned by chroniclers: Urse d'Abetot, Sheriff of Worcester, and Picot, Sheriff of Cambridgeshire. The author of the *Liber Eliensis*, written at Ely Abbey, could hardly find language sufficiently vituperative of Picot: 'ravening wolf, cunning fox'. When Picot was accused of robbing St Etheldreda, the virgin saint of Ely of her lands, and by extension the lands of Ely, Picot contemptuously replied 'Etheldreda, who is that Etheldreda of whom you speak' (Green 1982: 129). The sheriffs could easily abuse their position, and in 1076 or 1077 William the Conqueror set up a commission to look into their power which brought them more firmly into the king's orbit, a trend which was continued by kings thereafter. However, whilst some sheriffs may have overstepped the mark, the policy of William the Conqueror in appointing sheriffs of high calibre, with extensive powers and military knowledge over a wide geographical area, was an important part of the success of the Conquest (Green 1982: 129).

The duties and functions of a sheriff were numerous. They were responsible for the royal finances in the shires, executed royal justice, controlled the shire courts and the hundred courts, and were responsible for military matters such as raising local levies, keeping castles and organising local defence, as well as administering royal estates. As well as these general duties the sheriffs were expected to perform a whole host of other tasks. In 1074 *The Anglo-Saxon Chronicle* recorded that Edgar the Ætheling journeyed from Scotland to William in Normandy 'And the sheriff of York came to meet them at Durham and went all the way with them . . . until they got overseas to the king (Swanton 2000: 210).

Sometimes sheriffs could hold two or more positions at once. The pattern of holding more than one shrievalty was especially marked during Henry I's reign when Hugh of Buckland may have held as many as eight counties, and Richard Basset and Aubrey de Vere jointly held eleven between them (Green 1982: 134).

Family ties were also important, either through marriage or from father to son (though not usually directly). Ivo Taillebois' father Ralph was sheriff of at least two counties, and Ralph's niece married Ranulph, brother of Ilger, a future Sheriff of Huntingdonshire (Green 1982: 133). In Yorkshire son following father was not an uncommon occurrence, for example William de Stuteville (sheriff in 1201–3) was the son of Robert de Stuteville (sheriff in 1170–5), and Ansketil was sheriff from *c*.1115–28/9 and his son Bertram de Bulmer was sheriff 1128/9–30 (Ormrod 2000).

The turnover of sheriffs in office also varied and whilst many seem to have held the position for life, the holding of the position was at the king's pleasure and so sheriffs could be – and were – dismissed. The turnover of sheriffs between 1066 and 1086 was high, though in Henry I's reign the turnover rate dropped as he kept his more experienced officers in place (Green 1982: 133). The pattern under Henry II was one of remarkable stability, though the Inquest of Sheriffs in 1170 marked a change in policy. The Inquest revealed widespread abuses: twenty sheriffs were dismissed and only six remained in office (Heiser 1997: 7–8). Henry II initially had favoured sheriffs from the baronial classes, but after 1170 they were much more likely to be recruited from royal service. Once again the sheriffs were wholly dependent upon royal patronage. The inquiry was also supposed to cover 'archbishops, bishops, abbots, earls, barons, sub-tenants, knights, citizens and burgesses, their stewards and servants'. Only a few fragments of the

Inquest have survived, but in concept it rivalled any medieval administrative document and it would have been one of the glories of a very efficient and comprehensive administration of the twelfth century.

Richard I followed a very different policy and even though he was out of England, 'there are good grounds for believing that Richard played a substantial part in the appointment of sheriffs' (Heiser 1997: 7). Richard favoured a rapid turnover of sheriffs – sixty-five in total in a ten-year period (1189–99) – predominantly because of his constant need for money. Offices could be bought and in 1194, for the only time in England's history, the Archbishop of York, Geoffrey Plantagenet, bought the shrievalty of Yorkshire for 3,000 marks, thereby combining the two offices (Ormrod 2000).

The court system

The Anglo-Saxon court structure was well established and the Normans continued to use the basic system, though the new large estates, called 'honours', of the conquering nobles also had their own courts which cut across the ancient and geographic units of the Anglo-Saxon system. As well as these courts there was also a system of ecclesiastical courts (see below). The lay court system had been outlined in the law codes of King Edgar (I Edgar 1 and III Edgar 5) (Whitelock 1979: 433) which specified regular meetings of the courts: shire courts met twice a year, borough courts three times and hundred courts twelve times (Fleming 1994: 113). The same regularity is given in *The Laws of Henry I*, with the shire meeting twice a year, the hundred or wapentake twelve times a year, though the borough court was reduced to twice a year (Downer 1996: 101). The lowest level of court was the vill (roughly equivalent to a village) or the lord's manor court. Vills were grouped into four and between them were responsible for local law and order including the pursuit of criminals, known as hue and cry. The manor court allowed the lord to police his own territories, and gain revenue from them.

The hundred court has been called the 'maid of all work' (Loyn 1994: 98) in late Anglo-Saxon and Norman England. (A hundred was originally the area of land needed to support 100 warriors and their families.) It was this court that was the most relevant court to the vast majority of the population of England for it was where routine matters of justice were settled, whether boundary disputes, tithes or cattle theft. *The Laws of Henry I* state that attendance at the court was to include the 'lord, his steward and the priest and the reeve and the most substantial men' (Downer 1996: 99–101).

The next level up from the hundred courts were the shire courts, held twice a year. These were much grander occasions than the relatively humble hundred courts. The shire courts have been defined as 'great formal semi-political occasions, controlled and dominated by the crown' (Loyn 1994: 98). *The Laws of Henry I* give those who should attend as 'bishops, earls, sheriffs, deputies, hundredmen, aldermen, stewards, reeves, barons, vavassors, village reeves, and other lords of lands' (Downer 1996: 99) and it should meet at fixed times and at appointed places. Presumably, however, neighbouring counties would hold courts at different times to allow landlords who held land in both to attend.

The system of vill, manor, hundred and shire courts covered the vast majority of England but within this structure were the borough courts established within the more important towns. At first it was common for sheriffs to rule over the towns and preside over the borough courts. However, as the twelfth century progressed it became more common for the citizens to buy their freedom from the sheriffs control and to maintain their own courts without interference, though this was dependent upon the citizens paying a large annual sum to the king.

At the top of the hierarchy of justice sat the king, and his ability to make laws and impose his will was recognised by all. *The Laws of Henry I* state 'over and above everything stand the pleas of the royal court, which preserves the use of custom of its law at all times and in all places and with constant uniformity' (Downer 1996: 109). This statement explicitly makes the king not only the highest authority of the land, but also ties the royal authority into the Common Law (i.e. custom). In Anglo-Saxon England the king was a protector to the unprotected and this continued after the Conquest (Garnett 1985: 118). The king remained the protector of those who lay outside the normal 'web of lordship' or had no obvious kin, for example those in 'holy orders, strangers, poor people and those who have been cast out, if they have no one else to take care of them', and the king also had jurisdiction over highways and gallows (Loyn 1992: 18; Downer 1996: 109).

By Henry I's reign the authority of the king had reached into every court in the land and true autonomy of lordship may hardly have existed anywhere, except perhaps the border areas. Elsewhere both the hundred and the shire courts were accustomed to receive the royal writs (Hyams 1981: 83). Even in small disputes there was the strong possibility of the king's direct involvement, which had to be taken into consideration by the participants. The Pipe Roll of 1130 shows individual claimants appealing to the king (Hudson 1990: 77).

Even though the structure existed, there was no compulsion of fairness. In fact the mere presence of the lord, his steward, priest or reeve at a hundred court would probably force the decision in the lord's favour. Even if the lord had no personal concern in the judgement, he would still be looking for some sort of financial reward for the privilege of holding the court. It is perhaps for this reason that the author of *The Laws of Henry I* wrote that 'the vexations of secular legal proceedings are beset by wretched anxieties of such number and multitude, and are enveloped in so many fraudulences, that these processes and the quite unpredictable hazard of the courts seem rather things to be avoided' (Downer 1996: 99). Part of the reason for the hazardous nature of the courts was the role of the judge who was basically the king's or local lord's man. The judge was rarely an impartial observer, and those who were, were commended as such by various chroniclers. At a local level the judge was answerable to the local lord, who had put him into position, and at a higher level he was answerable to the king. As such the courts were never truly 'independent' but some had more royal involvement than others, which steadily increased after the Conquest.

Justice was both a source of substantial revenue and power, and the hundred courts were prizes well worth having control of. Generally the king gained all profits from justice within the hundred court but a substantial minority of courts were in private ownership. Before the Conquest figures for private ownership of hundred courts are difficult to determine, but after the Conquest nearly a quarter (about 150) of the hundred courts were in private hands. A lord or church who owned such a court controlled, and gained profit from, all justice within the hundred. Monastic houses such as Ely, Bury St Edmunds and Peterborough owned many hundred courts, sometimes scattered over a large area and there were also the concentrated areas of control by monasteries: the Abbot of St Albans possessed the nearby hundred of Cashio and its court (Loyn 1994: 98).

In Norman times the kings increasingly became involved in local issues and placed their own men, whether sheriffs or abbots or courtiers, within the court structure so that they could keep control of sensitive issues, and gain more revenue. The courts were also there to keep the peace (whether the king's or the local lord's) and to make sure their wishes were followed. In this way the king or lord could determine the outcome of trials or prosecutions.

The mechanisms of justice rested on a few documents in the Anglo-Saxon period, the most important of which was the writ. Whereas writs written by Anglo-Saxon kings seem to have been confirmation of a previous decision, after the Conquest they were used to make explicit the king's wishes to summon assemblies or courts to remedy disputes. From the Anglo-Saxon king's previous role of laissez-faire, the Conqueror and subsequent kings took more and more of a role in local communities and politics (Fleming 1994: 116). Following the Conqueror's lead, Rufus continued to impose his will by writ. Although the local courts had some remaining independence, the king's writ could now mandate the holding of county courts, investigate certain claims and determine the final resolution of complaints. Since the Conquest the king had gained an important foothold into the county and local court structure.

It was a dramatic change. As if to dispel any doubt in 1086 William the Conqueror gave the most powerful indication possible that he was interested in local communities by having Domesday Book compiled which listed every piece of land in England. By William's death even small amounts of land were signalled to be the concern of the king, as shown by the painstaking collection of information about landholdings throughout England.

The workings of the courts are shrouded in mystery for large periods of the twelfth century, but Fleming (1994) has analysed the workings of the courts in relation to the composition of Domesday Book. A basic source of information (though not the only one) was local knowledge, acquired for Domesday by the testimony of jurors, of whom 158 are known for Hertfordshire and Cambridgeshire. Where these men have been identified, they were minor tenants who presumably therefore had a detailed local knowledge. Although it is possible they could have been swayed in their testimony, especially if many jurors were under one lord, they had to swear a powerful oath to tell the truth, and perjury was heavily fined.

Punishments for crimes ranged from minor fines to mutilation or death. The death penalty (usually by hanging) was not uncommon. As well as the king's justices having the power to hang, so could lords or churches who owned their own courts and gallows. Mutilation was used for lesser crimes. Henry I had the hands cut off the moneyers who had minted counterfeit money (Swanton 2000: 255). Castration was used as a punishment for sexual crimes. The man who made the nun of Watton pregnant was castrated as a punishment (see Chapter 6) and blinding was a punishment for treachery (Chibnall 1997: 38).

The use of prisons was known and there are many references to enemies being imprisoned in the dungeon of a castle. The Constitutions of Clarendon imply that some counties had prisons. Monasteries too could have cells, and at Lewes a monastic prison cell has been discovered under the lavatorium (Anderson 1988: 9). Walter Map too describes a monk being put into iron bolts and left alone in the deepest dungeon for eloping with a wealthy widow and stealing the church's possessions. Map further describes the monk's conditions: that he changed his previous life of 'wine with water, his food with hunger, his excesses with a meagre diet, and to pay for his fine raiment with nakedness, for the softness of his bed with the roughness of the sand' (James *et al.* 1983: 325).

Ecclesiastical courts

The law of the church, Canon Law, rapidly developed between 1066 and 1215, as did the role of the church courts. Church courts had jurisdiction over two main areas: the morals and faith of the lay population, and second the clergy and church property. Before the Norman Conquest there is considerable evidence that ecclesiastical cases were heard in the lay courts of the shire and hundred. Following the Conquest there was an attempt to separate the lay and religious courts. In 1072 (though there is some dispute about the date) William the Conquerer commanded that 'no bishop or archdeacon shall henceforth hold pleas relating to the episcopal laws in the hundred court' and anyone brought to trial under episcopal laws 'shall come to the place which the bishop shall choose and name' (Douglas and Greenaway 1981: 657–8). By 1100 there is evidence of a separate jurisdiction for the church, though the exact nature of the courts is difficult to determine. Brett has suggested that during the reign of Henry I there were three broad classes of ecclesiastical court (Brett 1975: 152–61): first an assembly at which a bishop pronounced judgement, second when a bishop gave a judgement in chapter, and third in synod.

The law

On William's arrival at Hastings the law of England was not in existence as a codified, organised body of law, rather it was a patchwork of customs and conventional practices which were still being formed, moulded or being made into hard-and-fast rules that had been built up over the centuries (Holt 1997: 118). The vast majority was case law where individual cases had been settled which, given the sanction of a judgement, had become law. Length of time was a critical issue in the acceptance of common laws. A later definition from Edward I's reign (1272–1307) described a 'long custom' as ten or twenty years, 'very long' custom as thirty years and 'age old' custom as forty years or longer (Stenton 1965: 26–7).

Over the Anglo-Saxon centuries kings had had law codes written down in their names, but this tradition had effectively ended with Cnut. Even the law code purportedly written by Edward the Confessor (*Leges Edwardi Confessoris*) was in fact written in the early twelfth century and so gives an insight into early twelfth-century laws, rather than the laws of the last Anglo-Saxon king (Downer 1996: 6; Wormald 1999).

The Norman kings also had little interest in issuing laws in their own names – rather it was left to a small group of lawyers to try to disentangle the laws of the kingdom in the early twelfth century. One of the outstanding features of this group was that they had a keen interest in Anglo-Saxon laws. There are two texts surviving which have a pre-eminence amongst the early twelfth-century legal texts. The first is the *Textus Roffensis*, named after Rochester Cathedral where it was made. It has 235 leaves and is in two parts, a legal collection and then the Cathedral's cartulary. The legal material includes important pre-Conquest legislation and some post-Conquest by William the Conqueror ('The Laws of William the Conqueror') and Henry I (Wormald 1994: 243). The second great text is the *Quadripartitus* (Wormald 1994). From this legal collection it can be shown that Anglo-Saxon law codes were reaching early twelfth-century editors, and that, either through travel, discovery or other connections, the author was actively seeking out the texts. He had some powerful connections, such as Gerard, Bishop of Hereford and later Archbishop of York (Wormald 1994: 264).

The *Quadripartus* was an impressive undertaking which attempted to write down in four parts the laws and important documents of the kingdom, but only the first part, the Latin translation of the Anglo-Saxon law codes, was completed. However, it is possible that the other parts have survived in the *Leges Henrici Primi* (*The Laws of Henry I*), which was written by the same man (Downer 1996; Wormald 1999: 465). The modern editor of the *Laws* came to the conclusion that the unknown author was 'probably a minor official . . . a lawyer . . . by training and experience' (Downer 1996: 42) and that he was writing in the reign of Henry I at Winchester. Moreover, the author made a conscious effort to produce a lawyers handbook of laws, stretching back to the earliest Anglo-Saxon law codes of the kings (either copying the texts in *Quadripartus* or using the same source material) to contemporary times. The revival of interest in law and the Anglo-Saxon legal past indicates that for the first time lawyers were trying to codify and write down the current situation as they saw it during the reign of Henry I, which included the confusion of Anglo-Saxon, Norman and regional laws.

The *Leges Henrici Primi* mention distinct legal traditions. There were three basic regional groupings of different laws: 'English law is divided into three parts . . . one is the law of Wessex, another the law of Mercia, and the third the Danelaw' (Downer 1996: 97).

There were also different laws within individual counties, which the *Laws* claimed arose from the the 'rapacity and the evil and hateful practices of lawyers' (Hyams 1981: 81; Downer 1996: 99). Exactly what the differences or similarities were is not clear, or how the traditions worked is not clear either, but they added an overlay of difference between the areas.

Even after a dramatic century of legal change the author – known as Glanvill – writing between 1187 and 1189 complained about the 'confused multitude' of customs, which can be taken to mean that each lordship had different customs. It was from these variations that a uniformity of custom gradually emerged, producing a countrywide common law. However, whilst Glanvill may have been thinking of individual lordships, it is equally possible that he was considering different shire or regional customs. An alternative was that the customs were relatively uniform within strong English areas, or possibly the differences were between those lordships with strong Continental traditions and customs, such as in Yorkshire the Breton honour of Richmond, the Norman Lacies and the Flemish Gants (Hyams 1981: 83).

The influx of Normans and new traditions after the Conquest had an impact upon English law, though the extent of change is a matter of debate. Some of the changes were of emphasis rather than a rewriting of the law codes, for William saw himself as the natural and legal heir to Edward the Confessor. There were some legal innovations, notably trial by battle to resolve disputes and the forest law (see Chapter 7).

Before the Norman Conquest trial by battle was unknown, but after 1066 it was an alternative to the Anglo-Saxon judicial ordeals of trail by hot iron and trial by water. Whereas the judicial ordeals just involved the accused, trial by battle concerned both parties. Trial by water involved ducking the accused (normally men) into cold water to see if they sank or floated, and trial by hot iron (either men or women) involved the holding of a hot iron bar and then determining whether the healing process showed innocence or guilt. There were many determining factors, not least the experience and wishes of the decision makers as to what constituted sinking or floating, or the healing of the hands. The logic behind the Anglo-Saxon ordeals was that, in theory at least, the result showed God's judgement upon the accused. As such, there was a significant involvement by the church and God was invoked in the court room by a series of oaths, sworn on the gospels or relics, or by the priest blessing the iron bar, water or the shield and weapon used in the duel (Bartlett 1986; Kerr *et al.* 1992).

Between 1066 and 1164 there had been little interest by the kings of England in law codes, and any attempt at codification of the law was the work of scholarly individuals. However, in 1164 Henry II issued the Constitutions of Clarendon, which marked a turning point in royal interest in legislation (i.e. codification of the law). Moreover the laws were universal across society, rather than solely aimed at the nobility. The law did not become an aristocratic value system (Teunis 1989: 209). The impulse for such codification may have come from Henry II's Angevin and Continental background, for various commentators have emphasised that the Constitutions of Clarendon resembled similar legislation in France a few years later (Hyams 1981: 85).

In Henry II's subsequent reforms and laws there were three key elements. The first was the widespread use of the jury to decide the outcome of a dispute. However, unlike juries in modern court cases which are chosen because they are impartial, the juries under Henry II were chosen because they were already knowledgeable about the case. Before Henry II's reforms the jury system had had a long history of use in England to determine points of fact, but Henry extended the use of the jury system across a range of legal actions. Initially the jury system ran parallel to the continuing use of the ordeal to determine guilt, but in 1215 the Fourth Lateran Council forbade priests from taking part in ordeals and, without the sanction of the church and the inability to determine God's will, the ordeal withered in importance as a method of deciding guilt. The jury system, which had been growing in popularity as a quick, decisive method of determining truth took over from the ordeal in England.

The second key element in Henry II's reforms was the use of assizes (i.e. legal procedures or actions) which had the power to change customary law. (Unfortunately the word 'assize' has a range of alternative meanings: the sitting or session of a court, or an assessment for taxation. The word 'assessment' derives from the word 'assize'.) The two most important assizes instigated by Henry were the assize of *novel disseisin* and the assize of *mort d'ancestor*. As both concerned the possession of land they (and other less important assizes dealing with possession) were called 'possessory assizes'. The rightful possession of land, called seisin, was one of the most important legal concepts in the twelfth century. Only the king could be legally said to own land, whilst everyone else held land from the king directly or indirectly through lords. The assize of *novel disseisin* was a fast way to try and correct the situation of a lord or claimant physically seizing the land from the tenant, a feature of times of war, as had occurred during the Anarchy of Stephen and Matilda. Even in times of peace there were many opportunities for lands to be seized, as in the case of a lord taking land from a minor.

Before the assize there were various options: reverse the situation (when Henry II came to the throne he tried to reverse the landholding pattern to how it was before the Anarchy) and ordeal. With the assize of *novel disseisin* the jury was set the task of determining simple facts: 'was the plaintiff evicted unjustly and without judgement from an estate of which he was in peaceful possession'. The answer determined the outcome. The assize of *mort d'ancestor* occurred if there was a dispute about the possession of land following a person's death. Again the jury were to answer a series of questions, but *mort d'ancestor* had one big difference: objections could be raised by the sitting tenant, such as that the closest heir was illegitimate, or a villein and so could not hold free land. The raising of objections seems to have been new in English law (Warren 1983: 346). For those who lost their claim of either *novel deseissin* or *mort d'ancestor* there were usually damages and a court fine to pay. Possession, however, was easier to determine than who had the ultimate right to the land and for this reason another assize, called the Grand Assize, was created. Once again a jury was empowered to discover the facts and make the final decision.

The third change was the method of enforcing the new laws by experienced justices travelling around circuits acting on the king's behalf. This system of justices on eyre had been used piecemeal after the Conquest (most notably for the collection of information about Domesday Book), and more expansively by Henry I, but it was during Henry II's reign that the system was developed into a powerful form of government. Royal justices had an impartiality to local forces and imposed not only the king's will but also a more uniform system of law.

One important reason for Henry's reforms was the desire to strengthen the crown after the chaos of the Anarchy between King Stephen and Matilda. On Henry II's accession he rapidly produced a large number of 'acta' to confirm the churches in their possessions and by 1162 there was no cathedral church and only few monasteries which had not acquired Henry II's confirmation of their lands or rights. This had two effects. The first was that Henry stamped his authority onto the ecclesiastical world because by confirming their rights the churches recognised that he was the ultimate source of justice in any secular dispute. The difficulty came when church jurisdiction clashed with royal jurisdiction, a potent mix which resulted in the death of Thomas Becket. As well as the Anarchy, other historians (notably Searle) have pointed to the longer-term economic developments over the twelfth century to explain Henry's legal reforms. As the economic and social conditions changed, there was a growing tension within the underlying tenurial system between tenant and lordlord which needed to be resolved, one result of which was Henry's reforms (Searle 1979: 154).

An important commentator upon these reforms was Professor Milsom. He argued that Henry II was not a far-sighted genius who devised a carefully thought-through procedure and knew of its ramifications, but rather that Henry II was attempting to force the lords to enforce their own customs properly by outlining the correct procedures (Hyams 1981: 79). Milsom and others have argued that Henry achieved the reforms by making small, but far-reaching changes, within the existing framework (Thompson 1993: 222). The progressive incremental approach has also been taken by Holt, who pointed to Henry's dynamism in producing his 'acta' on gaining power (Holt 1997: 290). Furthermore, Hudson has emphasised that the aspirations and actions of Henry I and Henry II were much closer than some historians have thought (Hudson 1990: 80), thereby making Henry II's changes part of a long continuum of the crown acquiring more power for itself. Whether deliberate of not, Milsom further argued that the reforms set in motion a system which undermined baronial justice (Moss 1994: 193).

In contrast, some historians and common lawyers want to re-emphasise that Henry did indeed devise and implement the far-reaching reforms, knowing exactly what he was doing (Thompson 1993: 222). There are even stories of him staying up all night worrying about the precise wording of various laws (Warren 1983: 360) and that he explained his laws to Philip King of France, who listened intently (Hyams 1981: 85).

Once the procedures had been laid down, they could be applied widely by the king through previously autonomous courts and assemblies (Hyams 1981: 79). There was also a uniform system of legal standards and categories, especially concerning land. For the first time the king could enforce a common law to a common set of problems throughout England (Thompson 1993: 235). The king was also able to intervene directly between lords and tenants by citing a universal common law. The crown became not only the ultimate enforcer of the law but tenants could have a direct recourse to the law and if need be the king, thereby bypassing their immediate lord (Thompson 1993: 235). The royal–subject relationship was therefore made much stronger and threatened to bypass the magnates' control over local communities (Turner 1999: 317).

The reforms and changes were popular and the litigants came from a wide social spectrum (Turner 1999: 325). The cases dealt with by the justices in eyre involved local village life as well as the actions of the great lords. At the same time the actions of the justice system between 1194 and 1215 have been called the 'highpoint of royal authority in Medieval England' (Turner 1999: 317) as the king and government moved more and more towards a centralised state. Its ending can be seen in Magna Carta and thereafter with the growth of a council of nobles and Parliament from the thirteenth century onwards. Yet even so, Magna Carta reveals demands for more justice, not less, for example chapter 18 of Magna Carta calls for quarterly visits to the counties by royal justices (Turner 1999: 320).

By the end of the twelfth and into the thirteenth centuries two great codifiers and organisers of the law were at work: Glanvill (Hall 1965) and Bracton. The treatise ascribed to Glanvill is almost certainly not by him and there is no certain knowledge of the author's identity, but the highly ambitious royal minister and later Chief Justiciar, Geoffrey fitzPeter, may have contributed to it. The treatise was written at the end of the reign of Henry II and the issues described in the text reflect the author's interest in Anglo-French custom as administered within the king's lordship for the author has no real concern for non-royal courts, but excels in describing noble custom (Hyams 1981: 81–3). The second writer, Bracton (*c*.1210–68), wrote 'On the Laws and Customs of England' (*De Legibus et Consuetudinibus Angliae*), though it may be that he simply revised the text of others. Hyams argued that whereas Glanvill described noble and royal custom, Bracton described a kind of ideal written, authoritative law for a jurist. Furthermore, as Anglo-Saxon law remained basic to crime and the lower classes, so Bracton included material from the law codes (Hyams 1981: 82).

By the end of the twelfth century the haphazard nature of the description of English law had been codified and changed out of all recognition. The work of Glanvill and Bracton, compared with the fragmentary written *The Laws of Henry I*, shows the huge changes that had swept through the English legal system, from regional customs to an increasing national uniformity based on a fledgling codified system of law.

6 Religion

Between 1066 and 1215 the church grew substantially in power by becoming centralised, with a more defined hierarchy. A person asked in 1066 who the religious authority was might have wavered between the abbot of a local monastery or the bishop for the region and nationally there may have been indecision between the Pope or one of the two archbishops. The person's descendant in 1215 asked the same question would answer with much more certainty: the bishop was the most important religious figure regionally, nationally the Archbishop of Canterbury and internationally the Pope. The church had not only grown in power, but had begun to challenge the crowned heads of Europe. Between 1208 and 1212 the Papal Interdict against King John shut down churches across the kingdom, but in 1212 King John surrendered England to the overlordship of the Pope. The Pope had, temporarily, won the dispute between the King of England and the church, which had been a continuing source of tension throughout the twelfth century.

The power of the church

The power of the church rested upon the belief that through its actions divine vengeance or the gifts of God could be given to an individual. Theoretically the status of the individual did not matter, as the church had potential to help the soul of a peasant or king to heaven, or damn it to hell. Individuals could call upon the saints to act as personal intercessors between the human world and the divine. A saint had the power to influence life itself, whether by healing the sick, raising the dead or, alternatively, causing illness and ruin to an individual.

In order to influence saints or God to bring about divine wrath or displeasure the church had several weapons. The most severe was the rite of excommunication whereby an individual was separated not only from Christian society but also from the spiritual and physical protection of the church. The person was therefore alone and defenceless against the ravages of the devil. God's grace itself was withdrawn and an excommunicate person dying in such a state would be immediately drawn down into hell. A dispute recorded in the *Gesta Stephani* between Miles, Earl of Hereford and Robert, Bishop of Hereford, resulted in the bishop pronouncing:

> The dread sentence of the Church's condemnation, and by the severity of that sentence he so strictly bound all the surrounding region under his authority that it was unlawful to celebrate divine service or lay a body in the ground or plunge it into water or consume it with fire or even move it from the spot where death took place.
>
> (Potter 1955: 104)

Miles, the Earl of Hereford, died when he was shot through the heart whilst out hunting deer on Christmas Eve and the *Gesta Stephani* recorded that he 'perished wretchedly without profit of repentance' and his death as an excommunicate caused others to respect the church more. However, the results of being excommunicated varied. The Pope excommunicated King John and closed down the churches of England as part of a general Interdict. The situation lasted almost four years, but the King seems to have simply disregarded it. A more successful outcome occurred when Archbishop Anselm excommunicated Henry I during Henry's first full military campaign in Normandy: Henry's soldiers defected and his campaign faltered (Hollister 1983: 77).

Religious cursing by the church was also an option. In a famous example the Archbishop of York cursed the Sheriff of Worcestershire, Urse d'Abetot (Mason 1985: 166; for Ireland see Bitel 2000). However, cursing was a last resort when the rule of law broke down, and does not seem to have been effective. During the Anarchy *The Anglo-Saxon Chronicle* has the comment 'The bishops and clergy always cursed [the robbers], but that was nothing to them' (Swanton 2000: 265). Except in times of lawlessness, cursing by the church was generally diminishing by the late eleventh century, possibly because the power of central government increased. There were also a wide range of rituals to call for divine intervention, whether for help or vengeance. One such ritual occurred in 1122 when the monks of Winchester Cathedral complained about their bishop. In their attempts to reverse the current order, they processed backwards counter to the sun with their processional crosses turned upside down (Klukas 1983: 152). Bishop Giffard saw the potency of their actions and immediately conceded to the monks' demands (Greenway 1977: 10–12).

The church therefore had tremendous spiritual power, a power which could influence the soul's journey after death to heaven or hell. In the late eleventh and twelfth centuries these powers were used by the church, and especially the papacy, to become an influential political force across Europe.

The papacy, reforms and England

Two strong themes emerge between 1066 and 1215 connected with the church in England: the growth of the power of the papacy and church reform. Two of the most outstanding popes of the Middle Ages served during this time: Pope Gregory VII (1073–85) (Cowdrey 1998) and Pope Innocent III (1198–1216). A comparison between them shows the increase in papal power. Pope Gregory could only use propaganda or exhortation whereas by the end of Innocent III's reign the papacy had developed complex administrative systems allowing a consistent application of procedures and policy wherever the Pope held sway. The power of the papacy had grown to such an extent that Innocent III's Interdict against King John effectively closed down the churches of England for almost four years with wholesale compliance by the bishops and priests.

From the late eleventh and throughout the twelfth centuries there was a vociferous ecclesiastical reform movement, with the papacy in the vanguard. In the past, church reforms had often been as a result of pressure from the grass roots, but now the Pope himself was urging forward the speed of change. The reform movement had a number of basic aims, one of which was for a return to what was seen as the practices of the early church. This involved a rejection of worldly values (*contemptus mundi*) and the promotion of the monastic lifestyle. This also resulted in striving to separate the clergy from the temptations of society. The church began to think of itself as a distinct unit which should not be bound to lay society. In his treatise against simony, the monk Humbert wrote:

> Just as clergy are forbidden to interfere with secular business, so are laymen with ecclesiastical business . . . In the same way as clergy are distinct from laymen in their dress and profession, so they should also be in deeds and conversation . . . Thus laymen should arrange and provide for their own business, which is secular, and the clergy for theirs, which is ecclesiastical.

> (Morris 1989: 99)

As this ideal began to permeate through the church in the twelfth century, the effects were felt throughout England, for large numbers of churches were taken out of lay hands and given to the church (see below).

Another aim of the reforms was that of ensuring ritual purity when performing the Mass. To the reformers, ritual purity took precedence over everything else. Anything corrupting was banned. The greatest barriers to purity were clerical marriage or fornication, lay control over the church and simony. (Simony was the buying of an ecclesiastical office and was named after Simon Magnus who offered money for the power of the Holy Spirit and who was condemned by St Peter (Acts 8: 9–24).) Other factors, such as the lack of education or the incompetence of the priest were of little concern to the reformers. Stories therefore circulated of ritually unclean priests suffering divine punishments as they attempted to perform the Mass.

Following the Conquest, the Norman and Continental churchmen who arrived in large numbers in England viewed the Anglo-Saxon church as decadent. Stigand, the last Anglo-Saxon Archbishop of Canterbury, was even reputed by the chronicler Orderic Vitalis to have murdered someone and was held up as a prime example of the corruption of the English church. Stigand served under five kings (the first mention of him is in 1020 when he was a royal priest under Cnut) and he rose to become Archbishop of Canterbury under Edward the Confessor, a position he held for four years after the Conquest. He amassed a great fortune, owned lands in ten counties and controlled the two richest sees in England: Canterbury and Winchester. With the wealth came enormous power and a luxuriant lifestyle (Smith 1993: 199, 214). This view of a decadent Anglo-Saxon church, as portrayed by Norman chroniclers, can be overemphasised. Reform and changes under Edward the Confessor had been occurring, albeit slowly. The Norman churchman Robert of Jumièges was briefly Archbishop of Canterbury, and there were some priests from the German region of Lotharingia in the church who brought with them reforming ideas.

Stigand was deposed in 1070 and William the Conqueror appointed Lanfranc as his replacement. Whilst Lanfranc actively promoted the reform policies of the papacy, he 'neither expected nor welcomed direct intervention from Rome' (Morris 1989: 96) and was 'consistently unresponsive to Pope Gregory's approaches' (Cowdrey 1998: 465). Lanfranc did not allow himself to be dictated to by Rome. The reforms that he introduced were through his personal strength of character and owed little to external agencies.

The change in ecclesiastical personnel in England following the Conquest was dramatic. In just twenty years there was only Wulfstan of Worcester remaining as an Anglo-Saxon bishop (Mason 1985; 1990) and William the Conqueror appointed no Englishman into any important church post. Of the other fourteen bishops, eleven were from Normandy, two from Lorraine and one from Italy. Furthermore, at the time of their appointment the bishops tended to be young and so remained in post for decades: five remained in post for more than thirty years (Loyn 1987: 225). The new bishops and abbots also came with a consciousness that they were part of a new order. They had come from a dynamic and professional Norman church and were to bring many of the Continental practices to England, such as the holding of regular synods. Although this dynamism was to peter out in the mid-twelfth century, at the time of the Conquest the Norman bishops were a powerful ecclesiastical force (Loyn 1987: 234; Bates 1996: 212). Lanfranc and the other new churchmen had a profound effect upon the Anglo-Saxon church. National synods were called and Lanfranc successfully replaced the Anglo-Saxon monastic rule – the *Regularis Concordia* – in many churches with his own *Monastic Constitutions*, though they were not universally used.

Whilst Lanfranc could effectively ignore the papacy after the Conquest, over the next century the church in Rome increased its own power and influence. An important change was that it elevated its position from being the head of the western church, to being Christ's representative on earth. The Pope became Christ's vicar (i.e. deputy) on earth. The bishops became the vicars of Christ's apostles. This change gave the Pope a new power, for he and he alone could determine Christ's will on earth. This idea became widespread through the writings of Bernard of Clairvaux and was generally accepted after the new Pope Eugenius III declared it in 1153.

Evidence of papal power began to permeate throughout the church. Until the mid-twelfth century saints were created as the result of local accounts of miracles, followed by a decision of the local bishop. From the mid-twelfth century onwards the papacy became the single arbiter of canonisation. In 1163 when Pope Alexander III was at Tours he was petitioned to create six new saints, including Anselm, the former Archbishop of Canterbury, and Bernard of Clairvaux who had died in 1153.

Papal influence also began to be a consideration in national politics. When Anselm and William Rufus quarrelled at the end of the eleventh century the papacy did not intervene and papal influence was slight. As the twelfth century progressed, the papacy developed its own administration to deal with disputes between the church and laity, or within the church itself. By the 1130s the papacy had its own chamber and chancery, which grew as the number of appeals escalated during the twelfth century. By the late twelfth century it was common for disputes even at parish level to be referred to the papal authorities. At a national level the pope also delegated papal powers to local bishops, who were termed 'judge-delegates'. It is generally considered that Pope Innocent II (1113–43) first made widespread use of this process and Robert de Béthune, Bishop of Hereford (1131–48) was an early judge in England. Financially, the papacy also prospered, though its expenditure was often far greater. As well as the ancient contribution of a national collection in England to Rome called Peter's Pence (which raised about £200 annually), the Pope asked for 'gifts' from national or provincial groups of clergy with varying degrees of success. By the late twelfth century the papacy had the power to challenge and undermine royal control of churches (Harper-Bill 1999: 315).

The structure of the church in England

Bishops

In 1066 the English church was divided into two archbishoprics, the southern most and largest governed by the Archbishop of Canterbury and the northern by the Archbishop of York. Within the two archbishoprics were the dioceses (Map 6.1), which by 1133 totalled seventeen after the formation of the dioceses of Ely (in 1109) and Carlisle (in 1133). However, the number of dioceses within the provinces of Canterbury and York was very uneven as by the end of the twelfth century the Archbishopric of York only contained the dioceses of Carlisle, Durham and York. The archbishops of York were very aware of this disparity and during the twelfth century had fought hard, but ultimately unsuccessfully, to include within the archbishopric the dioceses of Worcester, Lincoln and those within Scotland, including the Northern Isles

Map 6.1 England, showing dioceses and important places.

diocese of Orkney. As the most senior bishops, the archbishops had the right to crown kings. Archbishop Ealdred of York crowned William the Conqueror, but normally the Archbishop of Canterbury performed the crowning ceremony. The argument between them as to whom was the most senior resulted in the primacy dispute (see below). Within their own dioceses the bishops were largely autonomous in their power and whilst the archbishops could apply pressure, there was little practically they could do.

During the late eleventh and twelfth centuries the bishop became increasingly powerful within his own diocese. This was a European phenomenon, but with the coming of the new wave of Norman and continental churchmen the impact was greater in England after the Conquest. The bishops constituted a powerful body, not least because they met regularly, either at the crown wearings of the king, or at councils called by the Archbishop of Canterbury (Brett 1975: 75–82). Many bishops also knew each other before arriving in England, or were related. At Bayeux in Normandy the cathedral chapter included three men who were later to become arch-bishops of York, Thomas I (1070–1100), Thomas II (1109–14) and Thurstan (1114–40). Other monks at Bayeux became bishops in England: William St Calias, Bishop of Durham (1081–96) and Samson, Bishop of Worcester (1096–1115) (Galbraith 1967: 86–101; Bates 1975: 13).

It has been suggested that it was the solidarity of the bishops after the Conquest, and the national power they wielded, that was a major factor in the permanent success of the Norman Conquest (Loyn 1987: 224). The scale of their activities is impressive. They were able administrators, oversaw the building of their new cathedrals (see Chapter 8) and were a powerful spiritual force for reform in England, though not all of them took on board the reforms personally: William of Thetford had a son who became an arch-deacon and the desire for sexual experience suffered by Maurice, Bishop of London was excused on medical grounds (Loyn 1987: 224).

The bishops did not always act as a unified body. During the twelfth century two issues dominated religious politics: the primacy dispute as to whether the Archbishop of Canterbury or York took precedence over the other, and the dispute between Henry II and Thomas Becket. The primacy dispute did not become contentious until after the Conquest when Lanfranc, Archbishop of Canterbury, promoted the interests of Canterbury above those of York – a move fiercely resisted by the Archbishop of York. A systematic collection of evidence was compiled to support Canterbury's allegedly superior position and any items which the monks of Canterbury thought should have existed, such as papal letters of support, were forged. At the papal court the forgeries were immediately spotted and when the request was made to show the originals the Canterbury monks said that they had been lost or destroyed, whereupon the court dissolved in laughter (Southern 1958; Gibson 1978; Philpott 1997: 194). In heated and sometimes farcical debates the arguments were played out with occasional fights and a great deal of posturing by both sides. The Pope refused to make a decision, but instead made the Archbishop of Canterbury a papal legate – a higher honour than any held by the Archbishop of York. This, coupled with the shrine of St Thomas at Canterbury whose popularity grew rapidly in the late twelfth century, sealed York's fate as the more junior of the two churches. The 'primacy dispute' was of major consequence to those who took part, but relatively unimportant to modern historians. However, it was part of a pattern of disputes across Europe between churches determining their relative status.

The bishop was responsible for the spiritual needs of the diocese. His duties included formally instituting a candidate to a benefice, the ordination

of priests, journeys to preach and convert through his diocese and the consecration of churches. As well as the work within their dioceses, bishops also
had a responsibility to the king to give sound advice and, when necessary, to
sit as judges in both lay and church courts. In times of war bishops were
required to lead armies. Archbishop Anselm of Canterbury camped with the
soldiers of Henry I before a prospective battle with Robert Curthose, Duke
of Normandy, and Archbishop Thurstan of York led the victorious English
army against the Scots at the Battle of the Standard in 1138. The most
famous ecclesiastical warrior was Odo of Bayeux who rode beside William
the Conqueror at the Battle of Hastings and is depicted in armour on the
Bayeux Tapestry.

Bishops were often cultivated and learned, promoting the arts and having
the power to raise individuals to positions of power. Some bishops were
amongst the richest men in England and were lavish patrons of the arts (see
Chapter 8), though they were open to criticism if they flaunted their wealth,
for example William of Malmesbury wrote that Roger, Bishop of Salisbury, was
too worldly (Smith 1993: 216). Bishops ranked alongside the powerful nobles
in wealth and status and they too had their own households. It is unfortunate
that the make-up of a bishop's household is unknown (Cheney 1950: 4), but it
would have included clerks and priests, all eager to climb the hierarchical
ladder, as well as the usual contingent of servants. Thomas Becket rose through
the ranks as part of the household of Theodore, Archbishop of Canterbury.

As the power of the bishops increased in the twelfth century the venerable
and once influential abbeys and monasteries began to loose their autonomy
because the bishops had to ratify decisions by abbots. The bishops also
licensed schools and preachers, giving them a much greater authority and
control of what went on in their diocese. In many ways this change of power
suited the monasteries (and especially the new Cistercian and Cluniac orders
of monks) who desired a withdrawal from the world in order to praise God
without worldly interference.

Bishops came into contact with monasteries in two ways. The first was the
extension of an Anglo-Saxon practice of creating monastic cathedrals where
monks, not secular canons, ran the churches whilst bishops governed the
dioceses. In the cases of the new dioceses, such as Ely and Carlisle (formed in
1109 and 1133 respectively), the cathedrals were founded with a monastic
community, whilst others had monks imposed upon them, such as
Rochester. That the imposition of monks may have been connected with
local politics in some cases can be seen from the example of Durham, where
the monks forcibly ejected the community of clergy who had for centuries
protected and venerated the shrine of St Cuthbert. The traditional community was probably seen as supporting the local uprising in Northumbria and
so its replacement by the community of Benedictine monks had a strong
political dimension of controlling the local area (Rollason 1992). In York the
reverse may have happened with Thomas of Bayeux deliberately instigating a
system of prebends whereby a secular canon received money from a parish

church and its land, in order to stop the church being taken over by Benedictine monks (Norton 2001).

Bishops were also responsible for the monasteries within their dioceses and a supportive bishop could lead to considerable patronage for monasteries, though patronage was rarely evenly distributed. Bishop Giffard of Winchester supported the monasteries in his diocese. Of the sixteen monastic houses, six were founded during his time in office, four others considered him very important in their foundation and he intervened in the running of three or four others. However, his patronage was not uniform and, if the surviving records are a representative sample, then the bishop had little involvement with the Augustinian and the Cistercian monasteries (Franklin 1990: 50, 60).

Whilst the bishops controlled the diocese, the cathedral chapters were responsible for the cathedral itself and its estates. There were often clashes between the bishops and their chapters for often both were reliant on the same resources. Before Henry of Blois, Bishop of Winchester, died he returned to the monastic chapter goods which he had unjustly taken from it. These included churches assigned for a specific purpose, such as the church of Ellendune, the money from which was to be used for the writing of books and the repair of the organ (Franklin 1990: 58).

The large size of many of the English bishoprics resulted in the formation of archdeaneries, whereby dioceses were subdivided into collections of parishes. This was proclaimed at the Council of Windsor in 1070 and the largest diocese, Lincoln, was subdivided into seven. Archdeaneries had an ancient history in France but seem not to have existed in England before the Norman Conquest. In Italy the system was not used at all, even in the large northern bishoprics. A subdivision of the archdeanery in England was the deanery, made up of fewer parishes.

A bishop was elected by the cathedral's chapter and without interference most chapters chose either local men or men from within their own chapters. However, English kings had the customary right to attend elections, either personally or through their agents, and they usually ensured the election of their chosen candidate. After the murder of Thomas Becket, Henry II filled three of the six vacant bishoprics with his supporters, and Thomas Becket himself had been chosen as Archbishop of Canterbury after pressure from Henry II. Royal relatives could also be placed in important positions: Henry of Blois, the powerful Bishop of Winchester, was Henry I's nephew (and later brother to the king when Stephen was crowned) and Geoffrey, Archbishop of York, was Henry II's son. Often it was also in a bishopric's interest to choose the royal candidate, as royal patronage could be lavish.

If a bishopric or abbey became vacant (i.e. through the death of the bishop or abbot or their exile overseas) the church's income flowed into royal coffers, which was an obvious incentive to keep the position vacant. In the previous Anglo-Saxon era the king had played little part in the administration of vacant abbeys, which were administered by the diocesan bishop or occasionally the prior, and if a bishopric fell empty, then the archbishop had custody

(Mason 1998: 115). The practice of kings acquiring the income of vacant churches seems to have been introduced after the Conquest (Crosby 1994: 362). This could be extremely lucrative and prolonged: the archbishopric of Canterbury was vacant between 1089 and 1093 and 1109 and 1113, whilst the archbishopric of York was vacant between 1181 and 1191.

Monasteries

Monastic life had been a feature of Christianity in Britain since at least the fifth century. Monks and nuns separated themselves from the secular world by – in theory at least – enclosing themselves in religious communities. In reality the separation between the religious and secular was probably not as distinct as many Anglo-Saxon church leaders would have wished. From the sixth century until about 1100 all English monks and nuns followed the Benedictine Rule, written by St Benedict (died 547) which was a simple set of rules outlining the monastic routine. The rule could be interpreted in a number of different ways and was flexible enough to be adapted by succeeding generations.

At the time of the Norman Conquest the Benedictine Rule dominated religious life in England. For both Lanfranc and Anselm, the first two archbishops of Canterbury after the Conquest, the 'Benedictine rule was the central principle of their lives' (Hollister 1987: 145). However, in 1066 Benedictine monasteries were confined to the south of England (see Chapter 1), but following the Conquest there was a conscious desire by Benedictine monks or patrons to establish new monasteries across England. One such foundation had symbolic significance as William the Conqueror founded Battle Abbey and insisted that the high altar was sited on the spot where Harold was killed.

The first Benedictine abbey to be founded in the north was at Selby, just south of York. The foundation narrative describes how Benedict, a monk from the French monastery of Auxerre, was told by St Germanus in a dream to journey to Selby. He originally misunderstood his instructions and ended up in Salisbury, but the amused saint once again directed him north. The reasons for Benedict's journey to Salisbury have never been fully explained, but the fact that Edward of Salisbury knew the north well was probably not coincidental (Williams 1997: 106).

During the Anglo-Saxon era, there had been no Benedictine monasteries further north than the Wash and the choice of Selby is therefore mysterious, especially as St Germanus named it as a targeted location. It may have been a conscious effort – possibly by either the church or Edward of Salisbury – to plant a settlement or holy man in the middle of a lawless area. Once Benedict had arrived at Selby, his probable intention of leading the life of a hermit disintegrated as he attracted followers and rich patrons in the form of the Sheriff of Yorkshire and William the Conqueror.

The most spectacular founding of post-Conquest monasteries occurred in north-east England when three monks, Reinfrid and Aelfwig (both of

Evesham Abbey) and Prior Aldwin of Winchcombe Abbey, journeyed to Northumbria. Reinfrid had first-hand knowledge of the north from his time in William the Conqueror's army and Aldwin knew Bede's *History of the English People* which described the Anglo-Saxon monasteries of Northumbria. Their intention may have been, like Benedict's, to live as hermits, but as they settled at former monastic sites their followers ensured that monasteries were refounded. The three monks journeyed north and settled at Jarrow. They then split, Aldwin and a clerk, Turgot, travelled north to Melrose, before being recalled to Monkwearmouth. In 1083 Benedictine monks from Jarrow and Monkwearmouth replaced the group of secular clerks who for centuries had been looking after the shrine of St Cuthbert to form the Benedictine monastery at Durham. Reinfrid then moved on to Whitby. A few years later a patron, William de Percy, harassed the community and so the group moved under the leadership of abbot Stephen, first to Lastingham and then to York.

There is only fragmentary evidence concerning religious communities in the north before the arrival of the Benedictines. Orderic Vitalis, who was born and brought up near Shrewsbury, described how the clergy wore no habit, took no vows, held private property, indulged in feasting and differed little from the laity (Chibnall 1984: 7). However, the Benedictine monks were often skilful users of propaganda and Orderic's account may be an example of this. The use of propaganda was not unusual and a particularly vivid example occurred at Mont St Michel in the eleventh century. The Benedictine author of the *Introductio monachorum* described the previous inhabitants as resisting reform and taking pleasure from feasting and hunting, in contrast to the more virtuous Benedictines who supplanted them (Potts 1990: 142).

From the Conquest to the early twelfth century the Benedictine revival in England carried all before it, as it had done in Normandy since the 1040s. Gradually, however, the Benedictine monasteries in England began to loose the initial impulse of their reforms. This dissatisfaction with traditional Benedictine lifestyle has led historians to coin the phrase the 'Crisis of Western Monasticism' which resulted in a movement away from establishing Benedictine houses to the founding of the monastic new orders, notably the Cistercians and the Cluniacs (see below). However, despite the new orders, the Benedictine monasteries gained recruits and remained an influential force until the late twelfth century. Only then did problems in recruitment and economies become evident when gifts from laymen began to dry up as the national economy began to experience inflation and other problems (Franklin 1990: 47).

Between 1066 and 1150 four new orders settled in mainland Britain: the orders of Tiron, Savigny (the Savignacs), Cluny (the Cluniacs) and Citeaux (the Cistercians). Each revised the Benedictine Rule, with the different orders believing that their own interpretation allowed them to get closer to God than any other. The order of Tiron was most prominent in Scotland under the patronage of the Scottish King David, with a few houses in Wales. The Savignac order founded its first monastic house in England at Tulketh in Lancashire in 1124, but then moved to a new site at Furness in 1127. The Savignac order was particularly popular in the 1130s and King Stephen founded Buckfast Abbey in Devon in 1136 and a few years later his queen, Matilda, established Coggeshall in Essex. By 1147 the Savignacs had fourteen houses in England and Wales, all except four founded directly from Savigny. But there were fundamental weaknesses in the order as a whole, especially that of a lack of control from the centre, which led to falling standards. The result was the subsuming of the Savignacs into the Cistercian order in 1147, a move which greatly increased the Cistercian presence in England. In the same year other small European orders, the Obazine and Coiroux, were also merged with the Cistercians (Thompson 1978: 227).

The two most important of the new orders in England were Cluny and Citeaux. The first Cluniac foundation in England was at Lewes in 1077, following a stay at Cluny by William de Warenne, the Lord of Lewes. There was then a period of rapid growth until 1100 in the south and Midlands, with outposts in the north at Pontefract and Monk Bretton and in Wales the monastery of St Clears. The links with the mother house of Cluny were formal and included payment of a yearly tax, but the order was loosely organised and there was no firm control from the centre (Burton 1997: 38).

It was the Cistercian order, however, that reached a pre-eminence in England, and throughout Europe. The first English Cistercian monastery was at Waverley, followed by one at Tintern. The arrival of a group of Cistercian monks in the north caused more of a stir and showed the tensions that could arise between the different orders. Cistercian monks on their way to Rievaulx near Helmsley stayed with the Benedictines at St Mary's Abbey, York, a contingent of whom were so impressed by the Cistercians that they rebelled and petitioned to make the monastery of St Mary's conform to a stricter lifestyle. The arguments between the reforming prior and the traditional abbot of St Mary's exploded into a heated debate in October 1132 with the result that the reformers left the abbey and were given land by the river Skell. This community was not at first Cistercian but soon after joined the Cistercian order and built Fountains Abbey near Ripon. From these initial monasteries the order in Britain grew.

The secret of the Cistercian success was a rigid organisational structure by which the mother house at Citeaux enforced the rules. There were annual visitations from Citeaux to the daughter houses and the abbots of all the Cistercian monasteries were expected to attend the annual General Chapter at Citeaux. Whilst the yearly General Chapter was feasible with a small number of abbeys, by 1152 there were over 300 Cistercian monasteries scattered throughout Europe, making the annual Chapter difficult to attend, so the Chapter was called once every four years. The rise of the number of Cistercian houses had been so rapid that in 1152 the Cistercian Chapter banned the foundation of new monasteries, an attempt not wholly successful as foundations in Wales flourished until 1200, but the main period of rapid growth in England had ended.

There were important differences between the new orders and the older Benedictine order. The Benedictine order was based on the independence of each house, with no one abbey controlling the others whereas the Cistercians were strictly controlled from their mother house at Citeaux. The Cistercians also devised a new system of using lay brothers as part of the monastic structure. The lay brothers worked on the agricultural granges set up at a distance from the monasteries instead of the monks who, whilst expected to work as part of their daily routine, were not expected to perform as much physical work as a lay brother. In the *Life of Ailred* by Walter Daniel, it is mentioned that there were 140 monks and some 500 lay brothers at Rievaulx Abbey (Powicke 1950: 38).

By the end of the twelfth century the new orders were themselves being criticised. In a long passage Walter Map castigates the Cistercians and other orders for their wealth and possessions, which they gained through gifts or simply by seizing lands which did not belong to them (James *et al.* 1983: 85–113). It is a salutary reminder that contemporaries did not always view monks, or indeed other churchmen, as holy.

During the twelfth century communities of women voluntarily followed the Cistercian Rule and way of life, but were not affiliated to the order. In 1147 the Cistercians rejected the desire of Gilbert of Sempringham to place his nunneries under their auspices and by extension the Cistercians rejected all other female houses. However, by the end of the twelfth and early thirteenth centuries the Cistercian abbots were relenting and the nunneries were given official recognition as part of the order in 1213, though seven years later the Statute of 1220 dictated no more convents were to be incorporated. There is an inconsistency in the figures, however, because between 1213 and 1220 only six nunneries are mentioned as being formally incorporated, whilst there is evidence of twenty-nine Cistercian nunneries in total (Thompson 1978: 232–40).

Canons

As well as the Benedictine Rule, there was one other popular rule, that of the Augustinian Rule, named after St Augustine, the Bishop of Hippo from *c.*396 to 430. The Augustinians, who were called canons (rather than monks), based their rule on a passage in the Acts of the Apostles, which states that: 'all who believed were together and had all things in common. And sold their possessions and goods and parted them all to men as every man had need' (Acts II: 45). Augustine argued that the true apostolic life had no private property and that all should live in common. The Augustine Rule had formed by the sixth century from some of Augustine's works, and later material, though it was only in the later eleventh century that it gained widespread popularity. There were major differences between the Augustinians and the orders following the Benedictine Rule. The Augustinian Rule was for groups of priests living in common who also undertook pastoral duties in local communities, whilst the Benedictine Rule, and especially that of the Cistercians, emphasised the desire to escape the pressures of life and live in the wilderness. The Augustinian Rule had several advantages for the church authorities, because groups of celibate priests lived in a community, whilst actively participating in pastoral work within towns. The Rule was especially favoured by collegiate churches and hospitals. There were a few pre-1100 houses under the Augustinian Rule in England, but from 1100 the order flourished, especially from the royal patronage of Henry I and his Queen Matilda.

Mixing the orders: the Premonstratensians and the Gilbertines

Whilst the Benedictine Rule and the Augustinian Rule had similarities (for example they both kept monastic hours which dictated the pattern of the day, dividing it into periods of prayer, work and sleep), they had different structures and concepts. However, two groups, the Premonstratensians and the Gilbertines, combined elements of both rules. The Premonstratensians were founded by Norbert of Xanten in France and basically followed the Rule of Augustine, although they later came to incorporate elements from the Benedictine Rule as followed by the Cistercians. The Cistercian influence resulted in a more austere lifestyle, but with a desire not only to live apart from society, but also – paradoxically – to carry out service, so the Premonstratensians ran hospitals and worked in the parishes. The first house in England was founded in 1143 at Newhouse.

The second order, the Gilbertines, was the only purely English order. Gilbert was a priest at Sempringham (Lincolnshire) when a group of women in his parish requested that he set up a cell for them adjoining the village church. The nuns lived by the Cistercian Rule and were Cistercian in all but name, but Gilbert's attempt to get the Cistercians to accept the nuns into their order in 1147 was refused. Gilbert was therefore forced to compile his own regulations for the women and men who had swelled the ranks of the order. From these small beginnings the order grew with double houses for both men and women, with canons and lay brothers and also nuns and lay sisters (the 'illiterate'). The nuns followed the Benedictine Rule, the lay brothers followed Cistercian customs while the Gilbertine canons followed the Augustinian Rule, allowing them to attend to the spiritual needs of the nuns as well as serving the local community. The order expanded in the decades after 1147, but it remained an English order, with houses in Scotland and Rome both failing. As well as the double houses, male only houses were founded of the Gilbertine canons. The biographer of Gilbert compared his order to the chariot of God: 'which has two sides, that is one of men and one of women; four wheels, two of men, clerics and laymen, and two of women, literate and illiterate; two beasts dragging the chariot, the clerical and monastic disciplines' (Constable 1978: 218).

Double houses were rare and more often there were completely separate monasteries and nunneries. There was a real fear of contact by the order's hierarchy, and especially sexual contact, between canons and nuns. The most famous case of sexual liaison between a canon and nun occurred at the Gilbertine double house at Watton where a canon or a lay brother made a nun pregnant. The consequences were horrific. The nun was forced to castrate her lover and was then placed in irons. The following investigation dismayed Abbot Ailred of Rievaulx who felt the sexes were not separated rigidly enough (Constable 1978: 207).

Gilbert himself was well aware of the temptations that existed. Gerald of Wales related how in old age Gilbert was looked upon with lascivious eyes by a Gilbertine nun. After preaching about the virtue of chastity, he completely disrobed and 'hairy, emaciated, scabrous and wild' walked around, and pointing to Christ on the Cross said ' "Behold the man who should be duly desired by a woman consecrated to God and a bride of Christ". He then went on pointing to himself "Behold the body on account of which a miserable woman has made her body and soul worthy of being lost in Hell" ' (Constable 1978: 222).

Nunneries

As has been stated, in 1147 the Cistercian General Chapter refused a request by Gilbert of Sempringham to accept Gilbert's two nunneries into the Cistercian order. The Cistercian order saw itself as exclusively male. The division between male and female was often as strict as the division between religious and lay.

Until the last few decades of the twentieth century male houses dominated historical research. There were several reasons for this. There are few surviving records for nunneries, whether charters or foundation histories, and because nunneries were usually poor there are few records of their economic activity. However, in the past few decades nuns and nunneries have become a serious source of historical and archaeological study, despite the paucity of evidence. The general pattern of development of nunneries through the twelfth century seems to be that of flexible and changeable organisations becoming highly disciplined institutions. This was especially the case in the double houses of monks or canons and nuns where early flexibility was replaced by strict segregation (Constable 1978: 219).

Sources are more plentiful for noble or royal nuns. Following the Conquest many aristocratic Anglo-Saxon widows entered monasteries, either through material hardship or fear, and both Edward the Confessor's widow, Queen Edith, and King Harold's daughter entered the monastery at Wilton. The nunnery has been described as the 'most famous refuge of English noblewomen after the Conquest . . . [and] one of the greatest repositories of English tradition in the country' (Southern 1966: 182–3). Nuns who were noble or royal were common throughout the twelfth century, for example

King Stephen's daughter, Mary, was Abbess at Romsey (Franklin 1990: 53).

There was always the possibility, however, that women entered a nunnery because of force or duress. Abbot Ailred discovered a girl who had been placed there by Archbishop Henry Murdac of York at the age of four and who had turned out to be a 'frivolous and lascivious woman' who ignored all attempts at her correction (Constable 1978: 206). There was, however, the problem of whether women who entered under such circumstances should be able to leave. Lanfranc's answer was that women who had entered the nunnery as children (oblates) or had made their profession were to remain, whilst those who fell outside these categories were to be sent home until their vocation was investigated (Clover and Gibson 1979: 167). Lanfranc's motive may have been to return the women home so that they could help to make peace between the different political factions following the Conquest (Searle 1980).

One of the most famous cases of a political refugee in a nunnery was Edith (later renamed Matilda), daughter of the Scottish King Malcolm Canmore and his Queen Margaret, who entered the nunnery of Wilton where probably her aunt, Christina, was Abbess. Edith was unhappy: 'I . . . went in fear of the rod of my aunt Christina . . . and she would often make me smart with a good slapping and the most horrible scolding, as well as treating me as being in disgrace.' It was Christina who, to protect her niece, put a veil on her head. Edith's reaction matched her father's fury – 'I did indeed wear [it] in her presence, but as soon as I was able to escape out of sight, I tore it off and threw it on the ground and trampled on it . . . I used to vent my rage and hatred of it which boiled up in me' (Baker 1978: 123–4). The issue became urgent when Henry I determined to marry Edith for political reasons of dynastic unity. The investigation by Archbishop Anselm resulted in Edith's release and freedom to marry because she had entered unwillingly and had never made her profession (Southern 1966: 182–90). In exceptional circumstances a nun could be forcibly removed from a nunnery. King Harold's daughter, Gunhilda – also a nun at Wilton – was abducted by Count Alan of Richmond as part of a political marriage strategy (Southern 1966: 185–6; Searle 1980: 167).

The foundation of many nunneries remains hidden, but some at least seem to have been formed from hermitages where small groups of women, or women and men, were living together. In England the most detailed description of such a community is that given in the account of Christina of Markyate (Talbot 1959). In France the hermit Robert of Arbrissel gathered around him both men and women, and from this group grew the monastery of Fontevrault, with both men and women being part of the double house, although, unusually, the women took precedence in the running of the organisation (Smith 1978).

With many royal and noble women in nunneries it is not surprising that some convents became centres of learning. The lack of records is frustrating but there is tentative evidence for a flourishing scriptorium at the Winchester nunnery of Nunnaminster in the twelfth century and the problems of identifying the origins of where manuscripts came from may mean there were others. The prohibitions in the Gilbertine Rule in the early thirteenth century probably show what in reality happened in the late twelfth century. In the prohibitions nuns were not allowed to copy or commission any books (except service books) without permission of the master of the order, nor could they employ scribes nor invite them to the church without permission. The nuns may also have been preparing parchment for there is a clause allowing nuns to enter the kitchen only in order to dry their parchment (Robinson 1997). Some saints lives were also probably written in monasteries – a *Life of Edward the Martyr* – was probably written by one of the nuns at Shaftesbury during the 1080s and 1090s (Hayward 1998: 85).

Relations between and within monasteries

The solid and imposing architecture of the monasteries that survive today gives the impression that the communities of monks and nuns had always remained settled on the same spot. However, the early years of many monasteries were spent in upheaval, with some communities not finding a suitable patron or site for many years. The experience of the monks who eventually settled at Byland Abbey in North Yorkshire shows the uncertainty that could exist. Originally members of the community at Furness, a group of thirteen monks left to found a house at Calder in Cumbria in 1134. Three years later the settlement at Calder was burnt to the ground during a Scottish raid. The monks fled back to Furness, only to be denied entry – the Furness monks were worried about feeding the extra monks from Calder and the abbot of the Calder monks refused to give up his privileged position. The Calder monks went across the Pennines to approach Archbishop Thurstan. On their way they met Gundreda, mother of Roger de Mowbray, who persuaded her son to become their patron. Even with his patronage the monks moved four times before settling at their final destination of Byland Abbey in 1177, forty-three years after leaving Furness. Although the number of sites for the Calder monks was exceptional, their difficulties were not unusual.

Even after the monastic community had become settled on a site, there were often internal tensions. In some cases an entire monastery could decide to adopt the rule of another order and so change allegiance, but more often an individual or group of monks from one house could leave to join another order. An interesting example occurred at the small Augustinian house of Kirkham Abbey in Yorkshire where a failed attempt was made to change allegiance from the Augustinian Rule to that of the Cistercians (Burton 1995). A more successful attempt was made by a group of Benedictine monks who left St Mary's Abbey York and soon after joined the Cistercian order. Another possibility was for a group within an established house to revolt, causing severe tensions within a particular order. This occurred in the

Gilbertine order in the mid-1160s when a group of lay brothers revolted against Gilbert (Harper-Bill 1984: 148–9).

Royal influence could have a part to play in the internal workings of monasteries. During the revolt of the Gilbertine lay brothers Henry II supported Gilbert in his dispute and when the Benedictine house at Amesbury (Wiltshire) was disbanded after a scandal, it was reconstituted by Henry II and given to the order of Fontevrault as a penance for his part in the murder of Thomas Becket (Burton 1997: 97).

Parishes

Whilst the cathedrals and monasteries were the spectacular churches with an intellectual dynamism, at a local level it was the parish church that was the focus for the religious worship of the majority of the population. Quantification of the numbers of churches is difficult to assess, for the first surviving documentary reference to them might come decades after they were built, and archaeological excavation can rarely give a precise date for a church's foundation. However, from contemporary accounts, the period following the Norman Conquest and into the twelfth century seems to have been when increasing numbers of parish churches were built. In a famous quote William of Malmesbury wrote that: 'you may see everywhere churches in villages, in towns and cities monasteries rising in a new style of architecture' (Mynors *et al*. 1998: 460).

The parish priest was part of the local community. Although church councils attempted to differentiate clergy from the laity by their dress, manner and celibacy, these teachings made little headway in the remoter parishes. Most priests had little training and were barely literate, whilst their examination before being appointed might be basic in the extreme. Even though a hierarchical structure existed within the church, there was little close supervision of the parish priests. Many bishops were unclear of their rights in reprimanding clergy and many archdeacons rarely ventured far from their cathedral. Even though church law refused marriage to priests, many had female 'companions of the hearth' (*focaria*) or concubines. In practice, priests often had children. In a vivid passage, Gerald of Wales describes the 'houses and hovels of parish priests filled with bossy mistresses, creaking cradles, newborn babes and squawking brats' (Warren 1983: 460).

Patronage: the church and the laity

The relationship between a patron and his or her church was two-way. The patron was willing to provide money, lands and gifts in return for prayers, which in turn would help his or her soul to heaven. The church required a strong patron in order to protect itself against external attack or political influences and also to increase its wealth in order to survive. However hard the Cistercians and other orders wished to divorce themselves from matters of the world, in the end they and the entire church were dependent upon the wealth and patronage of the laity.

The relationship between church and patron was a dynamic one, which could fracture or thrive depending on circumstance. Considerable historical exploration has taken place to investigate the patrons' motives for founding churches but less work has been undertaken concerning the strategies that the monks used to manipulate the ties of kinship, lordships and friendships to strengthen the position of their own houses (Potter 1998: 192). The relationship between patron and community was often influenced by members of the patron's family also being part of the community. This could cause internal tensions, for example when Anselm wanted William of Beaumont as his next prior, many of the community disagreed, which has been seen as benefactors trying to influence the election through their relatives who were monks (Potter 1998: 185).

The patronage of an important noble would also encourage the noble's tenants to give to their lord's monastery. It has been said of the tenants of Richard of Clare that they 'were free to grant property to their lord's religious foundation, though they may not have been equally free to withhold it' (Mortimer 1980: 141). A similar pattern emerges with the Cluniac foundation of Thetford where the tenants followed the Bigod family not only by giving donations, but also by attacking the rival church of St Benet Holme (Harper-Bill 1979: 67; Cownie 1994: 148).

Time was an important element between a lord and his church. The lord and his tenants would be remembered, potentially forever, in the prayers of the church community and in the act of remembrance the bond between the lord and church would be maintained. Furthermore, the church itself began to guarantee title of the lord's lands into the future, which was supported by a network of church courts and administrative documents in an attempt to bind patrons and donors to the church (Thompson 1993: 232–3).

The need to found or give to religious houses was felt by all levels of society. For the lords and those who could afford it, foundations and patronage were also a significant sign of prestige and status. There were also social pressures and expectation that a lord would show his importance by founding a religious house. This expectation was summed up by Orderic Vitalis: 'Every one of the great men of Normandy would have thought himself beneath contempt if he had not made provision out of his estates for clerks and monks to serve in the army of God' (Chibnall 1984: 47). It was as much a sign of feudal privilege as having estates, a household and rights over tenants (Colvin 1951: 32) and it was taken for granted that the spiritual obligation of a wealthy family included the foundation of religious houses. What better way of reaching heaven than having a monastery full of monks regularly praying for the founder's or patron's soul? Sometimes pressure could be brought to bear on lords by individuals or the church. The father of Orderic Vitalis, Odelerius, persuaded his lord Earl Roger of

Montgomery to found a new independent abbey at Shrewsbury in 1083 (Chibnall 1984: 16).

The patronage of royalty or a great lord could transform the fortunes of a house. Immediately after the Conquest, royal interest in the monasteries at Abingdon and Gloucester was decisive in the continued prosperity of these Benedictine houses (Cownie 1994: 157). Patronage by its nature was not uniform, with some houses receiving the attentions of great patrons whilst others relied on less important men in the locality. Some patronage was spectacular in scale, for example that of William, Count of Mortain, who founded Montacute Priory about 1100 (Golding 1980: 74). The foundation endowment consisted of the Montacute parish church, the borough and market, the castle and castle chapel, William's demense orchards and vineyard, the manor and its mill and the local fair on Hamdon Hill. The manors and churches of Tintinhull, Creech St Michael, East Chinnock, Closworth and West Mudford were also included as well as lands and churches in Somerset, Dorset, Devon and Cornwall.

The aspiration of every church was to have substantial royal patronage. Immediately following the Conquest the new Norman landlords and nobles still preferred to patronise their own houses on the Continent with new lands and churches in England. The greatest number of new monastic foundations were priories linked to abbeys on the Continent, and so they received the name of 'alien priories' (Cownie 1995: 57). This process was made easier by William the Conqueror being both King of England and Duke of Normandy, so the allegiances of Norman nobles were not divided. One notable exception to this was William the Conqueror's foundation of Battle Abbey in memory of his victory over Harold. Battle Abbey can be characterised as a royal church, or 'eigenkloster', for it was emphasised that it was William's private abbey, dependent upon him alone and surrounded by a league of land immune from the jurisdiction of all other men (Searle 1979: 154). The process of giving lands and foundations to alien priories altered when William Rufus became King of England because his brother Robert Curthose was Duke of Normandy. There was a decisive shift in patronage by the king and nobles to English Benedictine monasteries (Cownie 1995: 58). By 1100 there were approximately eighty-eight religious houses, whether monasteries or nunneries, in England. (The number is approximate because some foundation dates are unclear.) This number comprised both pre-Conquest Anglo-Saxon foundations and the newer, post-Conquest houses. Whereas the foundations had been a trickle up to 1100, the twelfth century saw an explosion in numbers. Between 1100 and 1136, 105 religious houses were founded, and a further 114 during the years of Anarchy between 1139 and 1154. Thereafter there was a tailing off in foundations, with thirty-three being founded between 1154 and 1175 (Knowles 1966: 711).

The reasons for the phenomenal growth during the Anarchy had everything to do with politics combined with an outward spirituality. Few foundations did not have a political dimension to their existence. The interconnectedness of foundations is shown by a group in Yorkshire and Lincolnshire involving different patrons seemingly vying with each other over the number of foundations and type of order. In 1147 Eustace Fitz John founded the Premonstratensian monastery in Alnwick (Northumberland), but then in the early 1150s he founded two Gilbertine priories in Yorkshire at Malton (*c*.1150) and Watton (1150–3). The choice of location and order has been seen as odd, for these were the first Gilbertine houses in Yorkshire and it was unusual for such a powerful figure to patronise the order, especially when there were Cistercian and Augustinian houses in the area. It may be that the Gilbertine houses were founded both in order to win favour with the Cistercian Archbishop of York, Henry Murdac, and as an act of reconcilaition with the powerful Lord Gilbert II de Gant, the overlord of Gilbert of Sempringham. As well as attempting to win favour, the foundations were a probable counterbalance to the powerful Earl of York (William Aumale) who founded the Cistercian Abbey of Meaux in 1151 in East Yorkshire. Furthermore, Earl William co-founded a house of Gilbertines at North Ormesby in Lincolnshire. Unfortunately the date of foundation lies between 1148 and 1154 so it may have been a precursor or response to Fitz John's foundations. Finally the foundations and patronage of both Eustace Fitz John and William Aumale were probably part of a local power battle, often seen in Stephen's reign, where foundations were seen as strengthening a local power base (King 1990; Dalton 1996: 374).

The role of patrons within the life of the church could vary enormously. Some patrons kept a close eye on the church from its foundations upwards. Henry I's Queen Matilda founded the Augustinian house of Holy Trinity Aldgate and as well as numerous gifts took her son along to play so that he might be inspired to remain a lifelong patron of the new foundation (Huneycutt 1990: 91). Matilda was following her mother's example for Queen Margaret of Scotland liaised with Lanfranc over the reforms for the Scottish church (Clover and Gibson 1979: 160–3), though opinions vary as to her importance in the changes brought about (Barrow 1973: 196; Baker 1978: 126).

However, whilst some patrons actively helped their foundations, others founded churches by using lands that were in dispute, which led to complaints and lengthy legal procedures. A cause célèbre occurred between William of Ypres and Hugh of Dover, the Lord of Chilham. William was described by Archbishop Theodore as 'that notorious tyrant and most grievous persecutor of our church' and William had managed 'by some means or other' to take possession of Chilham church from Hugh and attempted to grant it to the monks (Eales 1985: 100).

There was a delicate balance however between the patrons' wishes and what the churches thought acceptable, a balance which could be stretched and broken. Eadmer quoted William Rufus as saying that the monasteries were his, to do what he liked with (Mason 1998: 114), a view often tacitly held by various patrons, especially in the eleventh century. This view also incorporated the view that the monasteries were a great source of wealth, which could be taxed and financially exploited. William Rufus forcefully exercised his rights over the lands of the vacant bishoprics and abbeys. The exercising of rights by Rufus was therefore a significant change and one which following kings willingly followed.

Whilst the great lords were important politically, donations of money, land or gifts were always welcome from a lord's tenants or the surrounding populace whose names would be entered into a book. Lists of names survive from three places: Thorney Abbey, Durham Cathedral Priory and Hyde Abbey. The lists either form a necrology for the remembrance of the dead or the names are of the living who have helped or served the churches in some way. The latter is the most likely as the Thorney Book has a provision for Hugh de Beauchamp 'to take the cowl' (Clark 1984: 55). These books, which became numerous in the following centuries, show the importance of the survival of the memory of an individual or family at all levels of society.

One of the basic concepts behind the reforms of the twelfth century was the separation of religious and secular power, which included the wresting of churches out of the hands of the laity and into the control of the church. Many churches had been set up on private estates for the needs of the lord and his family over the centuries (Williams 1992: 233). There is also a noticeable pattern of important towns pre-1100 having many small churches which had been established by leading townsmen (Morris 1989: 188). By the twelfth century a patchwork of parishes covered the country, comprising around 8,500 in England and around 950 in Wales (Morris 1989: 276). Founders and owners of churches were often reluctant to give up their churches easily as churches were a profitable source of income, from the rights of baptism, burial and the tithes of the church.

Reformers wanted to take churches out of lay hands not only for reasons of spiritual purity, but also to make the divide between church and laity more defined. An obstacle to this was those churches which had become hereditary possessions within one family. A married priest with a son naturally sought to provide for him and one way was to pass on the church to his son. A further appeal of churches was that they could be financially profitable and it was not unknown for the ownership of churches to be divided into half or smaller fractions. In 1188 Abbot Samson divided the advowson (the living) of the church of Boxted between himself and Robert of Coddenham (Harper-Bill 1988: 122).

The combination of the insistence upon clerical purity (which was emphasised by clerical celibacy), the forbidding of clerical marriage and the desire to separate church and secular matters, led to pressure on families to hand the ownership of their churches to the church. During the twelfth century the laity gave the church a large number of parish churches. One such was Walter son of Fagenulf who gave two churches to St Leonard's Hospital in York in the middle of the twelfth century.

However, despite ecclesiastical pressure throughout the twelfth century, an estimated figure of one-quarter of all churches were still in lay hands in 1200. Even though the lay owners may have had their rights curtailed, many still took a keen interest in their churches and the grip of the church upon the parish churches can be exaggerated. One example is that of Ralph Nuvel in York, who insisted that the church of All Saints, Peaseholme Green, was in his ownership. In support of his claim the citizens of York signed a document and attached to it the first known seal of the city (Kemp 1980; Harper-Bill 1988: 113; Daniell 1995; Burton 1997).

The Jews

Following the Norman Conquest the first Jewish community was established in London, probably from the large Norman Jewish community in Rouen. From London small Jewish communities moved into towns across England, and there is some evidence to suggest that they deliberately settled in towns where there was a significant mint (see Chapter 7). Although small in number, these communities had a powerful influence both economically and in the popular imagination. Part of their power was their 'otherness' to the Christian population and this may have led to a reputation for spells or magic. In the life of Christina of Markyate, Christina's mother called upon a Jewess 'who wanted to harm Christina with tricks which were more power-ful' than the previous love potions and charms that Christina's mother had paid for (Talbot 1959: 75). The Jews lived and worked amongst the Christian population, though probably for their own security they tended to live in specific areas in the heart of towns. Their presence led to streets being named after them, and in York the present-day 'Jubbergate' is a corruption of the medieval 'Jew Bret Gate'.

Until 1215 the clothing of the Jews does not seem to have been different to that of the Christian population, but in that year the Fourth Lateran Council declared that Jews and Muslims 'shall be publicly distinguished from other people by their dress'. In death, however, Jews had always been segregated, for they were buried in their own cemeteries beyond the city walls. Initially they were only allowed to be buried in London even though they might live elsewhere, but in 1177 Henry II granted them permission for burial outside the walls of cities in England. The largest excavation of a Jewish cemetery in England has taken place in York, where 482 individuals were excavated at Jewbury (Lilley *et al.* 1994).

Legally the Jews were the king's personal property. The king provided security, for a price, but being his property also meant that the king could force them to pay into his own coffers. King John charged the Jews 8,000 marks (£5,333 6s 8d) in 1207 alone, plus one-tenth the value of the debts owed to them (Bartlett 2000: 351–4). Despite the king's protection, the Jews were potentially at risk from attack, although the physical evidence of bladed injuries to skeletons in the Jewish cemetery is comparable to Christian cemeteries (Daniell 2001).

The events following the coronation of Richard I proved how vulnerable the small communities of Jews could be to Christian persecution. From the mid-twelfth century anti-Semitism spread through England, fuelled by spurious tales of the death of Christian children by Jews. Some of the victims were made into saints. Such stories occurred at Norwich in 1144, following the death of a boy named William who was made into a local saint (Anderson 1964). The coronation of Richard I in 1189 marked the beginning of attacks and massacres against the Jewish communities. The first attack, against two prominent Jews from York, occurred during the coronation itself. The anti-Semitic movement spread rapidly throughout the eastern seaboard, with outbreaks in (King's) Lynn, Stamford, Bury St Edmunds, Norwich and Lincoln. That the worst attacks took place in these eastern trading communities, with little happening for example in Bristol, probably shows the close co-operation of the east coast trading communities.

The most fearsome attacks took place in York, a major port in its own right. A combination of events heightened the anti-Semitic atmosphere. Local nobles and traders had become indebted to the Jews and the crusading zeal which was sweeping the kingdom in anticipation of the Third Crusade, which Richard I himself led, created a potent mix. It was also the beginning of Lent, which highlighted the death of Christ by the Jews. Jews and their property were attacked and so for safety they fled to the royal castle. They gained access to the keep (today called Clifford's Tower), whilst below in the bailey there was the baying Christian mob. The Christians besieged the Jews and far from being a short-term incident, the siege lasted nearly a week. The attackers even had time to build and set in place siege engines. Local authority completely broke down, with the Sheriff of Yorkshire, John Marshall, unable to control the situation. After almost a week the situation was so desperate that the Jews decided to take their own lives. The men slitting the throats of the women and children first and then their own. Those that survived were offered safe passage the following morning by the Christians, who then reneged on their promises and killed the survivors. Elated with success the Christians marched on York Minster where the Jewish bonds were stored for safe keeping and burnt them in the middle of the nave (Dobson 1999).

As the Jews were crown property King Richard exacted his revenge by levying fines upon the participants and the leading figures of the cities and towns involved. Long term, however, many of the citizens retained their positions and continued to be influential in local politics. The Jewish communities survived (in York's case a community re-established itself) and remained a prominent source of money for the king until the mid-twelfth century, when they began to be taxed too heavily. By the time of their forcible expulsion from England by Edward I in 1290 the Jewish communities were impoverished.

Popular religion

Not surprisingly the official teachings of the church and the actions of the church hierarchy dominate the religious history of the twelfth century, partly because of their crucial role in the history of the country, but also because of the huge number of records that have been left behind. The beliefs and actions of the non-noble laity are harder to determine.

However, the *Life of Christina of Markyate*, shows how the lay and spiritual members of a community in the first half of the twelfth century could interact (Talbot 1959). The impression given is of considerable spontaneous interaction between important lay people and the church. Christina's trials and tribulations were considerable as her parents (Autti and Beatrix) tried everything in their power to change her decision to follow a religious life. In the course of their attempts they, or Christina, approached a host of eminent ecclesiastics of local or national importance. Some ecclesiastics occurred in the account almost by accident, such as Ranulf Flambard, the Bishop of Durham who attempted to seduce Christina and Christina's maternal aunt Alveva was his mistress. Other ecclesiastics were deliberately approached, such as the Archbishop of Canterbury, the Abbot of St Albans and the bishops of Durham and Lincoln. In Huntingdon there was frequent liaison between Christina's family and Fredebert, the abbot of the Augustinian monastery who at one point even approached Bishop Robert of Lincoln with the noble citizens of Huntingdon on Autti's behalf. At a most local level there were numerous minor clerics who feature in the account, such as Edwin, Sueno and a solitary but telling reference to Autti's personal chaplain. The family visited the shrine of St Alban when Christina was young, and also as a family visited the local Augustinian monastery in Huntingdon. Even though they were women there is no indication that Beatrix or her daughters were not freely admitted into them and welcomed. It was to be expected that ecclesiastics would feature prominently once Christina had chosen to become a recluse, but the account shows a remarkable interaction between a prominent citizen and a wide range of ecclesiastical figures at all levels. Admittedly the family were rich, but even so it is unlikely that there would be such flexibility, and almost casual contact, by the thirteenth century.

Villagers were expected to go to Mass every Sunday, but there is little evidence about actual attendance. The congregation played no part in the Mass and so people talked during the service or walked in and out, a task made much easier by the lack of seating in the central part of the nave, though there may have been benches along the walls. It was widely recognised that the most important moment was the elevation of the host, when the priest held the host above his head, thereby changing the bread into the body of Christ through a miraculous process called 'transubstantiation'. This was also repeated when the wine turned into the blood of Christ. The literal truth of the change had long been believed and the first miracle story about transubstantiation was recorded in the seventh century *Life of St Gregory the Great*, and miraculous stories concerning the Eucharist were well known in twelfth century England (Rubin 1991: 110–11). Communion by the congregation was once a year on Maundy Thursday. Before taking communion they were expected to confess their sins.

Confession had long been part of the church's teaching but until the middle of the twelfth century only the exceptionally religious had made confession. However, with heresies such as Catharism growing in southern France and northern Italy the church became increasingly concerned about a person's beliefs and actions and promoted confession widely amongst the laity and churchmen themselves. Confessions had to be inaudible to anyone but the priest, but in full public view. If the person repented of their thought or action, then a penance was given which in theory reflected the seriousness of the crime. To help confessors, manuals were written which detailed procedure and indicated appropriate penances.

The laity could be taught through a variety of mediums. Preaching tours by bishops could draw crowds but were infrequent. The most famous tour was by Baldwin, the Archbishop of Canterbury, whose tour in 1188 of Wales was recorded in detail by Gerald of Wales. The tour was intended to gain recruits for the Third Crusade. Monks from monasteries might preach in their localities, or the village priest might instruct his flock, though as most were illiterate and largely uneducated their theological message might be garbled. Other sources of instruction included plays, art and sculpture based on religious themes (see Chapter 8) and anecdotal miracle stories.

An individual could help his or her soul by a series of actions. Pilgrimage grew in popularity as the twelfth century progressed for it was seen as both a spiritual journey of the soul and an arduous physical journey. The sites of the major cults drew pilgrims from across Europe. The most difficult and dangerous to reach, but the most spiritually rewarding, were the sacred places of the Holy Land which had been made accessible by their capture by the crusaders. Nearer to home was the shrine of St James at Compestella, but the cult of Thomas Becket and his shrine at Canterbury rapidly became one of the most important shrines in Europe. There was increasing recognition amongst church authorities that a cult was beneficial both in terms of spiritual power and as inducement to pilgrims to visit and leave donations. The site of a saint's shrine was a place of heavenly power on earth where prayers could be offered to the saint for intercession or thanks for deliverance. Despite the growing interest in saints, only four English saints were canonised during the period 1066–1215 (Edward the Confessor in 1161, Thomas Becket in 1173, Gilbert of Sempringham in 1202 and Wulfstan of Worcester in 1203). Many Anglo-Saxon saints were promoted after the Norman Conquest (see Chapter 1) and many local cults were started in the twelfth century based on a particular holy person, such as the boy martyr William of Norwich who died in Norwich in 1144. Once formed, the saint's church promoted the cult as widely as possible with proof of the saint's intervention through miracle stories and visions. Some cults, such as that of Thomas Becket, gained immediate and instant success internationally, whilst others only slowly gained momentum. Archbishop William of York died in 1154 and miracles associated with him only began in the mid-1170s. He was eventually canonised in 1226, but his cult was only prominent around York.

However, whilst the writings of church leaders often give the impression of a purely Christian society, in many areas there was a mixture of Christian, pagan and frankly bizarre beliefs. In his journey through Wales, Gerald of Wales recorded many folk beliefs, traditions and wonders. Many involve the natural world, such as a doe with horns or fighting fish (Thorpe 1978: 78–9). Such signs, and miracles in general, were seen as evidence of God's power on earth. It was thought that by piecing together such instances the underlying purpose of God's will on earth could be uncovered. One miracle showed God's intervention in a particular event, the collection of miracles was hoped to reveal God's purpose.

There was also a darker side, a side which revealed the workings of the devil or sorcery. Gerald of Wales records many instances of the devil's work. A Welshman called Meilyr could see the devil and other unclean spirits and regularly talked with them, thereby being able to prophesy the future (Thorpe 1978: 117). Other spirits too were abroad in the world. An incubus, which had made love to a young woman, talked to Meilyr and he was therefore able to have foreknowledge of secrets and events. Gerald does, however, reveal his puzzlement about these events saying that:

> It seems most odd to me . . . that Meilyr was able to see these demons clearly with the eyes in his head. Spirits cannot be seen with our physical eyes, unless they themselves assume corporeal substance. . . . [As they] have made themselves visible, how was it that they could not be seen by other individuals?
>
> (Thorpe 1978: 117)

At a local village level devils and superstition could play an important part in spiritual life. The chronicler William of Newbrugh wrote of several encounters by Ketell, a man gifted with the power to see devils: 'Ketell used to say that some demons were large, robust and crafty, and, when permitted by a superior power extremely hurtful; others were small and contemptible, impotent in strength and dull in understanding.' Ketell saw devils all around and a pair were responsible for him falling off his horse. Furthermore,

> he once entered a public house, and saw devils . . . in the likeness of apes, sitting on the shoulders of all who were drinking, voiding their spittle into the cups, and deriding the stupidity of these men . . . And when prayers were said (as is customary) . . . they leaped off affrighted, being unable to endure the virtue of that sacred name.
>
> (Stevenson 1996: 474)

A remedy for the deviousness and visitation of the devil and his cohorts was through prayer or reciting the Gospels. In the case of Ketell, prayers were said in the public house, and at other times if the name of the name of the Saviour was said, the devils backed off. In the case of Meilyr, when he was harassed beyond all endurance by devils the Gospel of St John was placed in his lap and unclean spirits flew away (Thorpe 1978: 117).

Other darker elements include witches and ghosts, and both begin to enter the literature in the twelfth century. A mid-twelfth-century tradition stated that when the Normans attacked Hereward the Wake in his fenland fortress they used a witch to help them. She said her incantations three times, and at the end of each she uncovered her rear and pointed in the direction of Hereward and his men (Thomas 1998: 226). As this tale is anti-Norman it has been portrayed as comically obscene magic, but it is an early reference to a witch and witchcraft. During the twelfth century tales of ghosts became increasingly common, with ghosts appearing to warn of the terrors of the afterlife, a fate which should be avoided by the recipient of the ghost (Finucane 1984: 60).

There were many other beliefs and superstitions. Gerald records how the Fleming community in Wales could foretell the future by examining the shoulder blades of rams (Thorpe 1978:146). Other superstitions were prevalent, such as the link between sneezing and divining the future (Short 1995: 153). Orderic Vitalis related how William Rufus, on the eve of his death, rejected divine warnings through dreams with a contemptuous reference to the English faith in the snore and dreams of little old women (Thomas 1998: 226).

Omens could have a powerful impact. At times of stress everything could be seen as an omen. During the preparations for the Conquest Halley's Comet could be seen clearly in the night sky – it is shown on the Bayeux Tapestry – and it was taken as an omen by both sides. Working out whether an omen was good or bad was not always easy and often depended on the quick reactions of individuals. Other omens before the Battle of Hastings included William slipping on the beach and bloodying his nose, which was instantly taken as a bad omen; many men were very frightened until William FitzOsbern reversed the meaning of the omen 'do not take this as unlucky; it is really an omen of success. See, he has claimed England, taking possession of it with both hands, and he has consecrated it as his inheritance by his own lineage by marking it with his own blood' (Searle 1980b: 35).

7 Economy and society

Details of everyday life begin to multiply in the twelfth century, both through historical sources and archaeology. However, whilst the details are important, there are some dominant issues which develop as the century progresses: the economy, specialisation and the use of space. Individuals at the time may not have been aware of these in particular, but with historical hindsight they are clearly visible.

The economy and economic trends

From the Norman Conquest onwards the English economy can, for the first time, be studied in detail as the wealth of information available grows. A key question is whether the amount of trade increased or remained static in comparison with the population, which in turn would answer the problem of whether the country was becoming increasingly commercialised. If the amount of commerce did grow significantly, then did it affect the power structures which were initially largely based on service by tenants after the Conquest? There are two key sets of economic records for the period between 1066 and 1215 which give an economic snapshot across the country: Domesday Book of 1086, and from the mid-twelfth century the Pipe Rolls. There are also numerous single or fragmentary texts, from charters to account rolls, which also cast light on the situation.

Domesday Book and Pipe Rolls

Domesday Book is the starting point for all detailed debate about the economy. *The Anglo-Saxon Chronicle* relates that when William the Conqueror was at Gloucester at midwinter 1085, he met with his councillors 'and held very deep conversation with his council about this land, how it was occupied, or with which men' (Swanton 2000: 216). The reasons for the survey, and the questions included, have never fully been explained, though various explanations have been given (Loyn 1978: 122; Wormald 1992: 61; Kappelle 1992), including that of a 'vast administrative mistake' (Richardson and Sayles 1963: 28). The most obvious explanation is that it is a tax register, but if that was all, then it could have been much simpler in style and content. An alternative explanation is that the Domesday survey was a register of land following the upheavals of the Conquest, sorting out the legal issues, or at least highlighting them, but its primary purpose does not seem to have been of 'a sustained campaign to clarify the tenurial confusion left by the Norman Conquest' (Wormald 1992: 74). Whether deliberately or not, the survey emphasised William the Conqueror's control over the country by making the royal presence known in every village in the land (Hyams 1986: 134–6).

Fortunately, the details of compilation either have survived or can be worked out. The information was collected by king's commissioners – the only names surviving are of the commissioners for Worcestershire, which included the Bishop of Lincoln and three leading barons who did not hold land locally. The information for separate counties varies considerably, but the consistent details between groups of counties allow the seven circuits to be determined: Circuit I contained the counties of Kent, Surrey, Sussex, Hampshire and Berkshire. However, even within a circuit there are marked differences between counties, for example there are no tenants recorded in Kent, whilst a large number are recorded in Surrey – this was probably due to the methods of collection and compilation of the data rather than a real difference of landownership (Mortimer 1980: 131).

Before the circuit commissioners visited the shire towns a lot of information had already been gathered. Following William's decree at Gloucester, the tenants-in-chief compiled their own information and the royal sheriffs gathered information about the king's estates. Harvey's work has shown that the Anglo-Saxons must have had their own surveys (the mechanisms of collection the Normans probably used), and some information probably already existed from previous Anglo-Saxon surveys (Harvey 1971, 1975, 1985). The information was then passed to the county courts where it was checked by county jurors who also may have added details. Whereas landholders gave information according to their landholdings, the jurors' responsibilities were within the hundreds of counties, and so the information was re-arranged from landholder into geographical order by county. Various documents have survived from the early stages of the Domesday investigations which show the process in action. The *Inquisitio Comitatus Cantabrigensis* is a record which lists the jurors from thirteen of the sixteen Hundreds of Cambridgeshire. The jurors' testimony was most likely to be oral, given under oath. Others who may have given oral testimony included a range of people from the sheriff, to barons, priests and peasants from every in village the county or from more local courts (Fleming 1994: 101). The survey did not rely on oral evidence alone. Archbishop Lanfranc wrote a letter to 'S' (probably a Domesday commissioner) confirming that 'in those counties in which you have been assigned the duty of making an inquest I have no demense [i.e. directly farmed] land' (Clover and Gibson 1979: 170–3). Unless this letter is an aberration, many other such letters would have been sent to the circuit commissioners (Loyn 1978: 122).

From the county courts, the returns were sent to circuit centres where draft circuit returns were compiled by rearranging the county entries into lists of the most important landholders. One draft circuit return survives, that of the the Exon (or Exeter) Domesday, which covered Circuit II (Wiltshire, Dorset, Somerset, Devon and Cornwall). By this stage the collection of information was complete and over 90 per cent of information was included from the Exon Domesday into the final Great Domesday. Not every circuit may have had such a volume. Draft returns were probably produced for every circuit and then, it is assumed, they were sent to Winchester to be compiled into its present form, the Great or Exchequer Domesday. The final product consisted of two large volumes, containing six circuits. Circuit VII, which covered East Anglia (Norfolk, Suffolk and Essex), is contained in a fair provincial volume, instead of a draft, which still survives and is known as Little Domesday (or Domesday II). It is much more detailed than Great Domesday Book, though why it survives as a separate volume is puzzling.

The survey was completed at lightning speed, certainly by William's death in September 1087 and probably by August 1086. In that month an assembly of the chief landholders of England met at Salisbury to swear their loyalty to William. The Salisbury Oath may well be the key to explain why Domesday Book was compiled because it may have been the formal recognition of the nobles' titles, given in return for their oath (Holt 1997: 137–8), though as Kappelle (Kappelle 1992) points out it is odd that such an oath was not required before. It may be, however, that the oath was required for the succession of William Rufus (much in the same way that Henry I demanded oaths of loyalty from the nobles for his daughter Matilda) for England and Normandy would be split between William Rufus and Robert Curthose, creating divided loyalties between nobles with lands either side of the Channel.

Domesday Book admittedly contains many puzzles, inconsistencies and omissions, for example the northern counties beyond North Yorkshire were omitted, which contained an estimated 8 per cent of England's population (Snooks 1995: 31). Even so, it is a phenomenal record of the country in 1086. It is the starting point for all economic assessment for the eleventh and twelfth centuries and beyond. The survey also reveals many sidelights of England, including the earliest extant record of approximately 40 per cent of English place names and it is the largest single corpus of eleventh-century English personal names (Clark 1992: 317). Other recent studies on information within Domesday Book include slavery (Moore 1988), language interpreters (Tsurushima 1995) and law disputes (Wormald 1992).

In terms of the economy Domesday Book allows some estimate of the size of the population. Population size is an important aspect of the economy, and its growth – or decline – allows for a greater understanding of the commercialism that was taking place in the country. Although Domesday allows an assessment of population, there is an element of guesswork and many checks and balances have to be built in (Moore 1996). Domesday Book generally records the landholders, and sometimes a priest or other individual, but apart from the named individuals, there is little indication of the additional population such as women, children and the elderly. The quantification of these additional people varies considerably between historians. A reasonable, if conservative figure, is a population of 1,500,000 across the country, though this has been revised upwards in recent years to 2 million people (Moore 1996: 334).

As well as establishing the population in 1086, there is also the issue of population growth. A quadrupling of population, which Snooks suggests (Snooks 1995: 51), would cast a very different light on the growth of the economy and the process of commercialisation compared with a population which remained static as Bridbury suggests (Bridbury 1992). A static population would equate with a very high commercialisation of society, whereas a quadrupling of the population means that the greater number of people would have needed to trade more in any case. Both are at the extremes of what most historians envisage, especially as there is a generally agreed population of 5–6 million by 1300.

After Domesday Book, the information about the population and the economy fades away to small pieces of evidence which has to be pieced together. However, through the cumulative evidence (King 1996) there is the impression of, and some evidence for, increased economic activity, whether through the foundation of towns, the growth of older established towns, the increase in the known markets and fairs, or the clearance of forest and the drainage of marshland by lords improving their lands. This impression may, however, be overstated by the parallel growth in the quantity and quality or the records. Furthermore, huge areas of land were made into areas of forest (see below) and strictly controlled, with the result that previously unrecorded land would have been subject to documentation and corrective action. To some extent economic activity in the forests may have actively decreased during the reign of Henry II, as he steadily increased the area technically described as forest (see below).

The greatest source of information about the king's income and expenditure in the second half of the twelfth century are the Pipe Rolls. These record the annual revenue and expenditure which passed through the exchequer, though they do not include the more important chamber accounts (see Chapter 5). As a group the Pipe Rolls are the best source of nationwide economic data as year on year, county by county, the Pipe Rolls reveal in detail income and expenses of the exchequer. The number of entries steadily increases as the century progresses. Entries are generally grouped and include the payments by sheriffs for their power in the county (the sheriff's farms), as well as specific payments of fines, forest revenues and other payments to the king. The earliest Pipe Rolls dates from 1129–30 (with entries going back to 1125) and then in continuous sequence from 1154–5 onwards, with a short break at the end of King John's reign, before they resume under Henry III.

The individual Pipe Roll entries follow a set pattern: the name of the person, what the payment (usually some sort of fine) was for and then three amounts of money: the amount owed in the year, the amount paid and the remaining balance. It is not uncommon for the full amount never to be paid, which may be due to death of the debtor, or alternatively, as Hollister has described, royal patronage. Royal favourites may pay little or nothing over a long period of time, and are sometimes excused payment altogether, a feature which often occurs during the reign of Henry II (Hollister 1979: 103).

Analysis of the Pipe Rolls has shown huge fluctuations year on year, but with a general upward trend, though some of this would have been accounted for by a rise in inflation (see below). Considerable analysis has been undertaken on the Pipe Roll of 1129–30 (Hollister 1979: 98; Green 1989b: 51–94). About £24,200 is recorded as being paid to the treasury and about £5,500 being exempted, whether through pardons, exemption of the Danegeld tax or the effects of patronage. The Pipe Roll of 1129–30 stands as an isolated piece of evidence for the king's revenue and expenditure, but this may have been deliberate, as it recorded a very high amount of revenue (which was not exceeded until the end of the twelfth century).

One of the advantages of the Pipe Rolls of England and Normandy is that they can be compared, both with each other and as a basis for English/French records. English income and expenditure was just under 3.5 times greater than that of Normandy (Moss 1994: 194). Calculations made for the year 1180 showed that income from England was significantly higher than that from Normandy alone, but that the income from Normandy was significantly more than the French kings from their lands (Bates 1994: 32).

Sources of wealth

The king depended on income to rule effectively. A poor king could not give significant patronage to encourage loyalty nor could mercenaries be bought to protect the king's interests. Warfare was expensive. The building of castles and defences increasingly became more complicated and costly during the twelfth century and in one year (1197–8) one castle (Andeli in Normandy) alone cost nearly £49,000 (Allen Brown 1955).

The king had three main ways to raise money. The first was through the income and rents from his own lands and possessions. The second way was through his feudal rights as the greatest lord in the land – he could legally demand money from his tenants, just as any lord could (see Chapter 4). These rights also included the income from justice in the courts. The income from justice could be substantial and the fees and fines contained within the earliest Pipe Roll of 1130 contributed about 10 per cent towards all English royal revenues. In King John's reign income from justice rose to unprecedented levels after the autumn of 1210 (Turner 1999: 326). The third way was through taxation (see below).

Kings rarely had enough money for their desires, but comments by chroniclers show how the amounts in royal treasuries could rise or fall. Several chroniclers reported that by 1139 King Stephen had exhausted the well-stocked treasury of Henry I, and the aftermath of the Anarchy saw Henry II in a perilous financial position (Prestwich 1954: 37–42; Eales 1985: 102). The administrative machinery of accounting seems to have lapsed during Stephen's reign, to the extent that Nigel, the Bishop of Ely, was brought out of retirement to resurrect the financial machinery. The low receipts and disorder of the first years of accounting during Henry II's reign show how the previous system of accountability had broken down. It is, however, conceivable that Stephen had simply switched to an alternative system, the details of which are now lost, for he was able to continue effectively the costly business of warfare (Green 1991: 113).

The biggest source of income came from the royal lands. At the time of Domesday in 1086 over a quarter of the land was managed directly for the king (demesne lands), but through the reigns of William Rufus and Henry I the amount of demesne land steadily decreased as both kings alienated land to reward their followers, which in turn meant a considerable loss of revenue (Green 1979). By the start of the reign of Henry II the chronicler Gerald of Wales estimated that so much land had been granted from the royal demesne that the returns to the treasury were only £8,000 a year (though Henry II was considered wealthy by his other income). The nature of rent also changed. Payments had traditionally been in kind, particularly food, which allowed for plentiful food supplies for an itinerant king journeying around his kingdom. However, in the twelfth century, payment in kind was commuted into a monetary payment, a change which probably happened during the reign of Henry I (Green 1979: 348).

The period of the turbulent civil wars of the Anarchy between King Stephen and the Empress Matilda are difficult to assess in terms of the economy because the systems of centralised record-keeping ceased. It is notoriously difficult to define the period of the Anarchy in terms of any quantitative calculation of physical destruction, for the calculations have to be made by the later actions of Henry II. It may even be that Henry II's measures exceeded those which were needed for a return to the status quo of Henry I's reign. When Henry II gained the throne he immediately set about re-establishing the wealth of the crown. The machinery of central government was re-established and Nigel, Bishop of Ely, was reinstated to run the exchequer – a position Nigel had held during Henry I's reign. Crown lands were recovered which had either been lost by encroachment (purprestures) or when land had been granted out and then not returned when the owner died without any heirs (escheats). A major restocking of royal manors was also started. In 1156 the cost of restocking was £1,178 – or 30 per cent of total expenditure of the Pipe Roll – which suggests either war damage or that the manors had been severely neglected (Green 1991: 103–4; King 1996: 20).

Part of the disruption may have been 'simple inertia', with payments not being made because it was known that no checks would be carried out (King 1996: 19).

Henry also reintroduced the national tax known as the Danegeld, though it could not be collected in the many places which were described as 'waste' – a term which could include the effects of war, disputes as to who owned the land or out of date assessments. The Danegeld had been originally instigated by the Anglo-Saxon kings as a method of paying off the Vikings and it has been described as 'the first system of national taxation in Western Europe' (Douglas 1977: 299) because it was based on the land assessment of the number of hides a local community had. The reasons for the tax had become redundant by the twelfth century although collections were still being made. King Stephen was alleged to have promised to abolish the tax in 1139 (Green 1991: 104) but it was Henry II who allowed it to lapse after 1162. Why such a system of national taxation was discontinued is puzzling, especially as in 1162 it still raised over half of what was possible (Warren 1983: 377). The tax was attempted again in 1173 and 1174 and in Richard I's reign, but it was deeply unpopular and so was dropped.

By the 1170s the taxation scheme had fundamentally changed from a national land tax of the Danegeld to a wealth tax, based on the knight's fee, or payments due from the 'feudal incidents' (such as payments for the knighting of a son, or as a ransom, or on the marriage of a daughter). During Henry II's reign three levies were raised for the Crusades in 1166 and then in 1185 and 1188. The 1188 tax was particularly heavy and was known as the 'Saladin Tithe'. Collectors were appointed to receive 10 per cent of a person's revenues and movable goods with a local jury checking that people had paid correctly. The tax was deeply unpopular and William of Newbrugh commented that it was a 'heavy tax' upon England. Even so, the one-off taxation on a percentage of a person's wealth for particular reasons was a blueprint which was copied extensively throughout the Middle Ages.

The king also received income from towns and cities, either from payments to maintain their liberties, or as fines for misdemeanours. These could be substantial. In 1191 the Pipe Roll records that York citizens paid £100 for half a year as part of the city's 'farm' (the payment made for the continuation of privileges), a £10 increase ('cremento'), the city's guild of weavers paid £10, the sheriff paid 78s for an encroachment ('propresturis'), the citizens owed 10 marks (a mark is two-thirds of one pound), and the burgesses owed 200 marks for their liberties. There were also the fines upon the individual townsmen, such as Wiardus the wine seller who was fined 20s for selling wine 'against the assize' (either outside the legal time of the market or short measure). In 1195 the citizens were required to pay 300 marks as a 'gift' to free Richard I from imprisonment. It has been suggested that the urban wealth was of critical importance in maintaining the civil war between Stephen and Matilda, for Stephen could seek revenue or loans from London, Winchester, York and (for a time) Lincoln, whereas the Earl of

Gloucester, Matilda's key supporter, controlled Bristol with its growing trade (Green 1991: 106).

Other forms of income included loans. There was a range of sources available, for example from Christians, such as William Cade (Jenkinson 1913), Jews, military orders (such as the Knights Templar) or overseas. The Jews were an important part of the economy, for they were a major source of credit and, as they were debarred from many occupations, money lending was their main source of livelihood. The scale of their operations could be vast. When Aaron of Lincoln died in 1186 his debts were taken over by the crown and there was so much money involved that the 'Exchequer of Aaron' was established. Many people across society borrowed money from the Jews, but the interest charged was high: 22 per cent, 44 per cent or 66 per cent per annum (one, two or three pence per week per pound).

Following the Norman Conquest the Jews settled in London and may have been instrumental in funding many of the building programmes and influencing the English Exchequer (Loyn 2000: 145). Small groups of Jews began to move out from London, and Stacey (1995) has suggested that the Jews first became serious moneylenders in England during King Stephen's reign, where the disruption of trade and the chaos of war encouraged people to take out loans and to pawn objects. By 1159, however, a definite pattern had emerged: the Jews were geographically defined in those areas which were both in King Stephen's control and where there were important mints and fairs. The links between the Jews and the mints can be explained by the huge quantities of silver bullion needed for minting money.

In the mid-twelfth century the Jews were not the only moneylenders and a group of powerful Christians were also lending money at interest, a group which included William Cade, William fitz Isabel and Gervase and Henry of Cornhill. Amongst this group interest could be charged, but more often a penalty was imposed if payment was not made by the due date. After about 1190 the Christian group faded away, probably because both church and crown were beginning to punish severely Christian usurers (the king claimed the estates of usurers).

Between 1200 and 1250 money lending seems to have been left entirely to the Jews. The Jews of England were a unique community in Europe for they had their own exchequer in which they could register bonds and could have assistance in collecting their debts, for a price. Moreover, they were the legal possessions of the king, who protected them – for a price – and he could levy tax upon the Jewish community at will. The king regularly taxed the Jews, for example in 1210 King John taxed the Jews 66,000 marks (Bolton 1999: 37).

The church did not escape the attentions of kings who needed to raise money and in times of crisis heavy tax burdens were put upon churches, sometimes as obligatory 'voluntary aids'. Work on William Rufus's policy of financial exaction of monasteries has shown that the king was selective in his exactions, pressing the more wealthy monasteries and cathedrals (Rudd

1988: 252). Individual royal servants could increase the pressure and Orderic Vitalis described how Ranulf Flambard went so far as to measure monastic lands with a rope to make sure the boundaries of lands were correct (Mason 1998: 141). An alternative was simply to seize property, for the churches contained a huge amount of gold, silver and jewellery. King Stephen was told he would never lack money whilst the monasteries were full of treasure. The monastery of Abingdon was raided on Stephen's orders and the Abbot of St Albans had to melt down treasure for the royalist cause (Green 1991: 105).

However, there does seem to have been an appeal process whereby what was seen as excessive taxation was challenged by the monasteries, or in cases of exceptional expenditure the requirement for payment was relaxed. Ramsey and Whitby seem to have made challenges, and Thorney challenged its assessment so successfully that a writ was sent to Ranulf Flambard and Urse d'Abetot ordering them 'to assess the abbey . . . as leniently as any honour in England possessing the same amount of land' (Mason 1998: 139). Exceptional allowable expenditure was various, but included church building and repair. Perhaps because of the building works and repairs to Thorney Church, the abbey was exempted from toll on its clothing, food and materials for the church roof, and in the same vein, Abbot Baldwin of Bury St Edmunds was given the right to transport by water the necessary building stone for the church toll-free (Mason 1998: 139).

A nobleman's revenue could come from a variety of sources, with the most important being from his estates. The wealthiest nobles or churches owned extensive estates across many counties. The estates of the Bishop of Winchester as given in Domesday Book included over 100 mills and 970 plough teams scattered over southern England and the Midlands, estates which had the valuation of £1,325 (Lennard 1959: 77). These lands were a combination of estates managed directly (the demesne lands) or the rents from those leased out. The organisation of estates tended to follow a general principle following the Conquest, which was first noticed by Lennard (1959), who discovered that the lord tended to keep direct control over his most valuable manors, a situation that can be replicated many times. Even regional nobleman followed this pattern and in Devon Judhael of Totnes directly managed fourteen out of twenty of his most valuable estates, including the five largest. There was no geographical unity to the pattern and the only feature linking the estates was their high value. He leased out his other estates to tenants, so in total he held 47 per cent of total land value directly, a figure comparable with landholders of the first rank across England (Williams 1993:278). A consequence of keeping the most profitable estates was that Judhael had to reward his followers with a greater number of smaller estates, thereby producing large clusters of lands held by one person or family, a pattern also noticed for major tenants-in-chief by Le Patourel and Mortimer (Williams 1993: 278–9).

Accounts connected with farming and estates are rare, though fragments have survived. A fragment survives concerning the estate of Robert II de Lacy between his death and the succession of Roger, Constable of Chester 1194–5. However, as the date of his death or succession is not known precisely the length of time the roll covers could be as little as six weeks or over seven months (Wightman 1966: 95). Occasionally information about estates is given in the Pipe Rolls when a person's goods and lands are under the king's supervision. An example of this is the description in the Pipe Rolls (23 Henry II, pp. 81–2) of the estate of Count Conan, which included pigs, sheep, horses and hawks. A fuller set of accounts is that of the Bishop of Winchester's estates for the years 1204, 1208–9, 1211, 1218, 1219, 1220, 1224 and 1225. The 1208–9 accounts include details of the number of sheep, oxen and cows, as well as the cost of a millstone (24 shillings), digging in the gardens (8s 5d), spreading six acres with dung (6d), making a dovecote (22s 11½d) and making two gates for the sheepfold (2s). Although a proportion of animals and produce would be used by the great household with its ever-consuming needs, in reasonable conditions there would be enough to trade locally in the markets and there is reference to the numbers of animals bought, sold or died – of the 104 oxen from the previous year in the current year (1208–9) 17 were bought, 12 sold, 21 died, leaving 91. There are similar statistics for the cows, sheep, hogs and chickens. The workings of such estates can be seen by the rules set out in the mid-thirteenth-century estate books, such as the *Seneschaucy* and *Husbandry* by Walter of Henley (Oschinsky 1971).

However, whilst estates can be described and pinpointed through the evidence of charters, a large proportion of the wealth-making activities of trade is lost as the day-to-day business of merchants is unrecorded. One indication of the growing power of merchants as a collective unit is the widespread formation of guilds, particularly the Guild Merchant. Guilds as drinking assemblies had been known in the late Anglo-Saxon period, but following the Conquest they became more specialised. In particular weavers formed guilds in many major cities during the early twelfth century, such as at Oxford, Winchester and Lincoln. However, the Guild Merchant was the most important single guild in most towns. The workings of the guilds remain largely hidden, although one feast is recorded in the *Life of Christina of Markyate* (Talbot 1959: 49). Christina's father and mother had the place of honour and Christina as their 'eldest and most worthy daughter' had the honour of being cup-bearer. The presence of Christina and her mother show that such occasions were not male-only affairs. However, records about Christina's family also show how the general pattern of the records are heavily influenced towards land and property. The family was of ancient Anglo-Saxon stock, had survived the Norman Conquest and had remained wealthy and influential in the area around Huntingdon. Yet despite their standing – being part of the influential Guild Merchant of Huntingdon and having substantial contact with the bishops of Durham and Lincoln (Ranulf Flambard, Bishop of Durham, had Christina's maternal aunt as his mistress) – there is only one possible reference to Christina's father, Autti, in any surviving records apart from the account of Christina's life. The solitary record concerns Autti of Huntingdon giving the church of Shillington in Bedfordshire to the Abbot of Ramsey (Talbot 1959: 10–11). It is a sobering, but necessary, realisation that wealthy people may not enter records of the twelfth century at all unless a land transaction was involved or they transgressed and so were fined.

The only source of comparative trade figures on a national scale are the Pipe Rolls covering the period July 1203 to 29 November 1204 which list the money paid by ports around the east and south coasts of England. London comes top, having paid £836, followed by Boston (£780) – (presumably so high through the export of wool), and then Southampton (£712). The total figure for all the thirty-five ports is £4,958. As the tax collected was a fifteenth of the total, the total amount of trade was £74,375 (Poole 1955: 96). The figures of the ports stand alone as a tantalising glimpse of the amount of otherwise unrecorded trade.

Although there are no comparative figures for inland towns and cities, there was recognition by lords, both secular and ecclesiastical, of the importance of towns in generating revenue from rents or trade. The definition of a town can be measured either by economic activity (such as markets or fairs) or by legal foundation documents which defined the privileges of the townspeople. Between 1066 and the 1220s over 125 planned towns were founded in England, but they were not founded at an even rate nor proportionally by the same groups of people. Between Domesday Book of 1086 and 1100 one in three (32 per cent) towns were founded by the king, 40 per cent by laymen and 24 per cent by ecclesiastical authorities (either bishops or monasteries). In the period between 1101 and 1188 the kings founded only 19 per cent of towns with laymen founding 60 per cent. The location of towns also varied, with 80 per cent of towns between 1066 and 1100 being set alongside castles. Thereafter more towns were situated in commercial locations, such as the new town of Boston in Lincolnshire which by 1204 had become one of the great trading ports of the east coast (Beresford 1967: 335). Not all flourished and the failure rate is considered to be one in seven (Hindle 1990: 8). Monastic new towns have occasionally left plentiful evidence through surveys, charters and other records. Domesday Book of 1086 records the foundation of some towns, as at Bury St Edmunds where 342 houses had been built on land that had been arable land in the time of Edward the Confessor (Gransden 1981: 74). A well-documented example is that of the town which grew up around Battle Abbey. The Abbey laid out plots of land with generous frontages (35–40 feet) and deep gardens. Gradually a community formed and within twenty years a town was geographically recognisable (Searle 1990: 1). The towns attracted people to them and a rental of *c*.1100 for Battle shows over 100 burgage tenants, the majority of whom were local families though some came from overseas, a pattern repeated at Colchester (Clark 1978: 242). At Battle town traditions and institutions were started. There were two guildhalls which were 'almost certainly the common breweries of the town' and so used for feasting, but the guilds probably also discussed communal matters such as peace-keeping (Searle 1990: 6).

Towns were also the natural location for weekly markets and annual fairs. Whilst the majority of markets have unrecorded origins, some can be shown to be definitely post-Conquest, such as the market William the Conqueror's queen, Matilda, set up in Tewkesbury before 1086, and those markets which started outside the gates of post-Conquest castles or monasteries. From the mid-twelfth century markets and fairs became seen as a valuable financial commodity, for stalls and trading rights could be rented or sold, and the king could grant the right to hold a fair (Britnell 1993: 10–28). One such example is Henry de Lacy who bought the right from Henry II for an eight-day fair at Pontefract during the feast of St Giles, which probably increased both his own and the town's wealth (Wightman 1966: 93). Areas in towns also began to be designated for specific activities, such as the meat market (macello) held in York (probably the meat market in the Shambles), as recorded in Domesday Book.

Most of the nation's trade consisted of individuals buying and selling goods either in the markets or by hawking them around the countryside. Such hawkers rarely make it into the literature as they were a lowly part of society, though a rare reference to a pot seller occurs when Hereward the Wake disguises himself as one and enters a kitchen (Thomas 1998: 226). The account does not imply it was a regular round, but rather an ad hoc visit. A more detailed example is that of Godric, who later became St Godric of Finchale. He began life trading small commodities and rose to become a substantial merchant, but would have been unknown if his life had not been written by Reginald of Durham, who gives a vivid description of Godric's life as a trader:

> he began to follow the chapman's way of life, first learning how to gain in small bargains and things of insignificant price; and thence, while yet a youth, his mind advanced little by little to buy and sell and gain from things of greater expense. For, in his beginnings, he was wont to wander with small wares around the villages and farmsteads of his own neighbourhood; but, in process of time, he gradually associated himself by compact with city merchants. Hence, within a brief space of time, the youth who had trudged for many weary hours from village to village, from farm to farm, did so profit by his increase of age and wisdom as to travel with associates of his own age through towns and boroughs, fortresses and cities, to fairs and to all the various booths of the market-place.
>
> (Coulton 1918)

Another example given by Walter Map describes the different gradations of merchant. Sceva and Ollo, 'boys of low birth', with a small capital became 'first hawkers of small commodities, and then by continued success of large ones. From packmen they rose to be carriers, from being carriers to be masters of many waggoners' (James *et al.* 1983: 393).

Most of the great traders of the twelfth century remain unknown, though the Pipe Rolls, which record amounts paid to the exchequer, may give hints. These payments may either be fines for illegal action (such as smuggling), but equally they might be payment for the right to trade. A case in point occurred in 1174–5 (Pipe Roll 22 Henry II, p. 104) when six men, two of whom were from Scarborough, were fined for having wool from Flanders. Whether they were paying for the right to trade, or being fined for smuggling, is unclear. Equally unclear is whether they formed a consortium to bring in the wool, or were trading individually, but the amounts owed were substantial at around £10 each. Two were described as 'prepositus' which, as a position in the church hierarchy, may indicate church involvement in the wool trade with Flanders.

During the late eleventh and twelfth centuries the opportunities for foreign trade grew rapidly. The Norman Conquest and then the creation of the Angevin Empire opened up Europe to English trade in a way unprecedented since the Roman Empire. It is unfortunate that the overseas trade records for the twelfth century are fragmented and conclusions have to be drawn from scraps of information. The impression from twelfth-century records is that trade is dominated by the Low Countries, France and across the North Sea. By far the most important commodities for export were wool and cloth. The great Cistercian monasteries were beginning to build up their flocks which were to become so important in the later medieval centuries. Wax was often brought from abroad to be used for government business to seal documents as well as for candles, and as early as 1157–8 1,000lb of wax was brought into the country (Latimer 1999: 49).

The single greatest amount of any artefact still surviving which can show trade is that of pottery, dug up from the numerous archaeological excavations around the country. Pottery can be a wonderful indicator of overseas contacts and conquests, but in the case of the Norman Conquest there is no evidence of the Conquest in the pottery record at all (Mahany and Roffe 1982: 216). It is only occasionally that the style of pottery in the twelfth century is so markedly different to local wares that foreign influence can be seen, as at Castle Neroche in Somerset and also London, where distinctive sherds, confined to local areas, represent Continental potters being brought into the country. More tangible evidence occurs at Canterbury where a pottery kiln of mid-twelfth-century date (*c*.1145–75) has been excavated. The pottery recovered was recognised to be 'quite different from local East Kent ceramic traditions. The assemblage resembled contemporary North French ceramics and, accordingly, it was suggested that the kiln was established by a French potter who had possibly been brought to the city to produce quality wares at the behest of the church (Cotter 1993: 1). The kiln also seems to have had an impact on the local pottery manufacture as poor copies of the foreign styles began to circulate, as well as the innovation of the potter's wheel. However, the styles quickly became assimilated and any clear distinction becomes blurred (Cotter 1993: 98).

Trade was dominant commercially, but there were other methods of moving goods, notably gift exchange. The dynamics of gift exchange have been studied in detail across many cultures. Gifts not only have monetary value, but also social value. In some cases gifts can be a form of aggression, especially as gifts were expected to be reciprocated and if the receiver did not have a gift of similar value, then the receiver was in a socially awkward position (Warren 1998: 263). This was no different in the twelfth century, but gifts could form a wide variety of functions. At the bottom end of the scale gifts were a form of flattery. In 1210–11 Bishop Peter des Roches provided cheese and a bacon pig for the Queen and he spent 32d in buying song birds for her (Vincent 1999: 194). Gifts could also be symbolic, under-lining proper authority and social control, for instance following a dispute Judhael of Totnes received a horse and a cup from Guarinus, which high-lighted Judhael's superiority (Barton 1994: 59). Higher up the scale of value, gifts were a form of patronage: the Empress Matilda sent to the monastery of Bec a large number of very valuable items, including two golden crowns (one of which had been used to crown her husband, the Holy Roman Emperor), two golden chalices and a gold cross decorated with stones (Chibnall 1987: 48). Such gifts had more than monetary value, for they created a lasting bond, not only between the giver and the religious institution, but also the gifts had spiritual value for a bond between the giver and God had been created (Warren 1998: 263).

There was often a thin line between generosity of giving between equals and aggressiveness where one person deliberately sent a gift which could not be matched by another, thereby putting the giver in a socially higher position. A gift exchange of King Arthur's sword, Caliburn (Excalibur), between Richard I and Tancred, King of Sicily, shows the powerful impact of a gift between rulers. Tancred showered gifts on Richard for four days, but Richard, seeing the danger of accepting them, refused them all, except for a small ring 'as a sign of mutual esteem', but in giving Caliburn to Tancred Richard was showing his social superiority, despite his financial difficulties (Warren 1998: 267).

The most quantifiable aspect of the economy is that of coins, though the exact quantities have to be extrapolated from single discoveries and coin hoards. Each coin has an image of the monarch on the front, with a design, the name of the moneyer and the mint on the back. (There was a hiatus in this system during Stephen's reign, when, apart from the king, others minted coins in their own name, whether the Empress Matilda, Henry of Anjou or individual barons (Green 1991: 102; Blackburn 1994).) The infor-mation on the coin allows a detailed picture of the mints and who was working there to be built up. However, it is only in 1220–2 that actual records survive from two mints (London and Canterbury) which show that they were minting 4,000,000 pennies per annum (Blunt and Brand 1970). Before this the output of the mints is educated guesswork, but nevertheless is probably broadly accurate. In 1086 £37,500 is estimated to be in circulation (equals 9,000,000 coins), which if the population was between 1.75 and 2 million would equate to 5d or 4½d a head. By the 1170s and 1180s the number of coins had probably risen to 24,000,000 pennies (£100,000) and by 1205 probably 60,000,000 pennies (£250,000) (Dolley quoted in Bolton 1999: 31).

The amount of coinage in circulation also had a potential effect upon inflation and by the end of the twelfth century inflation had become a serious economic issue. Harvey (1976) suggested that a rising population and a massive influx of silver brought to England by the wool trade brought rapid inflation in prices and wages between 1180 and 1220. Since then further analysis has refined the details of the period of inflation with the sharpest rise being between 1199 and 1204, followed by a slight decline. The price surge can be identified through the prices paid for commodities in the Pipe Rolls and scattered references. The price surge occurred across a wide range of commodities, for example sheep, oxen, cloth, wine, grain, lead and wax, but after *c.*1205 the different commodities varied in their susceptibility to inflationary pressure (Latimer 1999: 42, 54).

This period of rapid inflation may have been caused by the relatively low level of John's demands upon the English economy between 1199 and 1203, whereas before and after these years King Richard and King John took huge amounts of coin out of circulation. King Richard's ransom to the Holy Roman Emperor cost 100,000 marks. Military campaigns were often exorbitantly expensive and Roger of Howden recorded that Hubert Walter sent 1,100,000 marks abroad in 1196 (175,999,920 silver pennies). This figure is probably an overstatement (some of the money may have come from Normandy) but it does show the huge flow of silver out of England (Bolton 1999: 33). The lack of coins meant that buying and selling was more difficult, simply because of the lack of coin, thereby keeping inflation down. Once money was no longer being sent overseas in huge quantities the brake upon inflation was released for several years, but then was reasserted when John once again took huge amounts of money out of circulation for his campaigns which in turn resulted in a lack of credit and rising indebtedness. It has been suggested that expansion of England's internal economy started once again after 1220 (Bolton 1999: 40).

Rapid inflation caused rents to fall in real terms (especially as many estates were let on long leases) and costs to rise. Landlords therefore began to directly manage their own estates, rather than renting them out. This was an important change, for until the late twelfth century landlords had rented out lands to tenants. This is trend indicated by how Glastonbury Abbey managed its estates. In *c.*1135 the abbey had thirty-three of a total of thirty-nine manors at farm (i.e. leased out), in 1171 'the overwhelming majority were still farmed out', but by 1198 sixteen manors had been brought back under the direct management of the abbey (Stacey 2001: 17–19). By the early and mid-thirteenth century other ecclesiastical landlords such as Westminster, Ramsey, Peterborough and Thorney abbeys all bought land to add to their directly managed (demesne) land (Britnell 1993: 115).

Specialisation and categorisation

The second dominant theme of the twelfth century is that of specialisation, by which is meant the desire to create small specialised units, which in turn had a defined role within a hierarchy. The trend was almost universal and can be seen as the start of the intellectual pursuit of categorisation and definition – shown clearly in the educational syllabus (see Chapter 8) – even to the point that there was increasing interest in individuals – the smallest single unit that existed.

The concept of the individual came to prominence during the twelfth century (Morris 1995). The individual's inner desire for self-knowledge, and outward wish for self-expression was manifested by the increase in personal portraiture, poetry and art. Self-expression was also recognised in the growth of romantic love, whether it was one person's unrequited love or the love of two individuals. This love could take the form of physical passion, but love was also a strong religious concept and many of the great religious thinkers of the age, such as Bernard of Clairvaux or Ailred of Rievaulx, discussed the nature of love and friendship between themselves and other monks. Self-knowledge, self-expression and religion came together in the increasingly common use of confession in the twelfth century as individuals' knowledge of their own actions and sins were spoken of and then absolved.

As well as the emotional concept of the individual, the human body too began to be categorised, whether through disease or medical treatment. Whilst there had been medical treatises in the Anglo-Saxon era, there was a growth of interest in disease and the body. The prime example was leprosy. The disfigurement of the body was seen as an indication of sin and its treatment gained in importance during the twelfth century. Whereas in the late eleventh century leprosy could be described vaguely, by the end of the century it was being described in detailed terms. Specialist hospitals for lepers began to be built with money coming from many of the most wealthy in society and some royal queens, such as Henry I's Queen Matilda took an especial interest, not only founding the leper hospital of St Giles in London, but going so far as to wash and kiss the feet of lepers.

Whilst leprosy was the cause célèbre of the twelfth century, there was a rapid growth of doctors and hospitals for general illnesses, especially with the growth of monasteries and their associated hospitals. Interest in practical medicine was particularly strong in the first half of the twelfth century.

Between 1066 and 1100 there were only eleven identifiable physicians in England, but over the next fifty years ninety have been discovered (Newman 1988: 24). In York three are known between 1100 and 1149, eight between 1150 and 1199 and ten between 1200 and 1249 (Stell 1996: Table 1).

It is possible that hospitals specialised to a degree, for example the hospital of the Gilbertine Priory in York may have been responsible for those who were injured or died in trial by combat (Daniell 2001). The predominant work of most hospitals, however, was to care for the old, insane and infirm, rather than the acutely ill, a conclusion also reached from evidence discovered at St Mary's Spitalfields, London, where archaeologists discovered fewer than thirty-five burials, less than one a year for the cemetery's existence (Thomas *et al.* 1997: 23–4). These conclusions support the theory that the hospital was not a place for the acutely ill at this date, otherwise the number of graves would have been higher. Even so, a place had been created which cared for people in a specialised environment away from the home, and the popularity of founding hospitals grew during the twelfth century. St Mary's was one of a number of twelfth-century hospitals in London, which included St Giles before 1118, St Bartholomew's in 1123, St Katherine's *c.*1148 and St Thomas of Acre *c.*1189–91.

Men also began to form into specialist groups. Guilds were known in the Anglo-Saxon period (as at Cambridge in 1000), but they became more widespread in the later eleventh and twelfth centuries. Although, as at Battle, they were originally 'assemblies of drinkers' their role evolved into a more general one of limited government within towns. Craft guilds also formed, to aid the fortunes of their members, but also to exclude foreigners (a term used for people from other areas in England as well as overseas). The guild merchant was an early form of civic government, being made up of leading merchants and burgesses and such guilds were widespread across England by the middle of the twelfth century. The first documented instance was at Leicester in William the Conqueror's reign. Weavers were the first craft to form guilds across England. By 1130 there were weavers' guilds at Oxford, Winchester, Huntingdon and Lincoln.

The distinction between men, and how they were categorised, became of increasing concern during the late eleventh and twelfth centuries. Such distinctions were nothing new, of course, and in the Anglo-Saxon period there were different levels of fines for different classes of men in the law codes, but distinctions became increasingly defined by wealth and status in the twelfth century. Richard I laid down a scale of charges for those participating in tournaments: a count or earl was charged 20 marks; a baron 10 marks, a knight with land 4 marks and a knight without land 2 marks (Bartlett 2000: 243). Differences in clothing were also becoming noticeable, especially with the increasing use of armorial devices. By the 1170s the college of heralds had formed to supervise mock tournaments and it rapidly came to oversee the rules of heraldry (Ailes 1992). Heraldic devices were an excellent method of identifying individuals, but they also proclaimed an individual's status and by the end of the twelfth century had begun to be used as a general symbol of wealth and power rather than just on armour in battle. At the lower end of the social spectrum there was increasing concern to specify status of tenants – whether they were 'unfree' or free. In Domesday Book the term 'villein' meant villager, but by the end of the twelfth century a social and economic division had been made, with 'villeins' being classed as 'unfree'. Such a status meant that a person could be traded or sold. Rules also began to be applied to different ranks in the ecclesiastical hierarchy. The fourth canon of the Third Lateran Council (1179) stipulated that on visitations archbishops should not take more than forty or fifty horses, cardinals twenty or twenty-five, bishops twenty or thirty, archdeacons five or seven, and deans only two horses.

In government too the processes became more refined. Whereas William the Conqueror controlled the government of England and Normandy from his own court, by the late twelfth century the functions of government had become specialised to the extent that the exchequer, whilst still careful to depict itself under the king's control, had its own administrative procedures which did not rely on the king. Furthermore, the king's household was also becoming more departmentalised, with the chamber and associated exchequers, and the chancery. The records too illuminate how a general mass of administration was being broken down into categories (see Chapter 5).

Agriculture dominated the wealth of England, but the patchy survival of records make trends difficult to determine. Some farms were beginning to specialise, for example Mortimer has identified an upward trend in the great demesne farms keeping sheep, for instance at Clare there had been sixty sheep in 1066 and 480 in 1086. This was not a Norman importation, but the process does seem to have increased following the Conquest (Mortimer 1980: 133). The specialist keeping of sheep increased markedly in the late twelfth century when the Cistercians began to build up huge sheep flocks in Yorkshire and elsewhere across the country (Lennard 1959: 262). Sheep were kept for both their wool and milk: Adam de Poningis granted 'the whole tithe of my sheep-runs' to Lewes Priory (*c.*1170) which was probably milk of sheep (Anderson 1988: 33). Whereas the Anglo-Saxons seem not to have distinguished between different types of horses, the Normans did (see Chapter 1) and by the end of the twelfth century there was a broad range: sumpter (i.e. pack) horses, rounceys, palfreys, hunters, chasers and destriers – the palfrey being the most common in the records (Latimer 1999: 52). Furthermore, there was increasing experimentation and specialisation in agriculture and farming. Robert of Bellême introduced Spanish horses into his Shropshire property, probably as breeding stock (Thompson 1990: 284) and there are mentions of stud farms in Domesday Book, for example the stud farm at Brendon in Devon had 104 horses (Lennard 1959: 266).

There were also technological breakthroughs and specialisation. Mining was a growth industry, with the Forest of Dean being described as the Birmingham of the twelfth century. Lead production rose dramatically, though it seems to have peaked in the twelfth century and declined in the thirteenth century (possibly because of European competition), whilst the monastic ironworks in Yorkshire of Rievalux, Fountains and Bylands abbeys all mined and forged iron. The demand was substantial with the crown purchases giving an insight into the range and quantity of material: weapons, nails and, in 1194, 50,000 horseshoes (Miller and Hatcher 1995: 59–61). Other industrial processes included the mining or creation of salt in saltpans which was widespread in coastal areas – there are sixty-one places in Norfolk – and some villages had more than one. Watermills could also be a great source of income for a lord, especially as his tenants often were forced to use the mill and pay for the privilege. One extreme case was at Battersea where the manor's worth was £75 of which the seven mills contributed £42. One innovation of the mid-twelfth century was the introduction of windmills, the first of which was built before 1137 on crown land with windmills becoming popular after 1180. They were a predominantly east coast phenomenon and were particularly popular in Norfolk. By the end of the century fifty-six examples are known, with over forty more in the early thirteenth century (Kealey 1987: 55–7).

Specialisation had, of course, also been evident in Anglo-Saxon society, for example some guilds had formed in towns, but following the Norman Conquest the trend noticeably quickened, as has been seen above. However, there were exceptions. In the archaeological record the number of different types of burial reduce from many different customs in the eleventh and twelfth centuries into a uniformly homogeneous style of burial after the early thirteenth century (Daniell 1999: 187–90). Some attempts at specialisation also failed. The most notable examples were the small monastic orders which formed but then could not remain independent. They therefore merged into a larger grouping, such as the Savignacs merging with the Cistercians. The Cistercians are the prime example of how a huge, pan-European group, controlled from the centre, could survive and prosper in a world where the trend was for fragmentation. Despite these exceptions the theme of increasing specialisation was exceptionally strong from the Conquest onwards.

Space

The third concept which dominated the twelfth century is that of space: whether personal or private; urban or rural; ecclesiastical or secular. In some ways the post-Conquest use of space could be seen as a further theme of specialisation, for it too became fragmented and personalised.

Following the Conquest two aspects of change became apparent: the use of castles for individual lords, and the annexation of large areas of land under forest law (see below). The introduction and development of castles marked a change from a communal system of town defence deployed by the Anglo-Saxons to a system where individual lords built defensive castles purely for the defence of themselves and their followers. The change was also visibly emphasised by the towering motte with the keep on top, in which a lord could be secure. A communal system had been radically changed into that of a lord's personal defence. Moreover, the space was a highly defined one, with gradations of importance – the least significant outer world, the more important bailey and then the most prestigious – and highest – part, the motte with the keep on top.

The lowest point of a castle was potentially its prison or dungeon. This was no accident, because being isolated permanently from society was in itself seen as a punishment. The descriptions of prisons indicate that they were usually for one person, who was completely dependent upon outside agents, whether to raise a ransom, or simply to supply food.

Urban and personal space

Towns became the focus of administration and defence in a way not seen since Roman times. The locations of cathedrals moved into towns, a process which had started in Anglo-Saxon times but which quickened after the Conquest, with the Council of London of 1075 specifying that cathedrals should be within town or city walls. Both the sheriff and bishop of regions were now located in towns or cities and as the king's men they were expected to keep order.

The emphasis which the Normans put upon towns can be seen by the example of York, which underwent a huge programme of building works within the city, which fundamentally changed its topography. Two castles were built, one either side of the river, destroying one of the seven Anglo-Saxon shires in the city. Associated with the larger castle, later called Clifford's Tower, was a large dam which blocked the Foss, with watermills positioned at the sluices. Behind the dam the build up of water formed the King's Fishpool. The Fishpool, or the Marsh, stretched round one side of York forming an impenetrable barrier to invading forces, but also providing a good supply of fish to the city. The Normans also instigated other massive building campaigns, especially of churches. The Anglo-Scandinavian Minster was dismantled and the Norman Minster was built by Thomas of Bayeux, the new Archbishop of York. St Mary's Abbey and the refounded monastery of Holy Trinity on Micklegate were also built. These building schemes not only required huge capital investment but also drew in skilled carpenters, masons and other workmen to the country (Holt 1997: 5–6). At York the motte and bailey castle dominated the city at one end, whilst the huge Norman cathedral dominated the skyline at the other. A similar pattern can be seen at Canterbury with the two institutions at opposite ends of the city. The alternative arrangement of the castle and cathedral close together also occurred, for example at Lincoln. Towns were becoming defined and institutions were becoming grouped within them in a new way.

Sharp defining boundary walls separating town and country also began to appear, though this tended to be a gradual process and was often not fully achieved until the thirteenth century. In York, surrounding the Minster on two sides, were the strong and impressive walls of the Roman legionary fortress. The other two sides of the legionary wall were in a state of complete decay, having been broken down to make way for houses. In the Walmgate area of the city a hedge seems to have been the extent of the defences in the twelfth century. The main areas of defence are likely to have been the gateways into the city, both as a military defence, but on a day-to-day basis more importantly as a stopping place for traders to pay their tolls and taxes. Militarily, a hedge or ditch on its own was useless, but they were all that was needed to stop a merchant with a cart gaining access to the city and thereby avoiding tax.

During the late eleventh and twelfth centuries towns began to grow in people's consciousness. The Heavenly City (associated with Jerusalem) came to prominence both as a physical reality during the Crusades and as a symbol of divine action and order. By the middle of the twelfth century Geoffrey of Monmouth considered that founding towns was one of the proper activities of a good king, as was building roads, encouraging agriculture or issuing laws, 'so when Brutus and his followers first arrived in England they founded a city – New Troy' – the mythical foundation of London (Thorpe 1966: 73–4). The presence of towns was also seen as a distinguishing feature of civilisation. William of Malmesbury contrasted Ireland with England and France. The English and French 'live in market-orientated towns enjoying a more cultivated style of life', whereas the Irish live in rustic squalour, without proper cultivation of their land (Gillingham 1990: 108–9).

During the twelfth century for the first time descriptions of towns are given in some detail, with the best known being William FitzStephen's description of London which opens the *Life of Becket*. However, far from being an objective portrayal, the description is modelled on classical sources about Rome (Staunton 1998: 199). For some others, however, towns were outside their mental scope. The monastic chronicler Orderic Vitalis shows little interest in urban history and his ideological world consisted of knights, peasants and clergy, wars and politics, rather than urban history or trade. For those in rural monasteries major towns were outside their normal experiences.

Within the larger towns there was a wide diversity of trades and specialised areas grew up. In Domesday Survey for York in 1086 there were areas for defence (the castles), religion (the Minster, St Mary's Abbey and the other churches), food production (mills) and the selling of meat, probably in the Shambles. There was also a range of influences, from the Sheriff, the Archbishop of York, the Bishop of Durham (who held lands in the city), the native Anglo-Scandinavian residents and the new Norman inhabitants. Occupations too are shown in more detail than before, with judges, moneyers, reeves, a carpenter and a crossbowman (Palliser 1990; Miller and Hatcher 1995: 260–1). The complexity of London and Winchester in 1086 were such that the entries were probably not compiled, and certainly were not copied into Domesday Book. Both cities had broken the bounds of knowledge and expertise, though Winchester was later surveyed (Biddle 1976).

There is evidence of urban property speculation, a risky but potentially profitable occupation. One of the best known speculators was Thomas Becket's father, Gilbert, who lived well from his income from property (Barlow 1986: 15). A detailed study of Winchester property has shown a group of private landlords (190 from a household total of *c.*1200) and a thriving property market in the city (Biddle 1976: 371, 440). Fortunes could be made and lost quickly. Fire was a constant danger and Gilbert Becket was probably reduced to straitened circumstances by destruction of his properties by fire (Barlow 1986: 15). In York fire was specifically mentioned in some charters: when Roger the cook and his wife Eva rented a house from Roger de Wynchon, the precentor at the Minster, a clause stated that 'if the buildings are burnt down by fire or are destroyed or deteriorate for any other reason' the house should be rebuilt to the value of 20 marks. For a combination of safety and prestige, houses constructed of stone gradually became more common. Two such houses have substantially survived in Lincoln and are today known as the Norman House and the Jews House (Plate 7.1), while other fragments of stone houses have survived elsewhere, such as in York.

In the twelfth century the concept of personal space began to be accepted for the richest in society. Previously the lord and his retinue would all eat and sleep together in the hall, and whilst some rooms could have specific uses, for example as kitchens or for animals, the use of rooms purely as private space for a lord's use was rare. Gradually through the twelfth century spaces began to be divided into rooms with regular functions and as private rooms for those in the upper levels of society. In high status and manorial complexes there often seem to have been two main buildings, separated from each other: the ground-floor hall and the first-floor chamber, which was reached by an external staircase (for a review of the debate see Grenville 1999: 66–88). From literary evidence both seem to have been used for the same functions – the reception of visitors, banquets and public occasions – but as the chamber was smaller than the hall, the chamber functions were more intimate. Furthermore, from French evidence it is possible that there was also a gender distinction made – the chamber for women and the hall for men (Barthémy 1988: 421). In the very wealthiest royal households there were further subdivisions. At Westminster in 1177 Henry II's architect was paid 101 shillings for building a wardrobe room to keep the king's personal treasure and clothing. The French king too had a wardrobe where he might sleep or, as in the case of the Louis IX, where he washed the feet of paupers in a secret act of holiness (Barthélemy 1988: 420). The English kings also began to have separate rooms to withdraw to, but they were rarely truly alone, for a servant would sleep either at the bottom of the bed or just outside the door. Most of the evidence about the internal layout of space begins to occur at the end of the twelfth century from a small number of surviving buildings, but there is important literary evidence from earlier in the century within the account of the life of Christina of Markyate (Talbot

Plate 7.1 The Jews House, Lincoln.

1959). In the descriptions there are two separate accounts of bedrooms. In the first, Christina's parents were in the hall ('aula') getting drunk and Christina was invited to the chamber of Ranulf Flambard, Bishop of Durham. In the chamber ('cameram') there were beautiful tapestries. Following his advances she managed to escape through the door, bolting it on the outside. (From the description the door seems to have bolts both inside and outside.) In Christina's parents' house there was a separate bedroom ('thalamum' or 'cubiculum') which had a hanging on the wall, behind which she hid whilst people searched for her. She eventually escaped through the room's external door, much as she had done during the episode with Ralph Flambard. Such rooms have not been identified by architectural historians in the few surviving stone buildings, and although in the accounts there were doors in the partition walls, the walls themselves may have been made of wood.

Slowly during the twelfth century the life of the richest individuals was becoming separated into private and public – a theme which continued down the social scale over the following centuries.

The forest

The greatest area set aside for an individual's personal use was that of the king's forests (Map 7.1). The Anglo-Saxons had cleared areas of woodland

Map 7.1 The forests of England.

mainly for agriculture, a process which is indicated by the Anglo-Saxon place names ending in 'den' or 'ley' (meaning a clearing in the forest). The Normans, however, changed the use of the forest to hunting. Usually the areas declared as forest were the most heavily wooded, although it was not always the case, for example the entire county of Essex was legally considered to be a forest (Young 1979: 5). The forest areas often included scrubland and settlements, though the inhabitants were not allowed rights of hunting or the cutting of trees.

The Anglo-Saxons had also been keen on hunting and Cnut had issued some laws concerning hunting rights, but the Normans brought with them new laws and draconian punishments for infringements. The forests stood outside the normal rule of common law and instead had their own forest law and courts. Forest law was intended primarily to protect the animals of the forest and prevent encroachment by landowners keen to increase their own lands. *The Anglo-Saxon Chronicle* recorded how

> He [William the Conqueror] set up great game preserves, and he laid
>   down laws for them,
> that whoever killed hart or hind
> he was to be blinded.
> He forbade hunting [the harts], so also the boars;
> He loved the stags so very much,
> as if he were their father,
> also he decreed for the hares that they might go free.
> His powerful men lamented it, and the wretched men complained of it
> but he was so severe that he did not care about the enmity of all of them,
> but they must wholly follow the king's will.
>
> (Swanton 2000: 221)

It was a common theme during the twelfth century and when William of Newburgh evaluated Henry I's reign he wrote that Henry 'was immoderately attached to the beasts of the chase, and, from his ardent love of hunting, used little discrimination in his public punishments between deer killers and murderers' (Stevenson 1996: 408). These laws, however, were designed to protect the animals and the trees, but hunting itself was an inherently dangerous occupation. The most famous death was that of King William Rufus who died on a hunting expedition in the New Forest when Walter Tirel shot him accidentally with an arrow. His death can be viewed as a plot, especially as Rufus's younger brother Henry instantly rode to Winchester to seize the treasury and was crowned in three days. However, forest accidents were not uncommon. Orderic Vitalis related how Curthose's own son, Richard, was also accidentally killed in the New Forest whilst on a hunting expedition (Chibnall 1975: 14).

During the late twelfth century the laws of the forest were codified in three assizes. Historians have considered that the second, the 1184 Assize of Woodstock, embodies the fundamental forest law. The Assize deals with a range of issues, for example punishments, trespass ('No person shall have bow, arrows or dogs within the royal forests'), the cutting and selling of wood, the inspection of the forest, the hearing of pleas concerning the forest, and the keeping of the venison and 'vert' (a general term for trees and undergrowth) (Young 1979: 27–9).

The boundaries of the forests contracted and expanded depending on the political situation. The king occasionally gave areas of forest to nobles as a gift or could seize lands to be made into forest. Henry I was powerful enough to increase the size of the forests, whilst Stephen lessened the extent of the forest, either by gifts or allowing encroachment. Henry II was determined to restore the forests as they had been in Henry I's time, and pursued such a vigorous policy that the forests and forest law covered the greatest extent of England before or after: between one-quarter and one-third the land area of England.

Forests had the potential to be very profitable through fines and the sales of rights. During the reigns of Henry II's sons, Richard and John, the forest areas diminished as rights were sold or granted. The sale of the right of deforestation, thereby enabling land to be brought into cultivation, was a very profitable venture. In 1204 when King John's need for money was particularly desperate the rights for the deforestation of Devon were sold for 5,000 marks, Cornwall for 2,200 marks and part of Essex for 500 marks.

In order to protect the forest area from encroachment and the animals within, the forest areas also had their own hierarchy of officials, directly answerable to the king. The foresters were the most important officials. Some references to them occur during Henry I's reign, but they become better documented under Henry II, with families sometimes becoming hereditary foresters. The structure of the administration was local foresters, answerable to a chief forester, who in turn was answerable directly, and only, to the king. The foresters had widespread powers and the 1184 Assize of Woodstock defined their role. Foresters were expected to maintain the forests and the forest law, hear pleas, have a care for the woods of knights and others which were within the forests. The power that foresters had, however, could be abused, for example by harsh punishments for petty offences or by destroying the forests themselves. The Assize recognised this latter point and stated that the forester could be arrested for any unexplained destruction.

At periodic intervals in the late twelfth century a tour of the country's forests was undertaken by the justices. These forest eyres, which took place in 1166–7, 1175, 1179, 1185, 1198 and 1212, generally resulted in a substantial increase of royal income through fines. The 1175 forest eyre was considered exceptionally harsh and brought in £12,305 whereas the next highest in 1212 only produced £4,486 and the lowest amount of £502 occurred in 1166. Any loud complaints generally went unanswered. The power that could be wielded by the king through the rescinding of forest rights was graphically illustrated in 1200 when twelve Cistercian abbots threw themselves at King John's feet and begged him to allow them to pasture their animals in the forest otherwise they would be ruined. Another source of profit was from payments made to the king for partial or full exemption from the forest law, with the exceptional amount of £333 6s 8d being paid by the Abbot of Dore in order to bring 300 acres of royal forest under cultivation. Payment for exemptions rose considerably during the reigns of Richard and John and further reduced the area of forest. Other payments included forest rent [known as 'census' or 'cesses'] which was due annually and probably included the sale of timber, cattle farms, the cutting of turf, and pannage – i.e. a payment made for pigs to feed in the forest which was charged on the number of pigs. The forest was financially profitable, as well as being a good source of animals for the king's sporting pleasure and table.

The experiment of separating the forest law and common law came to an end with Magna Carta. King John was forced by the rebel barons to allow others than the king and his officials to examine and inquire into the forests. The complete dependency of the forests upon the king's will had gone. Others could now have their voice heard. The issue was formalised by removing the clauses to the forest in Magna Carta when it was reissued in 1217 and making a new charter, the Forest Charter, which was issued in November of that year. It was by comparison of size with the Forest Charter that Magna Carta was called 'Great'. The Forest Charter provided a fixed body of law against which crimes could be judged, rather than the more fluid legislation of the twelfth century.

Theological space

The same trends within secular society of increasing division and specialisation were also occurring both within the church and its theology, and also in the church's attempts to impose its rules upon lay society. One of the most obvious divisions in the upper echelons of the English church was the argument between the archbishops of Canterbury and York as to which had the greater authority.

Perhaps more fundamentally for society was the increasing emphasis on the difference between the clergy and laity, a difference which eventually led to the trauma of Henry II's reign with the death of Thomas Becket (see Chapter 2). Becket led the movement which demanded a firm and unwavering distinction between clergy and the laity. The separation of the secular and ecclesiastical worlds became more and more defined, with priests required to be celibate, unmarried, and wear distinguishing clothes. The church also attempted to differentiate Sunday as a holy day by banning Sunday trading. The attempt failed and in York the archbishop preached against Sunday trading as late as 1322 when Sunday markets were formally prohibited.

In theology, space was also becoming compartmentalised. Towards the end of the twelfth century the concept of purgatory as a third possible destination in the afterlife became formalised. Whilst there had been notions of the purgatorial fires to cleanse the spirit, Le Goff has forcefully argued that purgatory as a physical space was developed in the schools of Paris in the 1180s (Le Goff 1984). Purgatory became defined as a place between heaven and hell where sins were cleansed before the soul went to heaven. The full impact in this revolutionary concept of the afterlife only made itself felt from the mid-thirteenth century onwards, but there were signs of a growing awareness that actions on earth could help the soul on its way to heaven. One result was the growing awareness that Masses said for the soul would be beneficial so that altars for individuals with attendant priests became common. These chantry chapels and priests meant that money was directed away from the major religious houses into more personal or family endowments within non-monastic churches. The first chantry chapels were recorded *c.*1235 at Lincoln Cathedral (Cook 1947: 16). The idea of personal action had replaced the notion of large benefactions to monastic institutions in return for prayers for a community of souls.

Before the Conquest in England all monasteries were Benedictine, often based in towns, but the new monastic orders actively sought the wilderness, in particular the Cistercians.

There is a considerable literature about the 'wilderness' foundations of the Cistercians which points out that the accounts are literary constructs, and that whilst the sites may have been desolate they also owed their descriptions to spiritual ideals of taming a landscape to make it habitable, and emphasising the poverty of the monks (Otter 1996: 62–5; Menuge 2000). Furthermore, the reality is that whilst the actual location might be desolate, often the foundation was not far from an important settlement. Fountains Abbey is only three miles from Ripon, and similarly Rievaulx is only a few miles from the town of Helmsley.

At the margins of space and society were the hermits. They deliberately excluded themselves from society and sought out isolated places for their devotion. This also meant rejecting their own families, and their own chastity meant that they deliberately abandoned the future of their own family line. This concept was made more forceful because they chose a path of chastity at a time when heirs and family lines had become crucial in the world of the nobility. Hermits were also on the margin between heaven and earth, as they fought with the devil through their prayers. In one way, however, hermits might have bonded elements of society, for it is noticeable that in mid-twelfth-century England many hermits have Anglo-Saxon or Anglo-Scandinavian names, such as Wulfric of Hazelbury or Godric of Finchale. There is the possibility that they, and other hermits, might have been ministering to people who felt alienated by the new Norman culture, both in society and in the church (Holdsworth 1978: 202–3). Hermits were considered an important part of society, playing an active part in it, even if they did live on the margins (Mayr-Harting 1972).

8 The arts in England

Twelfth-century Renaissance and education

The explosion of new learning and thought during the twelfth century has led to the term 'the twelfth-century Renaissance' being used to convey the range, quantity and quality of the new thinking which was generated in Europe between 1050 and 1250. The Renaissance was fuelled by a revived interest in the classical authors of Greece and Rome, the learning encountered in the Byzantine Empire and the lands bordering the Mediterranean, either through the Crusades or individuals searching out knowledge. In Europe groups of scholars congregated to discuss new ideas, with Paris being especially important.

One of the keys to understanding the Renaissance is that of the *'translatio studii'* ('a transmission of learning') (Chenu 1997: 2) from ancient Greece and Rome to the cultures of northern France and Anglo-Norman England. The natural language of transmission and discussion throughout Europe was Latin – the language of the church and classical Rome – and to a lesser extent Greek. Yet there was also a countermovement towards producing texts in vernacular languages. This 'vernacularisation' of written texts has been seen as an important aspect of the new humanist learning (Short 1991: 230) though the crushing of a previously vibrant Anglo-Saxon language and culture mitigates this view. The search for knowledge by Christian scholars led to Arab and Jewish writings being discovered, translated and discussed widely in intellectual circles. One man who actively sought out information was Adelard of Bath who journeyed to Syria via Italy, Sicily and Greece. The most important manuscripts that Adelard acquired were the thirteen books of Euclid's *Elements* which had been translated into Arabic from the Greek (Cochrane 1994: 32–4).

The transmission of texts and their consequences in European thought were twofold. The first was the intellectual pursuit of trying to determine the answers to problems by reason. One of the most important proponents of this method of scholarship was Abelard. In a seminal work *Sic et Non (Yes and No)*, Abelard sets out 158 questions about the Christian faith and ethics, and then cites the various opinions of the authorities (whether biblical or those of the Church fathers), without giving a definitive answer. It is up to readers to decide the outcome by their own reason and by their study of other sources. Abelard drew some of his ideas from the works of the Greek philosopher Aristotle (d. 322 BC). The transmission of Aristotle's works had opened up a world of logic and reason to the twelfth-century mind. Aristotle's and Abelard's methods of working were also used by Peter Lombard, Bishop of Paris (d. 1164) who built on Abelard's work to create the textbook *Sententiae* (*Sentences*) which detailed the theological arguments; it remained an important work until the sixteenth century.

The second outcome was the opposite: a repudiation of the notion that logic and reason can determine the answers to theological questions. Rather it was the mystery of the faith and divine revelation that solved problems. Bernard of Clairvaux attacked Abelard for trying to understand the mysteries of the divine by reason and without any moral feelings or humility. Bernard launched a vicious campaign against Abelard and secured his conviction as a heretic, thereby ruining Abelard, but it was Abelard's methods that were accepted by many theologians and gained ground throughout the century.

A fundamental part of the twelfth-century Renaissance was education, so much so that 'the educational transitions . . . give . . . overall coherence to . . . [the] period of "renaissance"' (Swanson 1999: 12). It was a European-wide interest and, following the Conquest, the Continental churchmen who entered the English church brought new ideas to be taught in the schools. There were two types of schools: monastic and secular (usually attached to a non-monastic cathedral). The monastic schools were designed to pass on the information to the next generation of monks, and the method of learning was therefore one of acceptance and assimilation. Although questions may arise, answers were assumed to be known within the church or, where none existed, would be revealed by divine intervention, an approach favoured by Bernard of Clairvaux (Swanson 1999: 13). In order to pass on information (or revelations) the monasteries became powerhouses of finding and copying classical and religious texts. One estimate is that over 800 manuscripts were copied or acquired by English churches between *c.*1066 and *c.*1125 – this is a greater number than all the Anglo-Saxon manuscripts of the previous four and a half centuries (Gameson 1998: 230). The principal concern was to acquire the church fathers and nearly half the volumes (356 out of 800) fall into this category. The works of Augustine were the most popular and his writings occur in nearly three times as many manuscripts as those of Jerome, the second most popular author (Gameson 1998: 235–40). Other authors commonly found in monastic libraries were Ambrose, Anselm, Bede and Gregory the Great. Some contemporary works were instantly popular being copied and then passed on, in particular Bernard of Clairvaux's mid-twelfth-century sermons on the Song of Songs. As the quantity of religious commentaries grew, compendiums, or 'sentences', were compiled which listed the views of religious authorities on a wide range of subjects, both theological and practical to everyday life (Chibnall 1984: 91, 98).

Education within the secular cathedrals schools concentrated more on a basic education, including teaching literacy and rhetoric. As many clerks and priests were destined for government posts, there may also have been an emphasis on administrative skills and etiquette. Few details of such secular schools survive, but they did not operate in isolation of each other and the theological school at Lincoln Cathedral had close connections with the school at York, and with scholars in Oxford. The excellence of the schools at York and Lincoln, combined with Lincoln being a centre of book production, led to the creation of a series of fabulous bestiaries, which illustrated and described animals of the known world (Muratova 1986). There was also a fertile cross-over between all sections of the church, with teachers and texts moving between different schools and clergy moving into positions within government.

The reputation of a particular teacher can be shown by Gilbert Crispin's description of Lanfranc, Archbishop of Canterbury, when he was at the monastery of Bec:

> clerics came running, the sons of dukes, the most renowned masters of Latin learning; powerful laymen and many men of high nobility through their love of him bestowed a great deal of land on that same church. Instantly Bec was enriched by adornments, by possessions, by high-born and honourable persons.
>
> (Potter 1998: 181)

However, despite the teachers' very best efforts, not all their students were satisfactory. Herbert de Losinga, Bishop of Norwich, wrote to two monks Oto and Willelm: 'Lay aside your drivelling; and then ye shall find in your verses nothing more than an ass covered with a lion's skin. I am weary of your nerveless verses, which, like flowers, are fair only on the outside, and are not distinguished by any weight or solidity of sentiment' (Goulburn and Symonds 1878: Letter XXXIX). Furthermore, there were constant sources of distraction, as Herbert forcefully reminded his clerks Samson and Roger: 'See that ye waste not your days, and waste not also the money of your parents, by laying it out upon vanities and useless articles of self-indulgence. I sent you [to school] to learn, not to play' (Goulburn and Symonds 1878: Letter XX).

The teachers were almost exclusively men of a wide range of abilities. The role of women as educators is hidden from view, though there are odd references to people learning as children, probably taught by their wet-nurses. St Godric of Finchale 'learned the Lord's Prayer and the Creed from his very cradle [and later] he oftentimes turned them over in his mind' (Coulton 1918). There was probably private education, though details are scarce. At the lowest level the parish priest might teach children the basic alphabet and rudimentary Latin, with progressively better teaching and the study of theology the higher up the ecclesiastical echelons a student went. In the highest reaches of learning were the trivium and quadrivium which formed the seven liberal arts. Herbert de Losinga wrote that he who lacks these 'in vain professes himself a philosopher' (Goulburn and Symonds 1878: Letter XLIX). The trivium was based upon language and comprised grammar, rhetoric, dialectic or logic, whereas the quadrivium was the study of four different aspects of mathematics: arithmetic, music, geometry and astronomy. Hugh of St Victor gave a reason for these seven being called 'liberal' as 'these sciences pursue subtle inquiries into the causes of things' (Taylor 1968: 75). These seven were matched against the seven mechanical sciences which were concerned with the 'artificer's product': fabric making, armament, commerce, agriculture, hunting, medicine and theatrics (Taylor 1968: 74). The mechanical sciences were rarely taught in the monastic and secular schools, though hunting was a great favourite amongst the nobility and medicine became of increasing interest during the twelfth century.

In the twelfth century the largest group of scholars and teachers was in Paris, which was renowned for its teaching and learning. There were two general teaching techniques, lecturing to an audience (albeit probably a small one) and disputing, which involved arguing about the difficult subjects. There were four basic divisions of subjects in Paris which became increasingly defined, each with its own expert teachers: theology, canon and Roman law, medicine and the arts. Gerald of Wales wrote that he studied these subjects, except medicine, when he was in Paris during in the 1160s and 1170s (Baldwin 1985: 143). A glimpse of one teaching technique is given, for Peter of Poitiers in Paris reproduced key texts on large animal skins which he hung on the classroom wall for reference and to help those clerks too poor to buy books (Morey 1993: 16).

The standard of English learning and teaching between 1179 and 1215 can be shown by the geographical origins of the masters in Paris. Of the forty-seven known masters, the largest group of sixteen came from England, followed in size by ten from the French Royal Domain. The high numbers of English masters may be a consequence of the unsettled times in England, especially under the reign of John, but also speaks of the esteem in which they were held. Masters increasingly became important in English diocesan chapters. In London and York the chapters comprised 47 and 46 per cent respectively of masters and the entourage of the Archbishop of Canterbury between 1193 and 1205 may have comprised as many as 63 per cent of masters (Baldwin 1985: 155). The English crown also employed greater numbers of masters as justices and in government than their French counterparts. To achieve the title of 'magister' opened the door to further advancement, at least in England.

Although the twelfth-century Renaissance can be identified by the increase in education and knowledge, the geographical boundaries of the Renaissance are difficult to identify. It has been suggested that rather than a European phenomenon the Renaissance was in fact a series of regional advances in learning which, whilst distinct, were linked together through the church or personal contacts. If this is correct then 'we [may] have to construct a hierarchy of regions, of places which had "more of a renaissance" than elsewhere' (Swanson 1999: 6).

One area that can be studied in detail is Yorkshire. Before 1066 it is difficult to find evidence of any classical learning or even libraries in Yorkshire. The largest church – York Minster – had once had a famous library but there is no evidence that it had survived the Viking occupation and settlement of the city. The one Anglo-Saxon manuscript that is known to have been at the Minster before 1066, the *York Gospels*, was not written in York. Elsewhere in Yorkshire there is only evidence from inscriptions on sundials of the use of a rudimentary and crude Latin which is interspersed with Anglo-Scandinavian.

One hundred years on and by the late twelfth century, a large number of monasteries had been founded in Yorkshire, from the increasingly wealthy Benedictine and Cistercian abbeys, to many smaller monastic houses. Even in the small houses there was the potential for great learning. Maurice, the Prior of Kirkham Priory, knew Hebrew (Burton 1995: 16), though at the other end of the scale was Helias, Prior of Holy Trinity in York, who 'apart from his memory of the psalms was almost completely a layman' (Neale 1984: 48). All the monasteries were building up their libraries and teaching Latin to the novices. In York Minster too, there were an important theological school (Muratova 1986: 131). How widespread this new learning was in Yorkshire is difficult to answer, though as churches were passed by the laity into the hands of the church (see Chapter 6) even poorly educated priests were linked into a powerful network of learning.

The church networks were not the only means of intellectual transmission. In contrast to the static monasteries at the centre of estates, there were the itinerant king and his court, which, as they travelled, spread culture and fashion throughout England. There is little direct evidence of this happening in Yorkshire, even though kings, from William the Conqueror onwards, visited York and Yorkshire at infrequent intervals. However, the nobles also had their own contacts and were becoming more literate and educated. Walter Espec, who founded both Kirkham Priory and Rievaulx, bought a book of Arthurian romances for Dame Constance, the wife of Ralf fitzGilbert, Lord of Scampton (Powicke 1950: lxxxviii).

Languages

England after the Conquest was a country of many languages. At court French or Norman-French was spoken, Latin was the language of the church and the most commonly written language, whilst Anglo-Saxon was most widely spoken especially amongst those of middling or lower social status. Documents written in Latin initially may have been spoken in French, and finally read to the recipient in English (Clanchy 1987: 154). Whilst this outline is broadly correct, the difficulty comes in defining the social boundaries of each language. Noblemen might speak Anglo-Saxon in order to discuss estate matters and servants might have a smattering of Norman-

French in order to converse with their masters. It is from the clash of languages over time that two words have survived from Anglo-Saxon and Romance languages for some animals and foods, such as lamb and mutton, ox and beef. It has been suggested that 'linguistic skill was a key component in social mobility of the period' (Hyams 1981: 92). For French speakers there were fewer barriers in the secular world as they could be understood with relative ease either side of the Channel. What is clear, however, is that the Anglo-Saxon language often grated on the ears of Latin or Norman-French speakers. William of Malmesbury did not list pre-Conquest saints lives because the names 'grate outlandishly on the ear' (Short 1995: 161) and the chronicler Orderic was given the surname Vitalis as Orderic sounded harsh to the Norman monks of Saint Evroul.

In the countries and regions around England there were a host of other languages. In Scotland there was French at court, Gaelic in the Highlands and Lowland Scots elsewhere, with some Norwegian spoken in the islands (as they were ruled by the Norwegian kings). Welsh and Cornish were spoken in their respective areas, and Gaelic in Ireland. Even though English was nominally spoken throughout England, the strong regional dialects were at times incomprehensible even in neighbouring regions: Abbot Samson, a native of Norfolk, preached in the county, but was incomprehensible to his Suffolk congregation (Legge 1979: 115). Scattered throughout England were Jewish communities who spoke Hebrew.

The number of languages spoken by churchmen varied greatly. William Longchamp, Bishop of Ely, could only speak French (Clark 1978: 225) and St Hugh of Lincoln could not speak English. The comments occasioned by these rare examples probably show that bilingualism, or even trilingualism, of English and/or Latin and French was the norm (Short 1995: 159). A recorded example of trilingual preaching took place in the later twelfth century when Abbot Odo of Battle preached in Latin, in French ('Gallico') and in the 'mother tongue' which can only be English (Clark 1979: 32). This was not a common skill and although Abbot Samson of Bury St Edmunds exhorted his priests to preach in English, he allowed them to preach in French as a second best (Legge 1979: 115). At the lowest end of the ecclesiastical scale the parish priest may well have had halting Latin and all English churchmen would have initially grown up speaking Anglo-Saxon or later Middle English. Even such an eminent churchman as Ailred, in his dying words, mixed Anglo-Saxon and Latin: 'Festinate, for crist luve' ('Hurry, for Christ's love'), which acts as a reminder that he was the son of a Northumbrian priest (Legge 1979: 111).

The use of language amongst the nobility is more difficult to assess. French was the language of culture, social power and was dominant in court. However, the complexity of discovering the language used by the nobility has been highlighted by the account of the murder of Hugh de Moreville, one of Becket's murderers. Moreville's wife, Helewisia, pretended to help an Englishman, Liulf, to murder her husband. As Liulf approached she called out in English: 'Huge de Moreville, ware, ware, ware, Lithulf heth his swerd adrage' ('Hugh de Moreville, beware, beware, beware, Lithulf has his sword drawn'). This is normally taken as evidence that husband and wife spoke English together on a day-to-day basis (rather remarkable for a couple of such high status), but an alternative explanation is that Helewisia was actually warning Liulf and indicating she had betrayed him to her husband (Legge 1979: 111). A further possibility is that all three spoke English, and the husband and wife could have been bilingual.

The Norman-French of the conquerors was a new language in England to all but the highest levels of Edward the Confessor's previous Anglo-Saxon court. The invaders made French much more widespread within England and it commanded social respect. Every king of England between William the Conqueror and John either was brought up in French-speaking areas (William the Conqueror, Stephen, Henry II) or had French-speaking parents. Some kings may have had a smattering of English (William the Conqueror unsuccessfully tried to learn it and Henry II may have had basic English) but it was not their mother tongue and was probably not that important to them. As has been seen, the nobles on their estates probably needed some English, but French was the language of the court, and therefore power. It was that patronage of French-speaking nobles at court in England that resulted in the production of a large and diverse French literature, both religious and secular. It has even been suggested that French literature was invented in England because far more was produced than in Continental France. Reasons for this may be the extreme wealth of some of the nobles in England, combined with a desire to remember their origins. The *Song of Roland* originated in the Anglo-Norman realms by 1080–1100 and the earliest surviving manuscript comes from England (Mason 1979: 131; Owen 1997: 115). *The Voyage of St Brendan* by Benedict, which has been described as the first surviving Anglo-Norman text (Noble 1994: 69), was dedicated to Henry I's queens, Matilda and then Adeliza. Benedict may well have been bilingual for within the poem are English words, such as 'ropes' and 'hasps', which were incomprehensible to a Continental audience (Short 1995: 155).

Gradually the languages and literary norms diverged between England and France. Even during Henry I's reign (1100–35) the Anglo-Norman poet Philippe de Thaon wrote 'in a distinctly insular (i.e. non-Norman) French' (Short 1995: 155). From the middle to the end of the twelfth century there was a marked divergence between the French spoken in England and France. In the vernacular work of Jordan Fantosme, his chronicle of the Young King's Revolt of 1173–4 was far removed from Continental-style French poetry (Johnston 1981: 154). In a famous example the nun of Barking describes her *Life of St Edward* (*Vie de saint Edouard*) as 'false French', which was written towards the end of the twelfth century (Short 1995: 156). The term used for bad or rustic French was 'Marlborough French' after Walter Map's description: 'At Marlborough . . . there is a spring of which they say that whoever tastes it speaks bad French ['Gallice barbarizat']' (James *et al.* 1983: 496–7).

After the early years of the Conquest Latin dominated the written language of government and church, sweeping away the previously dominant Anglo-Saxon language. This process can be clearly seen in the *Peterborough Chronicle*. After a disastrous fire at Peterborough, a copy of *The Anglo-Saxon Chronicle* was acquired from Canterbury Cathedral and copied until 1122, but thereafter the *Peterborough Chronicle* is unique. There are two distinct sections. The first, known as the 'First Continuation', runs from 1122 to 1131. There is then a gap until someone in 1155 filled in the missing years (the 'Second Continuation'). The author of the First Continuation has been described as 'one of the early masters of English prose' whereas the author of the Second Continuation only shows 'a fair command of language' (Clark 1970: lxxix, lxxxiv).

However, between the middle and the end of the twelfth century there appears to be a gap in the English literary record, though the group of manuscripts assigned to *c.*1200 are difficult to date precisely and may have been written slightly earlier. By 1200 there is also a substantial change in the grammar, from the inflected Anglo-Saxon words which could be in almost any order to a word order of subject–verb that is more recognisable today. The absence of literature in the late twelfth century in English composition effectively signals the change from Anglo-Saxon to Middle English. Anglo-Saxon had evolved – with input from French – into a very versatile and poetic language.

From around 1200 onwards English literary enterprise flourished and gained increasing importance in English culture. The works in English range from the religious to the secular. There appears to be a special concern with works for and about women, for example the saints' lives of Katherine, Margaret and Juliana and later in the century the *Anchoresses' Guide*. Amongst secular works is the beautiful and poignant *The Owl and the Nightingale*, where the two birds hold a dialogue about their respective virtues. Although each work is difficult to date precisely they form a group which shows Middle English emerging and becoming a powerful literary language.

Literature and drama

There were two main themes in the literature of the time: religion and romance. Before and after the Conquest there was a strong tradition of hagiography (the writing of saints' lives), though after 1066 the lives written by English communities were an attempt to highlight the worth of their English saints to the new Norman prelates. The sudden production of these written texts has been seen as analogous to communities forging charters. Both the forged charters and the new saints' lives were attempts to put down in writing oral traditions in an attempt to convince those in power about the worthiness of the particular cause (Hayward 1998: 89). In order to convince Maurice, Bishop of London (1086–1107), of the holiness of the nunnery of

Barking, the nuns commissioned the monk Goscelin to write the lives of their saints. Between 1086 and 1100 Goscelin wrote the *Life of St Aethelburg*, the *Life of St Wulfhild*, a set of lessons about St Hildelith, and an account of Abbess Ælfgiva's translation of three saints.

The tradition of writing saints' lives also influenced the production of vernacular literary texts. Theobald of Vernon, a canon of Rouen, translated many saints' lives into the vernacular and put them to music (van Houts 1989: 236). It is unfortunate that none survives. During the reign of Henry I, Geoffrey of Le Mans journeyed from Normandy to St Albans and on his way stayed at Dunstable where he organised a miracle play of St Katherine (Axton 1974: 162).

Drama and plays became increasingly popular in England and throughout Europe as the twelfth century progressed. The common thread was the role played by the church in promoting the plays, or the religious nature of the plays. The church had many pre-Conquest ceremonies which were semi-dramatic in structure, such as the dedication of a church in which, after a procession round the church, the bishop has a formal exchange with a cleric hidden inside the building. The most popular and widespread enactment was the Easter 'Visitation of the Sepulchre', which took place in many churches throughout Europe: the three Marys (played by clerics) discover Christ's tomb is empty and converse with the angel (Axton 1974: 61–74). Other liturgical themes were acted out, such as the Christmas story, a play of which occurred in York in 1220–5: 'Item, one will contrive stars with all things pertaining to them except the rushes . . . : one on Christmas night for the shepherds and two on Epiphany night if the presentation of the three kings be done' (Johnston and Rogerson 1979: 687).

As well as the Latin plays, vernacular dialogues and plays began to emerge in the twelfth century. The most important in England is the Anglo-Norman *Le Mystère d'Adam*, which has been described as an 'astonishing work, a fusion of separate traditions: ecclesiastical and popular, liturgical and apocryphal, sung and spoken, Latin and vernacular' (Axton 1974: 112). The play contains a location (a churchyard or near the church) and stage directions where paradise is a garden and hell is a kitchen with cauldrons. It is a first in its complexity, its theme (there are no known previous plays involving the Fall or Cain and Abel), and the skills demanded of the actors (Axton 1974: 112–30).

There may also have been elements of drama in the villages. Gerald of Wales records how he saw villagers dance in the church and around the graves, and then in a trance mime workday occupations forbidden on the Sabbath – 'This man is imitating a cobbler at his bench, the man over there is miming a tanner at work' – before going into church where they 'recover' (Thorpe 1978: 93). Gerald writes that this happens every year on the feast day of St Eluned when great crowds assemble at the church. Here was a stage (church and churchyard) with actors and audience, and possibly a narrator to describe the mimes. However, it is possible that the use of mime was inspired by the monastic everyday sign language for the many occasions when monks were not allowed to speak.

A very popular literary subject which grew exponentially during the twelfth century was that of the Arthurian romances. Both in England and across the Channel, for example in Normandy and Brittany (Chibnall 1987: 46), the tales flourished. The greatest exponent in England was Geoffrey of Monmouth who wrote his *History of the English Kings* in the middle of the twelfth century (Thorpe 1966). The nobility avidly read the tales and passed manuscripts between themselves, and the tales were known in the community. Ailred, Abbot of Rievaulx, related how a novice said he had been moved to tears by the exploits of Arthur. As well as the romantic and chivalric subject matter there were other reasons for the popularity of Geoffrey's *History*, not least that he consciously transferred the twelfth century into the past. Contemporaries would have recognised Arthur's three annual crown wearings and, like Rufus and Henry I, Vortigern seized the treasury on coming to power (Tatlock 1950; Prestwich 1981: 31).

However, the Arthurian legends seem to have been more popular in some regions than others. In Yorkshire the tales were known, but the nobles of Yorkshire do not seem to have taken to the myths as people of other areas did. The lack of interest in the Arthurian stories is perhaps surprising as Geoffrey wrote that Arthur visited York. Yorkshire nobles did not name their children after Arthurian characters, whereas those in other regions did, for example a charter of 1161 written at St Andrew's Cathedral in Scotland has as signatories a Master Arthur and a Master Merlin (Owen 1997: 24).

Despite the supposed factual nature of Geoffrey's *History* not everyone accepted his work uncritically. At the end of the century William of Newburgh decried the Celtic matter in Geoffrey's *Historia* as 'fables from ancient fictions of the Britons, acquired by means of the illusions of divinators'. He also declared that 'in our own times has started up and invented the most ridiculous fictions concerning [the Britons, and giving] in a Latin version, the fabulous exploits of Arthur . . . and moreover, he has unscrupulously promulgated the mendacious predictions of one Merlin' (Stevenson 1996: 398). Even the great storyteller Gerald of Wales cast derision on Geoffrey of Monmouth's work. He described how when the Gospel of St John was placed on the Welshman Meilyr's lap the unclean spirits left him, but when Geoffrey of Monmouth's work was placed on his lap 'the demons would alight on his body, and on the book, too, staying there longer than usual, being even more demanding' (Thorpe 1978: 117). One reason for the criticism may be that chroniclers were taking Geoffrey of Monmouth's tales literally and copying them verbatim, as in the case of chroniclers Diceto and Gervase of Canterbury, both writing *c.*1188–1200 (Gillingham 1990: 100). Other works too came in for criticism. An anonymous scribe who copied the adventures of St Brendan wrote 'this work is fabulous; it is not true nor even probable . . . these fabulous tales ought to be consigned to the fire' (Ó Néill 1997: 182).

Art

During the twelfth century there were two different contemporary views of art. The first, as represented by the monastic federation of Cluny and the Benedictine abbeys, was that art could be elaborate, decorative and attractive. Abbot Suger of St Denis in France wrote that the main altar had 'golden panels on either side and adding a fourth, even more precious one, so that the altar would appear golden all the way round . . . we installed there two candlesticks . . . we added hyacinths, emeralds and sundry precious gems' (Panofsky 1979: 61). The opposing opinion was that of the Cistercians, and in particular Bernard of Clairvaux. In his 'Apologia' Bernard wrote 'I say naught of the vast height of your churches, their immoderate length, their superfluous breadth, the costly polishings, the curious carvings and paintings which attract the worshipper's gaze and hinder his attention' (Holt 1981: 19). Bernard complained that the elaborateness of the art detracted from prayer and devotion, and that monks 'have now come forth from the people . . . [and should have left] all the precious things of the world for Christ's sake' (Holt 1981: 19). It was not only the decoration which Bernard complained about, but also the subject of the images:

> To what purpose are those unclean apes, those fierce lions, those monstrous centaurs, those half-men, those striped tigers, those fighting knights, those hunters winding their horns? Many bodies are there seen under one head . . . Here is a four-footed beast with a serpent's tail, there a fish with a beast's head . . . [therefore] we are more tempted to read in the marble than in our books, and to spend the whole day in wondering at these things rather than meditating the law of God.
>
> (Holt 1981: 21)

But then Bernard ends with a parallel concern: that of the expense 'For God's sake, if men are not ashamed of these follies, why at least do they not shrink from their expense? [For the church is] beggarly in her poor, . . . her sons naked . . . [and] the needy find no relief' (Holt 1981: 20).

In the religious communities in England there was therefore a division of response between luxurious art and what might be called the anti-art movement. Bernard continually stressed the expense, but it remains to be seen whether the Cistercians were markedly more charitable in their alms-giving and charity than other orders. Ailred, the Cistercian Abbot of Rievaulx, followed the teachings of St Bernard and advised his recluse sister to meditate on the deposition of Christ by only having a cross in her cell, without any accompanying pictures. The alternative viewpoint is shown by the Benedictine-produced psalter for Christina of Markyate which was almost certainly made at St Albans. The psalter combines text and illustrations to stimulate meditation. As well as images of Christ, there are the labours of the months, the signs of the zodiac and forty full-page miniatures. Initial letters at the beginning of passages are decorated to show the spiritual implications of the text and by visual and textual references also help the texts to be memorised. The manuscript also includes Gregory the Great's defence of images in Latin and Anglo-Norman and the Anglo-Norman poem 'Chanson d'Alexis' – a tale which had recently been translated from Byzantine sources. It was highly appropriate to Christina's situation as in the story the hero left his wife on their wedding night, as Christina had left her husband on their wedding night to follow a religious life (Holdsworth 1978: 190–3; Alexander 1992: 1).

It is rare to find accounts of the artist's motivation behind the depiction of the monsters and other images that Bernard castigates, though Walter Map gives an interesting description of a monk who was plagued by Morpheus:

> The monk was a painter and a sacrist of his monastery, and every time that he chanced to be vexed by nightly phantasies, of which he knew Morpheus to be the presiding genius, he heaped on him every possible abuse, and on every opportunity that was given him, portrayed him upon walls, hangings and glass windows in the ugliest form and with relentless accuracy. Morpheus repeatedly ordered and besought him in dreams not to uglify his figure and make him such an object of popular derision.
>
> (James *et al*. 1983: 323)

This account highlights several issues. The first is the range of mediums that an artist might work in, for the monk drew Morpheus 'upon walls, hangings and glass windows'. The second is that the monk deliberately made the demon ugly in order to make him 'an object of popular derision' – Morpheus was not ugly, but was made so in order to be derided. The idea of derision and contempt may be the reason why so many devils and monsters are portrayed upon parish churches across England.

Architecture

The period between 1066 and 1215 covers three major architectural movements and styles in England: Anglo-Saxon, Romanesque and Gothic. In most cases the boundaries are confused as one style merges into another, with remnants of the former styles often still in evidence in later styles. However, a definitive event marks the start of the Gothic period in Europe, the building of St Denis Cathedral in the Île-de-France by Abbot Suger (see below).

There is no such clear-cut start date for the Romanesque style in Europe. As the name suggests, the Romanesque was based on Roman principles of architecture and art. It was introduced into Normandy by an Italian, William de Volpiano, who eventually became Abbot of Bernay Abbey, where he died in 1028 (Zarnecki 1978: 170). After William, the Abbot of Bernay was Thierry of Dijon. Both abbots brought with them the latest architectural ideas, based on Roman ideas, and it was at Bernay that the first important

Romanesque sculpture workshop was founded (Baylé 1982: 2, 3). The first church with significant Romanesque influence in England was Westminster Abbey, started by Edward the Confessor and with architectural features which closely resemble the Abbey of Jumièges in Normandy. The link between the two was through Roger Champart, who was successively the Abbot of Jumièges, where he started the great rebuilding of Jumièges in 1040, then Bishop of London in 1044 and Archbishop of Canterbury in 1051 (Gem 1980: 54).

The Norman Conquest was devastating for Anglo-Saxon art. Large numbers of manuscripts were transported across the Channel to Normandy (see Chapter 3), but of more political significance was that the Normans destroyed the larger Anglo-Saxon churches. No English cathedral or large monastic church is known to have any Anglo-Saxon masonry in it at all (Fernie 1994: 105). The destruction of the Anglo-Saxon cathedrals contrasts starkly with the practice of previous or later centuries when churches were altered in size by additions over the centuries. It could be argued that the Anglo-Saxon churches were inadequate for the purposes of the new church liturgies brought in by the Norman reformers. However, the complete absence of Anglo-Saxon cathedral architecture suggests that there was a political decision to sweep away symbols of the Anglo-Saxon church and impose a new order (Fernie 1994: 105; Fernie 1998). One of the most dramatic instances of this process occurred in York, with the complete destruction of the Anglo-Saxon cathedral, to the extent that even today the site is unknown and can only be guessed at. A strong possibility is that the Anglo-Saxon cathedral lay behind the present Minster with its Norman foundations. (Norton 2001). If this is correct, then it was a powerful symbol of Norman dominance over the city, for the Norman church would have slowly grown in front of the Anglo-Saxon building, dwarfing it in scale and magnitude.

Yet whilst the destruction of the cathedrals was total, elsewhere less significant churches survived, showing that the Normans were not intent upon destroying all things Anglo-Saxon. Some Anglo-Saxon churches exist today only in plan as all their fabric has been replaced, as at Marston St Lawrence in Northamptonshire (Franklin 1984: 77), but large numbers exist scattered throughout the countryside (Taylor and Taylor 1965). As well as the churches, large amounts of Anglo-Saxon sculpture survives. Furthermore, Anglo-Saxon sculpture and monuments were sometimes built into new Norman churches, and often the sculpture was positioned to be seen. In particular tympana (the area over a doorway, which was often decorated with images), which have been thought to be a post-Conquest feature, may in fact be re-used Anglo-Saxon sculpture (Tudor-Craig 1989: 221).

There are probably many reasons for the demolition and rebuilding of the major churches of Anglo-Saxon England. Late in the twelfth century Henry of Huntingdon described the changes in terms of the moral domination of the Norman church (Holt 1997: 12). In some cases the buildings may have been in a bad state of repair, following years of neglect or attack. When Thomas of

Bayeux arrived at York, he discovered the church had been burned, and its ornaments, charters and privileges were consumed or lost (Norton 2001). A second reason was that the Anglo-Saxon churches did not conform to the new Norman liturgy. Klukas has argued strongly that the simplicity and regularity of the forms of some of the new Norman churches were directly related to Archbishop Lanfranc's influence and the use of his *Decreta* (his *Monastic Constitutions*) (Klukas 1983: 167). Not every church followed Lanfranc's liturgy and there were alternative liturgies available such as that of Rouen or Mont St Michel which some English churches followed, such as St Augustine's Canterbury, Winchester, Bury St Edmunds and Worcester (Mason 1985: 170). Three distinctly different liturgies were in use in England – Norman, Anglo-Saxon and Lotharingian – which in turn led to variations in architectural design, and it is important to note to which liturgical family each church belonged (Klukas 1983: 137). Churches, especially monastic churches, could also follow the plan of their mother house, for example the Cluniac Lewes Priory of the mid-twelfth century deliberately copied the style of the third rebuilding of Cluny (Anderson 1988: 9). The third reason for demolition was political pressure. This can be seen most clearly at Worcester, for Wulfstan is said to have wept when his cathedral was pulled down to rebuild it in the new Norman style (Mason 1985: 170).

In certain cases ecclesiastical politics may have determined differences in architectural style. After the Conquest, William I granted Waltham Abbey to Walcher, Bishop of Durham, and although Waltham Abbey regained its independence the links were maintained with the result that the architecture of Waltham Abbey is very similar to Durham Cathedral (Fernie 1985; Rogers 1992: 167). The cathedral at York was the only large building without aisles, and although Norton (2001) has shown that the archbishop, Thomas of Bayeux, based it on his old church at Bayeux, there might also have been a deliberate attempt to make York's church as different as possible from Lanfranc's cathedral in Canterbury (Fernie 1986: 77).

The example of York conforms to three other trends connected with this huge Norman rebuilding campaign. The first is that all the inspiration for the designs came from the Continent. The design of Canterbury Cathedral, masterminded by Lanfranc, was closely based on the design of St Etienne in Caen, and also north Italian elements were included, such as the raised choir. Further expansion by Anselm was based on the Santa Maria in Kapitol, Cologne (Fernie 1994: 109–10).

The second trend was the massive increase in scale from the previous Anglo-Saxon churches. Everything about the Norman churches was huge, from the length of the naves to the towering walls and towers. The new churches were different to anything seen in England before, with the exception of Westminster Abbey started just before the Conquest. The churches were powerful symbols of the strength, permanence and power of the new Norman presence (Grant 1994: 120–1). If the church meant to portray itself as the new religious force in the land, allying itself with the Norman conquerors, it surely succeeded. The size of the churches was not simply an imitation of Norman parallels for in virtually every case the churches were bigger than those in Normandy, and many rivalled the largest examples in Europe. The four largest churches in Europe during the eleventh century were: St Peter's in Rome (built 320), measuring 133m × 124m; Speyer Cathedral (1030–60), 128m × 123m; Cluny Abbey (from 1088), 172m × 118m; and fourth Walkelin's Winchester Cathedral (from 1079) which measured 157m × 114m (Fernie 1994: 108). The internal length of Westminster has been calculated as 98.2m (Gem 1980: 44), which itself was longer than any church in Normandy or France, with Rouen at 82.4m and Chartres 85m.

The third trend which York embraced was elaborate architecture and masonry. The new Norman architecture concentrated upon elaborate decorative motifs – indeed so universal was this trend for motifs rather than figural sculpture on architecture during the period 1066–1120 that it has been suggested there was a general 'iconophobia' both in the context of buildings and manuscripts. Patterns that exist are often simple and geometric, such as painted masonry lines giving an impression of stonework (Park 1983: 234). However, as in any general trend there are exceptions. The most important was the Bayeux Tapestry, which is dominated by figures, movement and action. Other examples exist, such as the Lewes group of church paintings. Some documentary evidence exists concerning paintings which have since been lost, as in Canterbury Cathedral (Dodwell 1982: 226–7) and when Gilbert the Sheriff founded Merton Priory in 1114, the priory was described as 'handsomely decorated with paintings and other images as was customary' (Heales 1868: 2; Salzman 1967: 160–1; Park 1983: 235). There is also a solitary capital in Durham Castle representing St Eustace and the stag (Zarnecki 1978: 186).

Apart from the exceptions, the period was dominated by decorative motifs. Durham Cathedral demonstrates the full visual impact of an elaborately decorated and patterned shapes with geometric designs cut into the nave piers. Geometric designs were a feature of Anglo-Saxon architecture in the chronologically distant past, such as the spiral lines in the crypt at Repton, but there are no known architectural examples in eleventh-century Anglo-Saxon churches. However, the chevron pattern does occur on some tombs and sculpture between the seventh and mid-eleventh centuries, for example at Auckland (church of St Andrew), Jarrow and Norton (Cramp 1984). There are more contemporary parallels in the Low Countries at Utrecht and Deventer which could account for the sudden use of them at Canterbury, Durham and York (Fernie 1994: 110). The use of geometric ornament was in some cases a Norman importation, for example chevron ornament (also called zigzag) was first used in Normandy at Cérisy-la-Florêt, twenty years before Durham (Zarnecki 1978: 181). The geometric decoration in Normandy remained favoured throughout the eleventh and twelfth centuries, indeed Normandy still favoured such decoration when neighbouring areas, such as the royal domain of the French kings or Anjou and Maine, had adopted new styles (Zarnecki 1978: 169). As Normandy persisted in using geometric ornamentation whilst other areas changed their styles, it may be that it was consciously continued as a Norman style, deliberately independent from other areas. The meaning of the interlace or geometric patterns is obscure, although where the style appears on fonts one explanation is that it signifies running water and eternity (Baylè 1982: 6, 14).

The most common area for extensive decoration within a Romanesque church of any size is externally around the main doorway. The doorway was the threshold between the outside world and the internal holy world, and was an integral part of many liturgical practices, and as such was symbolic. The chancel arch is another clear favourite for decoration. The curving shape of the arch conveniently simulates the rise and fall of the year and so lends itself to showing the labours of the months or the signs of the zodiac (as on the arch at Westmeston) (Park 1983: 210). Other areas commonly decorated were the tower arch and, externally, the corbel table just under the roof. Whilst the decoration might not be explicable, it was designed to be seen by the laity. Few doorways have internal decoration, but the decoration upon the chancel, or tower arches, usually faced the nave where the laity sat.

Another feature of English twelfth-century architecture was that it was experimental: the massive west fronts of cathedrals such as Lincoln, Peterborough and Ely have no parallel. The ground plans of many churches were complex, with a multiplicity of towers overhead. Rib vaults too were probably developed in England at Durham (though there is an academic debate that an alternative origin was at Lessay in Normandy). The development of rib vaults was a major structural breakthrough allowing a wider expanse of ceiling and it was used widely in England, such as at Gloucester, Peterborough and Lincoln. Rib vaults have been described as 'a technological and artistic development which is a part of the history of north-west Europe at large: Durham was not on the periphery but in the centre of Romanesque history' (Brooke 1986: 3). Generally, however, whilst the church designs in England expanded and experimented, the church designs of Normandy were more reserved with little innovation (Grant 1994: 120–1, 126–7).

From the early twelfth century the use of figural sculpture and images became more common. The decipherment of the meanings of images can be multilayered and a feature of Romanesque art is that it is concerned with bringing together ambiguities, for example life through death or victory through defeat. One charming example occurs on a corbel of Kilpeck Church where a floppy-eared hound is next to a startled-looking hare (Plate 8.1). On one level this is just a fun juxtaposition, on another it symbolises a secular hunt theme, and on another it has a religious connotation, with contemporary bestiary descriptions describing dogs as preachers, while the hare represents men who fear God (Thurlby 1999: 59). The theme of cock-fighting has been studied in depth (Forsyth 1978). The image shows an everyday scene familiar to contemporaries, but the cock also represented regeneration and also the clergy themselves. There are therefore secular and

Plate 8.1 Hound and hare corbel, Kilpeck Church, Herefordshire.

religious explanations but to concentrate on only one is to miss the ambiguity. The overlapping secular and religious themes amplified the total meaning. Churchmen were well aware of this pattern. Guibert of Nogent urged preachers to use multiple senses in their interpretations of scripture both to relate to the listeners, and also to arrive at the higher truth (Forsyth 1978: 252).

Within architectural studies as a whole there are two major and recurring problems: dating and whose ideas or influences are represented. At present dating can only be achieved by comparisons of architectural and artistic styles, unless in very rare instances enough wood survives for dendrochronological dating. Some general trends are, however, evident in architectural history. In Normandy the great period of Norman building was between 1020 and the Conqueror's death in 1087. Thereafter the trend was to refashion or repair existing buildings, which means that there are rarely documentary records related to the consecrations, dedications or burials which can give evidence about the date that the feature was built. Therefore authorities disagree, for example the nave at Bayeux has been dated *c.*1120 and 1163–5; both dates represent different interpretations of the limited evidence available (Grant 1994: 119). In England the great period of widespread church building started after the Conquest in 1066. The middle of the twelfth century, during the wars known as the Anarchy, can be seen as a period of stagnation in building. However, there is no automatic reason why building work should cease, for the campaigns were sporadic, affecting limited areas. Moreover it could be argued that in times of trouble the great lords who financed building campaigns might have wanted to make a statement of status and building a church was a good way to achieve this, and there was an enormous growth in the number of monasteries during the Anarchy (see Chapter 2). The Anarchy, and the seizure of Normandy by Geoffrey of Anjou, did, however, split regions and families and it has been suggested that King Stephen's strong connections with Flanders and Boulogne brought new influences and styles into England. Whilst church building continued in England, in Normandy a new phase started under the impetus of the Empress Matilda and then Henry II, which concentrated upon the areas of upper Normandy and Rouen (Grant 1994: 119–20, 129).

Whilst the general outline and the building phases of the great churches are relatively well documented, the lesser churches are more difficult to date. The transition between recognisably Anglo-Saxon and Norman architecture is one of the great problem areas of style and dating. Double splayed windows have been claimed as evidence of Anglo-Saxon influence after the Conquest, and so they might be, but they became part of the architectural repertoire for domestic and monastic buildings through the twelfth century (Gem 1983b: 243). One of the churches which stands as a classic example is All Saint's Wittering in Northamptonshire, which is variously placed in style between the late eleventh century and the 1150s because the church has both Anglo-Saxon and Norman features. However, each element is open to debate. Anglo-Saxon masons could have adapted their Anglo-Saxon designs easily or could have travelled to Normandy. Alternatively, Norman masons could have travelled to England. The most likely explanation, however, is that the architect or mason had seen other Romanesque buildings in the vicinity, possibly that of Steyning Church, which itself had links to the Normandy church of Fécamps (Gem 1982: 126). The copying or adapting of features from important local churches is a key consideration in the spread of styles. At parish level it is likely that Norman Romanesque influence was as a result of copying Romanesque buildings nearby, rather than an influx of Norman masons (Gem 1983a: 236; Fernie 1998: 2–5; Fernie 2000).

The more prestigious the patron and building the more influence it was likely to have locally and nationally. This can be seen by Henry I's royal foundation at Reading where the 'beakhead' ornament was probably first used in England. It then was used by Bishop Roger of Salisbury at Old Sarum and then Lincoln. It was copied from these churches and became used extensively in Yorkshire and Oxfordshire. The date of the first time a design is used is therefore important, because all copies must be dated afterwards. In the case of the beakhead introduced at Reading Abbey the style probably has a link with St Aubin in Anjou, following the marriage of Henry I's daughter Matilda to Geoffrey, Count of Anjou in 1128 (Grant 1994: 122).

In some cases the spread of a style or ideas was the result of deliberate copying. Henry of Blois, Bishop of Winchester, had based his designs for his palace in Winchester on Abbot Suger's Abbey of St Denis. The evidence for this is the exceptional similarities between sculpture at both sites. Bishop Alexander of Lincoln also used St Denis as a model for Lincoln Cathedral, and followed Henry of Blois in importing a large marble font from Tournai (Plate 8.2). Whilst not provable, the 'suspicion that he [Alexander] was emulating Henry becomes irresistible' (Zarnecki 1986: 162).

What is clear, however, is that there were regional schools of architecture and sculpture in certain regions. The way that the schools worked is unclear: either the masons moved around from project to project, or they were based in one place and moved when there was a demand for a church to be built. The Herefordshire school is the best example (Thurlby 1999) and there is a Yorkshire school, assumed to be based at York.

Sources of inspiration

The sources of inspiration for any particular piece of art or architecture are often difficult to unravel. Manuscripts were an obvious source, and the libraries of monasteries or churches were reservoirs of images and ideas. The usual method of acquiring ideas was to copy what had gone before (as has been seen by the beakhead ornament). The flow of Anglo-Saxon manuscripts across the Channel, and the interchange between artists and patrons, produced such similar styles of work that it would be 'more realistic to speak of an Anglo-Norman art of the period from 1070 to 1100 than to try and separate the paintings of England or Normandy' (Dodwell 1971: 86–9).

Indeed, the production of truly innovative work for its own sake was rare, for previous manuscripts acquired a status of authority which would then be copied. However, the artist copying the originals sometimes misunderstood

Plate 8.2 Tournai marble font at Lincoln Cathedral.

the picture or made slight but significant variations. These gave the images contemporary relevance and today allow art historians to see the changing emphasis of techniques and images.

The Conquest also opened up new contacts in Europe to the artists and patrons of England, which resulted in a far wider variety of sources and styles than ever before, whether through the cross-Channel travels of nobles and their entourages, or through ecclesiastical connections. The exchange of works of art between rich patrons, such as kings, nobles or churchmen, could be spectacular, with either gifts being given or items requested. A case in point is Ivo of Chartres who sought artwork from contacts across England, including royalty and other churchmen. Ivo requested from Queen Matilda 'an alb or some other priestly vestment such as befits a queen to give and a bishop to wear in celebrating the sacraments'; from Bishop Walkelin of Winchester he requested a chrism vessel in metalwork and from Samson of Worcester a pair of liturgical slippers (Barker 1990: 29).

English architecture had many different European influences and there was far more variation of styles than in Normandy. Initially the Norman influence in England was evident in many of the early churches – York was based on Bayeux, and Canterbury Cathedral was built on the scale and layout of St Etienne in Caen (Fernie 1986: 77). Other traditions are also apparent from the Rhineland, Flanders, Picardy and Italy. At Canterbury the choir was built in the Italian manner and cushion capitals were used, which were common in the Holy Roman Empire and Italy, but unknown in Normandy until later. The eastern arm of the cathedral, begun in 1093 by Archbishop Anselm, has been described as 'an exercise in the Anglo-Norman manner on a German design in particular [the influence of] the crypt of St Maria in Kapitol in Cologne'. Similarly, Canterbury Cathedral followed the Cologne church by having towers at almost every possible point (Fernie 1986: 77). Some churches have defied a solution as to their architectural derivation, a case in point being Tewkesbury Abbey, which has been explained with reference to Romanesque architecture of northern France, Germany, Burgundy and western France. Tewkesbury Abbey clearly stands outside the mainstream of architectural influence from Normandy (Fernie 1986: 84). Influence from returning crusaders who had seen Mediterranean architecture is impossible to assess, though one prisoner, Lalys, captured during the Crusades was an architect to Henry I (Harvey 1971: 28). Roman art – both classical and contemporary – held a continual fascination for churchmen travelling to Rome. After a visit to Rome, Henry of Blois, Bishop of Winchester, 'obtained permission before leaving to buy old statues at Rome and had them taken back to Winchester' (Chibnall 1956: 79). This is an interesting reference as it implies that the papacy kept a tight control on what could be taken. Many other artefacts and sculptures were influenced by Roman styles and models, including Bishop Alexander's frieze at Lincoln.

By the mid-twelfth century, Paris and its hinterland, the Île-de-France, had become the centre of fashion, and the architecture from the area inspired buildings in both England and Normandy. The changing centre of fashion can be shown by the patronage of the Tankerville family at Boscherville – in the 1120s William de Tankerville looked for inspiration to Reading and Caen, whereas in the 1160s his grandson William II imported sculptors from the Île-de-France for the new chapterhouse (Grant 1994: 129). The new architectural fashions had been formed by the Cathedral of St Denis built in the Gothic style around 1140 by Abbot Suger. The new Gothic style was a sensation for it allowed much thinner walls and larger stained glass windows, both of which were made possible by the use of the pointed arch. The building was an amalgam of many elements, for example the experimentation in England of rib vaults and early forms of flying buttress and an Italianate west front (Grant 1994: 122, 124) but the structure was greater in concept and design than the constituent elements. Immediately the new cathedral became famous throughout Europe and elements were widely copied.

In England the new orders of monks, such as the Cistercians and Cluniacs, brought different architectural styles with them from Burgundy. Links between England and Burgundy were close and Bernard of Clairvaux sent Geoffrey of Ainai 'an experienced and elderly monk . . . to instruct the religious in Cistercian observance', and no doubt he had views about what was required in terms of building style and decoration (Grant 1994: 122; James 1998: Letter 171).

It was through the Cistercian order that the principles of Gothic architecture became widely known in England, and especially the north of England, which in turn created a distinctly regional 'school' as the early Gothic style was amalgamated with Burgundian Cistercian architecture. Masons then spread the style to both the choir at York Minster and Ripon Cathedral. The joining together of the styles at York can be best explained by suggesting that the 'designer was of north French origin and that his most recent work had been at a northern Cistercian abbey' (Wilson 1986: 105). From York, Ripon and the northern Cistercian monasteries the Gothic style quickly spread in England, so much so that the Cistercian's leadership in the style only lasted a few years (Wilson 1986: 116).

Decoration

There is no doubt that the majority of Norman interiors, in both houses and non-Cistercian-influenced churches, were vividly coloured with figures and patterns. Little now survives of this colour, although a great amount of stone carving remains. In a few cases the decorative scheme survived in churches to show the detail and richness of colour and patterning. An important part of the decoration within churches was wall painting. There are two main types of wall painting: secco, painted on the wall when the plaster is dry, and fresco, painted on when the plaster is wet. Romanesque wall paintings generally tend to be in fresco, which also helped them to survive as the plaster and pigments chemically bond together (Tristam 1988: 76–83).

Remarkably, a group of five related schemes of wall paintings dated *c.*1080–1120 survive in five Sussex churches (Park 1983; Tristam 1988: 26–41). The five are known as the 'Lewes Group' and occur in the churches of Clayton, Coombes, Hardham, Plumpton and Westmeston. There are differences of opinion about the dating of the group, ranging from late eleventh century (Park) to *c.*1125–50 (Tristam). One link between all the churches is their patron, the Lord of Arundel, Roger de Montgomery (d. 1093). It is also beyond doubt that the paintings are of Cluniac workmanship, inspired by the Priory of St Pancras at Lewes (Tristam 1988: 26). The five paintings are considered to be the product of the same group of artists as there are numerous thematic and stylistic links between them. The five schemes give a rare opportunity to show how a workshop operated. The works at Clayton and Coombes may have been by one artist, whilst that at Hardham is probably the work of two or three different hands. In all there were between four and seven artists working on the Lewes Group. Although evidence is limited, the paintings, and those for most of the medieval period, were probably created by professional lay painters who travelled individually or in teams. The iconography is eclectic. The figures of Adam and Eve have parallels in Alsace, there is Byzantine influence in the scenes from the life of St George, the standing Virgin with arms raised is based on an Ottonian type. Anglo-Saxon iconography is also evident in the Last Judgement scenes,

Christ's wounds and the instruments of the Passion. Despite the different influences the group of paintings are pure Romanesque in style, characterised by their striped draperies and their formal monumental style which contrasts with the looser styles of Anglo-Saxon paintings

Surprisingly, less is known about stained glass in England during *c.*1100–75 than in the previous Anglo-Saxon era, because Anglo-Saxon glass has been archaeologically excavated (such as at the Anglo-Saxon monastery at Jarrow) and there are numerous documentary references (Marks 1993: 109–10). It is, however, known that there was Norman stained glass in use between 1100 and 1175 in even relatively minor monasteries such as Kirkham Abbey in Yorkshire (Marks 1993; Burton 1995) and a stained-glass angel, dated *c.*1100–35(?) has survived at Dalbury in Derbyshire. The two largest collections of twelfth-century English stained glass are at the cathedrals of Canterbury and York. The York stained-glass panels are fragmented, but include miracles of St Nicholas and the genealogy of Christ in the form of a Jesse Tree (Marks 1993: 113–17). Canterbury has the greatest and clearest iconographical programme of stained glass (Marks 1993: 118–24). The scheme appears to be the work of one man (possibly the prior, Benedict) and of the original eighty or more figures, thirty-five still survive. The stained glass at Canterbury is one of a number of superb northern French glazing schemes of the late twelfth and early thirteenth centuries which have similar traits, such as the lavish use of ornament and brilliant colouring (Marks 1993: 121).

Interrelationships

The interrelationship between architecture, sculpture, art and manuscripts is not a straightforward one. It is only in rare instances that the direct copying of an item made in another medium can be determined. The doorway at Alne (North Yorkshire) has around it a series of images from a bestiary which seems to be based on a bestiary manuscript, which itself has been described as of 'special importance' as a source of bestiary illustration (Muratova 1986: 120–1). One of the Romanesque wall paintings in Hardham (Sussex) is a Temptation scene, which is painted to simulate a textile hanging. The drapery folds are painted, with a rail with hooks and then loops to hold the wall hanging in place and it seems as though the wall painting was actually based on a wall hanging (Park 1983: 234). Wall hangings are known to have occurred in churches in the twelfth century and earlier (Dodwell 1982) and it is conceivable that the wall hanging was put up in the church so that it could be copied. One imaginative leap further leads to the wall hanging being originally in the patron's hall, thereby creating a direct link between the lord's secular and spiritual patronage. This is of course pure speculation, but if the wall painting was a direct copy of a wall hanging, the hanging must have been hung somewhere.

The influence of Anglo-Saxon manuscript art upon Norman architecture and sculpture has also been detected. A capital from Jumièges Abbey church has links with Anglo-Saxon illumination (Baylé 1982: 4) and the foliage motifs at Jumièges Abbey, rebuilt 1040–67 'follow English book illuminations of the Winchester School style' (Zarnecki 1978: 174). Norman influences can also be detected in England. In Canterbury the scribes of the scriptoria at Christchurch and St Augustine's used Norman-style initials in their manuscripts from 1090s onwards, and similar motifs can be seen in the carving on the capitals in the cathedral crypt of *c.*1100 (Zarnecki 1978: 184).

Some styles seem to be purely sculptural or architectural. The beakhead ornament around doorways, especially in Yorkshire, is not, so far as this author knows, repeated in any manuscript art, although monsters and beasts often figure in margins and as decoration in manuscripts. The cross-over between media has yet to be fully explored, especially between Norman manuscripts and Norman Romanesque sculpture (Zarnecki 1978: 184).

However, as well as the artists working from memory, it has been suggested that they had an extensive stock of models which they could use by using model books (Park 1983: 234). The use of templates and model books was not a new idea, for the Anglo-Scandinavian sculptors can be shown to have used such techniques (Bailey 1980: 242–56). The earliest 'pattern' sketchbook that is known to survive is from the early thirteenth century, and it is a book filled with design ideas and sketches. Masons probably kept their own books or had techniques of memorising particular features to copy later. If the use of such notebooks is accepted, then it is possible for the books to be given to other masons. This in turn means that designs could travel separately from the craftsmen. This is made slightly less likely by the probable personal nature of the books, and the desire to have them to hand.

Despite the wide variety of sources available to the artists and craftsmen of the time, and the authority of more ancient traditions, there was considerable leeway for new thought, methods and designs. Richard Gem (1986: 87–96) has shown how the Bishop's Chapel at Hereford was an innovative combination of German and Anglo-Saxon influence – the German influence came from Bishop Robert of Lorraine who, according to William of Malmesbury, based the design of the chapel on the chapel at Aachen, and the Anglo-Saxon from the master mason who did not understand the designs and so built the design with unique variations. Some of these styles were then used at Tewkesbury Abbey, which in turn influenced the design of Romsey Abbey. The synthesis between patron, Robert of Lorraine, and the Anglo-Saxon mason produced new designs which were then copied elsewhere.

Patrons, masons and materials

A key problem and point of discussion concerns the role and identity of the patrons. In some instances this is not a problem as individual patrons of great wealth and power are known, or can be inferred. When Thomas of Bayeux rebuilt York Minster, it is likely that he had the church of Bayeux in mind as a blueprint. Royal patronage of churches, such as Henry I's patronage of Reading Abbey, was highly significant, but wealthy churchmen too had extensive funds and Europe-wide contacts. Thomas Becket had a fine collection of jewellery and clothes, and was a patron of scholarly literature (Nilgen 1986), and Henry of Blois started the fashion for the use of expensive Tournai marble in England (Zarnecki 1986). Many bishops or abbots took an active role in supervising works and, as many had collected the money for repairs or new buildings, they had a vested interest in the outcome. When Norwich Cathedral was damaged by fire in 1171 Bishop William Turbe is reputed to have sat by the door collecting alms (Harper-Bill 1984: 152). However, as the social scale is descended the problems of defining the patron become more acute, especially in parish churches where the roles of the church, the lord of the manor and the masons who built the church could all become intertwined. Monks are known to have been builders and architects. A story about Gerald of Wales as a boy records how he and his brothers traced or built in sand 'towns, palaces [and in the case of Gilbert] designing churches or building monasteries' (Wada 1997: 223). Fernie has suggested that following the Conquest the range of styles and variations occurred because it was the patrons, rather than the masons, who changed their social positions and perspectives. The potential for alternative designs can be seen in the building of palace chapels, the main characteristic of which is the 'wayward variety of their designs' (Fernie 1998: 5).

The building materials, whether stone or wood, were an important and expensive commodity. The landowner who held the quarry or wood was in a powerful position to help or hinder the work. There are some modern studies about the use of quarries in the Middle Ages and the extent to which stone was used in the various regions (Parsons 1990), but there is little medieval documentary evidence between 1066 and1215 about what happened at the quarries. Later medieval images show the masons and carpenters all working on carving the stone at the site of the building, but there is a presumption that a lot of the cutting and sizing occurred at the quarry, so that as little as possible needed to be transported. One extension of this is that the doorways and windows were all designed and carved at the quarry and then transported to the site. If this interpretation is correct, then the masons at the quarry had a lot of influence about the design of particular buildings. It has been suggested that the architecture of All Saints Wittering was influenced in some way (as yet unspecified) by using stone from the major Barnack quarry only two miles away (Butler 1964; Gem 1982: 126). However, where records exist it appears that apart from providing stone there was little input by the quarrymen/masons into the architectural design. The Caen quarries in upper Normandy provided a great deal of stone for Canterbury in the mid-twelfth century, but there is no evidence of any influence from the workers in the quarries of Normandy upon the English masons within the designs, though there are sculptural similarities between Canterbury Cathedral and the church at Evreux (Grant 1994: 127).

Wood was the dominant building material of the time, for everything from humble dwellings to major castles. Little now remains through the ravages of time, though some survivals and literary references do cast some light on its use. In a description of Henry II's journey to Ireland the chronicler Roger of Howden wrote that the king: 'caused a royal palace to be built [in Dublin] for his own use, by his own command, [made] out of twigs after the fashion of that country; in which he held a royal feast on Christmas Day with the kings and seniors of Ireland' (Duffy 1997: 82). At the other end of the scale is a small survival of a wooden beakhead decoration from a church, the importance of which is that it shows that designs could cross between different media (Blair 1991).

The building of churches in wood, however, would explain why survival rates of Romanesque churches differ from area to area. A desk study of the survival of Romanesque and twelfth-century architecture in East Yorkshire churches, based on Pevsner's county-by-county lists of buildings, shows some regions without any surviving Romanesque or twelfth-century fabric, whilst others have a considerable amount (Map 8.1). The absence, it is suggested, is a result of wooden churches, which were only rebuilt after the twelfth century.

By 1215 the architecture had undergone two profound changes: first with the introduction of the Romanesque style and then from the middle of the twelfth century with the introduction of the new Gothic style. These architectural changes were one example of the close links between England and the Continent, though these links were largely severed by the loss of Normandy in 1204. Yet even between 1066 and 1204 England was not a mere follower of Continental fashion and there were many architectural innovations, such as ribvaults, which came about through new techniques and invention. Innovation was also evident in language as the combination of the Romance languages of Norman-French and church Latin, mixed with the native Germanic language of Anglo-Saxon, evolved by 1200 into the powerful and flexible Middle English. By 1215 the culture of England had been transformed and the foundations had been laid for the continuing flowering of the arts in the Middle Ages.

Map 8.1 Norman church architecture in the East Riding, Yorkshire. The map shows how churches are grouped into two basic areas, the northern and middle area predominantly having some Romanesque or twelfth-century architectural features in them, the southern area largely without. One possible reason is that the southern churches were built of wood and therefore features did not survive. Key: (F) means that although there is no Romanesque or twelfth-century features in the church, there is a Romanesque/twelfth-century font. In the case of Leconfield there is Anglo-Saxon architecture but no Romanesque or twelfth-century architecture. This map is based upon information in Pevsner's *Yorkshire: York and East Riding* volume in the Buildings of England series. New churches built between 1700 and 2000 have been omitted. It is recognised that descriptions and dating are often imprecise, but even so, noticeable groupings do exist.

Postscript

In the East Yorkshire village of Aughton there are the overgrown remains of a small motte and bailey castle. Little is visibly left of the castle, but a stone's throw away is a church. The whole site overlooks the flood plain of the river Derwent. This site is a microcosm of the Norman Conquest and its impact. The village existed before the Conquest but with the arrival of the new Norman lord, Nigel Fossard, the character of the village changed. At some time following the Conquest a motte and bailey castle was built, not only to impose the lord's authority upon the village but also to control the river Derwent which was accessible to shallow-draughted boats. The Derwent, like any river or road, had the potential to be used for attack, migration, trade and ideas.

Today the castle buildings have gone and the motte and bailey are covered by vegetation. After the twelfth century the necessity for defence began to wane and, probably in the thirteenth century, a new medieval moated manor house was built, followed, centuries later, by a Georgian country house. The tiny church, still on the same site, has been altered but not enlarged over the centuries and it still retains elements of its twelfth-century Romanesque fabric.

As one stands in the churchyard next to the castle, looking over the rich flood plain of the river Derwent in the gathering gloom, there is still a sense of the physicality of the changes wrought across England by the Norman Conquest. New foundations and ideas, radically different to those of the previous Anglo-Saxon centuries, were being laid which have helped to form modern society.

Appendix

Significant dates and facts about the monarchs of England, 1066–1216

Monarch	Born	Crowned	Died	Buried	Married	Significant children
William I the Conqueror	1028	25 Dec 1066	9 Sept 1087	Rouen	Matilda, d. of Baldwin V, Count of Flanders	Duke Robert Curthose King William Rufus King Henry I Adela, Countess of Blois
William II Rufus	1056	26 Sept 1087	2 Aug 1100	Winchester Cathedral	Not married	
Henry I	Sept 1069	5 Aug 1100	1 Dec 1135	Reading Abbey	(1) Matilda (Edith) (2) Adeliza of Louvain	William Matilda Robert of Gloucester (illeg.)
Stephen	c.1096–7	26 Dec 1135	25 Oct 1154	Faversham	Matilda of Boulogne	Eustace
Matilda	1101	Not crowned	10 Sept 1169	Fontevrault Abbey	(1) Henry V, Holy Roman Emperor (2) Geoffrey, Count of Anjou	King Henry II
Henry II	5 Mar 1133	19 Dec 1154	6 July 1189	Fontevrault Abbey	Eleanor of Aquitaine	King Richard I King John Geoffrey, Archbishop of York (illeg.)
Richard I	6 Sept 1157	3 Sept 1189	6 Apr 1199	Fontevrault Abbey	Berengaria of Navarre	
John	24 Dec 1167	27 May 1199	18 Oct 1216	Worcester Cathedral	(1) Isabella of Gloucester (2) Isabella of Angoulême	Henry III

Bibliography

Abels, Richard (1984) 'Bookland and Fyrd Service in Late Saxon England', *Anglo-Norman Studies* VII, 1–25.

Abrams, Lesley (1994) 'Eleventh-century Missions and the Early Stages of Ecclesiastical Organisation in Scandinavia', *Anglo-Norman Studies* XVII, 21–40.

—— (1997) 'The Conversion of the Scandinavians of Dublin', *Anglo-Norman Studies* XX, 1–30.

Abulafia, D. (1984) 'Normans in Africa, Majorca and the Muslim Mediterranean', *Anglo-Norman Studies* VII, 26–49.

Ailes, Adrian (1992) 'The Knight, Heraldry and Armour: The Role of Recognition and the Origins of Heraldry', in C. Harper-Bill and Ruth Harvey (eds), *Medieval Knighthood IV, Papers from the Fifth Strawberry Hill Conference 1990*, Woodbridge: The Boydell Press, 1–22.

Aird, W. M. (1993) 'St Cuthbert, the Scots and the Normans', *Anglo-Norman Studies* XVI, 1–20.

Alexander, J. J. G. (1992) 'Ideological Representation of Military Combat in Anglo-Norman Art', *Anglo-Norman Studies* XV, 1–24.

Allen Brown, R. (1955) 'Royal Castle-building in England, 1154–1216', *English Historical Review* LXX, 353–98.

—— (1980) 'The Battle of Hastings', *Proceedings of the Battle Conference on Anglo-Norman Studies* III, 1–21.

Altschul, M. (1965) *A Baronial Family in Medieval England. The Clares 1217–1314,* Baltimore: Johns Hopkins University Press.

Anderson, Freda (1988) 'St Pancras Priory, Lewes: Its Architectural Development to 1200', *Anglo-Norman Studies* II, 1–35.

Anderson, M. D. (1964) *A Saint at the Stake: The Strange Death of William of Norwich, 1144,* London: Faber and Faber.

Axton, Richard (1974) *European Drama of the Early Middle Ages,* London: Hutchinson University Library.

Babcock, Robert S. (1993) 'Rhys Ap Tewdwr, King of Deheubarth', *Anglo-Norman Studies* XVI, 21–36.

Bachrach, Bernard S. (1985) 'Some Observations on the Military Administration of the Norman Conquest', *Anglo-Norman Studies* VIII, 1–25.

Bailey, Richard N. (1980) *Viking Age Sculpture,* London: Collins.

Baker, Derek (1978) ' "A Nursery of Saints": St Margaret of Scotland Reconsidered', in D. Baker (ed.) *Medieval Women,* Oxford: Basil Blackwell, 119–41.

Baldwin, John W. (1985) 'Masters at Paris from 1179 to 1215: A Social Perspective', in Robert L. Benson and Giles Constable (eds) *Renaissance and Renewal in the Twelfth Century,* Oxford: Oxford University Press.

Barber, Malcolm (1998) *The New Knighthood. A History of the Order of the Temple,* Cambridge: Canto.

Barker, Lynn K. (1990) 'Ivo of Chartres and the Anglo-Norman Cultural Tradition', *Anglo-Norman Studies* XIII, 15–33.

Barlow, Frank (1986) *Thomas Becket,* London: Weidenfeld and Nicolson.

Barratt, Nick (1999) 'The Revenues of John and Philip Augustus Revisited' in S. D. Church (ed.) *King John: New Interpretations,* Woodbridge: The Boydell Press.

Barrow, G. W. S. (1973) *The Kingdom of the Scots,* London: Edward Arnold.

—— (1980) *The Anglo-Norman Era in Scottish History,* Oxford: Clarendon Press.

—— (1991) 'The Charters of David I', *Anglo-Norman Studies* XIV, 25–37.

Barthélemy, Dominique (1988) 'The Use of Private Space' in G. Duby (ed.) (trans. A. Goldhammer) *A History of Private Life', Vol. 2: Revelations of the Medieval World,* Cambridge, MA: Harvard University Press.

Bartlett, Robert (1986) *Trial by Fire and Water: The Medieval Judicial Ordeal,* Oxford: Clarendon Press.

—— (2000) *England Under the Norman and Angevin Kings 1075–1225,* Oxford: Clarendon Press.

Barton, R. E. (1994) 'Lordship in Maine: Transformation, Service and Anger', *Anglo-Norman Studies* XVII, 41–64.

Bates, David R. (1975) 'The Character and Career of Odo, Bishop of Bayeux (1049/50–1097)' *Speculum* L, 1–20.

—— (1978) 'The Land Pleas of William I's Reign: Penenden Heath Revisited', *Bulletin of the Institute of Historical Research* LI, 1–19.

—— (1981) 'The Origins of the Justiciarship', *Proceedings of the Battle Conference on Anglo-Norman Studies* IV, 1–12.

—— (1989) 'Normandy and England after 1066', *English Historical Review* CCCCXIII, 851–80.

—— (1992) 'The Conqueror's Charters', in Carola Hicks (ed.), *England in the Eleventh Century, Proceedings of the 1990 Harlaxton Symposium,* Stamford: Paul Watkins.

—— (1994) 'The Rise and Fall of Normandy, c.911–1204', in David Bates and Anne Curry (eds) *England and Normandy in the Middle Ages,* London: The Hambleton Press.

—— (1996) *Normandy before 1066,* London: Longman.

—— (1998) *Regesta Regum Anglo-Normannorum. The Acta of William I (1066–1087),* Oxford: Clarendon Press.

Baylé, Maylis (1982) 'Interlace Patterns in Norman Romanesque Sculpture: Regional Groups and their Historical Background', *Anglo-Norman Studies* V, 1–20.

Beech, George (1986) 'The Participation of Aquitanians in the Conquest of England, 1066–1100', *Anglo-Norman Studies* IX, 1–24.

—— (1992) 'A Norman–Italian Adventurer in the East: Richard of Salerno 1097–1112', *Anglo-Norman Studies* XV, 25–40.

Beeler, J. H. (1956) 'Castles and Strategy in Norman and Early Angevin England', *Speculum* XXXI, 581–601.

Bennett, Matthew (1982) 'Poetry as History? The "Roman de Rou" of Wace as a Source for the Norman Conquest', *Anglo-Norman Studies* V, 21–39.

—— (1986) 'Stereotype Normans in Old French Vernacular Literature', *Anglo-Norman Studies* IX, 25–42.

—— (1988) 'Wace and Warfare', *Anglo-Norman Studies* XI, 37–57.

—— (1992) 'Norman Naval Activity in the Mediterranean', *Anglo-Norman Studies* XV, 41–58.

Beresford, Guy (1981) 'Goltho Manor, Lincolnshire: The Building and their Surrounding Defences *c*.850–1150', *Proceedings of the Battle Conference on Anglo-Norman Studies* IV, 13–36.

Beresford, Maurice (1967) *New Towns of the Middle Ages*, London: Lutterworth Press.

—— (1983) *The Lost Villages of England*, Stroud, Gloucestershire: Alan Sutton.

Bernstein, David (1982) 'The Blinding of Harold and the Meaning of the Bayeux Tapestry', *Anglo-Norman Studies* V, 40–64.

Biddle, Martin (ed.) (1976) *Winchester in the Early Middle Ages: An Edition and Discussion of the Winton Domesday,* Oxford: Clarendon Press.

—— (1985) 'Seasonal Festivals and Residence: Winchester, Westminster and Gloucester in the Tenth to Twelfth Centuries', *Anglo-Norman Studies* VIII, 51–72.

Bishop, Edmund (1918) 'On the Origins of the Prymer', *Liturgica Historica*, 217–28.

Bishop, T. A. M. (1961) *Scriptoris Regis*, Oxford: Oxford University Press.

Bitel, L. (2000) 'Saints and Angry Neighbours: The Politics of Cursing in Irish Hagiography', in Sharon Farmer and Barbara H. Rosenwein (eds) *Monks and Nuns, Saints and Outcasts,* Ithaca: Cornell University Press.

Blackburn, Mark (1990) 'Coinage and Currency Under Henry I: A Review', *Anglo-Norman Studies* XIII, 49–76.

—— (1994) 'Coinage and Currency', in Edmund King (ed.) *The Anarchy of King Stephen's Reign,* Oxford: Clarendon Press.

Blair, John (1991) 'A Romanesque Timber Beakhead from Cameley, Somerset', *The Antiquaries Journal* LXX1, 252–8.

Bloch, Marc (1965) *Feudal Society,* London: Routledge and Kegan Paul.

Blunt, C. E. and Brand, J. D. (1970) 'Mint Output of Henry III', *British Numismatic Journal* 39, 61–6.

Bolton, Brenda (1978) '*Vitae Matrum*: A Further Aspect of the *Frauenfrage*', in D. Baker (ed.) *Medieval Women,* Oxford: Basil Blackwell, 253–73.

Bolton, J. L. (1999) 'The English Economy in the Early Thirteenth Century', in S. D. Church (ed.) *King John: New Interpretations,* Woodbridge: The Boydell Press, 27–40.

Bradbury, Jim (1983) 'Battles in England and Normandy, 1066–1154', *Anglo-Norman Studies* VI, 1–12.

—— (1996) *Stephen and Matilda: The Civil War of 1139–53,* Stroud, Gloucestershire: Alan Sutton.

—— (1998) *Philip Augustus, King of France 1180–1223*, London: Longman.

—— (1999) 'Philip Augustus and King John: Personality and History', in S. D. Church (ed.) *King John: New Interpretations,* Woodbridge: The Boydell Press.

Brand, Paul (1993) '"Time out of Mind": The Knowledge and Use of the Eleventh- and Twelfth-Century Past in Thirteenth-Century Litigation', *Anglo-Norman Studies* XVI, 37–54.

Brett, M. (1975) *The English Church Under Henry I*, Oxford: Oxford University Press.

Bridbury, A. R. (1992) *The English Economy: From Bede to the Reformation,* Woodbridge: The Boydell Press.

Britnell, Richard H. (1993) *The Commercialisation of English Society 1000–1500,* Cambridge: Cambridge University Press.

—— (1995) 'Commercialisation and Economic Development in England 1000–1300' in Richard H. Britnell and M. S. Bruce Campbell (eds) *A Commercialising Economy England 1086 to c.1300,* Manchester: Manchester University Press.

—— (1996) 'Boroughs, Markets and Trade in Northern England, 1000–1216', in Richard Britnell and John Hatcher (eds) *Progress and Problems in Medieval England,* Cambridge: Cambridge University Press.

Brooke, C. (1986) 'Introduction', in S. Macready and F. H. Thompson (eds) *Art and Patronage in the English Romanesque,* London: Society of Antiquaries.

Brooks, N. P. and Walker, H. E. (1978) 'The Authority and Interpretation of the Bayeux Tapestry', *Proceedings of the Battle Conference on Anglo-Norman Studies* I, 1–34.

Brown, Shirley Ann and Herren, Michael W. (1993) 'The "Adelae Comitissae" of Baudri of Bourgueil and the Bayeux Tapestry', *Anglo-Norman Studies* XVI, 55–73.

Bull, Marcus (1995) 'Origins', in Jonathan Riley-Smith (ed.) *The Oxford Illustrated History of the Crusades,* Oxford: Oxford University Press.

Burton, Janet, E. (1987) 'Monasteries and Parish Churches in Eleventh and Twelfth Century Yorkshire', *Northern History* 23, 39–50.

—— (1995) *Kirkham Priory from Foundation to Dissolution,* Borthwick Papers 86, York: University of York.

—— (1997) *Monastic and Religious Orders in Britain 1000–1300,* Cambridge: Cambridge University Press.

Burton, Janet and Stalley, Roger (1983) 'Tables of Cistercian Affiliations', in Christopher Norton and David Park (eds) *Cistercian Art and Architecture in the British Isles,* Cambridge: Cambridge University Press.

Butler, Laurence (1964) 'Minor Medieval Monumental Sculpture in the East Midlands', *Medieval Archaeology* 121, 111–25.

Carpenter, D. A. (1990) *The Minority of Henry III,* Berkeley: University of California Press.

Cheney, C. R. (1950) *English Bishops' Chanceries, 1100–1250,* Manchester: Manchester University Press.

Chenu, M.-D. (1997) *Nature, Man and Society in the Twelfth Century,* Toronto: University of Toronto.

Chibnall, Marjorie (1956) *John of Salisbury's Memoirs of the Papal Court,* London: Thomas Nelson.

—— (1973) *The Ecclesiastical History of Orderic Vitalis Books VII and VIII,* Oxford: Clarendon Press.

—— (1975) *The Ecclesiastical History of Orderic Vitalis Books IX and X,* Oxford: Clarendon Press.

—— (1977) 'Mercenaries and the Familia Regis under Henry I', *History* LXII, 427–42.

—— (1978) 'Feudal Society in Orderic Vitalis', *Proceedings of the Battle Conference on Anglo-Norman Studies* I, 35–48.

—— (1982) 'Military Service in Normandy before 1066', *Anglo-Norman Studies* V, 65–77.

—— (1984) *The World of Orderic Vitalis,* Oxford: Clarendon Press.

—— (1986) *Anglo-Norman England 1066–1166,* Oxford: Basil Blackwell.

—— (1987) 'The Empress Matilda and Bec-Hellouin', *Anglo-Norman Studies* X, 35–48.

—— (1988) 'The Empress Matilda and Church Reform', *Transactions of the Royal Historical Society,* 5th Series, 38, 107–30.

—— (1994) 'Monastic Foundations in England and Normandy, 1066–1189', in

David Bates and Anne Curry (eds) *England and Normandy in the Middle Ages,* London: The Hambleton Press.

—— (1997) '"Clio's Legal Cosmetics": Law and Custom in the Work of Medieval Historians', *Anglo-Norman Studies* XX, 31–43.

—— (1999) *The Debate on the Norman Conquest*, Manchester: Manchester University Press.

Church, S. D. (1998) 'The 1210 Campaign in Ireland: Evidence for a Military Revolution?', *Anglo-Norman Studies* XX, 45–58.

Ciggaar, Krijnie (1982) 'England and Byzantium on the Eve of the Norman Conquest', *Anglo-Norman Studies* V, 78–96.

—— (1986) 'Byzantine Marginalia to the Norman Conquest', *Anglo-Norman Studies* IX, 43–69.

Clanchy, M. T. (1987) *From Memory to Written Record*, London: Edward Arnold.

Clark, Cecily (ed.) (1970) *The Peterborough Chronicle, 1070–1154,* Oxford: Oxford University Press.

Clark, Cecily (1978) 'Women's Names in Post-Conquest England: Observations and Speculations', *Speculum* LIII, 223–51.

—— (1979) 'Battle *c.*1110. An Anthroponymist Looks at an Anglo-Norman New Town', *Proceedings of the Battle Conference on Anglo-Norman Studies* II, 21–41.

—— (1984) 'British Library Addition Manuscript 40,000 fflv–12r', *Anglo–Norman Studies* VII, 50–65.

—— (1992) 'Domesday Book – a Great Red-Herring: Thoughts on some Late-Eleventh-Century Orthographies', in Carola Hicks (ed.), *England in the Eleventh Century, Proceedings of the 1990 Harlaxton Symposium,* Stamford: Paul Watkins.

Clover, Helen and Gibson, Margaret (1979) *The Letters of Lanfranc, Archbishop of Canterbury*, Oxford: Clarendon Press.

Cochrane, Louise (1994) *Adelard of Bath: The First English Scientist,* London: The British Museum Press.

Colvin, H. (1963) *The History of the King's Works, Vols I and II: The Middle Ages,* London: HMSO.

Colvin, A. H. (1951) *White Canons in England,* Oxford: Clarendon Press.

Constable, Giles (1978) 'Aelred of Rievaulx and the Nun of Watton: An Episode in the Early History of the Gilbertine Order', in D. Baker (ed.) *Medieval Women,* Oxford: Basil Blackwell.

—— (1996 reprinted papers) *Culture and Spirituality in Medieval Europe,* Aldershot: Variorum.

Cook, David R. (1978) 'The Norman Military Revolution in England', *Proceedings of the Battle Conference on Anglo-Norman Studies* I, 94–102.

Cook, G. H. (1947) *Medieval Chantries and Chantry Chapels*, London: Phoenix House.

Coss, Peter (1988) 'Knighthood and the Early Thirteenth-Century County Court', *Thirteenth Century England* II, 45–57.

Cotter, John (1993) *A Twelfth-Century Pottery Kiln at Pound Lane, Canterbury,* Canterbury: Canterbury Archaeological Trust.

Coulson, Charles (1983) 'Fortress-policy in Capetian Tradition and Angevin Practice: Aspects of the Conquest of Normandy by Philip II', *Anglo-Norman Studies* VI, 13–38.

—— (1994) 'The French Matrix of the Castle: Provisions of the Chester–Leicester Conventio', *Anglo-Norman Studies* XVII, 65–86.

Coulton, G. G. (ed. and trans.) (1918) 'Reginald of Durham, "Life of St. Godric" ', in *Social Life in Britain from the Conquest to the Reformation*, Cambridge: Cambridge University Press.

Cowdrey, H. E. J. (1987) 'Towards an Interpretation of the Bayeux Tapestry', *Anglo-Norman Studies* X, 49–65.

—— (1998) *Pope Gregory VII, 1073–1085,* Oxford: Clarendon Press.

Cownie, Emma (1994) 'Gloucester Abbey, 1066–1135: An Illustration of Religious Patronage in Anglo-Norman England', in David Bates and Anne Curry (eds) *England and Normandy in the Middle Ages,* London: The Hambleton Press.

—— (1995) 'The Normans as Patrons of English Religious Houses, 1066–1135', *Anglo-Norman Studies* XVIII, 47–63.

Cramp, Rosemary (1984) *Corpus of Anglo–Saxon Stone Sculpture, County Durham and Northumberland*, Oxford: British Academy.

Crook, John (2000) *The Architectural Setting of the Cult of Saints in the Early Christian West c.300–1200*, Oxford: Clarendon Press.

Crosby, Everett U. (1994) *Bishop and Chapter in Twelfth-Century England,* Cambridge: Cambridge University Press.

Crouch, David (1990) *William Marshal, Court, Career and Chivalry in the Angevin Empire 1147–1219,* London: Longman.

—— (1994) 'Normans and Anglo-Normans: A Divided Aristocracy?' in David Bates and Anne Curry (eds) *England and Normandy in the Middle Ages,* London: The Hambleton Press,

Curnow, P. E. (1979) 'Some Developments in Military Architecture *c.*1200: Le Coudray-Salbart', *Proceedings of the Battle Conference on Anglo-Norman Studies* II, 42–62.

Dalton, Paul (1991) 'In Neutro Latere: The Armed Neutrality of Ranulf II Earl of Chester in King Stephen's Reign', *Anglo-Norman Studies* XIV, 39–59.

—— (1996) 'Eustace Fitz John and the Politics of Anglo-Norman England: The Rise and Survival of a Twelfth-Century Royal Servant', *Speculum* 71, 358–83.

Damian-Grint, Peter (1998) *'En nul leu truis encrit:* Research and Invention in Benoit de Dainte-Maure's *Chronique des dues de Normandie'*, *Anglo-Norman Studies* XXI, 11–30.

Daniell, Christopher (1995) 'Family, Land and Politics: Ralph Nuvel and Twelfth-Century York', *York Historian* 12, 2–20.

—— (1999) *Death and Burial in Medieval England, 1066–1550,* London: Routledge.

—— (2001) 'Battle and Trial: Weapon Injury Burials of St Andrew's Church, Fishergate, York', *Medieval Archaeology* XX, 220–6.

Davis, R. H. C. (1980) *King Stephen,* London: Longman.

—— (1987) 'The Warhorses of the Normans', *Anglo-Norman Studies* X, 67–82.

Davis, R. H. C. and Chibnall, Majorie (eds and trans.) (1998) *The Gesta Guillelmi of William of Poitiers,* Oxford: Clarendon Press.

Davis, R. H. C., Engels, L. J. *et al.* (1979) 'The Carmen de Hastingae Proelio', *Proceedings of the Battle Conference on Anglo-Norman Studies* II, 1–20.

Davis, R. R. (1991) *The Age of Conquest: Wales 1063–1415,* Oxford: Oxford University Press.

DeAragon, RaGena C. (1994) 'Dowager Countesses, 1069–1250', *Anglo-Norman Studies* XVII, 87–100.

Dobson, R. B. (1999) *The Jews of Medieval York and the Massacre of March 1190,* Borthwick Paper 45, York: University of York.

Dodwell, C. R. (1971) *Painting in Europe 800–1200,* Harmondsworth: Penguin.

—— (1982) *Anglo-Saxon Art,* Manchester: Manchester University Press.

Douglas, David (1943) 'Companions of the Conqueror', *History* XXVIII, 129–47.

—— (1964) *William the Conqueror,* Berkeley: University of California Press.

Douglas, David C. (1977) *William the Conqueror,* London: Eyre Methuen.

Douglas, David C. and Greenaway, George W. (eds and trans.) (1981) *English Historical Documents, Vol II. 1042–1189,* Oxford: Oxford University Press.

Douie, Decima L. and Farmer, Dom Hugh (eds and trans.) (1961) *The Life of Hugh of Lincoln, Vol I,* London: Thomas Nelson.

Downer, L. J. (ed. and trans.) (1996) *Leges Henrici Primii,* Oxford: Clarendon Press.

Duby, Georges (1990) (trans. Catherine Tihanyi) *The Legend of Bouvines: War, Religion and Culture in the Middle Ages,* Cambridge: Polity Press.

Duffy, Seán (1997) 'Ireland's Hastings: The Anglo-Norman Conquest of Dublin', *Anglo-Norman Studies* XX, 69–86.

—— (1999) 'John and Ireland: The Origins of England's Irish Problem', in S. D. Church (ed.) *King John: New Interpretations,* Woodbridge: The Boydell Press.

Dumville, David N. (1993) 'Anglo-Saxon Books: Treasure in Norman Hands?', *Anglo-Norman Studies* XVI, 83–99.

Dunbabin, Jean (1993) 'Geoffrey of Chaumont, Thibaud of Blois and William the Conqueror', *Anglo-Norman Studies* XVI, 101–16.

Duncan, A. A. M. (1999) 'King John of England and the King of Scots', in S. D. Church (ed.) *King John: New Interpretations,* Woodbridge: The Boydell Press.

Eales, Richard (1985) 'Local Loyalties in Norman England: Kent in Stephen's Reign', *Anglo-Norman Studies* VIII, 88–108.

—— (1986) 'The Game of Chess: An Aspect of Medieval Knightly Culture', in C. Harper-Bill and R. Harvey (eds) *The Ideals and Practice of Medieval Knighthood I,* Woodbridge: The Boydell Press.

English, Barbara (1991) *The Lords of Holderness 1086–1260,* Hull: Hull University Press.

—— (1998) 'Towns, Mottes and Ring-works of the Conquest', in Andrew Ayton and J. L. Price (eds) *The Medieval Military Revolution,* London: I.B. Tauris.

Everard, Judith (1997) 'The Justiciarship in Brittany and Ireland under Henry II', *Anglo-Norman Studies* XX, 87–105.

Faulkner, Kathryn (1996) 'The Transformation of Knighthood in Early Thirteenth Century England', *English Historical Review* CXI, 1–23.

Fernie, E. C. (1985) 'The Romanesque Church of Waltham Abbey', *Journal of the British Archaeological Association* 138, 48–78.

—— (1986) 'The Effect of the Conquest on Norman Architectural Patronage', *Anglo-Norman Studies* IX, 71–85.

—— (1994) 'Architecture and the Effects of the Norman Conquest', in David Bates and Anne Curry (eds) *England and Normandy in the Middle Ages,* London: The Hambleton Press.

—— (1998) 'Saxons, Normans and their Buildings', *Anglo-Norman Studies* XXI, 1–9.

—— (2000) *The Architecture of Norman England*, Oxford: Oxford University Press.

Finucane, R. C. (1984) *Appearances of the Dead*, London: Junction Books.

Flanagan, Marie Therese (1997) 'Strategies of Lordship in Pre-Norman and Post-Norman Leinster', *Anglo-Norman Studies* XX, 107–25.

Fleming, Donald F. (1990) 'Landholding by "Milites" in Domesday Book: A Revision', *Anglo-Norman Studies* XIII, 83–98.

Fleming, Robin (1986) 'Domesday Book and the Tenurial Revolution', *Anglo-Norman Studies* IX, 87–102.

—— (1991) *Kings and Lords in Conquest England,* Cambridge: Cambridge University Press.

—— (1994) 'Oral Testimony and the Domesday Inquest', *Anglo-Norman Studies* XVII, 101–22.

Foreville, R. (1996) 'The Synod of the Province of Rouen in the Eleventh and Twelfth Century', in C. N. L. Brooke *et al. Church and Government in the Middle Ages,* Cambridge: Cambridge University Press.

Forsyth, Ilene H. (1978) 'The Theme of Cockfighting in Burgundian Romanesque Sculpture', *Speculum* LIII, 252–82.

Franklin, M. J. (1984) 'The Identification of Minsters in the Midlands', *Anglo-Norman Studies* VII, 69–88.

—— (1990) 'The Bishops of Winchester and the Monastic Revolution', *Anglo-Norman Studies* XII, 47–65.

Fröhlich, Walter (1987) 'St Anselm's Special Relationship with William the Conqueror', *Anglo-Norman Studies* X, 101–10.

——(1992) 'The Marriage of Henry VI and Constance of Sicily: Prelude and Consequences', *Anglo-Norman Studies* XV, 99–115.

Fryde, Natalie (1999) 'King John and Empire', in S. D. Church (ed.) *King John: New Interpretations,* Woodbridge: The Boydell Press.

Galbraith, V. H. (1935) 'Literacy of Medieval Kings', *Proceedings of the British Academy* XXI, 201–38.

—— (1967) 'Notes on the Career of Samson, Bishop of Worcester', *English Historical Review* 82, 86–101.

Gameson, R. (ed.) (1997) *The Study of the Bayeux Tapestry*, Woodbridge: The Boydell Press.

—— (1998) 'English Book Collection in the Late Eleventh and Early Twelfth Century: Symeon's Durham and its Context', in David Rollason (ed.) *Symeon of Durham: Historian of Durham and the North,* Stamford: Shaun Tyas, 230–53.

Gardiner, Mark (1999) 'Shipping and Trade between England and the Continent during the Eleventh Century', *Anglo-Norman Studies* XXII, 71–93.

Garnett, George (1985) ' "Franci et Angli": The Legal Distinction between Peoples after the Conquest', *Anglo-Norman Studies* VIII, 109–37.

Gem, Richard (1980) 'The Romanesque Rebuilding of Westminister Abbey', *Proceedings of the Battle Conference of Anglo-Norman Studies* III, 33–60.

—— (1982) 'The Early Romanesque Tower of Sompting Church, Sussex', *Anglo-Norman Studies* V, 121–8.

—— (1983a) 'The "Lewes Group" of Wall Paintings: Architectural Considerations', *Anglo-Norman Studies* VI, 236–7.

—— (1983b) 'An Early Church of the Knights Templars at Shipley, Sussex', *Anglo-Norman Studies* VI, 238–46.

—— (1986) 'The Bishop's Chapel at Hereford, the Roles of Patron and Craftsman', in S. Macready and F. H. Thompson (eds) *Art and Patronage in the English Romanesque,* London: Society of Antiquaries.

Gibson, Margaret (1978) *Lanfranc of Bec,* Oxford: Clarendon Press.

Gillingham, John (1981) 'The Introduction of Knight Service into England', *Proceedings of the Battle Conference on Anglo-Norman Studies* IV, 53–64.

—— (1988) 'War and Chivalry in the *History of William the Marshal*', *Thirteenth Century England* II, 1–13.

—— (1990) 'The Context and Purposes of Geoffrey of Monmouth's "History of the Kings of Britain" ', *Anglo-Norman Studies* XII, 77–118.

—— (1994a) 'Historians without Hindsight: Coggeshall, Diceto and Howden on the Early Years of John's Reign', in S. D. Church (ed.) *King John: New Interpretations,* Woodbridge: The Boydell Press.

—— (1994b) *Richard Coeur de Lion: Kingship, Chivalry and War in the Twelfth Century,* London: The Hambledon Press.

—— (1997) 'The Travels of Roger of Howden and his Views on the Irish, Scots and Welsh', *Anglo-Norman Studies* XX, 151–69.

—— (1999a) 'William the Bastard at War', in Stephen Morillo (ed.) *The Battle of Hastings: Sources and Interpretations,* Woodbridge: The Boydell Press.

—— (1999b) 'Historians Without Hindsite: Coggeshall, Diceto and Howden on the Early Years of John's Reign', in S. D. Church (ed.) *King John: New Interpretations,* Woodbridge: The Boydell Press.

Gillmor, C. M. (1984) 'Naval Logistics of the Cross Channel Operation, 1066', *Anglo-Norman Studies* VII, 105–31.

Godfrey, John (1978) 'The Defeated Anglo-Saxons take Service with the Eastern Emperor', *Proceedings of the Battle Conference on Anglo-Norman Studies* I, 63–74.

Golding, Brian (1980) 'The Coming of the Cluniacs', *Proceedings of the Battle Conference on Anglo-Norman Studies* III, 65–77.

—— (1986) 'Anglo-Norman Knightly Burial', in C. Harper-Bill and R. Harvey (eds) *The Ideals and Practice of Medieval Knighthood I,* Woodbridge: The Boydell Press.

—— (1994) *Conquest and Colonisation: The Normans in Britain 1066–1100,* London: Macmillan.

Goulburn, Edward Meyrick and Symonds, Henry (1878) *The Letters of Herbert de Losinga,* Oxford.

Graboïs, Arveh (1975) 'The *Hebraica Veritas* and the Jewish–Christian Intellectual Relations in the Twelfth Century', *Speculum* 50, 613–34.

Graham Campbell, James (1991) 'Anglo-Scandinavian Equestrian Equipment in Eleventh-Century England', *Anglo-Norman Studies* XIV, 77–89.

Grainge, Christine and Grainge, Gerald (1999) 'The Pevensey Expedition: Brilliantly Executed Plan or Near Disaster?', in Stephen Morillo (ed.) *The Battle of Hastings: Sources and Interpretations,* Woodbridge: The Boydell Press.

Gransden, Antonia (1981) 'Baldwin, Abbot of Bury St Edmunds, 1065–1097', *Proceedings of the Battle Conference on Anglo-Norman Studies* IV, 65–76.

—— (1989) 'Traditionalism and Continuity during the Last Century of Anglo-Saxon Monasticism', *Journal of Ecclesiastical History* XL, 202–7.

Grant, Lindy (1994) 'Architectural Relationships between England and Normandy, 1100–1204', in David Bates and Anne Curry (eds) *England and Normandy in the Middle Ages,* London: The Hambleton Press.

Green, Judith (1979) 'William Rufus, Henry I and the Royal Demesne', *History* 64 (212), 337–52.

—— (1982) 'The Sheriffs of William the Conqueror', *Anglo-Norman Studies* V, 129–45.

—— (1989a) 'Unity and Disunity in the Anglo-Norman state', *Historical Research* 62, 1–17.

—— (1989b) *The Government of England under Henry I,* Cambridge: Cambridge University Press.

Green, Judith, (1991) 'Financing Stephen's War', *Anglo-Norman Studies* XIV, 91–114.

Greenway, Diana (1977) *Bishop William Giffard,* Winchester: Winchester Cathedral Record.

—— (1995) 'Authority, Convention and Observation in Henry of Huntingdon's *Historia Anglorum', Anglo-Norman Studies* XVII, 105–22.

Grenville, Jane (1999) *Medieval Housing,* Leicester: Leicester University Press.

Hadley, Dawn (1998) *Masculinity in Medieval Europe,* London: Longman.

Hall, G. D. G (ed. and trans.) (1965) *The Treatise on the Laws and Customs of the Realm of England Commonly Called Glanvill,* London: Nelson.

Hallam, Elizabeth M. (1982) 'Royal Burial and the Cult of Kingship in France and England, 1060–1330', *Journal of Medieval History* 8, 359–80.

Hamilton, Bernard (1978) 'Women in the Crusader States: The Queens of Jerusalem (1100–1190)', in D. Baker (ed.) *Medieval Women,* Oxford: Basil Blackwell.

Harfield, C. G. (1991) 'A Hand-list of Castles Recorded in the Domesday Book', *English Historical Review* 106, 371–92.

Harper-Bill, Christopher (1979) 'The Piety of the Anglo-Norman Knightly Class', *Proceedings of the Battle Conference on Anglo-Norman Studies* II, 63–77.

—— (1984) 'Bishop William Turbe and the Diocese of Norwich, 1146–1174', *Anglo-Norman Studies* VII, 142–60.

—— (1988) 'The Struggle for Benefices in Twelfth-Century East Anglia', *Anglo-Norman Studies* XI, 113–32.

—— (1999) 'John and the Church of Rome', in S. D. Church (ed.) *King John: New Interpretations,* Woodbridge: The Boydell Press.

Hart, Cyril (1999) 'The Bayeux Tapestry and the Schools of Illumination at Canterbury', *Anglo-Norman Studies* XXII, 117–67.

Harvey, John (1971) *The Master Builders,* London: Thames and Hudson.

Harvey, P. D. A. (1976) 'English Inflation of 1180–1120', in R. H. Hilton (ed.) *Peasants, Knights, and Heretics: Studies in Medieval English History*, Cambridge: Cambridge University Press.

Harvey, Sally P. J. (1971) 'Domesday Book and its Predecessors', *English Historical Review* 86, 753–73.

—— (1975) 'Anglo-Norman Governance', *Transactions of the Royal Historical Society*, 5th Series, 25, 186–93.

—— (1985) 'Taxation and the Ploughland in Domesday Book', in P. Sawyer (ed.) *Domesday Book, A Reassessment*, London: Edward Arnold, 86–103.

Haskins, C. H. (1916) *The Normans in European History*, London: Constable.

Hayward, Paul Anthony (1998) 'Translation-Narratives in Post-Conquest Hagiography and English Resistance to the Norman Conquest', *Anglo-Norman Studies* XXI, 67–93.

Head, Victor (1997) *Hereward,* Stroud, Gloucestershire: Alan Sutton.

Heales, A. (1868) *Records of Merton Priory,* London: H. Frowde.

Heiser, Richard R. (1997) 'Richard I and His Appointments to English Shrievalties', *English Historical Review* 112, 1–19.

Hermans, J. (1979) 'The Byzantine View of the Normans', *Anglo-Norman Studies* II, 78–92.

Hicks, Carola (1992) 'The Borders of the Bayeux Tapestry', in Carola Hicks (ed.), *England in the Eleventh Century, Proceedings of the 1990 Harlaxton Symposium,* Stamford: Paul Watkins.

Higham, N. J. (1997) *The Death of Anglo-Saxon England,* Stroud, Gloucestershire: Alan Sutton.

Hiley, David (1993) 'Changes in English Chant Repertoires in the Eleventh Century as Reflected in the Winchester Sequences', *Anglo-Norman Studies* XVI, 137–53.

Hindle, Brian Paul (1990) *Medieval Town Plans,* Princes Risborough: Shire Archaeology.

Hindley, Geoffrey (1990) *The Book of Magna Carta,* London: Guild Publishing.

Hockey, Frederick (1982) 'The House of Redvers and its Monastic Foundations', *Anglo-Norman Studies* V, 146–52.

Holdsworth, Christopher J. (1978) 'Christina of Markyate', in D. Baker (ed.) *Medieval Women,* Oxford: Basil Blackwell.

—— (1985) 'St Bernard and England', *Anglo-Norman Studies* VIII, 138–153.

Hollister, C. (1965) *The Military Organization of Norman England,* Oxford: Clarendon Press.

—— (1979) 'Henry I and the Anglo-Norman Magnates', *Proceedings of the Battle Conference on Anglo-Norman Studies* II, 93–107.

—— (1983) 'War and Diplomacy in the Anglo-Norman World The Reign of Henry I', *Anglo-Norman Studies* VI, 72–88.

—— (1987) 'St Anselm on Lay Investiture', *Anglo-Norman Studies* X, 145–58.

Holt, Elizabeth Gilmore (ed.) (1981) *A Documentary History of Art, Vol 1: The Middle Ages and the Renaissance,* Princeton: Princeton University Press.

Holt, J. C. (1961) *The Northerners,* Oxford: Clarendon Press.

—— (1974) 'Politics and Property in Medieval England', *Past and Present* LXV, 127–35.

—— (1983) 'The Introduction of Knight Service in England', *Anglo-Norman Studies* VI, 88–106.

—— (1994) '1153: The Treaty of Winchester', in Edmund King (ed.) *The Anarchy of King Stephen's Reign,* Oxford: Oxford University Press.

—— (1997) *Colonial England 1066–1215,* London: The Hambledon Press.

Hooper, Nicholas (1978) 'Anglo-Saxon Warfare on the Eve of the Conquest: A Brief Survey', *Proceedings of the Battle Conference on Anglo-Norman Studies* I, 84–93.

—— (1984) 'The Housecarls in England in the Eleventh Century', *Anglo-Norman Studies* VII, 161–76.

Hudson, John (1990) 'Life-Grants of Land and the Development of Inheritance in Anglo-Norman England', *Anglo-Norman Studies* XII, 67–80.

Huisman, Gerda C. (1983) 'Notes on the Manuscript Tradition of Dudo of St Quentin's "Gesta Normannorum"', *Anglo-Norman Studies* VI, 122–35.

Huneycutt, Lois L. (1990) 'The Idea of the Perfect Princess: The "Life of St Margaret" in the Reign of Matilda II (1100–1118)', *Anglo-Norman Studies* XII, 81–97.

Hyams, Paul (1981) 'The Common Law and the French Connection', *Anglo-Norman Studies* IV, 77–92.

—— (1986) ' "No Register of Title": The Domesday Inquest and Land Adjudication', *Anglo-Norman Studies* IX, 127–41.

James, Bruno Scott (ed. and trans.) (repr. 1998) *The Letters of Bernard of Clairvaux,* Stroud, Gloucestershire: Alan Sutton.

James, M. R. (ed. and trans.), revised by C. N. L. Brooke and R. A. B. Mynors (1983) *Walter Map De Nugis Vurialium, Courtier's Trifles,* Oxford: Clarendon Press.

Jenkinson, Hilary (1913) 'William Cade a Financier of the Twelfth Century', *English Historical Review* XXVIII, 209–27.

Johnson, Charles (1950) *The Course of the Exchequer by Richard, Son of Nigel,* London: Thomas Nelson and Sons.

Johnston, A. and Rogerson, M. (eds) (1979) *Records of Early English Drama*, York, Toronto: Toronto University Press.

Johnston, R. C. (1981) *Jordan Fantosme's Chronicle,* Oxford: Oxford University Press.

Jolliffe, J. E. A. (1963) *Angevin Kingship*, London: A. & C. Black.

Kappelle, William (1992) 'New Insights into the Domesday Book', *Essays in Medieval Studies* 9, 55–65.

Kealey, Edward J. (1987) *Harvesting the Air, Windmill Pioneers in Twelfth-Century England*, Woodbridge: The Boydell Press.

Keats-Rohan, K. S. B. (1992) 'The Bretons and Normans of England 1066–1154', *Nottingham Medieval Studies* 36, 42–78.

Keefe, T. K. (1983) *Feudal Assessment and Community under Henry II and his Sons*, Berkeley: University of California Press.

Keen, Laurence (1982) 'The Unfravilles, the Castle and the Barony of Prudhoe, Northumberland', *Anglo-Norman Studies* V, 165–84.

Kemp, B. R. (1980) 'Monastic Possession of Parish Churches in England in the Twelfth Century', *Journal of Ecclesiastical History* XXXI, 133–60.

—— (1993) 'Towards Admission and Institution: English Episcopal Formulae for the Appointments of Parochial Incumbents', *Anglo-Norman Studies* XVI, 155–76.

Kerr, Margaret H., Forsyth, Richard D. and Plyley, Michael J. (1992) 'Cold Water and Hot Iron: Trial by Ordeal in England', *Journal of Interdisciplinary History* XXII, 4, 573–95.

Keynes, Simon (1987) 'Regenbald the Chancellor *(sic)*', *Anglo-Norman Studies* X, 185–222.

—— (1990) 'The Aethelings in Normandy', *Anglo-Norman Studies* XIII, 173–205.

King, Edmund (1990) 'The Foundation of Pipewell Abbey, Northamptonshire', *Haskins Society Journal* 2, 167–77.

—— (1991) 'Dispute Settlement in Anglo-Norman England', *Anglo-Norman Studies* XIV, 115–30.

—— (1996) 'Economic Development in the Early Twelfth Century', in Richard Britnell and John Hatcher (eds) *Progress and Problems in Medieval England,* Cambridge: Cambridge University Press.

Klukas, Arnold William (1983) 'The Architectural Implications of the "Decreta Lanfranci"', *Anglo-Norman Studies* VI, 136–71.

—— (1984) 'The Continuity of Anglo-Saxon Liturgical Tradition in Post-Conquest England as Evident in the Architecture of Winchester, Ely and Canterbury Cathedrals', *Les Mutations Socio-Culturelles au Tournant des XI-XII Siecles,* Paris: Etudes Anselmiennes (IV Session).

Knowles, David (ed. and trans.) (1951) *The Monastic Constitutions of Lanfranc,* London: Nelson's Medieval Classics.

—— (1966) *The Monastic Order in England*, Cambridge: Cambridge University Press.

Latimer, Paul (1999) 'Early Thirteenth-Century Prices', in S. D. Church (ed.) *King John: New Interpretations,* Woodbridge: The Boydell Press, 40–73.

Lawrence, Anne (1994) 'Anglo-Norman Book Production', in David Bates and Anne Curry (eds) *England and Normandy in the Middle Ages,* London: The Hambleton Press.

Le Goff, Jacques (1984) *The Birth of Purgatory*, London: Scholar Press.

Le Patourel, J. (1976) *The Norman Empire,* Oxford: Clarendon Press.

Legge, M. D. (1979) 'Anglo-Norman as a Spoken Language', *Proceedings of the Battle Conference on Anglo-Norman Studies* II, 108–17.

Lendinara, Patrizia (1992) '*The Oratio de Utensilibus ad donum regendum pertinentibus* by Adam of Balsham', *Anglo-Norman Studies* XV, 161–76.

Lennard, Reginald (1959) *Rural England, 1086–1135. A Study of Social and Agrarian Conditions,* Oxford: Clarendon Press.

Lewis, C. P. (1984) 'The Norman Settlement of Herefordshire under William I', *Anglo-Norman Studies* VII, 195–213.

—— (1990) 'The Early Earls of Norman England', *Anglo-Norman Studies* XIII, 207–23.

—— (1993) 'The Domesday Jurors', *Haskins Society Journal* V, 17–44.

—— (1994) 'The French in England before the Norman Conquest', *Anglo-Norman Studies* XVII, 123–44.

Leyser, Karl (1990) 'The Anglo-Norman Succession 1120–1125', *Anglo-Norman Studies* XIII, 225–41.

Liddiard, Robert (1999) 'Castle Rising, Norfolk: A "Language of Lordship"?', *Anglo-Norman Studies* XXII, 169–86.

Lilley, J. M., Stroud, G., Brothwell, D. R. and Williamson, M. H. (1994) 'The Jewish Burial Ground at Jewbury', *The Medieval Cemeteries, The Archaeology of York* 12/3, York: Council for British Archaeology.

Lloyd, Simon (1995) 'The Crusading Movement, 1096–1274', in Jonathan Riley-Smith (ed.) *The Oxford Illustrated History of the Crusades,* Oxford: Oxford University Press.

Lomax, Frank (ed. and trans.) (1992, facsimile reprint of 1908) *The Antiquities of Glastonbury by William of Malmesbury,* Felinfach: J. M. F. Books.

LoPrete, Kimberley A. (1991) 'Adela of Blois and Ivo of Chartres: Piety, Politics, and the Peace in the Diocese of Chartres', *Anglo-Norman Studies* XIV, 131–52.

Loud, G. A. (1981) 'The "Gens Normannorum" – Myth or Reality', *Proceedings of the Battle Conference on Anglo-Norman Studies* IV, 104–16.

—— (1992) 'The Genesis and Context of the Chronicle of Falco of Benevento', *Anglo-Norman Studies* XV, 177–98.

Loyn, H. R. (1978) 'Domesday Book', *Proceedings of the Battle Conference on Anglo-Norman Studies* I, 121–30.

—— (1987) 'William's Bishops: Some Further Thoughts', *Anglo-Norman Studies* X, 223–35.

—— (1992) 'De Iure Domini Regis: A Comment on Royal Authority in Eleventh-Century England', in Carola Hicks (ed.), *England in the Eleventh Century, Proceedings of the 1990 Harlaxton Symposium,* Stamford: Paul Watkins.

—— (1994) 'Abbots of English Monasteries in the Period Following the Norman Conquest', in David Bates and Anne Curry (eds) *England and Normandy in the Middle Ages,* London: The Hambleton Press.

—— (2000) *The English Church 940–1154,* London: Longman.

Luscombe, D. E. (1995) 'Bec, Christ Church and the Correspondence of St Anselm', *Anglo-Norman Studies* XVIII, 1–17.

Maccarini, Pier Andrea (1983) 'William the Conqueror and the Church of Rome (from the Epistolae)', *Anglo-Norman Studies* VI, 172–87.

Mahany, Christie and Foffe, David (1982) 'Stamford: The Development of an Anglo-Scandinavian Borough', *Anglo-Norman Studies* V, 197–219.

McNeill, T. E. (1990) 'The Great Towers of Early Irish Castles', *Anglo-Norman Studies* XII, 99–117.

Maier, Christopher T. (2000) *Crusade Propaganda and Ideology: Model Sermons for Preaching of the Cross,* Cambridge: Cambridge University Press.

Mallory, J. P. and McNeill, T. E. (1995) *The Archaeology of Ulster: From Colonisation to Plantation,* Belfast: Institute of Irish Studies.

Marks, Richard (1993) *Stained Glass in England during the Middle Ages,* London: Routledge.

Martindale, Jane (1984) 'Aimeri of Thouars and the Poitevin Connection', *Anglo-Norman Studies* VII, 224–45

—— (1992) 'The Sword on the Stone: Some Resonances of a Medieval Symbol of Power (The Tomb of King John in Worcester Cathedral)', *Anglo-Norman Studies* XV, 199–241.

—— (1999) 'Eleanor of Aquitaine: The Last Years', in S. D. Church (ed.) *King John: New Interpretations,* Woodbridge: The Boydell Press.

Mason, Emma (1976) 'The Mauduits and their Chamberlainship of the Exchequer', *Bulletin of the Institute of Historical Research* 49, 1–23.

—— (1979) 'Magnates, Curiales and the Wheel of Fortune: 1066–1154', *Proceedings of the Battle Conference on Anglo-Norman Studies* II, 118–40.

—— (1985) 'Change and Continuity in Eleventh-Century Mercia: The Experience of St Wulfstan of Worcester', *Anglo-Norman Studies* VIII, 154–76.

—— (1990) *Saint Wulfstan of Worcester c.1008–1095,* Oxford: Basil Blackwell.

—— (1998) 'William Rufus and the Benedictine Order', *Anglo-Norman Studies* XXI, 113–44.

Mason, J. F. A. (1990) 'Barons and their Officials in the Later Eleventh Century', *Anglo-Norman Studies* XIII, 243–62.

Matthew, D. J. A. (1994) 'The English Cultivation of Norman History', in David Bates and Anne Curry (eds) *England and Normandy in the Middle Ages,* London: The Hambleton Press.

Maund, K. L. (1988) 'The Welsh Alliances of Earl Aelfgar of Mercia and his Family in the Mid-Eleventh Century', *Anglo-Norman Studies* XI, 181–90.

Mayr-Harting, H. (1972) 'Functions of a Twelfth-Century Recluse', *History* 62, 337–52.

Melazzo, Lucio (1992) 'The Normans Through their Languages', *Anglo-Norman Studies* XV, 243–50.

Menuge, Noel James (2000) 'The Foundation Myth: Yorkshire Monasteries and the Landscape Agenda', *Landscapes* 1, 22–37.

Miller, Edward and Hatcher, John (1995) *Medieval England: Towns, Commerce and Crafts 1086–1348,* London: Longman.

Moore, John S. (1988) 'Domesday Slavery', *Anglo-Norman Studies* XI, 191–220.

—— (1991) 'The Anglo-Norman Family: Size and Structure', *Anglo-Norman Studies* XIV, 153–96.

—— (1996) ' "Quot Homines?" The Population of Domesday England', *Anglo-Norman Studies* XIX, 307–33.

Morey, James H. (1993) 'Peter Comestor, Biblical Paraphrase, and the Medieval Popular Bible', *Speculum* 68, 6–35.

Morillo, Stephen (1999) *The Battle of Hastings: Sources and Interpretations,* Woodbridge: The Boydell Press.

Morris, Colin (1989) *The Papal Monarchy: The Western Church from 1050 to 1250,* Oxford: Clarendon Press.

—— (1995) *The Discovery of the Individual 1050–1200,* Toronto: University of Toronto Press.

Morris, Richard (1989) *Churches in the Landscape*, London: J. M. Dent and Sons.

Mortimer, Richard (1980) 'The Beginnings of the Honour of Clare', *Proceedings of the Battle Conference on Anglo-Norman Studies* III, 119–41.

—— (1985) 'Land and Service: The Tenants of the Honour of Clare', *Anglo-Norman Studies* VIII, 177–97.

—— (1990) 'The Charters of Henry II: What are the Criteria for Authenticity?', *Anglo-Norman Studies* XII, 119–34.

Moss, Vincent (1994) 'Normandy and England in 1180: The Pipe Roll Evidence', in David Bates and Anne Curry (eds) *England and Normandy in the Middle Ages*, London: The Hambleton Press.

—— (1999) 'The Norman Exchequer Rolls of King John', in S. D. Church (ed.) *King John: New Interpretations*, Woodbridge: The Boydell Press.

Muratova, Xenia (1986) 'Bestiaries: An Aspect of Medieval Patronage', in S. Macready and F. H. Thompson (eds) *Art and Patronage in the English Romanesque*, London: Society of Antiquaries.

Mynors, R. A. B., Thomson, R. M. and Winterbottom, M. (eds and trans.) (1998) *William of Malmesbury Gesta Regum Anglorum*, Oxford: Oxford University Press.

Neale, Ian (trans.) (1984) *A History of Selby Monastery to 1174 AD* (privately printed).

Nelson, Janet L. (1981) 'The Rites of the Conqueror', *Proceedings of the Battle Conference on Anglo-Norman Studies* IV, 117–32.

Neumann, J. (1988) 'Hydrographic and Ship-hydrodynamic Aspects of the Norman Invasion, AD 1066', *Anglo-Norman Studies* XI, 221–43.

Newman, Charlotte A. (1988) *The Anglo-Norman Nobility in the Reign of Henry I: The Second Generation*, Philadelphia: University of Pennsylvania Press.

Nilgen, Ursula (1986) 'Intellectuality and Splendour: Thomas Becket as a Patron of the Arts', in S. Macready and F. H. Thompson (eds) *Art and Patronage in the English Romanesque*, London: Society of Antiquaries.

Nip, Renée (1998) 'The Political Relations between England and Flanders (1066–1128)', *Anglo-Norman Studies* XXI, 145–67.

Noble, Peter S. (1992) 'Perversion of an Ideal', in C. Harper-Bill and Ruth Harvey (eds) *Medieval Knighthood IV, Papers from the Fifth Strawberry Hill Conference 1990*, Woodbridge: The Boydell Press.

—— (1994) 'Romance in England and Normandy in the Twelfth Century', in David Bates and Anne Curry (eds) *England and Normandy in the Middle Ages*, London: The Hambleton Press.

Norton, Christopher (2001) *Archbishop Thomas of Bayeux and the Norman Cathedral at York*, Borthwick Paper 100, York: University of York.

O'Brien, Bruce (1996) 'From "Mord-or" to "Murdrum": The Preconquest Origin and Norman Revival of the Murder Fine', *Speculum* 71, 321–57.

Ó Néill, Pádraig (1997) 'The Impact of the Norman Invasion on Irish Literature', *Anglo-Norman Studies* XX, 171–85.

Okasha, Elizabeth (1992) 'The English Language in the Eleventh Century: The Evidence from the Inscriptions', in Carola Hicks (ed.), *England in the Eleventh Century, Proceedings of the 1990 Harlaxton Symposium*, Stamford: Paul Watkins.

Ormrod, M. (ed.) (2000) *The Lord Lieutenants and High Sheriffs of Yorkshire 1066–2000*, Barnsley: Wharncliffe Publishing.

Oschinsky, Dorothea (1971) *Walter of Henley and Other Treatises on Estate Management and Accounting*, Oxford: Clarendon Press.

Otter, Monika (1996) *Inventiones*, London: University of North Carolina Press.

Owen, D. D. R. (1997) *William the Lion, 1143–1214, Kingship and Culture,* East Lothian: Tuckwell Publications.

Owen, Dorothy M. (1979) 'Bishop's Lynn: The First Century of a New Town?', *Proceedings of the Battle Conference on Anglo-Norman Studies* II, 141–53.

—— (1983) 'The Norman Cathedral at Lincoln', *Anglo-Norman Studies* VI, 188–9.

Palliser, David M. (1990) *Domesday York,* Borthwick Paper 78, York: University of York.

Panofsky, Gerda (1979) *Abbot Suger on the Abbey Church of St-Denis and its Art Treasures,* Princeton: Princeton University Press.

Park, David (1983) 'The "Lewes" Group of Wall Paintings in Sussex', *Anglo-Norman Studies* VI, 200–37.

Parsons, David (ed.) (1990) *Stone Quarrying and Building in England AD 43–1525,* Chichester: Phillimore.

Peirce, Ian (1987) 'Arms, Armour and Warfare in the Eleventh Century', *Anglo-Norman Studies* X, 237–57.

—— (1992) 'The Knight, his Arms and Armour *c.*1150–1250', *Anglo-Norman Studies* XV, 251–74.

Philpott, Mark (1997) 'Some Interactions between the English and Irish Churches', *Anglo-Norman Studies* XX, 187–204.

Piele, J. H. (trans.) (1934) *William of Malmesbury's Life of Saint Wultstan,* Lampeter: Llanerch Press.

Platt, Colin (1978) *Medieval England. A Social History and Archaeology from the Conquest to A.D. 1600,* London: Routledge and Kegan Paul.

Poole, A. L. (1955) *Domesday Book to Magna Carta 1087–1216,* Oxford: Clarendon Press.

Pope, Janet M. (1994) 'Monks and Nobles in the Anglo-Saxon Monastic Reform', *Anglo-Norman Studies* XVII, 165–80.

Potter, Julie (1998) 'The Benefactors of Bec and the Politics of Priories', *Anglo-Norman Studies* XXI, 175–92.

Potter, K. R. (1955) *Gesta Stephani,* London: Nelson Medieval Texts.

Potts, Cassandra (1990) 'Normandy or Brittany? A Conflict of Interests at Mont Saint Michel', *Anglo-Norman Studies* XII, 135–56.

—— (1992) 'The Early Norman Charters: A New Perspective on an Old Debate', in Carola Hicks (ed.) *England in the Eleventh Century, Proceedings of the 1990 Harlaxton Symposium,* Stamford: Paul Watkins.

—— (1995) ' "Atque Unum Ex Diversis Gentibus Populum Effecit": Historical Tradition and the Norman Identity', *Anglo-Norman Studies* XVIII, 139–52.

Poulle, Béatrice, (1994) 'Savigny and England', in David Bates and Anne Curry (eds) *England and Normandy in the Middle Ages,* London: The Hambleton Press.

Power, D. J. (1994) 'What did the Frontier of Angevin Normandy Comprise?', *Anglo-Norman Studies* XVII, 181–201.

—— (1999) 'King John and the Norman Aristocracy' in S. D. Church (ed.) *King John: New Interpretations,* Woodbridge: The Boydell Press.

Powicke, F. M. (1963) *The Loss of Normandy 1189–1204,* Manchester: Manchester University Press.

—— (ed. and trans.) (1950) *The Life of Ailred of Rievaulx by Walter Daniel,* London: Thomas Nelson.

Preston, Jean F. (1997) 'Mixed Blessings: A Twelfth-Century Manuscript from Waverley', in P. R. Robinson and Rivkah Zim (eds) *Of the Making of Books,* Aldershot: Scholar Press.

Prestwich, J. (1954) 'War and Finance in the Anglo-Norman State', *Transactions of the Royal Historical Society* IV, 37–42.

—— (1963) 'Anglo-Norman Feudalism and the Problem of Continuity', *Past and Present* 26, 39–57.

Prestwich, J. O. (1981) 'The Military Household of the Norman Kings', *English Historical Review* XCVI, 1–35.

Renn, D. F. (1973) *Norman Castles in Britain*, London: John Baker.

—— (1993) 'Burgheat and Gonfanon: Two Sidelights from the Bayeux Tapestry', *Anglo-Norman Studies* XVI, 176–98.

Reynolds, Susan (1991) 'Bookland, Folkland and Fiefs', *Anglo-Norman Studies* XIV, 211–27.

—— (1994) *Fiefs and Vassals: The Medieval Evidence Reinterpreted*, Oxford: Oxford University Press.

Richardson, H. G. (1959) 'Letters and Charters of Eleanor of Aquitaine', *English Historical Review* LXXIV, 193–213.

Richardson, H. G. and Sayles, G. O. (1963) *The Governance of Medieval England from the Conquest to Magna Carta*, Edinburgh: Edinburgh University Press.

Ridyard, S. J. (1986) '*Condigna Veneratio*: Post-Conquest Attitudes to the Saints of the Anglo-Saxons', *Anglo-Norman Studies* IX, 179–206.

Riley-Smith, Jonathan (1995) 'The State of Mind of Crusaders to the East, 1095–1300', in Jonathan Riley-Smith (ed.) *The Oxford Illustrated History of the Crusades*, Oxford: Oxford University Press.

Robinson, P. R. (1997) 'A Twelfth-Century *Scriptrix* from Nunnaminster', in P. R. Robinson and Rivkah Zim (eds) *Of the Making of Books*, Aldershot: Scholar Press.

Roesdahl, Else (1986) 'The Danish Geometrical Viking Fortresses and their Context', *Anglo-Norman Studies* IX, 208–26.

Roffe, David (1990) 'From Thegnage to Barony: Sake and Soke, Title and Tenants-in-Chief', *Anglo-Norman Studies* XII, 157–76.

Rogers, Nicholas (1992) 'The Waltham Abbey Relic-list', in Carola Hicks (ed.) *England in the Eleventh Century, Proceedings of the 1990 Harlaxton Symposium*, Stamford: Paul Watkins.

Rollason, David (1992) 'Symeon of Durham and the Community of Durham in the Eleventh Century', in C. Hicks, (ed.) *England in the Eleventh Century, Proceedings of the 1990 Harlaxton Symposium II*, Stamford: Paul Watkins.

Rowlands, I. W. (1980) 'The Making of the March: Aspects of the Norman Settlement of Dyfed', *Proceedings of the Battle Conference on Anglo-Norman Studies* III, 142–56.

—— (1999) 'King John and Wales', in S. D. Church (ed.) *King John: New Interpretations*, Woodbridge: The Boydell Press.

Rubenstein, Jay (1995) 'The Life and Writings of Osbern of Canterbury', in Richard Eales and Richard Sharpe (eds) *Canterbury and the Norman Conquest: Churches, Saints and Scholars 1066–1109*, London: The Hambleton Press.

Rubin, Miri (1991) *Corpus Christi: The Eucharist in Late Medieval Culture*, Cambridge: Cambridge University Press.

Rudd, Marylou (1988) 'Monks in the World: The Case of Gundulf of Rochester', *Anglo-Norman Studies* XI, 245–60.

Salzman, L. F. (1967) *Building in England down to 1540*, Oxford: Oxford University Press.

Sawyer, Peter (1985) '1066–1086: A Tenurial Revolution?', in Peter Sawyer (ed.) *Domesday Book: A Reassessment*, London: Edward Arnold.

Searle, Eleanor (1979) 'The Abbey of the Conquerors: Defensive Enfeoffment and Economic Development in Anglo-Norman England', *Proceedings of the Battle Conference on Anglo-Norman Studies* II, 154–64.

—— (1980) 'Women and the Legitimisation of Succession at the Norman Conquest', *Proceedings of the Battle Conference on Anglo-Norman Studies* III, 159–170.

—— (1985) 'Frankish Rivalries and Norse Warriors', *Anglo-Norman Studies* VIII, 198–213.

—— (1990) '"Inter Amicos": The Abbey, Town and Early Charters of Battle', *Anglo-Norman Studies* XIII, 1–14.

Shepard, Jonathan (1992) 'The Uses of the Franks in Eleventh-Century Byzantium', *Anglo-Norman Studies* XV, 275–306.

Short, Ian (1991) 'Patrons and Polyglots: French Literature in Twelfth-Century England', *Anglo-Norman Studies* XIV, 229–49.

—— (1995) '*Tam Angli Quam Franci*: Self-Definition in Anglo-Norman England', *Anglo-Norman Studies* XVIII, 153–75.

Smith, Frances Mary (1993) 'Archbishop Stigand and the Eye of the Needle', *Anglo-Norman Studies* XVI, 199–218.

Smith, Jacqueline (1978) 'Robert of Arbrissel: Procutaro Mulierum', in D. Baker (ed.) *Medieval Women,* Oxford: Basil Blackwell.

Snooks, Graeme Donald (1995) 'The Dynamic Role of the Market in the Anglo-Norman Economy and beyond, 1086–1300' in Richard H. Britnell and Bruce M. S. Campbell (eds) *A Commercialising Economy: England 1086 to c.1300,* Manchester: Manchester University Press.

Southern, R. W. (1953) *The Making of the Middle Ages,* London: Hutchinson University Library.

—— (1958) 'The Canterbury Forgeries', *English Historical Review* LXXIII, 193–226.

—— (ed. and trans.) (1962) *The Life of St Anselm,* London: Thomas Nelson.

—— (1966) *Saint Anselm and his Biographer,* Cambridge: Cambridge University Press.

—— (1973) 'The Sense of the Past', *Transactions of the Royal Historical Society* 23, 243–63.

Spear, David S. (1997) 'Power, Patronage, and Personality in the Norman Cathedral Chapters, 911–1204', *Anglo-Norman Studies* XX, 205–21.

Stacey, N. E. (ed.) (2001) *Surveys of the Estates of Glastonbury Abbey,* Oxford: Oxford University Press for the British Academy.

Stacey, Robert (1987) *Politics, Policy and Finance under Henry III, 1216–1245,* Oxford: Clarendon Press.

—— (1995) 'Jewish Lending and the Medieval English Economy', in Richard H. Britnell and Bruce M. S. Campbell (eds) *A Commercialising Economy: England 1086 to c.1300,* Manchester: Manchester University Press.

Staunton, Michael (1998) 'Thomas Becket's Conversion', *Anglo-Norman Studies* XXI, 193–211.

—— (2001) *The Lives of Thomas Becket,* Manchester: Manchester University Press.

Stell, Philip (1996) *Medical Practice in Medieval York,* Borthwick Paper 90, York: University of York.

Stenton, Doris Mary (1965) *English Justice between the Norman Conquest and the Great Charter 1066–1215,* London: George Allen and Unwin.

Stenton, F. M. (1944) 'English Families and the Norman Conquest', *Transactions of the Royal Historical Society,* 4th series, XXVI, 1–12.

—— (1961) *The First Century of English Feudalism 1066–1166,* Oxford: Clarendon Press.

Stevenson, Joseph (repr. 1996) *The History of William of Newburgh,* Felinfach: Llanerch Press.

Stewart, I. and Watkins, M. J. (1984) 'An Eleventh Century *Tabula* Set from Gloucester', *Medieval Archaeology* 28, 185–90.

Stratford, Neil (1986) 'Niello in England in the Twelfth Century', in S. Macready and F. H. Thompson (eds) *Art and Patronage in the English Romanesque,* London: Society of Antiquaries.

Strickland, Matthew (1989) 'Securing the North: Invasion and the Strategy of Defence in Twelfth-Century Anglo-Norman Warfare', *Anglo-Norman Studies* XII, 177–98.

—— (1992a) 'Slaughter, Slavery or Ransom: The Impact of the Conquest in Warfare', in Carola Hicks (ed.) *England in the Eleventh Century, Proceedings of the 1990 Harlaxton Symposium,* Stamford: Paul Watkins.

—— (1992b) 'Arms and the Men: War, Loyalty and Lordship in Jordan Fantosme's Chronicle', in C. Harper-Bill and Ruth Harvey (eds), *Medieval Knighthood IV, Papers from the Fifth Strawberry Hill Conference 1990,* Woodbridge: The Boydell Press.

Swanson, R. N. (1999) *The Twelfth Century Renaissance,* Manchester: Manchester University Press.

Swanton, Michael (2000) *The Anglo-Saxon Chronicles,* London: Phoenix Press.

Symons, Thomas (ed. and trans.) (1953) *Regularis Concordia,* London: Thomas Nelson.

Talbot C. H. (ed. and trans.) (1959) *Christina of Markyate*, Oxford: Oxford University Press.

Tanner, Heather J. (1991) 'The Expansion of the Power and Influence of the Counts of Boulogne under Eustace II', *Anglo-Norman Studies* XIV, 251–86.

Tatlock, J. S. P. (1950) *The Legendary History of Britain,* Berkeley: University of California Press.

Taylor, H. M. and Taylor, Joan (1965) *Anglo-Saxon Architecture*, Cambridge: Cambridge University Press.

Taylor, Jerome (1968) *The Didascalicon: A Medieval Guide to the Arts*, New York: Columbia University Press.

Taylor, Pamela (1991) 'The Endowment and Military Obligations of the See of London: A Reassessment of Three Sources', *Anglo-Norman Studies* XIV, 287–312.

Teunis, H. B. (1989) 'Benoit of St Maure and William the Conqueror's *amor'*, *Anglo-Alorman Studies* XII, 199–209.

Thomas, Christoper, Sloane, Barney and Phillpots, Christopher (eds) (1997) *Excavations at the Priory and Hospital of St Mary Spital, London,* London: Museum of London Archaeology Service Monograph 1.

Thomas, Hugh M. (1998) 'The *Gesta Herwardi*, the English, and their Conquerors', *Anglo-Norman Studies* XXI, 213–32.

Thompson, Benjamin (1993) 'Free Alms Tenure in the Twelfth Century', *Anglo-Norman Studies* XVI, 221–44.

Thompson, Kathleen (1990) 'Robert of Bellême Reconsidered', *Anglo-Norman Studies* XIII, 263–86.

—— (1995) 'The Lords of Laigle: Ambition and Insecurity on the Borders of Normandy', *Anglo-Norman Studies* XVIII, 177–200.

Thompson, Sally (1978) 'The Problem of the Cistercian Nuns in the Twelfth and Early Thirteenth Centuries', in D. Baker (ed.) *Medieval Women,* Oxford: Basil Blackwell.

Thompson, Victoria (1999) 'Kingship in Death in the Bayeux Tapestry', *Reading Medieval Studies* XXV, 107–21.

Thorpe, Lewis (1966) *Geoffrey of Monmouth: The History of the Kings of Britain,* Harmondsworth: Penguin.

—— (ed. and trans.) (1978) *Gerald of Wales: The Journey Through Wales/The Description of Wales,* Harmondsworth: Penguin.

Thurlby, Malcolm (1999) *The Herefordshire School of Romanesque Sculpture,* Little Logaston: Logaston Press.

Tristam, E. W. (1988) *English Medieval Wall Painting The Twelfth Century*, New York: Hacker Art Books.

Tsurushima, H. (1991) 'The Fraternity of Rochester Cathedral Priory about 1100', *Anglo-Norman Studies* XIV, 313–37.

—— (1995) 'Domesday Interpreters', *Anglo-Norman Studies* XVIII, 201–22.

Tudor-Craig, Pamela (1989) 'Controversial Sculptures: The Southwell Tympanum, The Glastonbury Respond, The Leigh Christ', *Anglo-Norman Studies* XII, 211–31.

Turner, Ralph (1999) 'John and Justice', in S. D. Church (ed.) *King John: New Interpretations,* Woodbridge: The Boydell Press.

Tyerman, C. J. (1995) 'Were there any Crusades in the Twelfth Century?', *English Historical Review* 110, 553–77.

van Houts, Elizabeth M. C. (1980) 'The Gesta Normannorum Ducum: A History without an End', *Proceedings of the Battle Conference of Anglo-Norman Studies* III, 106–18.

—— (1987) 'The Ship List of William the Conqueror', *Anglo-Norman Studies* X, 159–83.

—— (1989) 'Historiography and Hagiography at Saint Wandrille: The Inventio et Miracula S. Wulfranni', *Anglo-Norman Studies* XII, 233–51.

—— (1995) 'The Norman Conquest through European Eyes', *English Historical Review* 110, 832–53.

—— (trans.) (1998) 'The Anglo-Flemish Treaty of 1101', *Anglo-Norman Studies* XXI, 169–74.

Varga, Livia (1992) 'A New Aspect of the Porphry Tombs of Roger II, First King of Sicily, in Cefalù', *Anglo-Norman Studies* XV, 307–15.

Vaughn, Sally N. (1987) 'Eadmer's *Historia Novorum*: A Reinterpretation', *Anglo-Norman Studies* X, 261–89.

—— (1993) 'Anselm in Italy', *Anglo-Norman Studies* XVI, 245–70.

Vincent, Nicholas C. (1993) 'The Origins of the Chancellorship of the Exchequer', *English Historical Review* XXX, 105–21.

—— (1998) 'Warin and Henry fitz Gerald, the King's Chamberlains: The Origins of the Fitzgeralds Revisited', *Anglo-Norman Studies* XXI, 233–61.

—— (1999) 'Isabella of Angoulême: John's Jezebel', in S. D. Church (ed.) *King John: New Interpretations,* Woodbridge, The Boydell Press.

Wada, Yoko (1997) 'Gerald on Gerald: Self-presentation by Giraldus Cambrensis', *Anglo-Norman Studies* XX, 223–45.

Waley, D. P. (1954) 'Combined Operations in Sicily AD 1060–78', *Papers of the British School in Rome* XXII, 118–25.

Walker, David, (1978) 'The Norman Settlement in Wales', *Proceedings of the Battle Conference on Anglo-Norman Studies* I, 131–43.

—— (1982) 'Crown and Episcopacy under the Normans and the Angevins', *Anglo-Norman Studies* V, 220–33.

Walker, John (1998) 'Alms for the Holy Land: The English Templars and their Patrons', in Andrew Ayton and J. L. Price (eds) *The Medieval Military Revolution*, London: I. B. Tauris.

Ward, Jennifer C. (1988) 'Royal Service and Reward: The Clare Family and the Crown, 1066–1154', *Anglo-Norman Studies* XI, 261–78.

Wareham, Andrew (1994) 'The Motives and Politics of the Bigod Family, c.1066–1177', *Anglo-Norman Studies* XVII, 223–42.

Warren, Michelle R. (1998) 'Roger of Howden Strikes Back: Investing Arthur of Brittany with the Anglo-Norman Future', *Anglo-Norman Studies* XXI, 261–72.

Warren, W. L. (1983) *Henry II*, London: Methuen.

—— (1987) *The Governance of Norman and Angevin England 1086–1272*, London: Edward Arnold.

West, F. (1966) *The Justiciarship in England 1066–1232*, Cambridge: Cambridge University Press.

White, G. H. (1948) 'The Household of the Norman Kings', *Transactions of the Royal Historical Society*, 4th series, XXX, 127–55.

Whitelock, Dorothy (1979) *English Historical Documents I*, London: Eyre Methuen.

Wightman, W. E. (1966) *The Lacy Family in England and Normandy 1066–1194*, Oxford: Clarendon Press.

Williams, Ann (1978) 'Some Notes and Considerations on Problems Connected with the English Royal Succession, 860–1066', *Proceedings of the Battle Conference on Anglo-Norman Studies* I, 144–67.

—— (1980) 'Land and Power in the Eleventh Century: The Estates of Harold Godwineson', *Proceedings of the Battle Conference on Anglo-Norman Studies* III, 170–87.

—— (1985) 'The Knights of Shaftesbury Abbey', *Anglo-Norman Studies* VIII, 214–42.

—— (1988) 'A Vice-comital Family in Pre-Conquest Warwickshire', *Anglo-Norman Studies* XI, 279–95.

—— (1992) 'A Bell-house and a Burh-geat: Lordly Residences in England before the Norman Conquest', in C. Harper-Bill and Ruth Harvey (eds) *Medieval Knighthood IV, Papers from the Fifth Strawberry Hill Conference 1990*, Woodbridge: The Boydell Press.

—— (1997) *The English and the Norman Conquest*, Woodbridge: The Boydell Press.

Williams, John Bryan (1993) 'Judhael of Totnes: The Life and Times of a Post-Conquest Baron', *Anglo-Norman Studies* XVI, 271–89.

Wilson, Christopher (1986) 'The Cistercians as '"Missionaries of Gothic", in Northern England', in Christopher Norton and David Park (eds) *Cistercian Art and Architecture in the British Isles*, Cambridge: Cambridge University Press.

Woolgar, C. M. (1992) *Household Accounts from Medieval England*, Oxford: Oxford University Press for the British Academy.

Wormald, Patrick (1992) 'Domesday Lawsuits: A Provisional List and Preliminary Comment', in Carola Hicks (ed.), *England in the Eleventh Century, Proceedings of the 1990 Harlaxton Symposium*, Stamford: Paul Watkins.

—— (1994) 'Laga Edwardi: The *Textus Roffensis* and its Context', *Anglo-Norman Studies* XVII, 243–266.

—— (1999) *The Making of English Law, King Alfred to the Twelfth Century, Volume I: Legislation and its Limits*, Oxford: Blackwell.

Wright, Laurence (1986) 'The Role of Musicians at Court in Twelfth-Century

Britain', in S. Macready and F. H. Thompson (eds) *Art and Patronage in the English Romanesque,* London: Society of Antiquaries.

Young, Charles R. (1979) *The Royal Forests of Medieval England,* Leicester: Leicester University Press.

Zarnecki, George (1951) *English Romanesque Sculpture 1066–1140*, London: Alec Tiranti.

—— (1953) *English Romanesque Sculpture 1140–1210,* London: Alec Tiranti.

—— (1978) 'Romanesque Sculpture in Normandy and England in the Eleventh Century', *Proceedings of the Battle Conference on Anglo-Norman Studies* I, 168–89.

—— (1984) 'Sculpture', in *English Romanesque Art 1066–1200,* London: Weidenfeld and Nicolson in association with the Arts Council of Great Britain.

—— (1986) 'Henry of Blois as a Patron of Sculpture', in S. Macready and F. H. Thompson (eds) *Art and Patronage in the English Romanesque,* London: Society of Antiquaries.

Index